AF267226

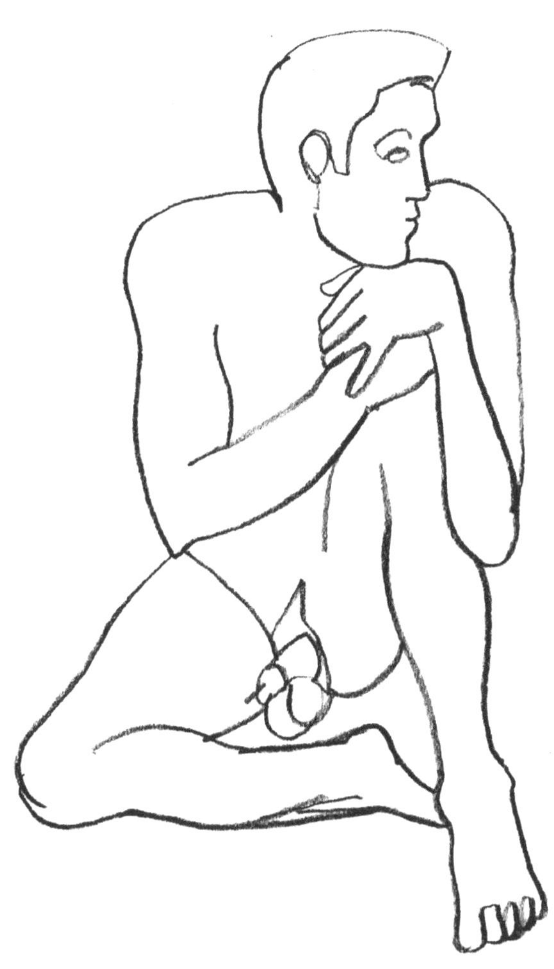

THE MALE NUDE

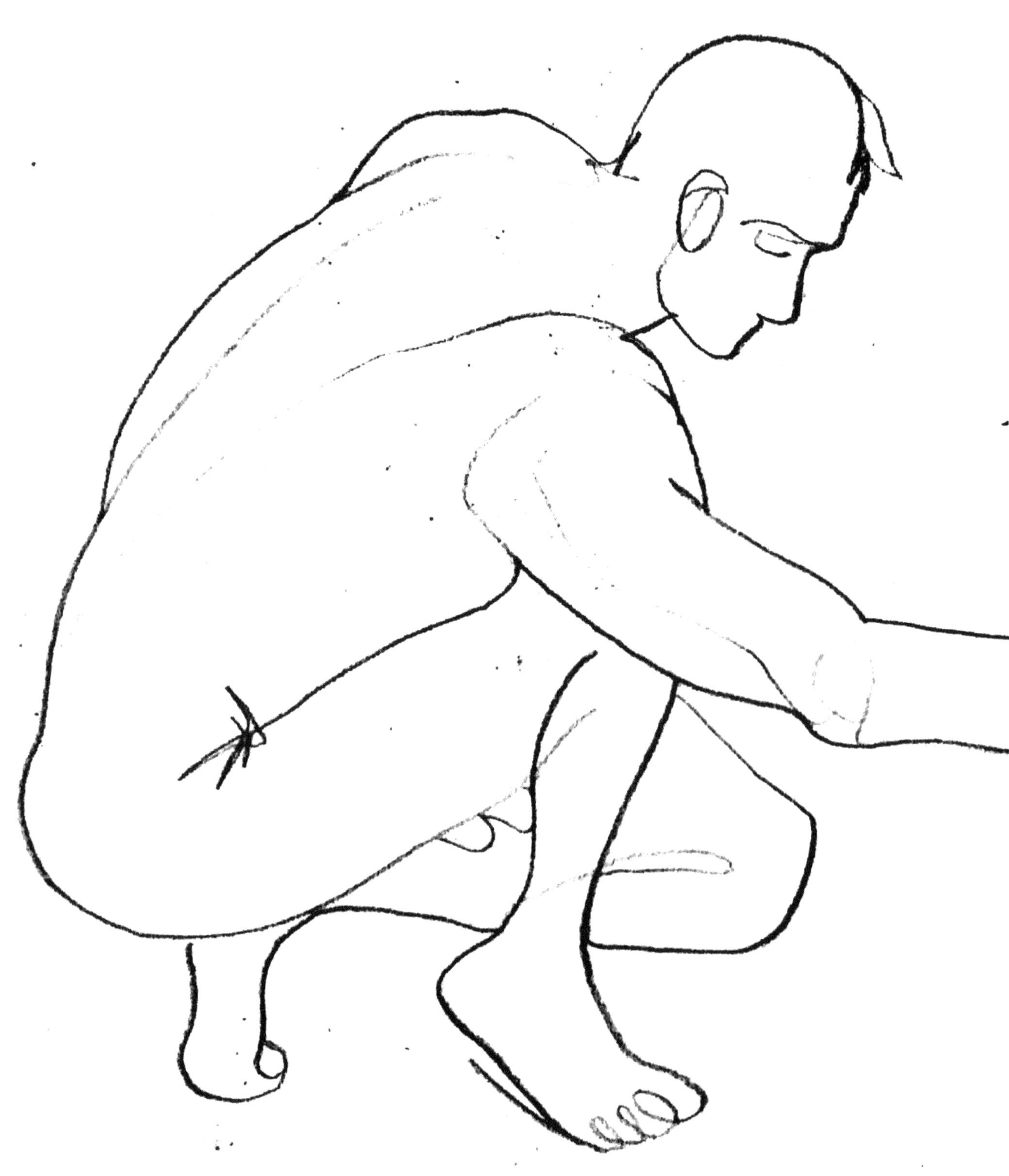

THE MALE NUDE

LINE DRAWINGS 2008–2018

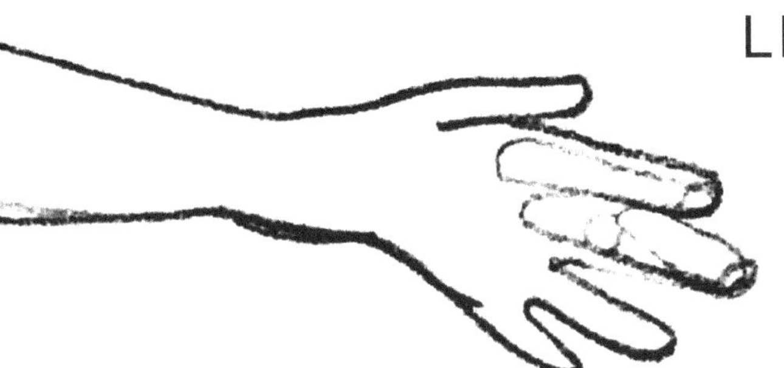

MICHAEL TICE

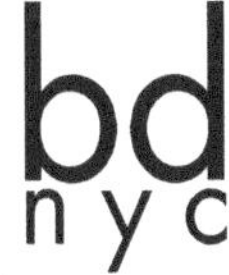

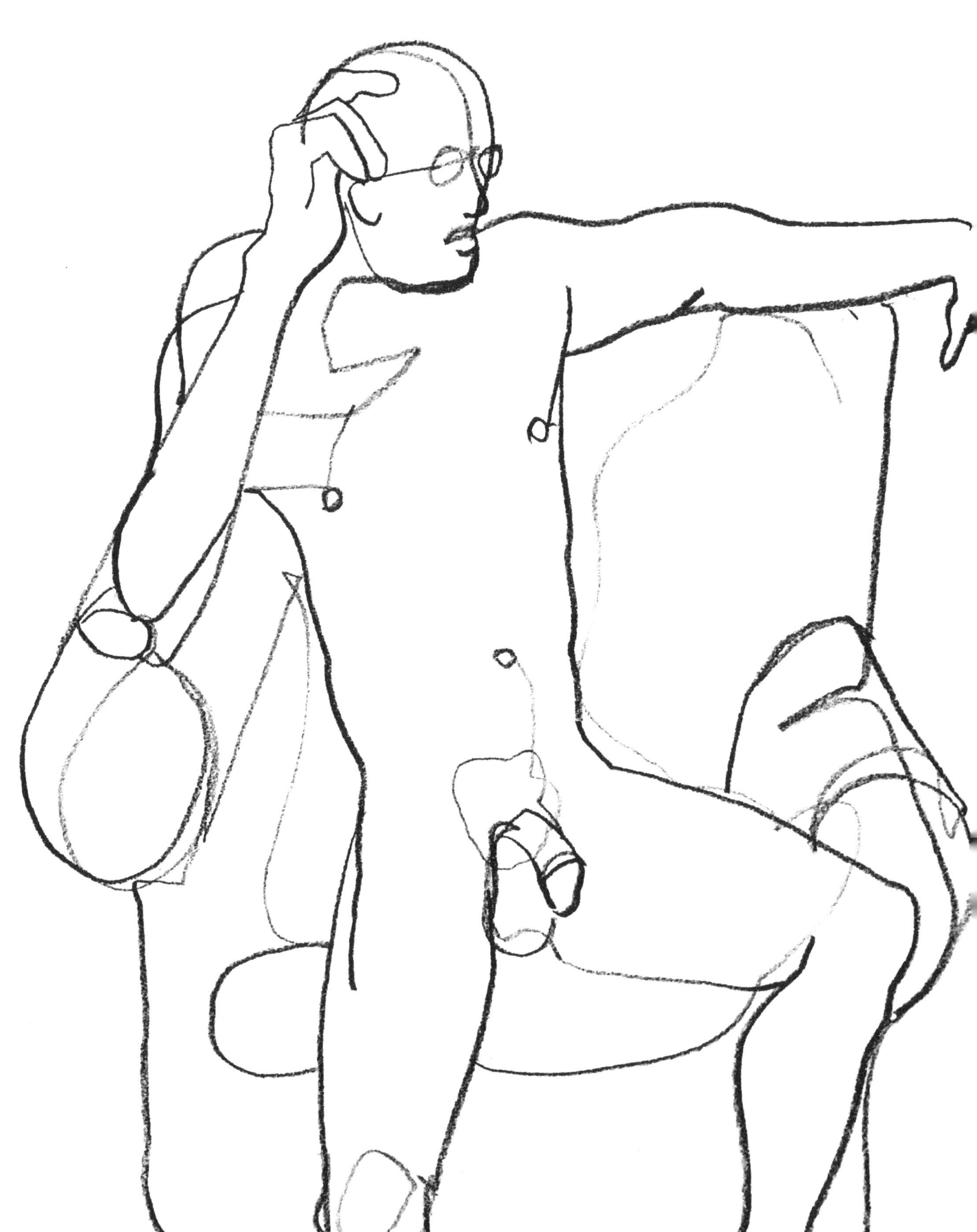

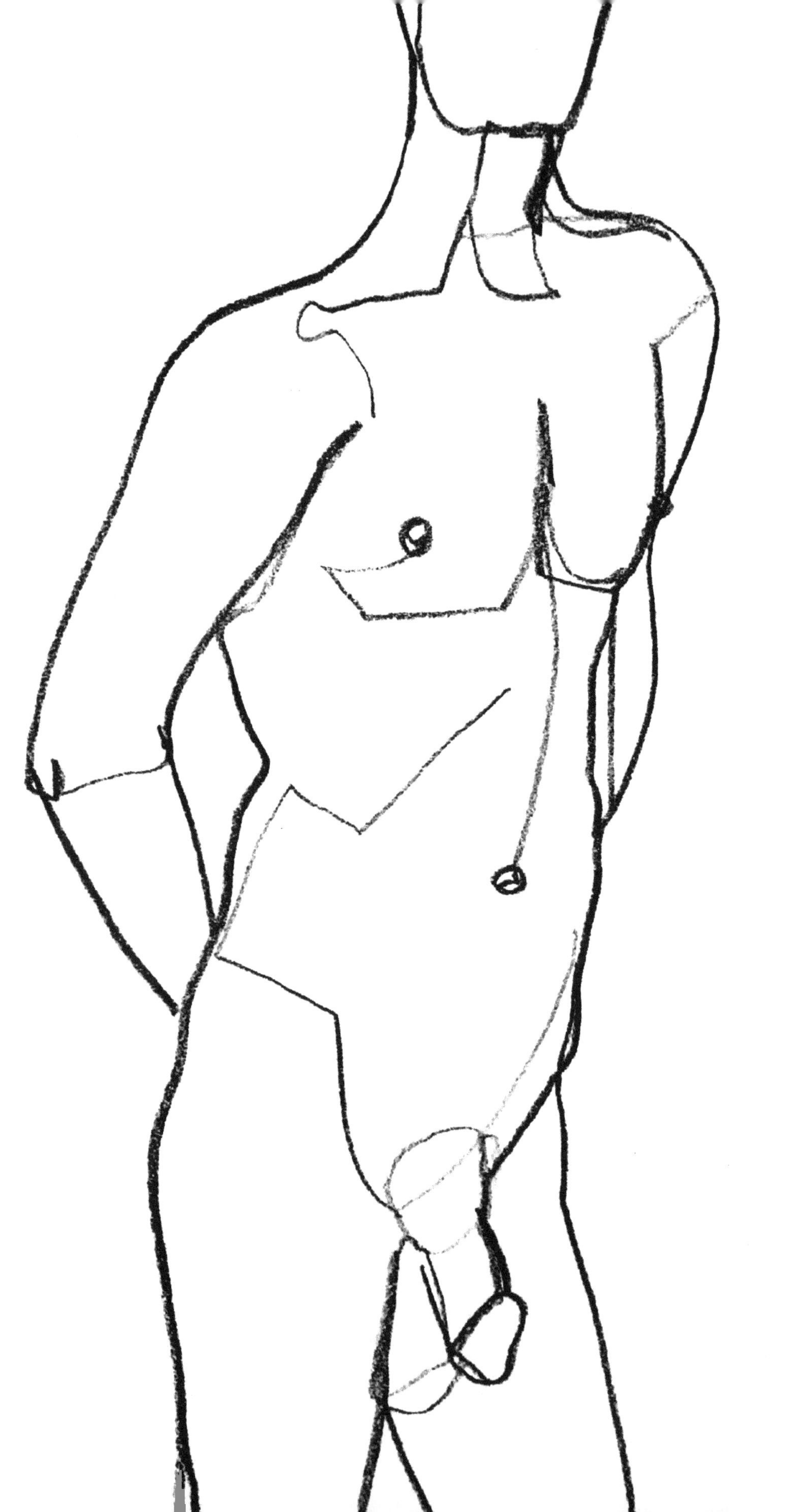

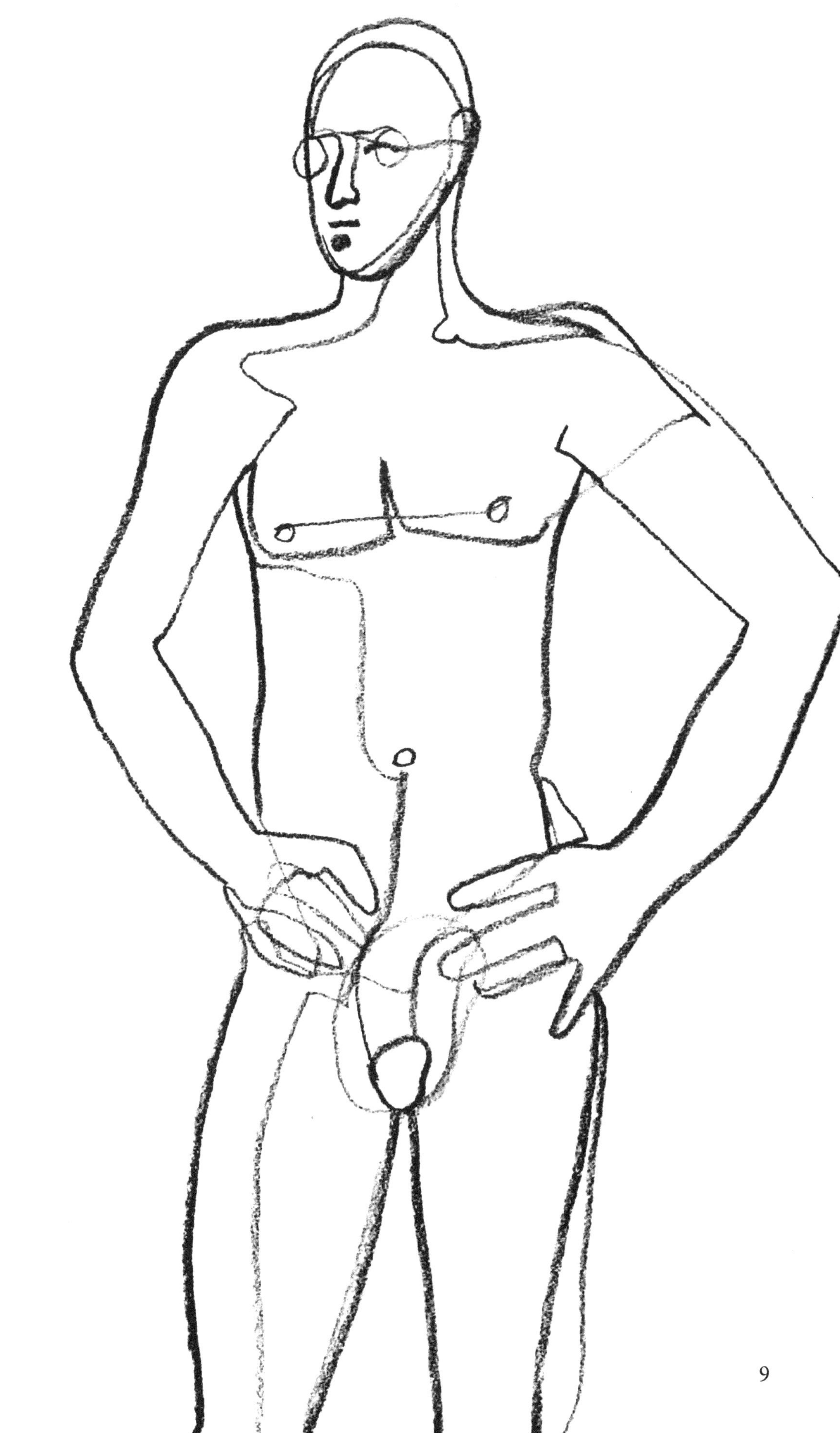

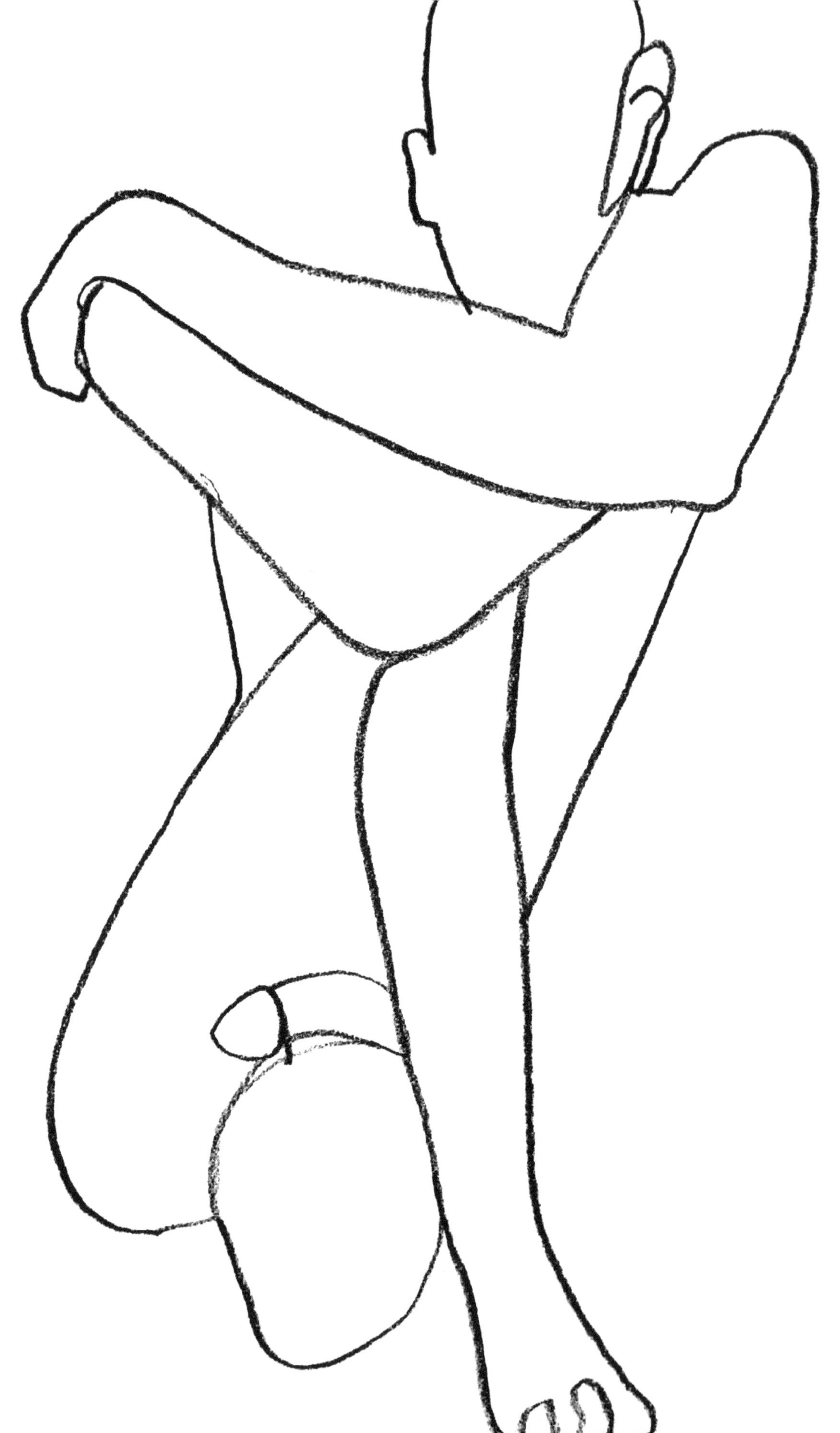

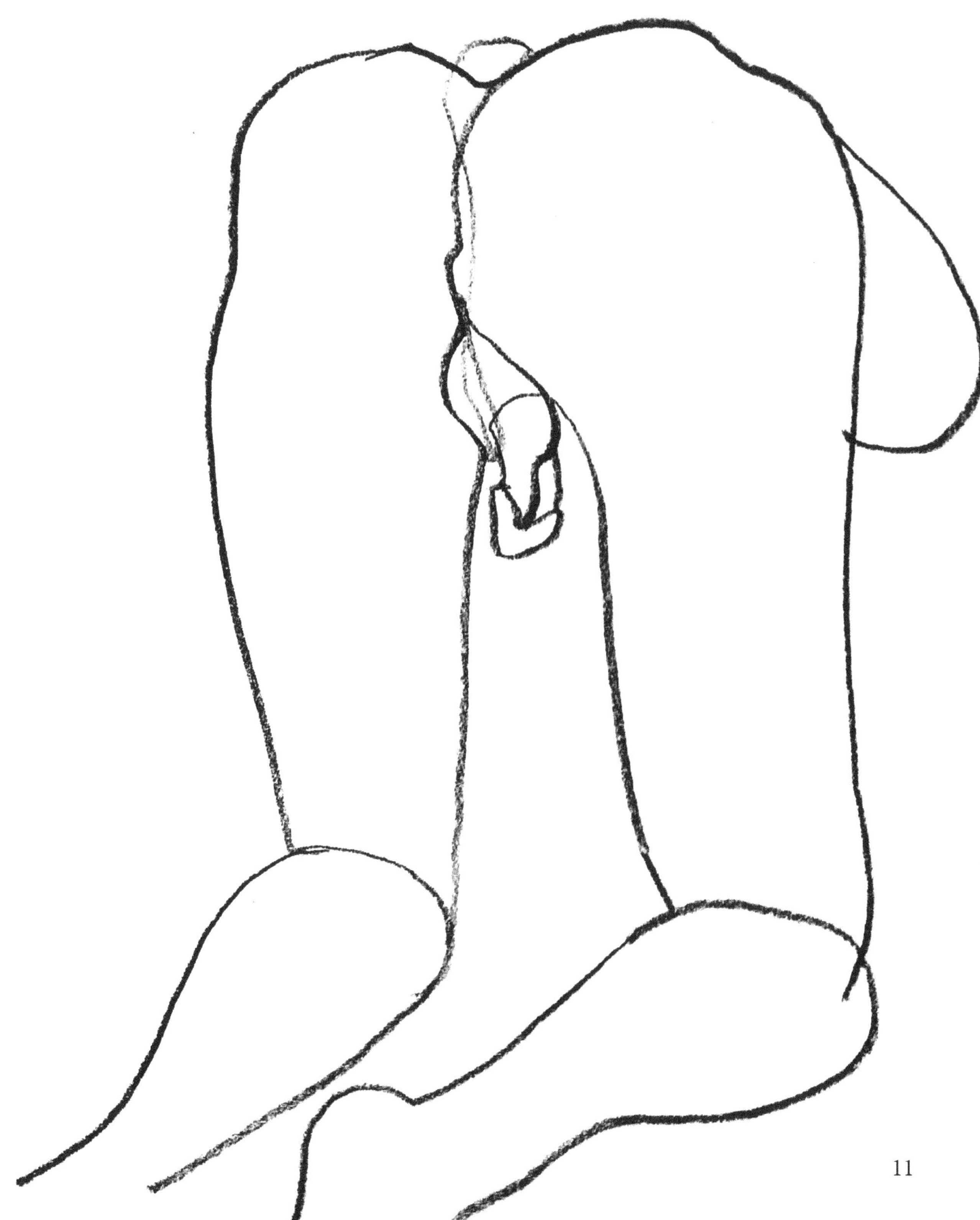

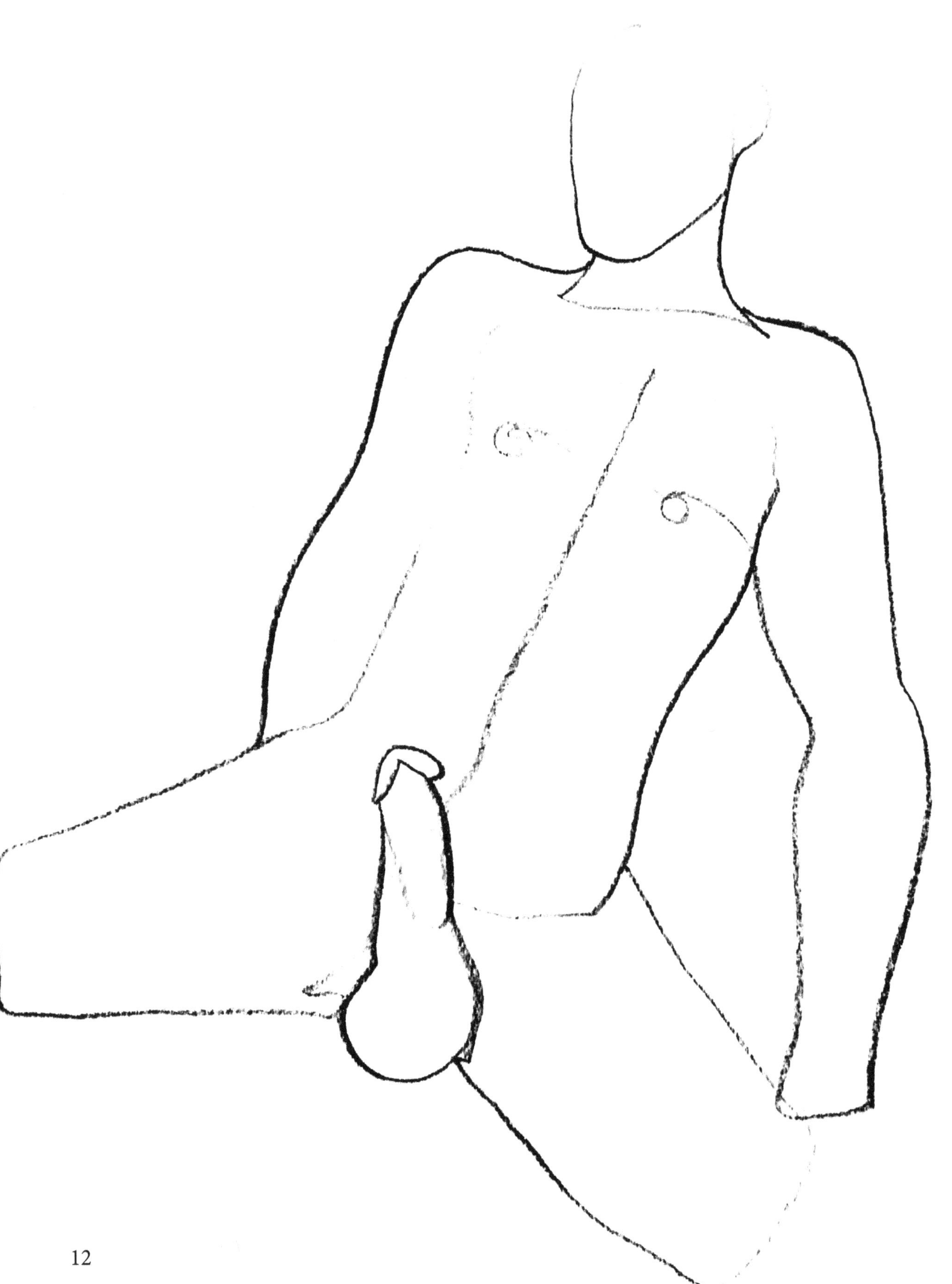

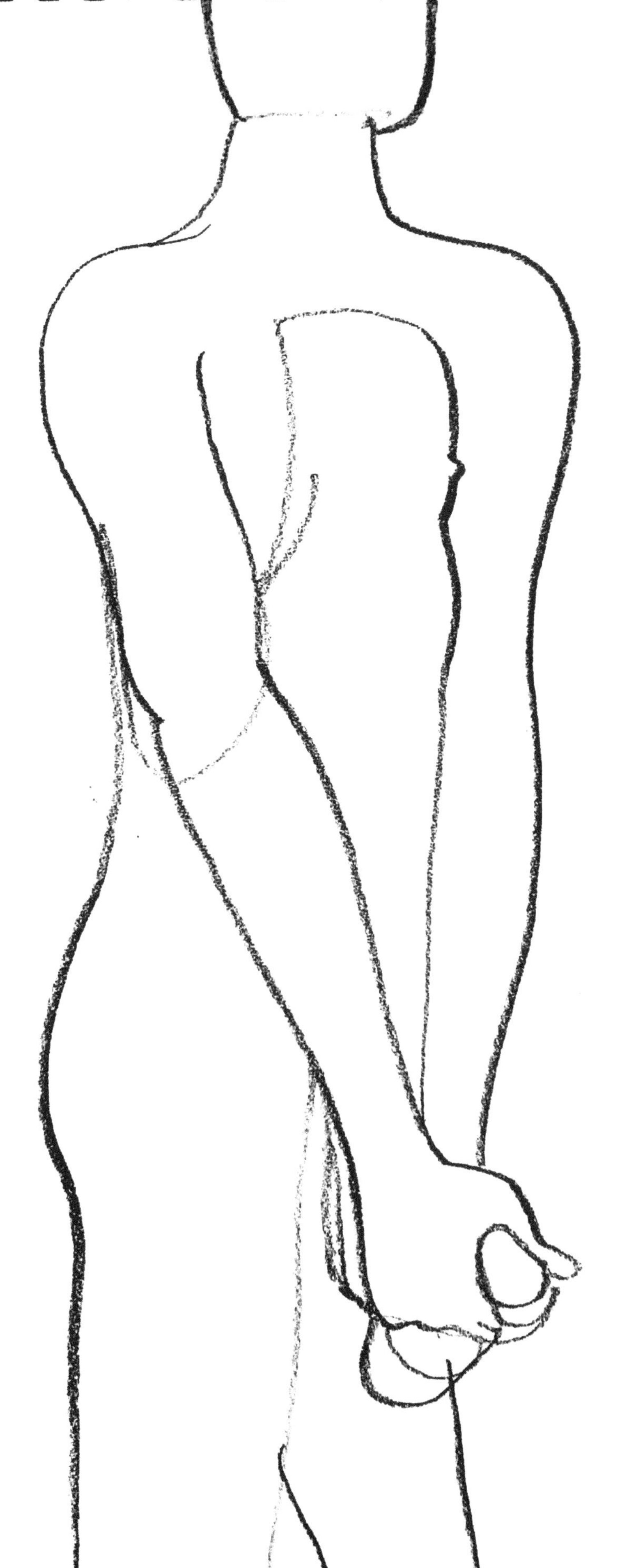

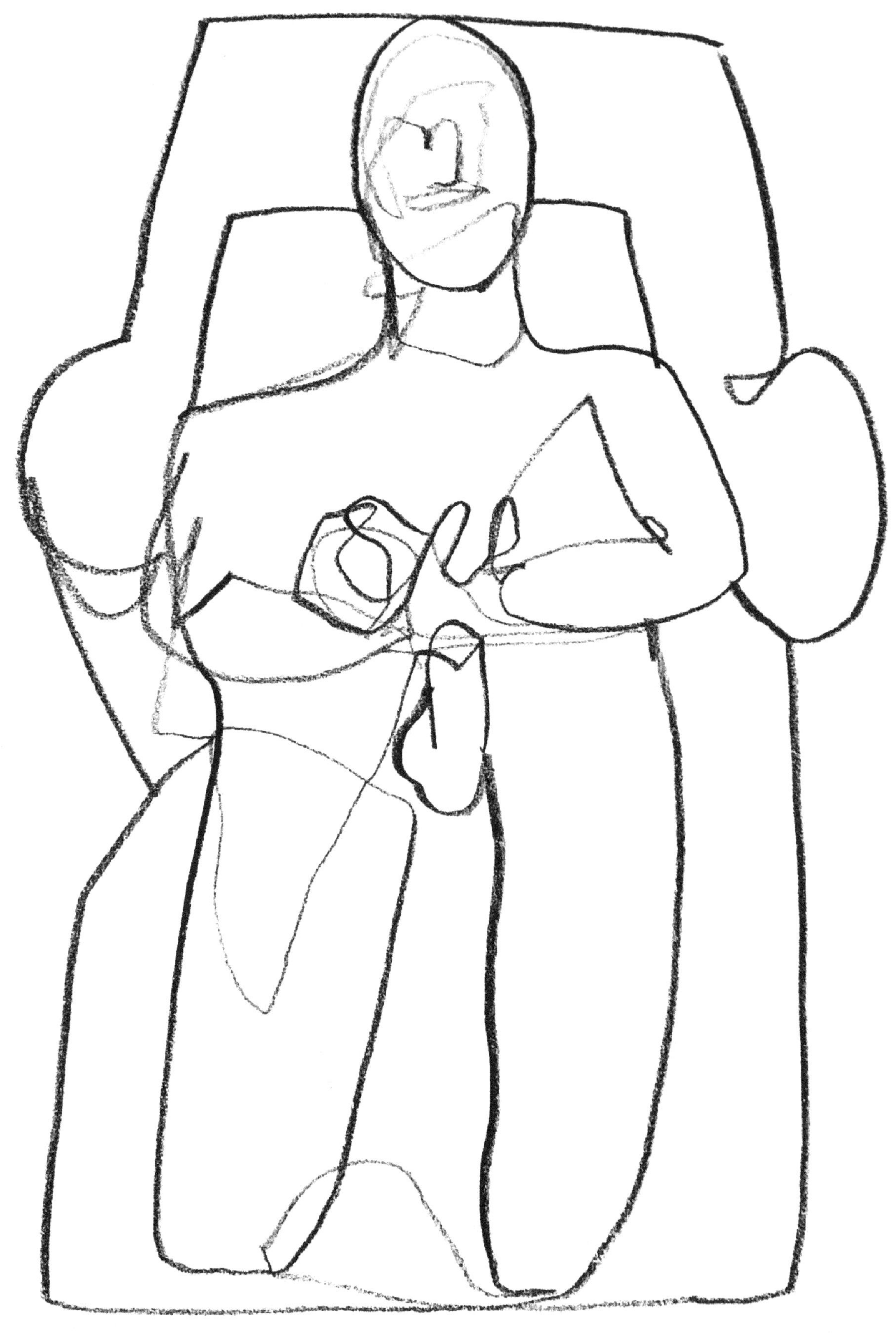

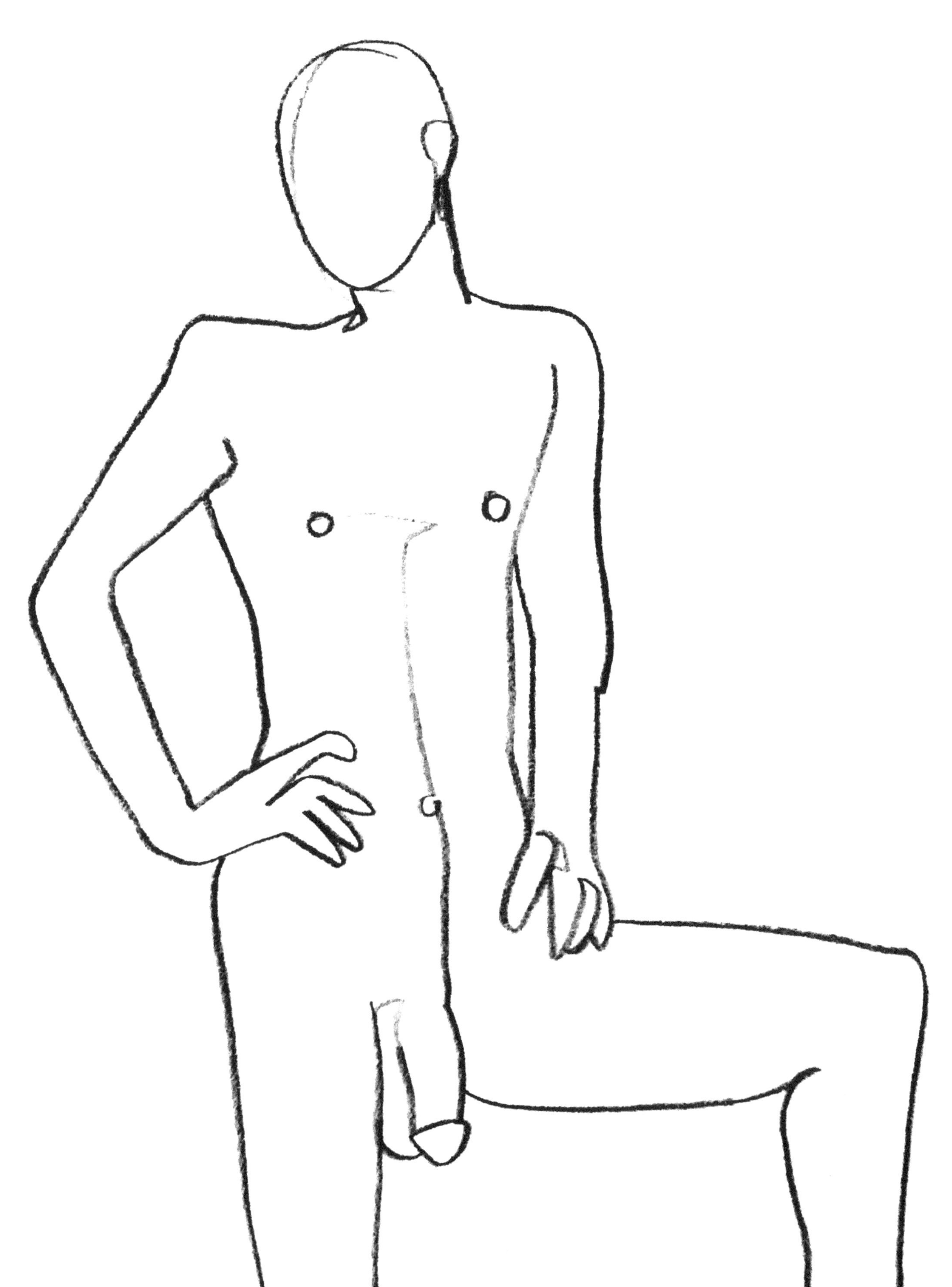

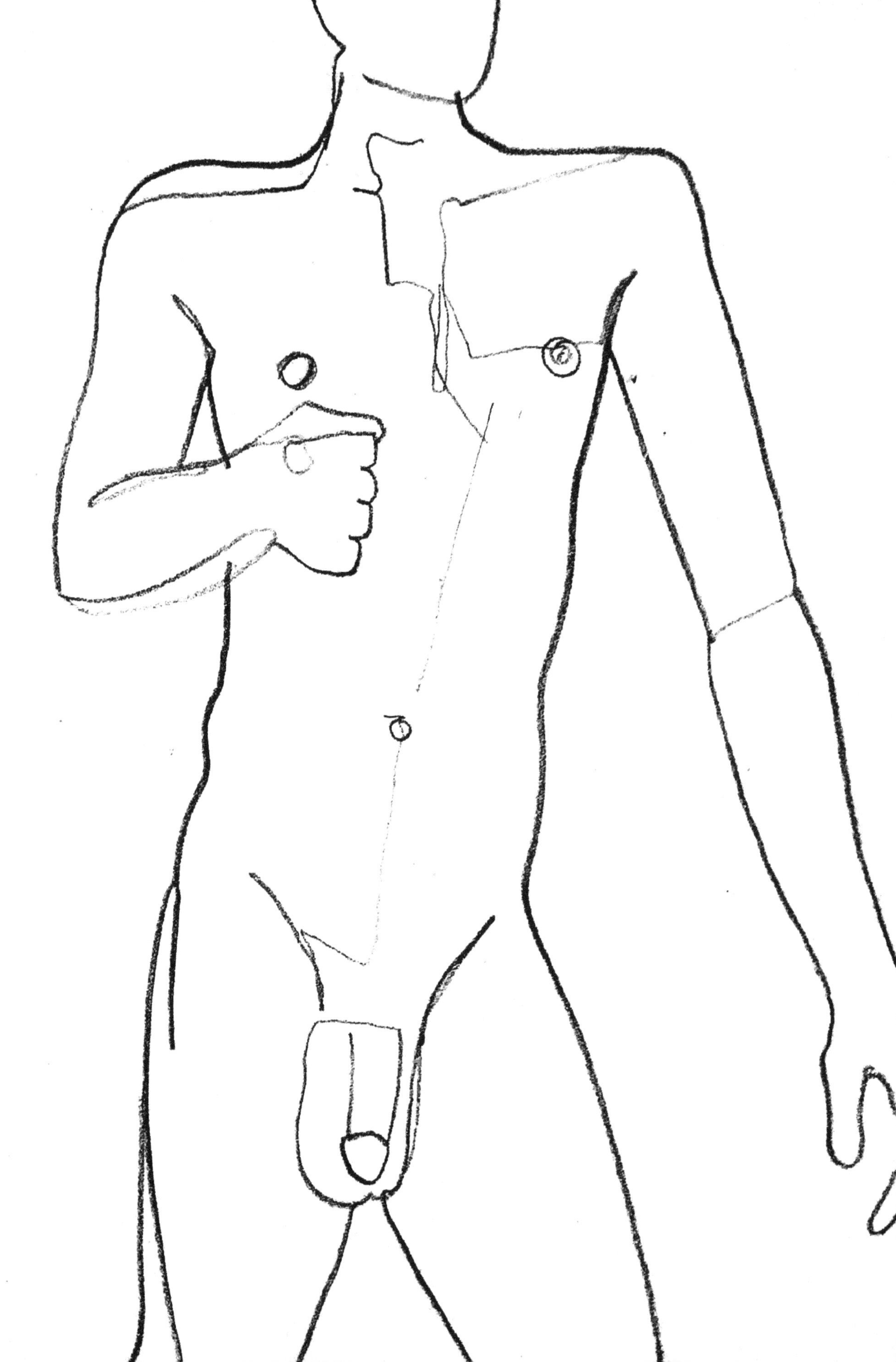

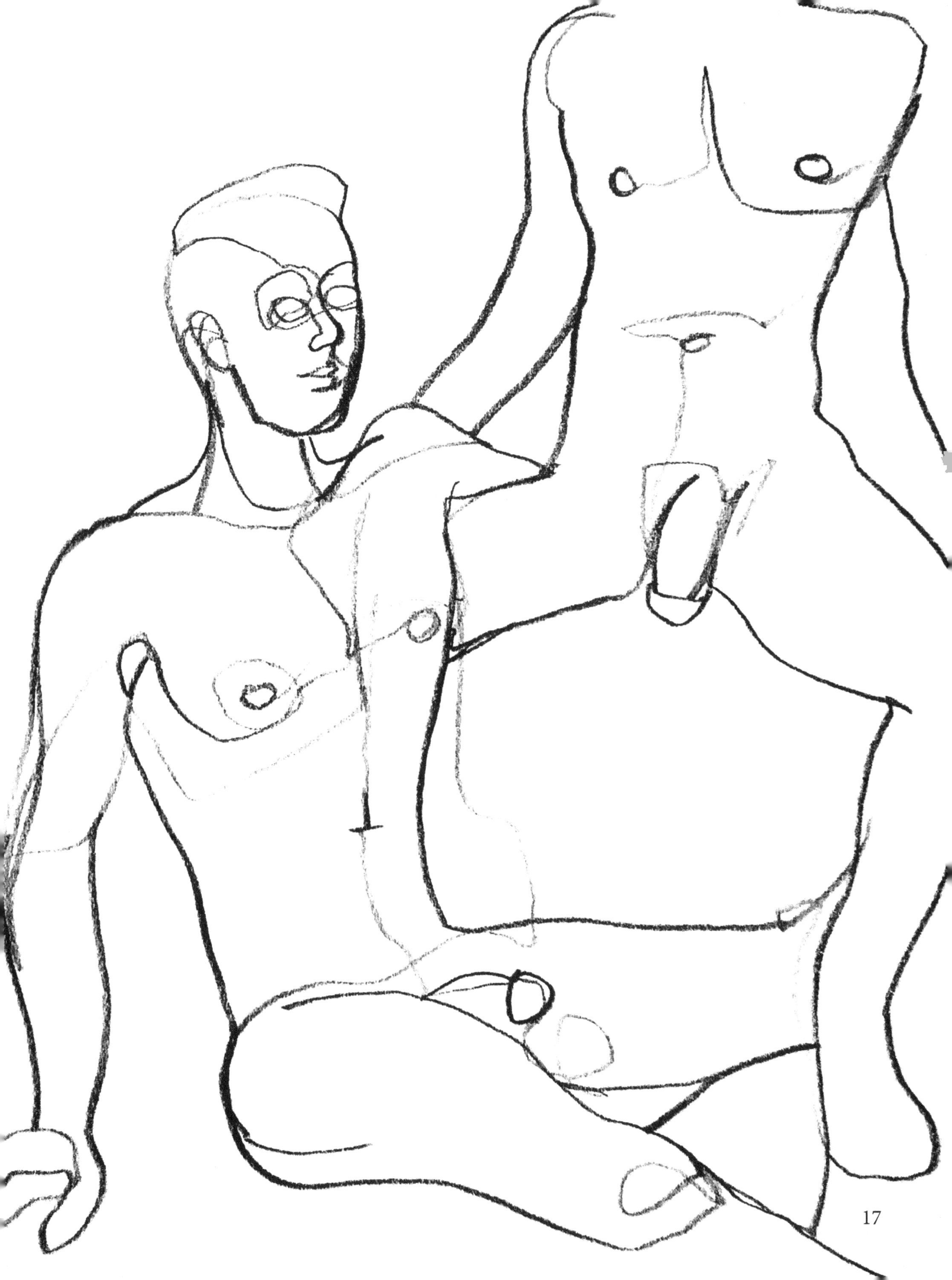

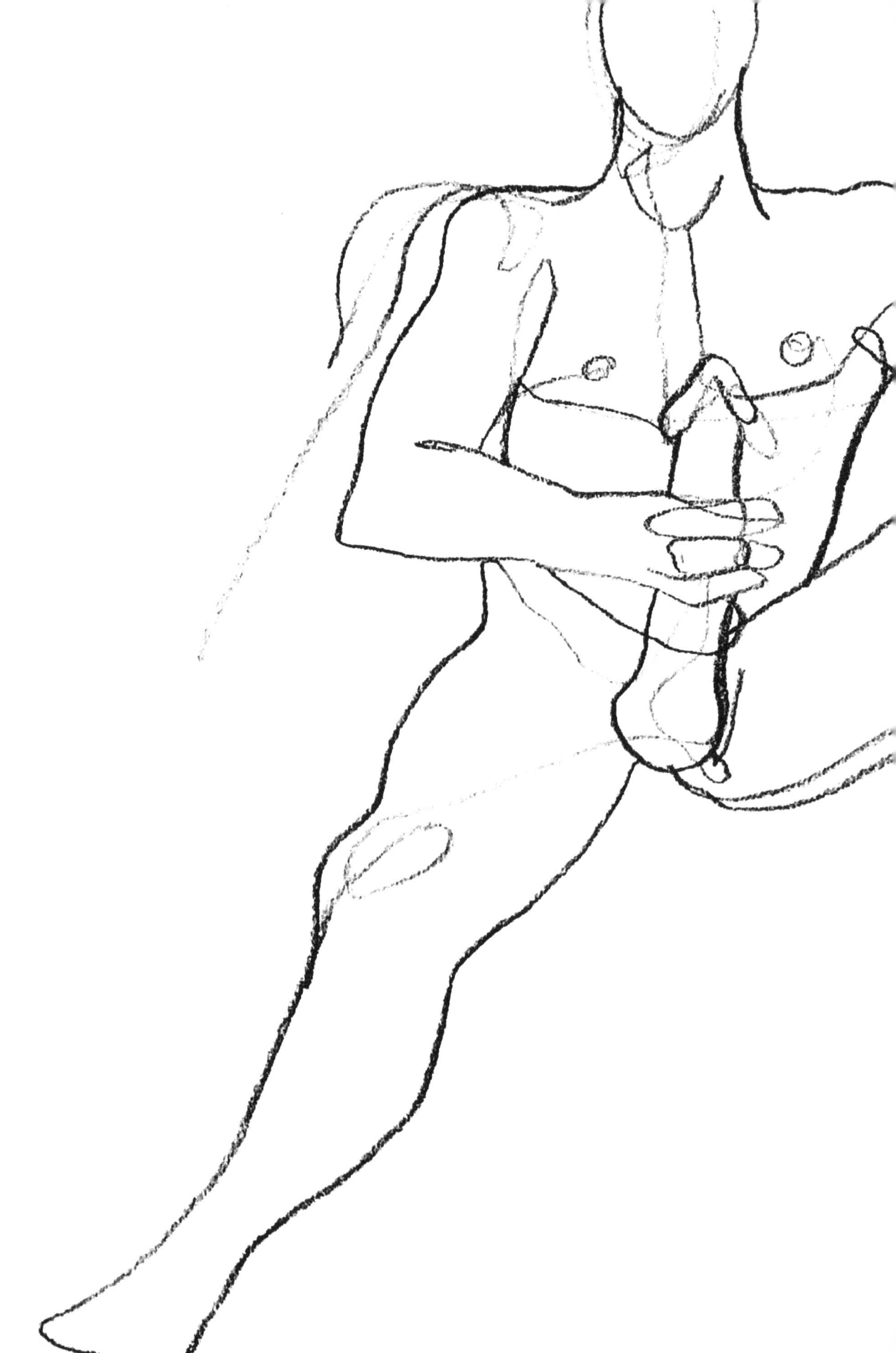

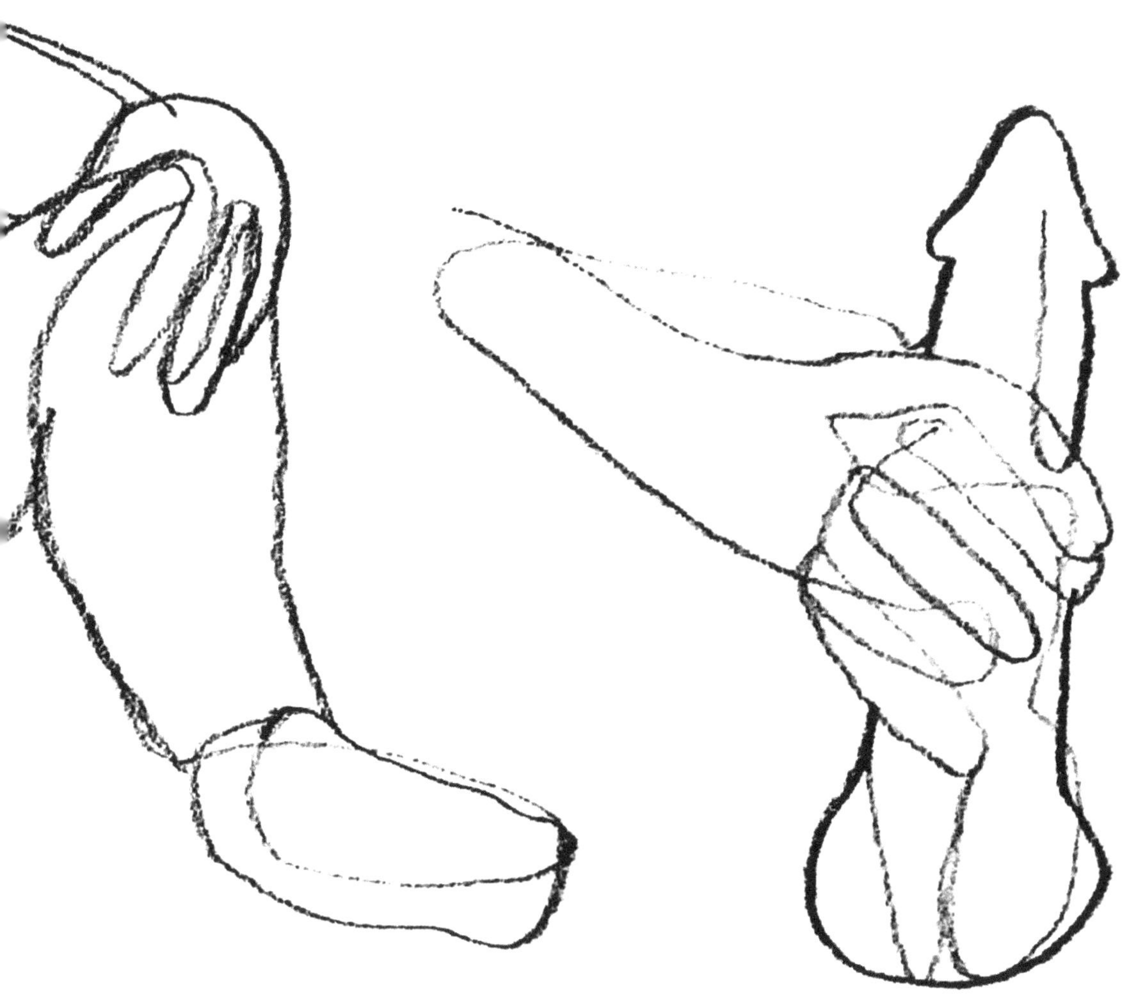

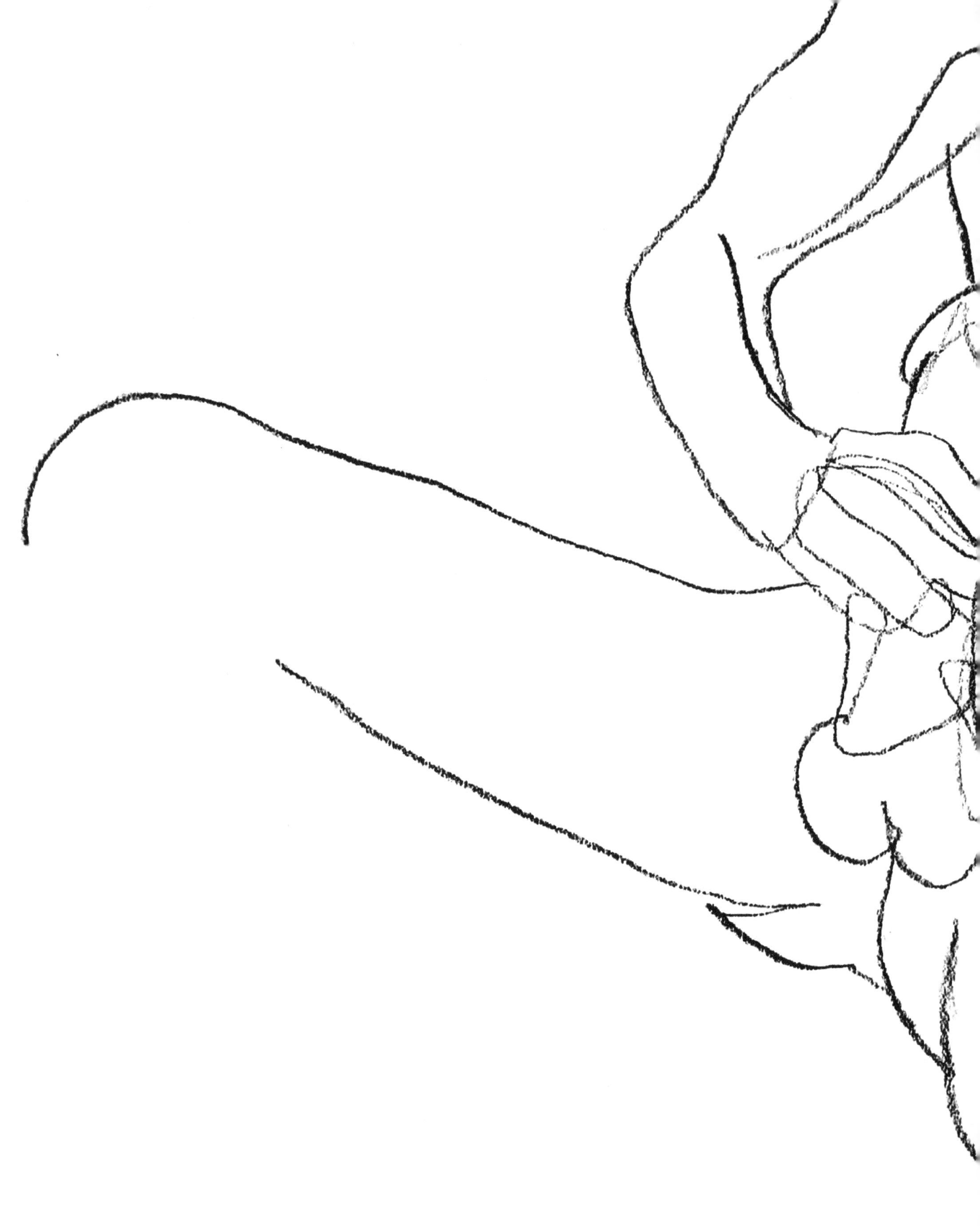

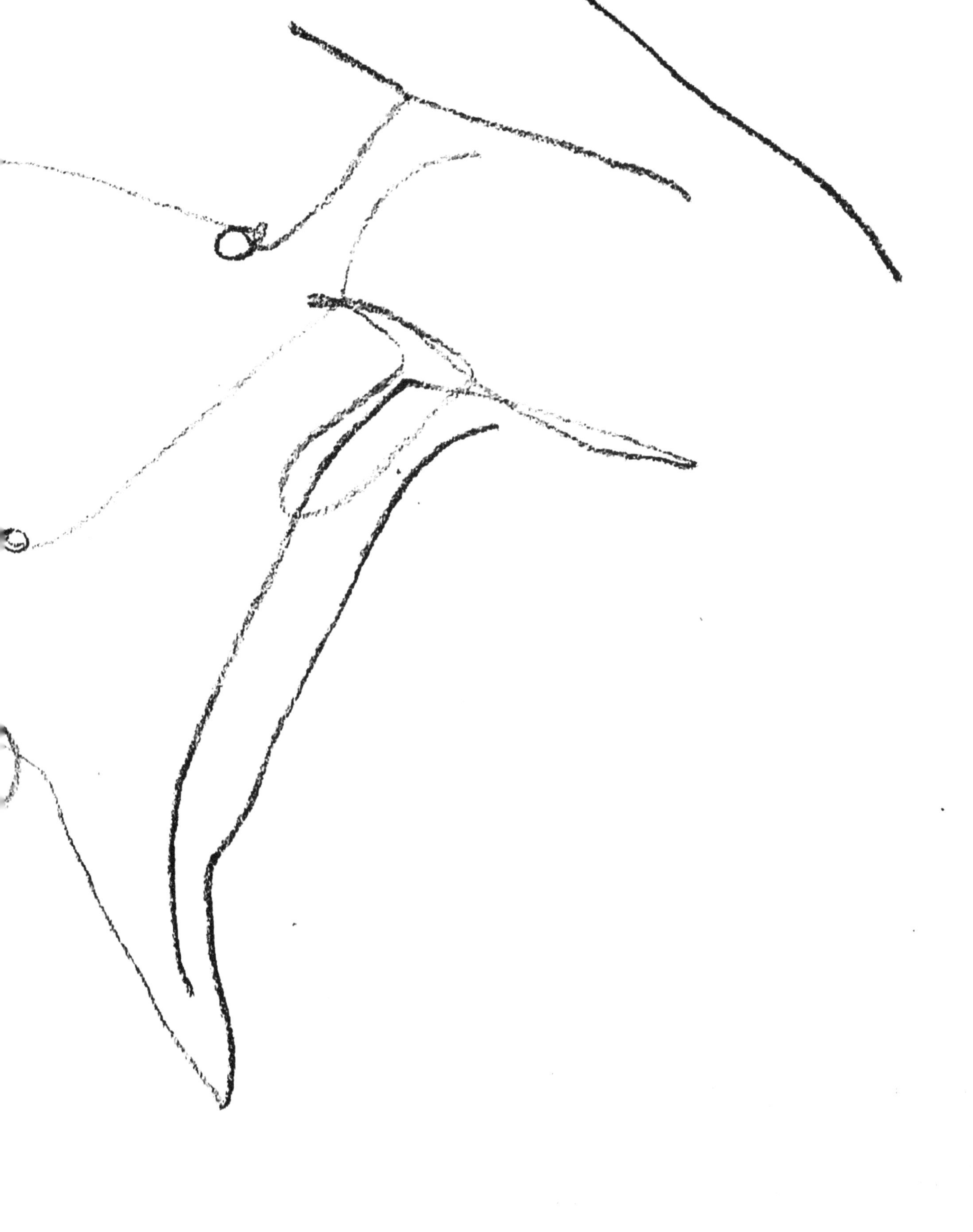

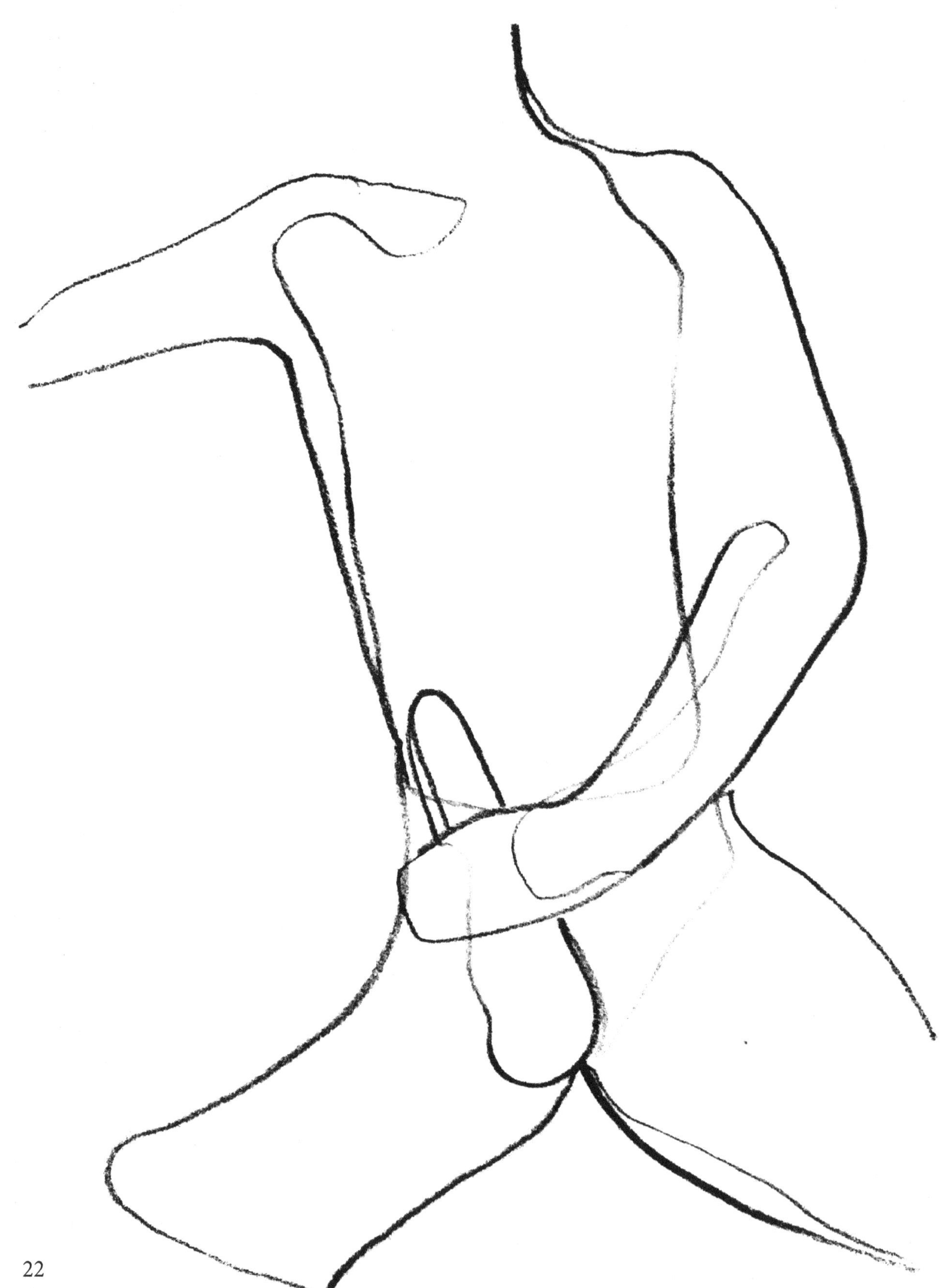

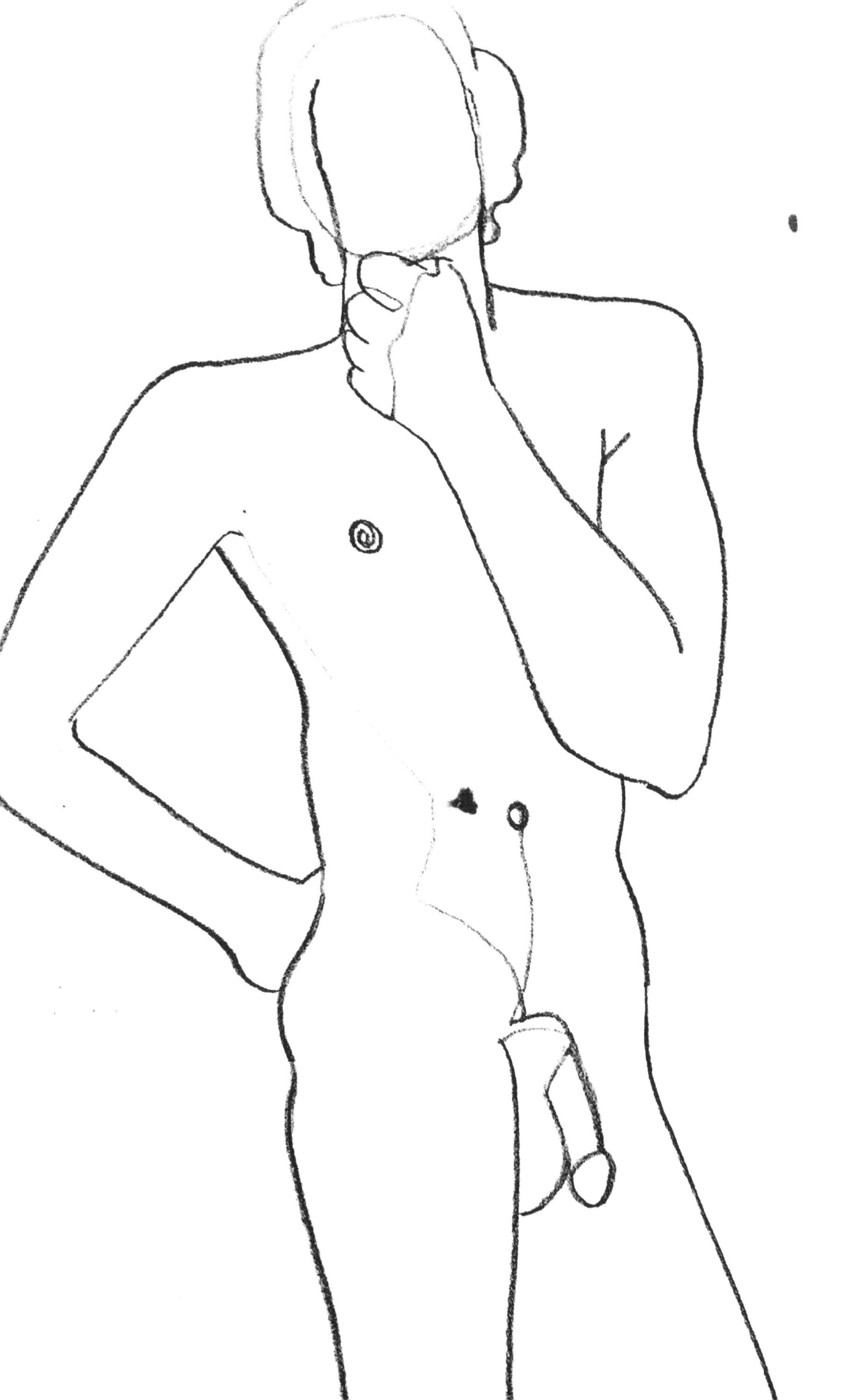

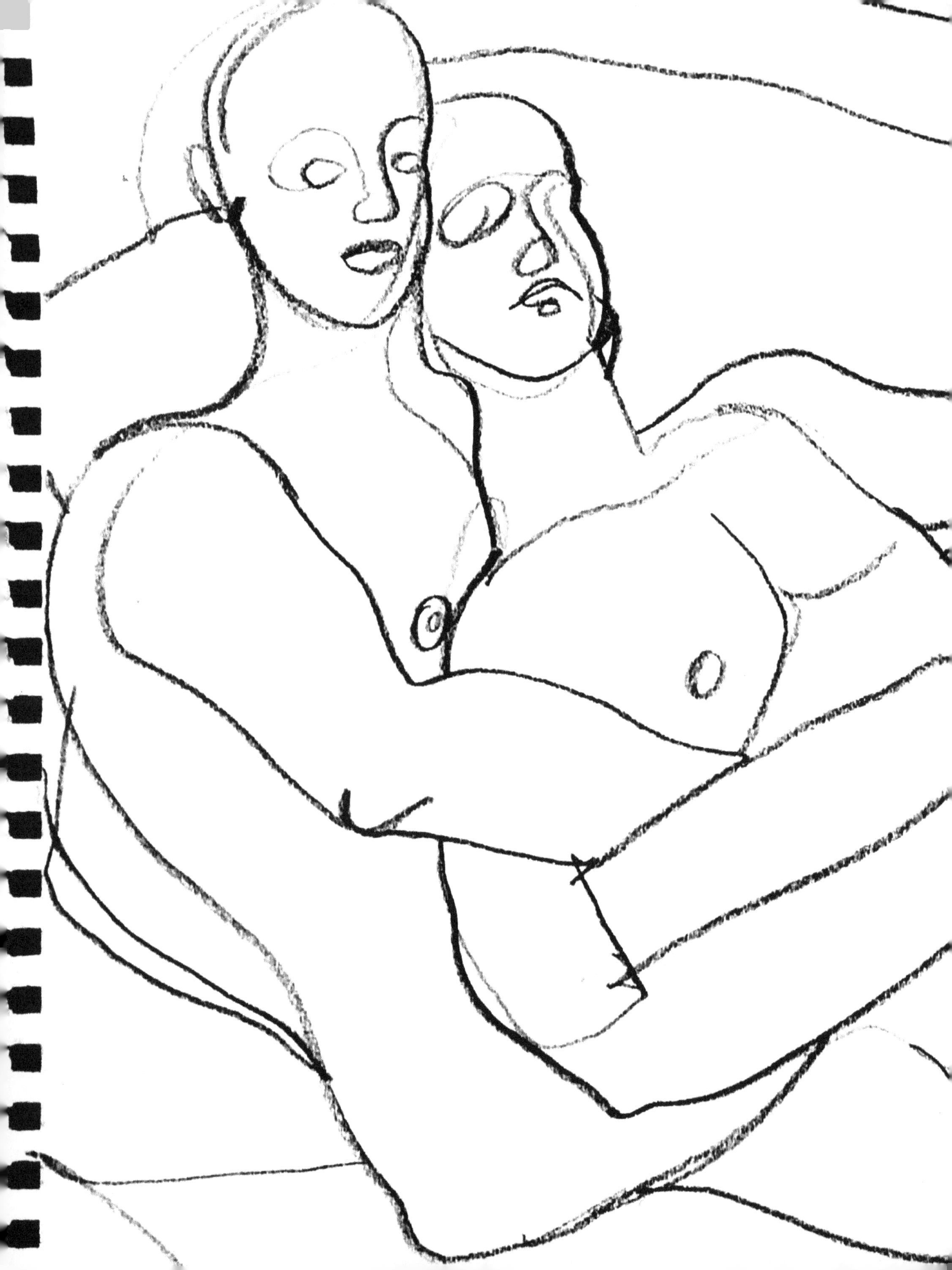

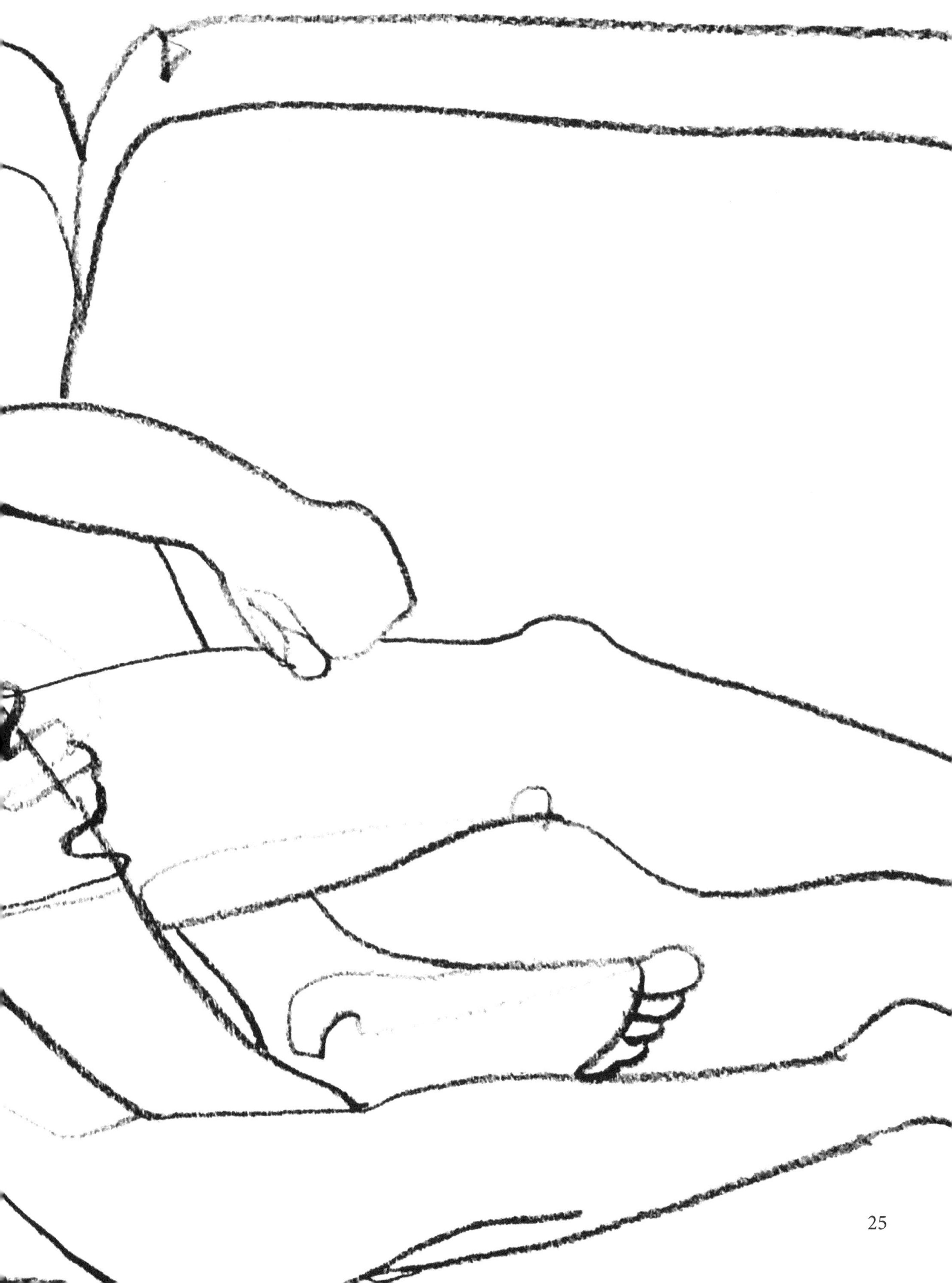

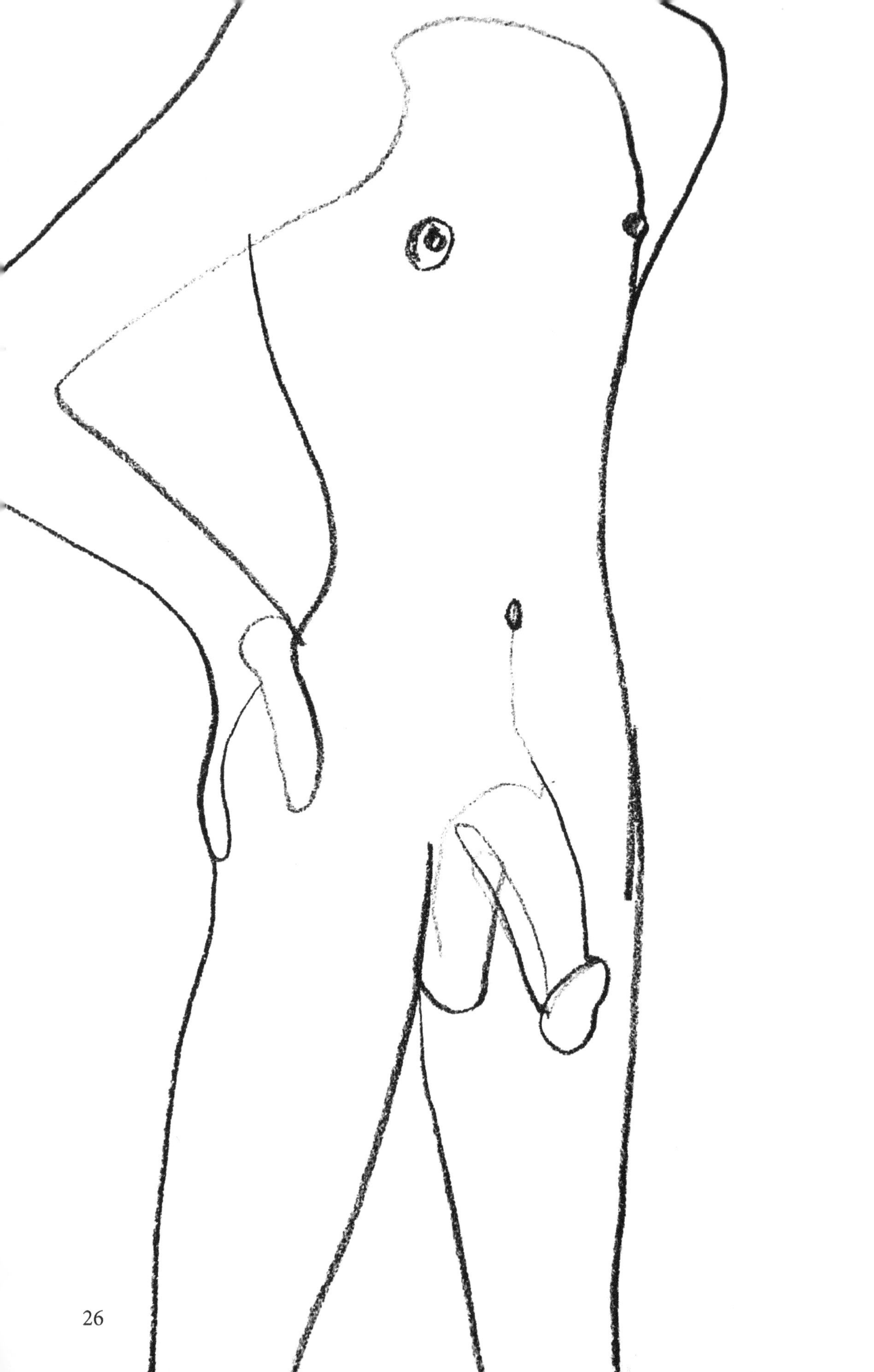

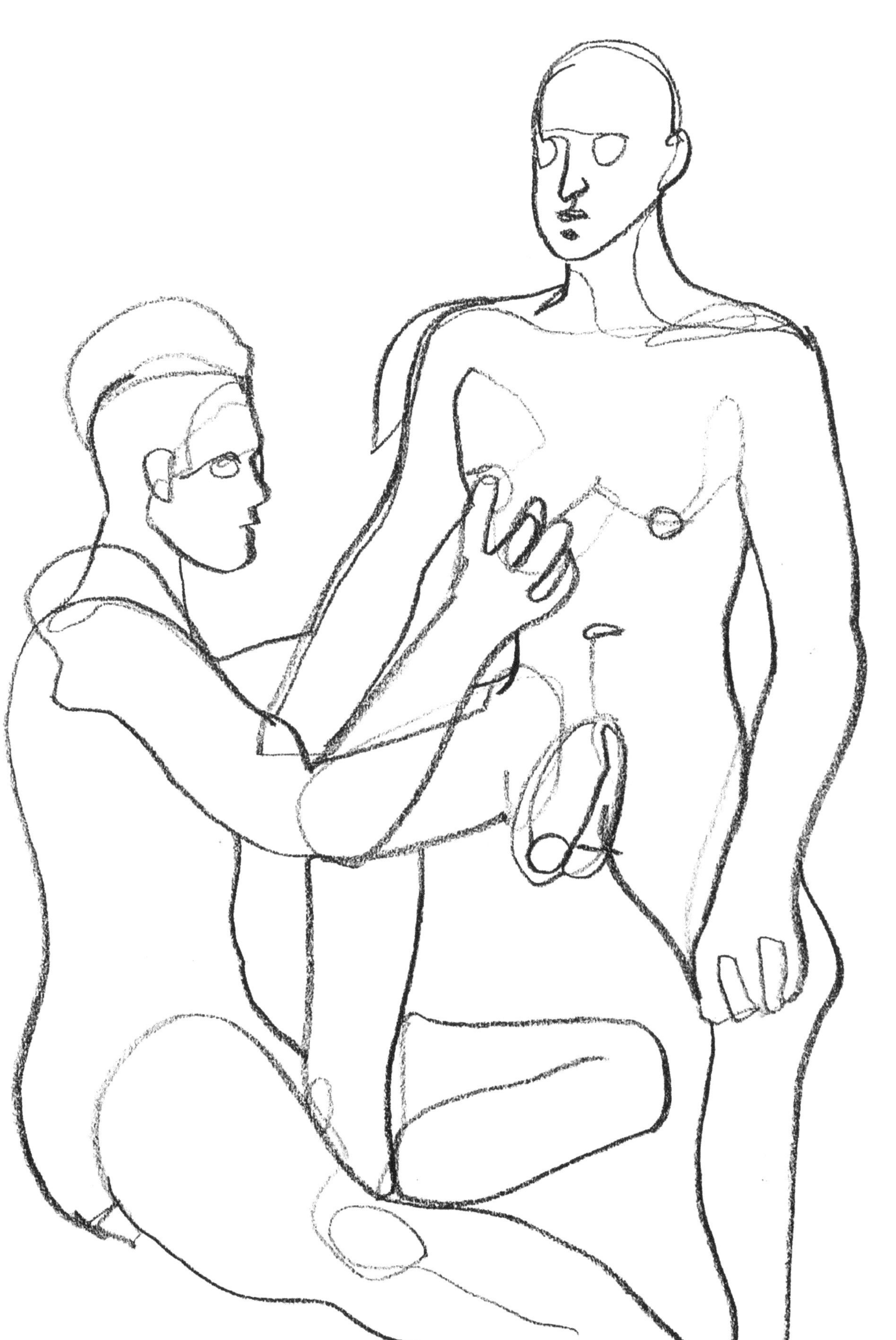

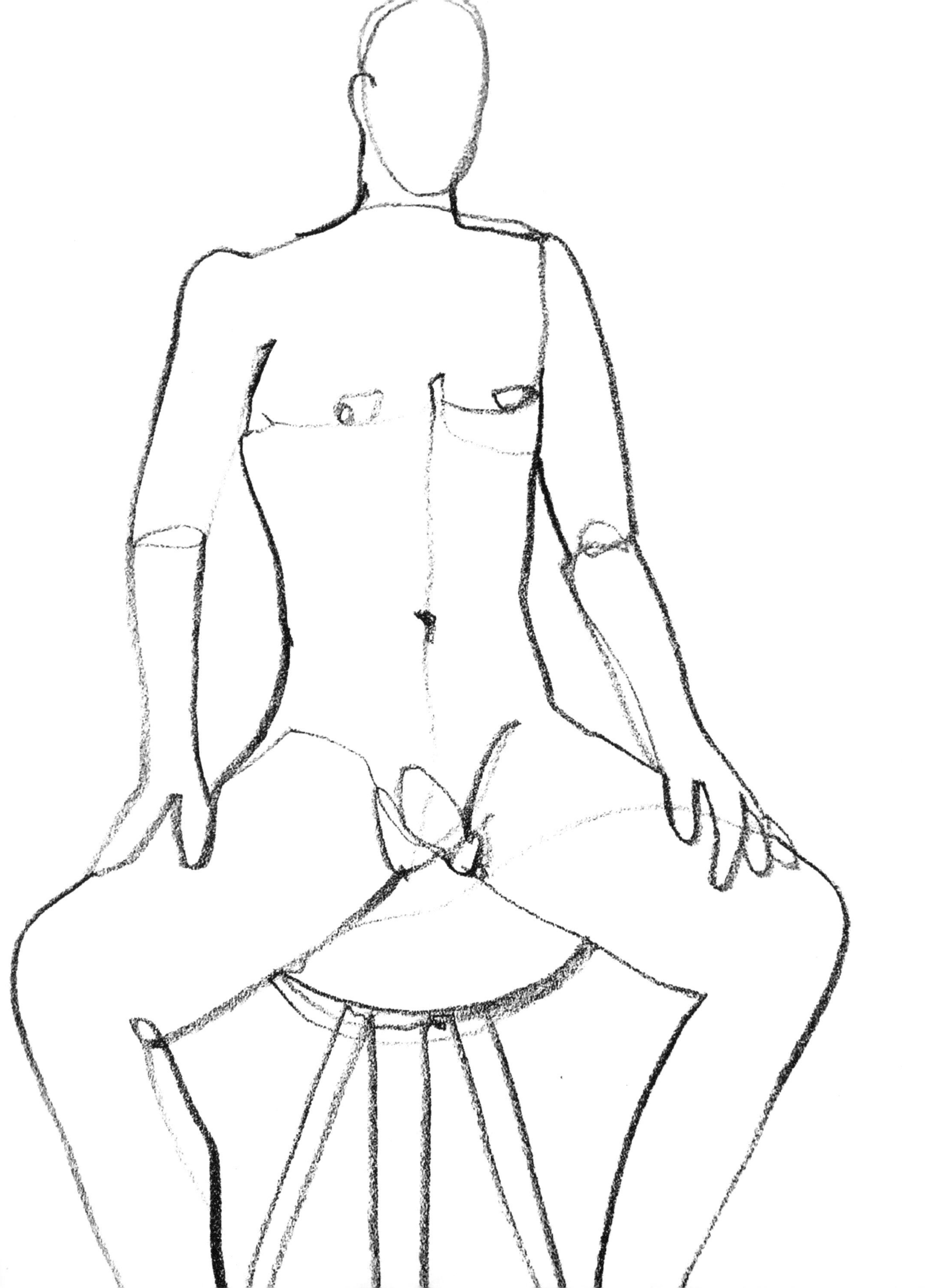

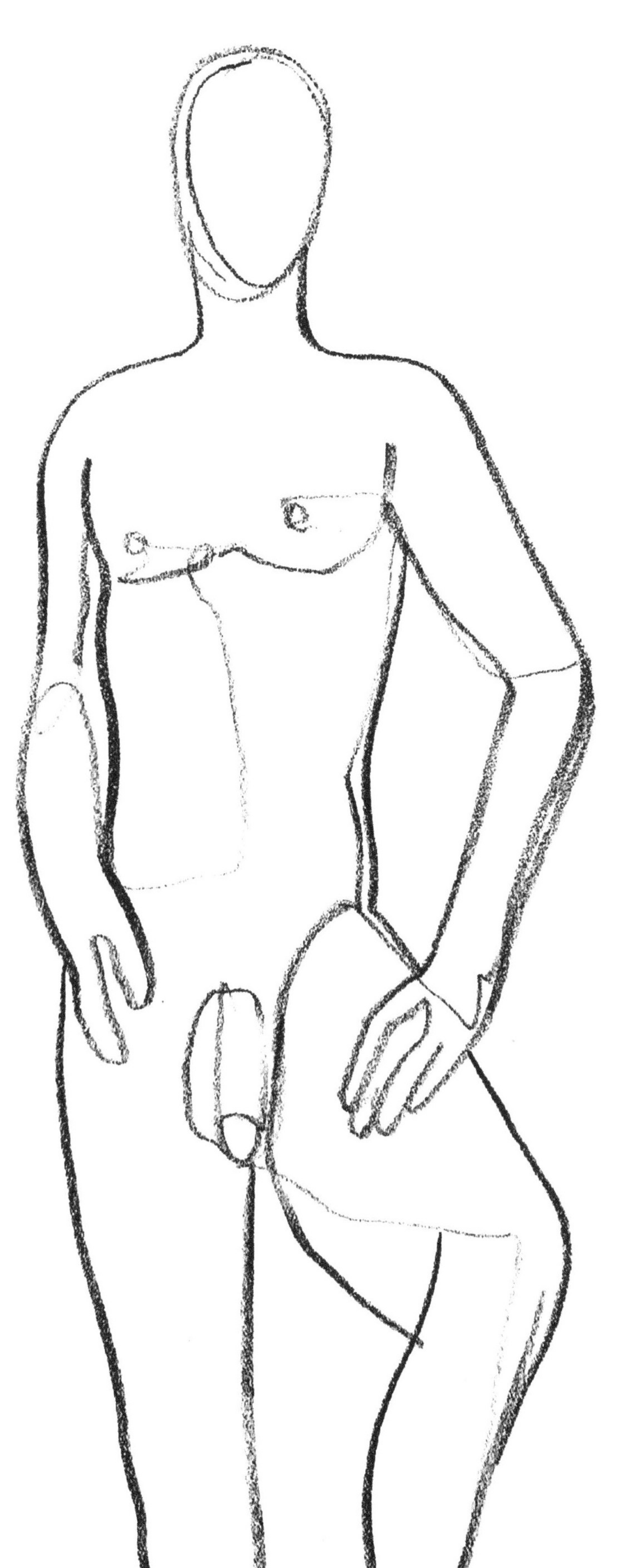

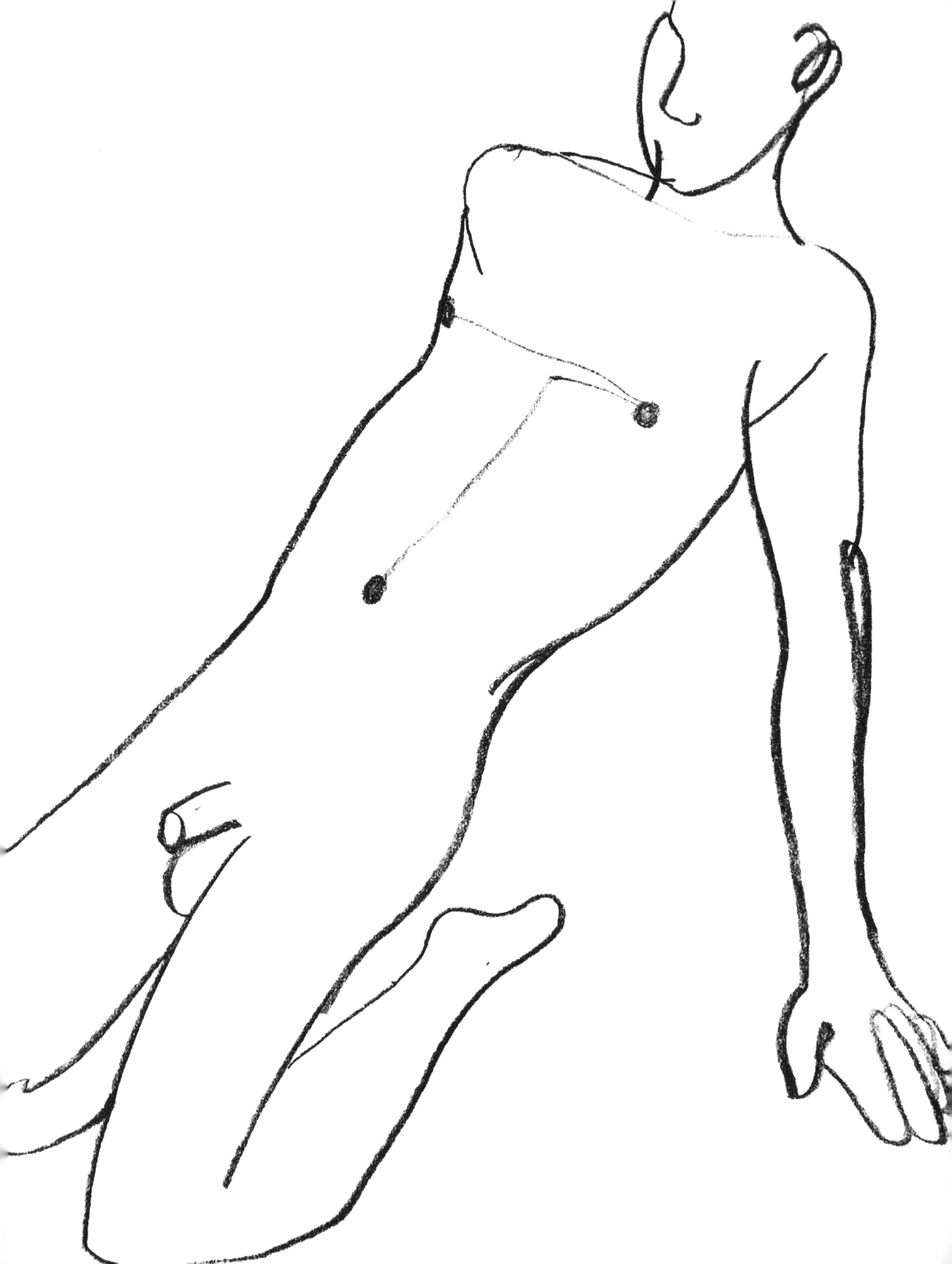

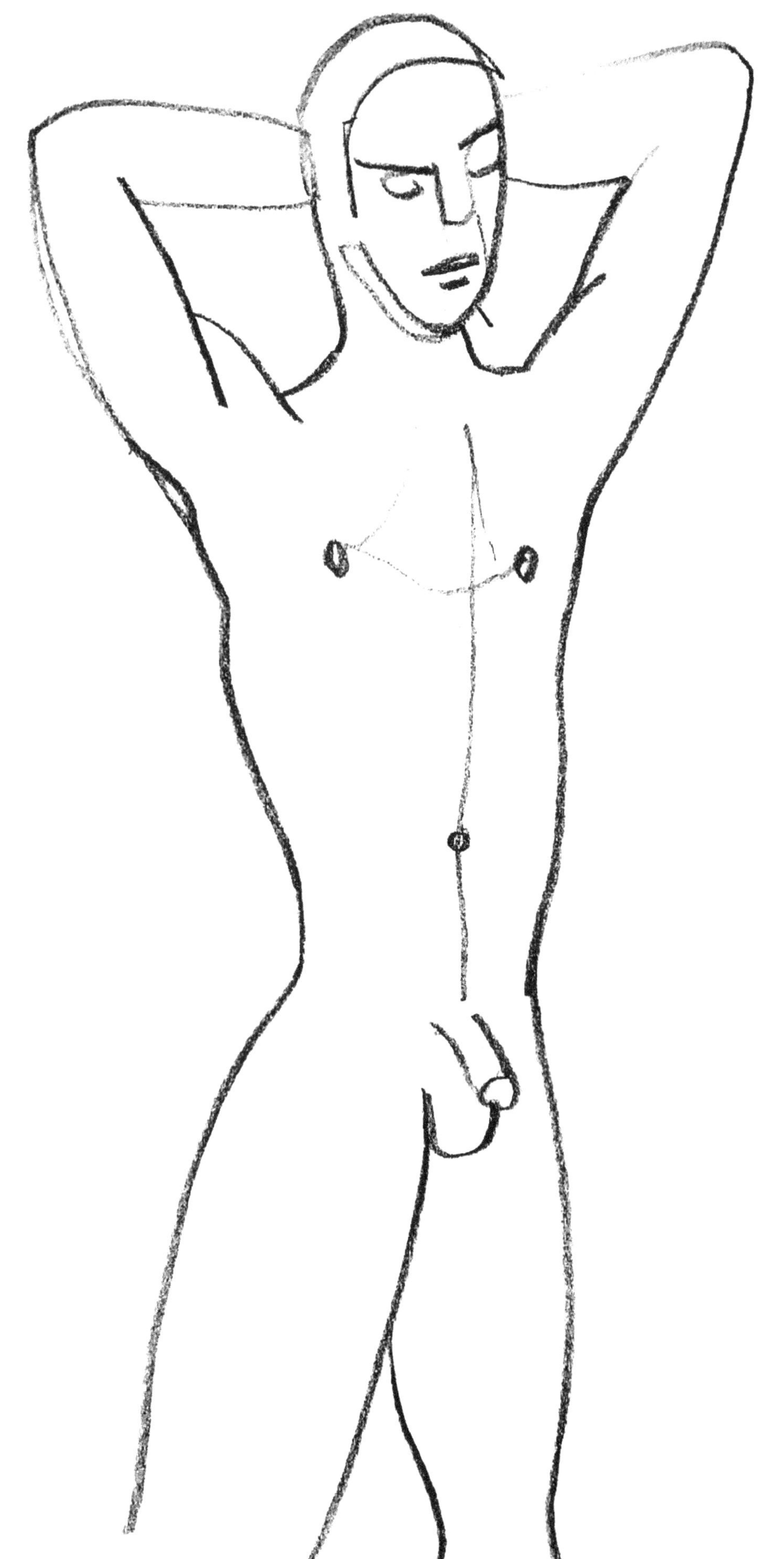

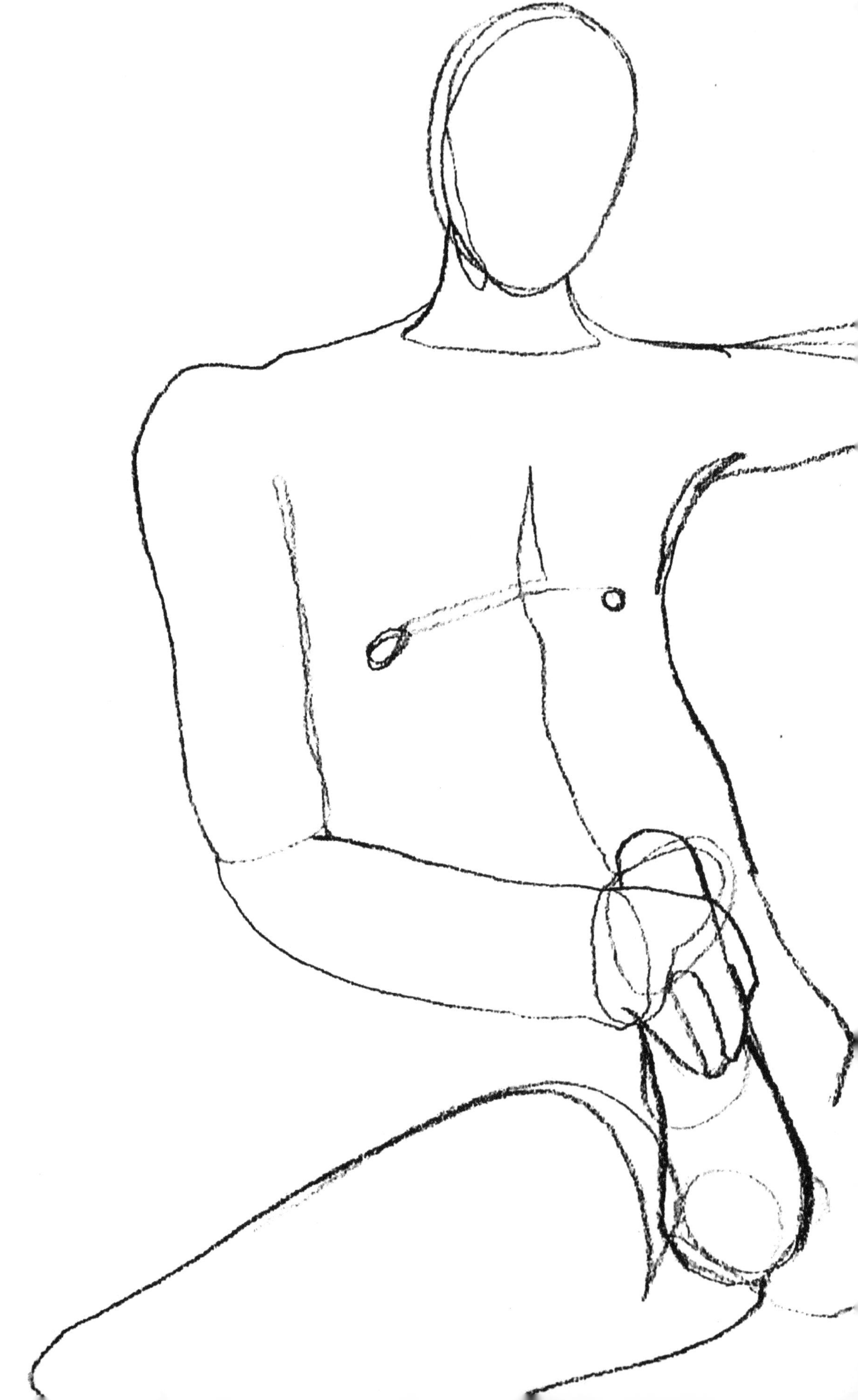

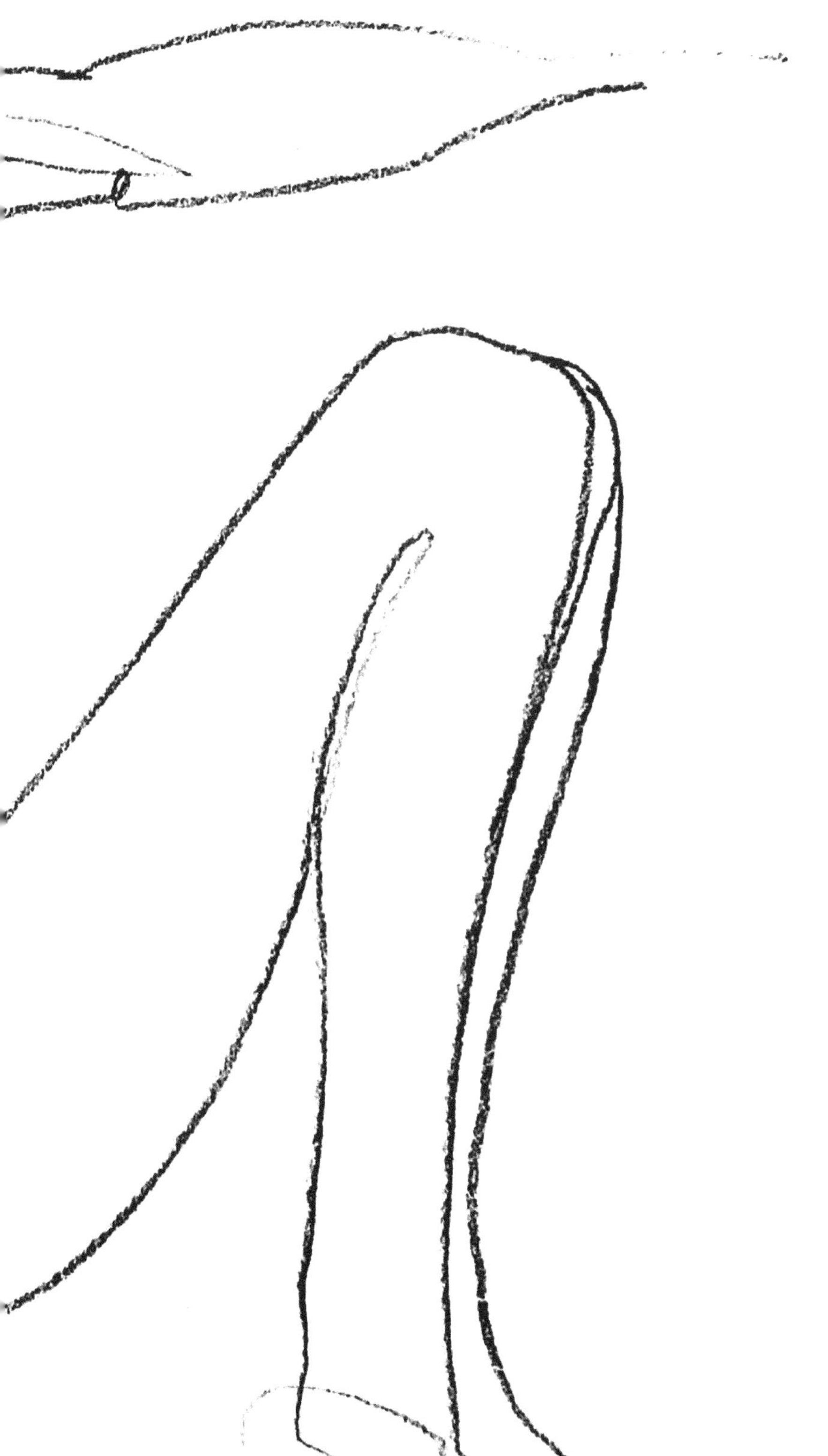

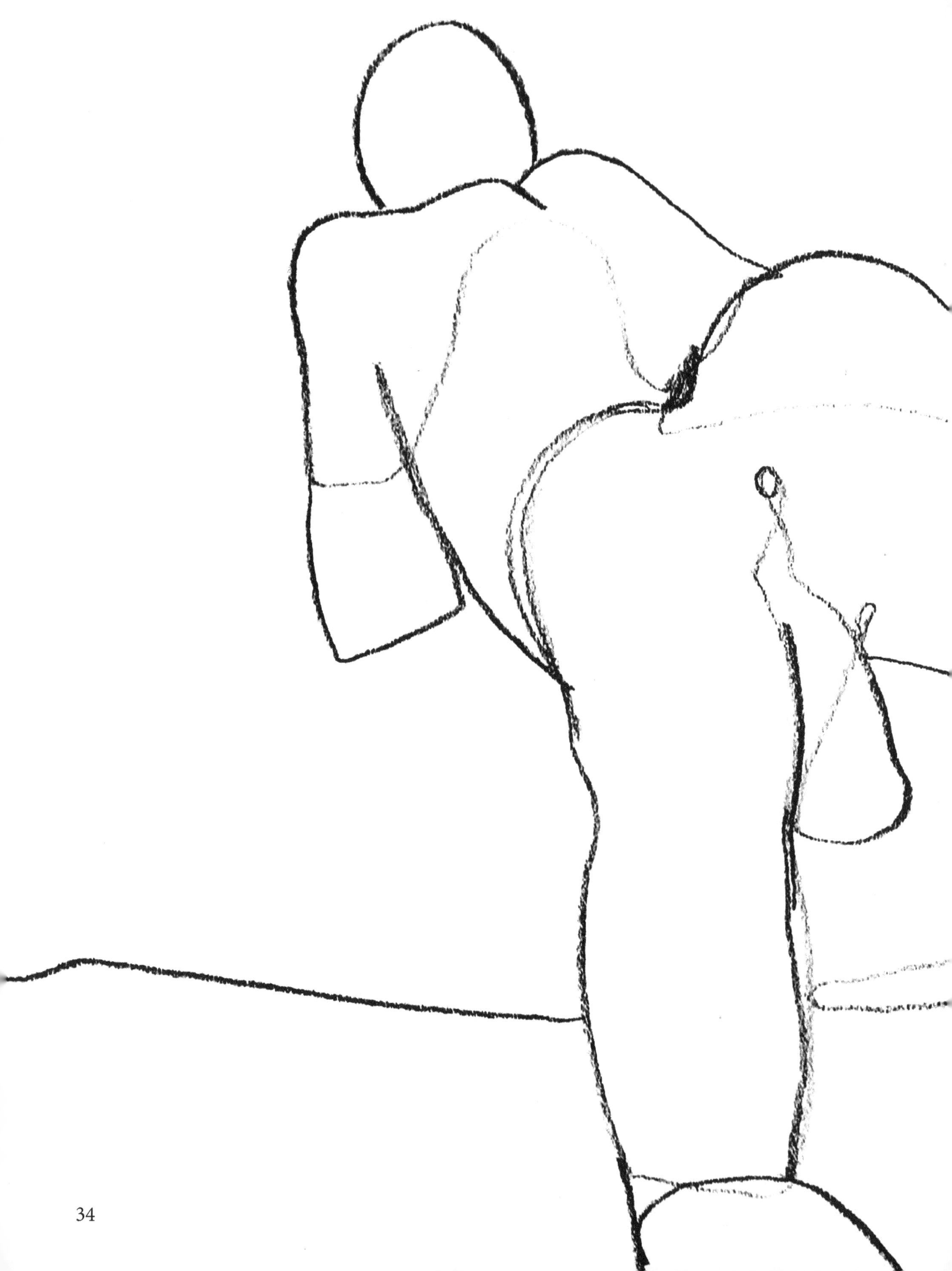

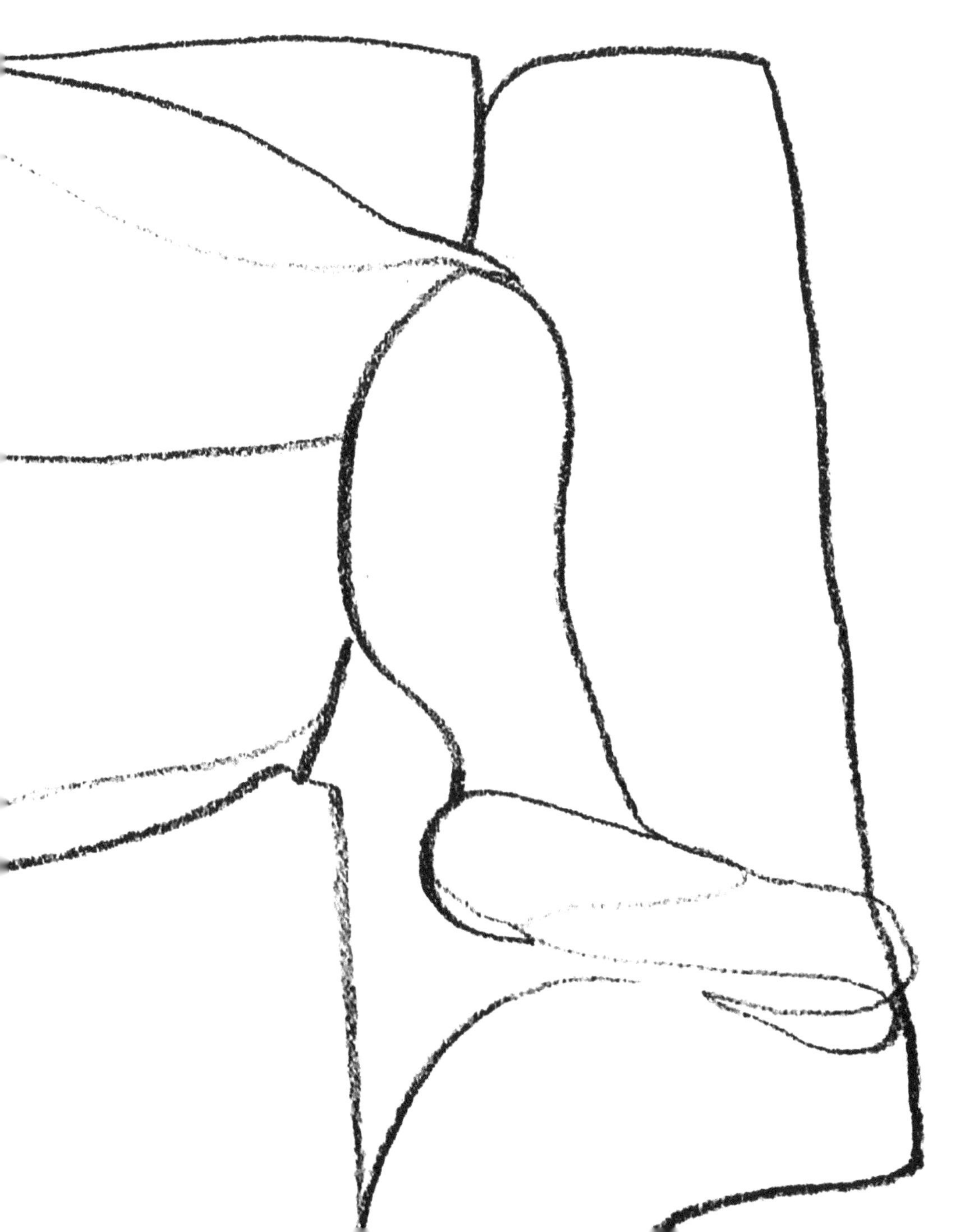

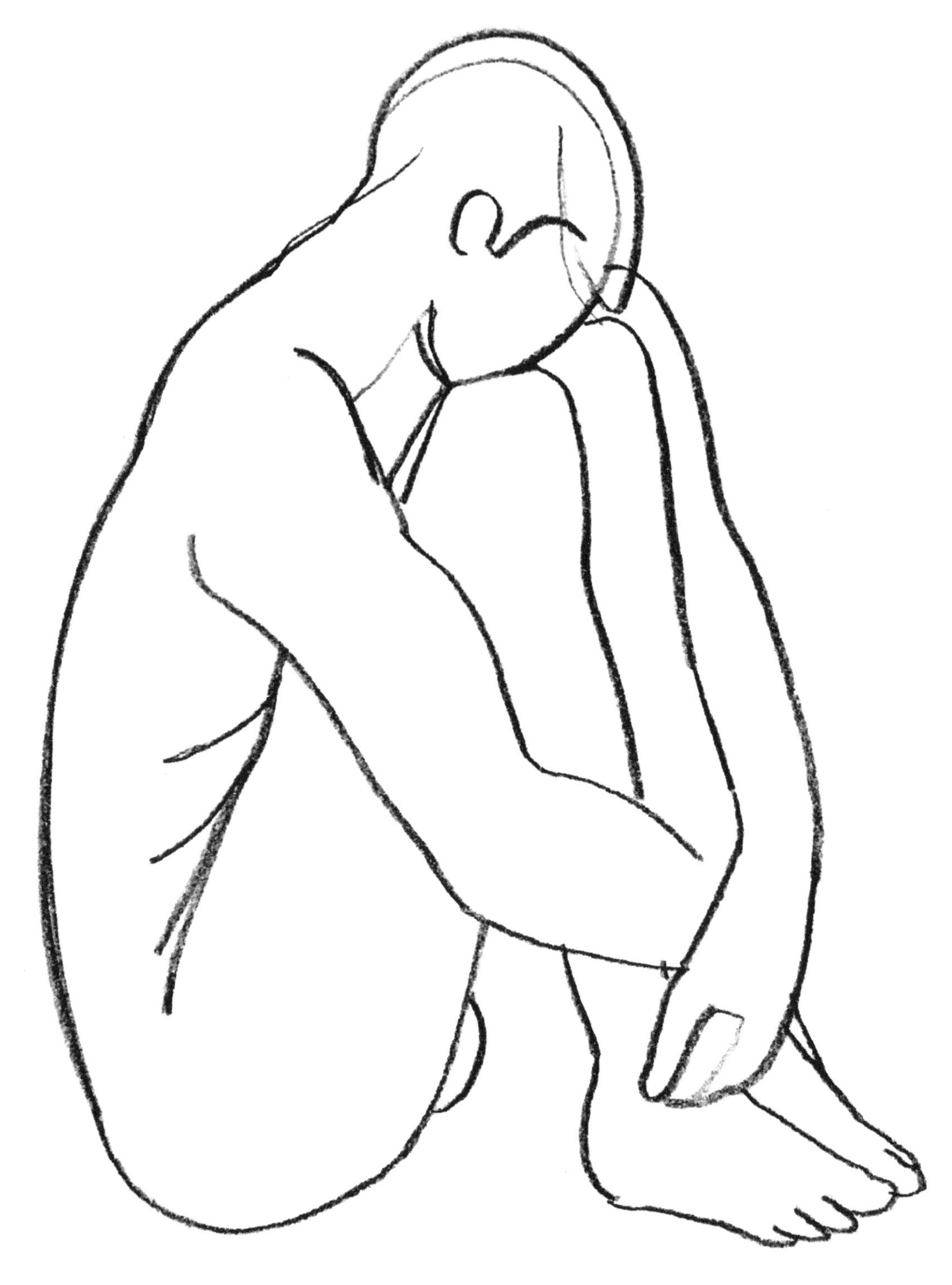

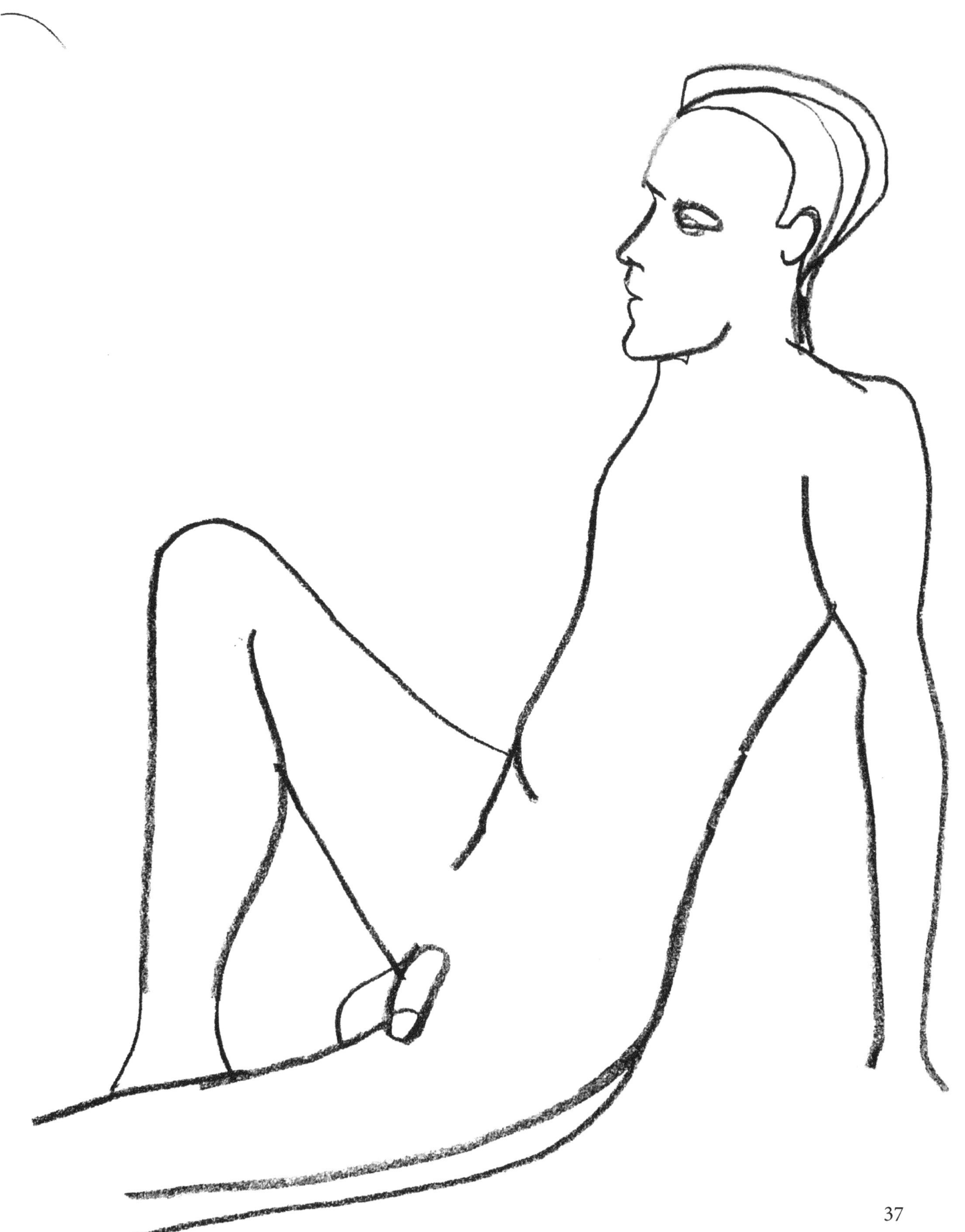

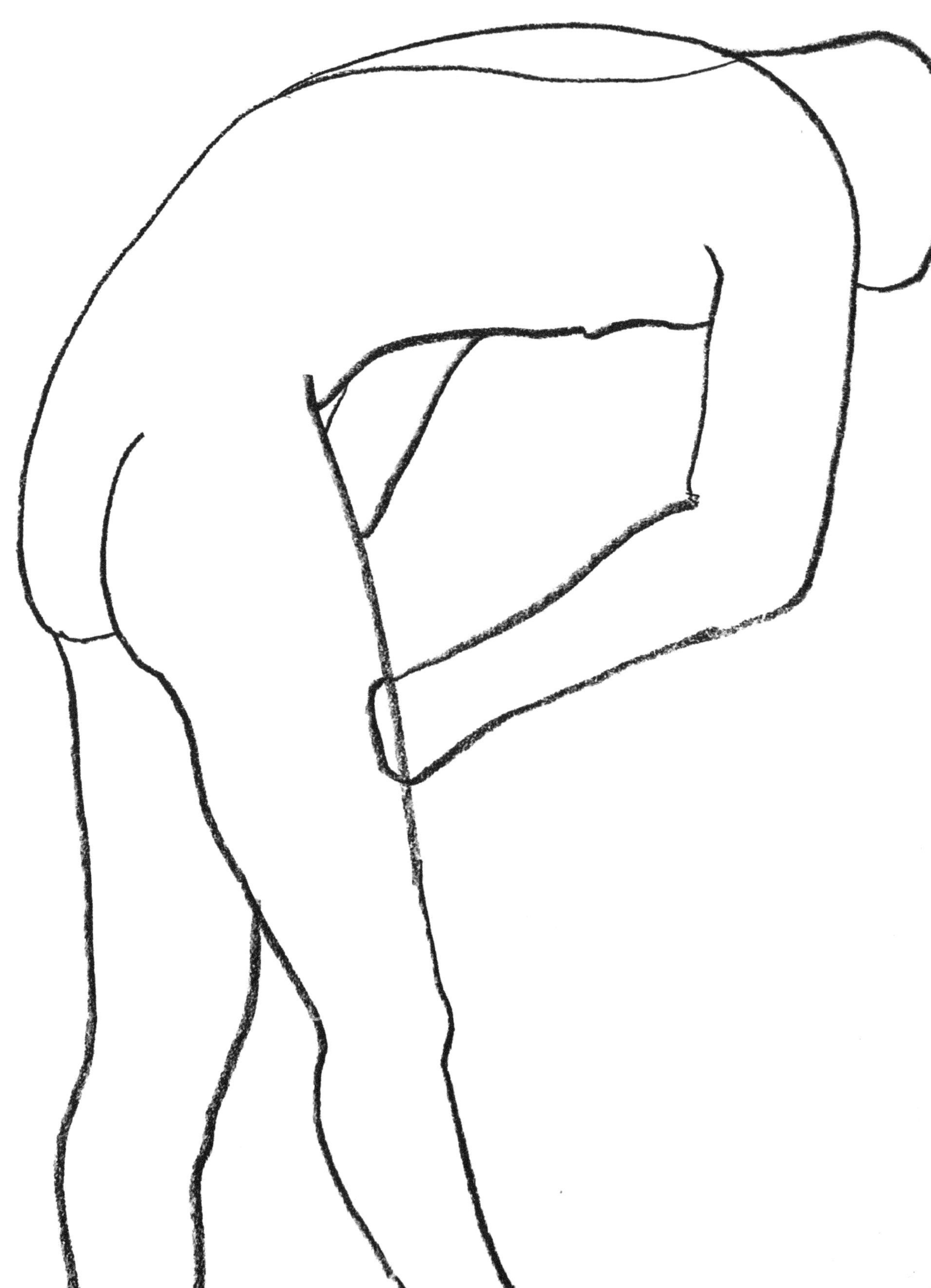

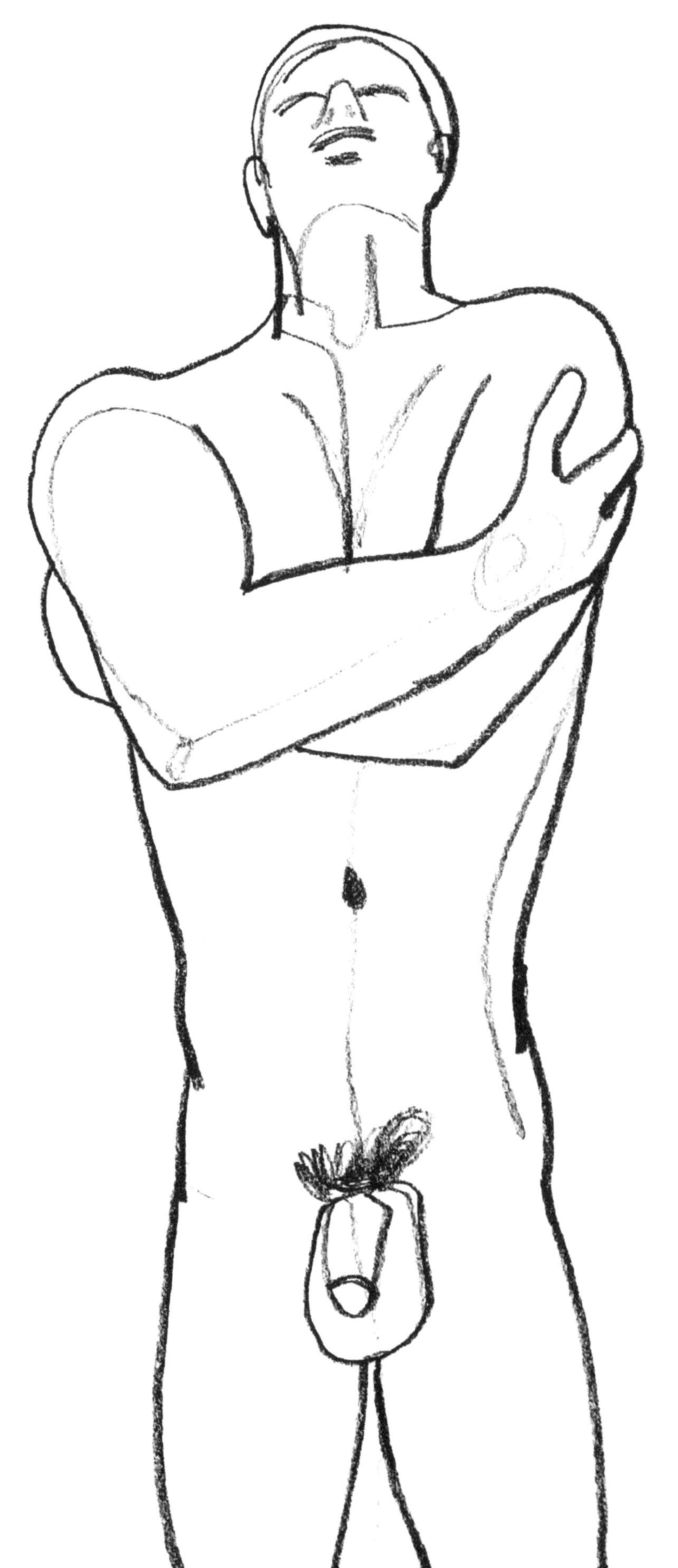

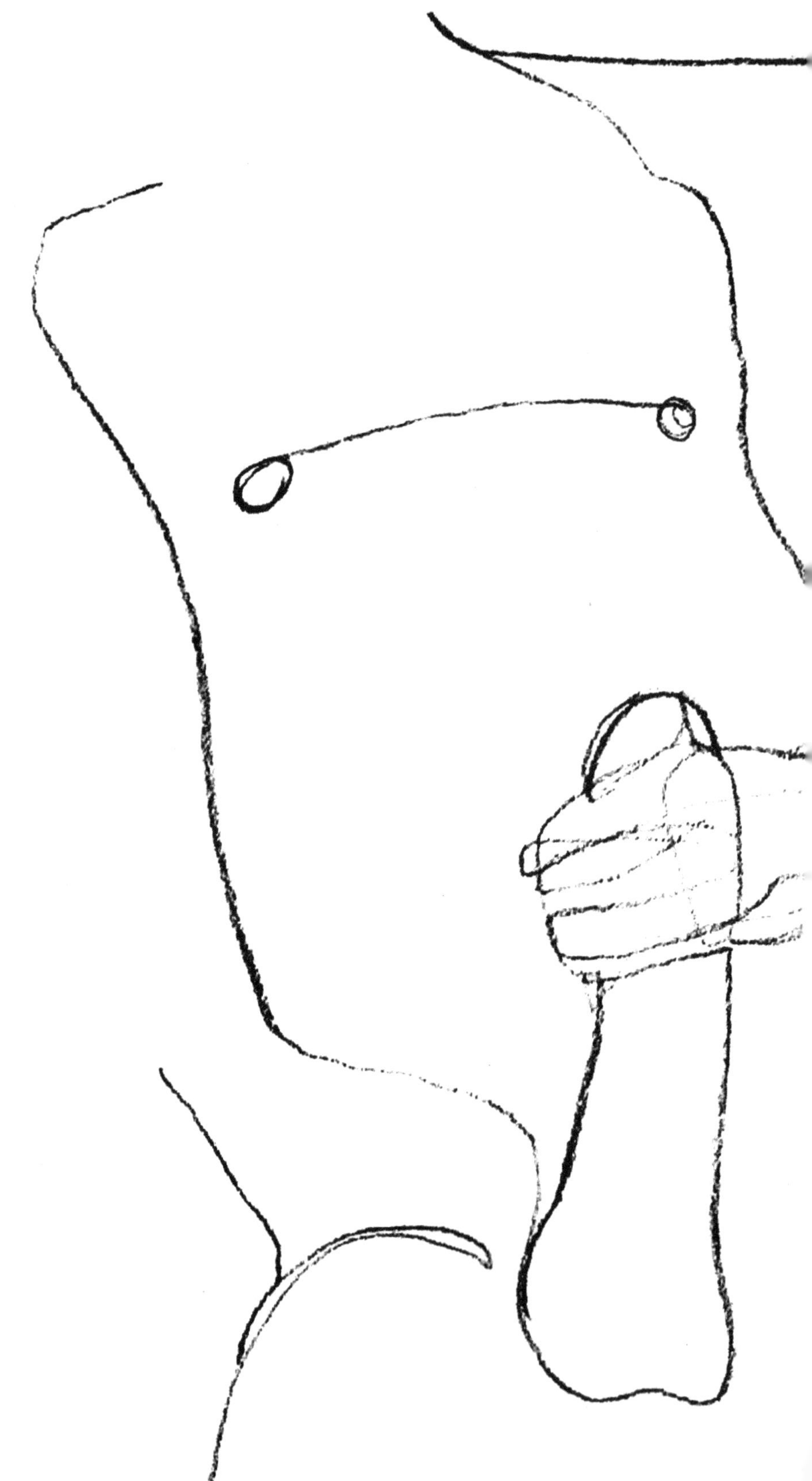

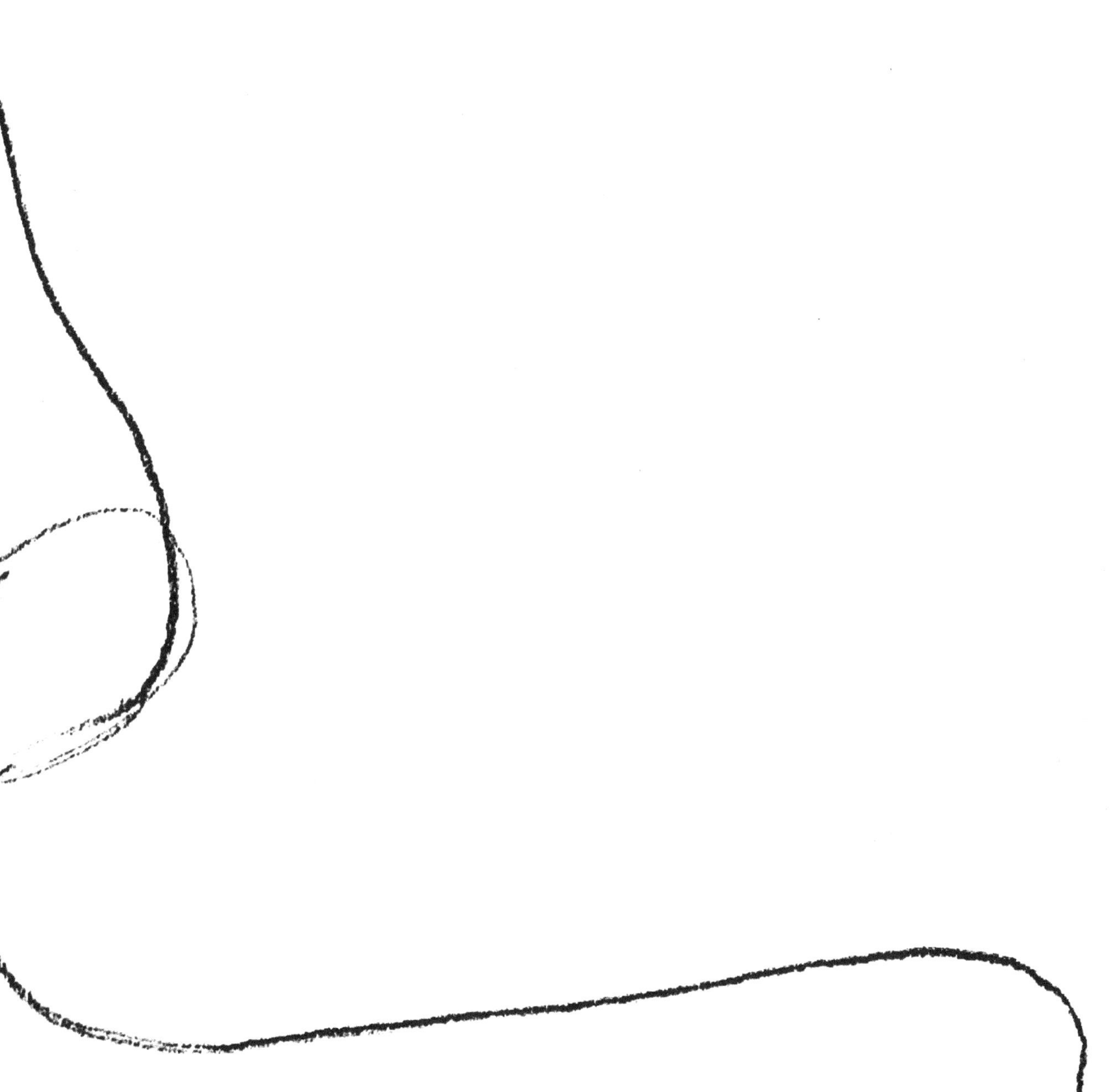

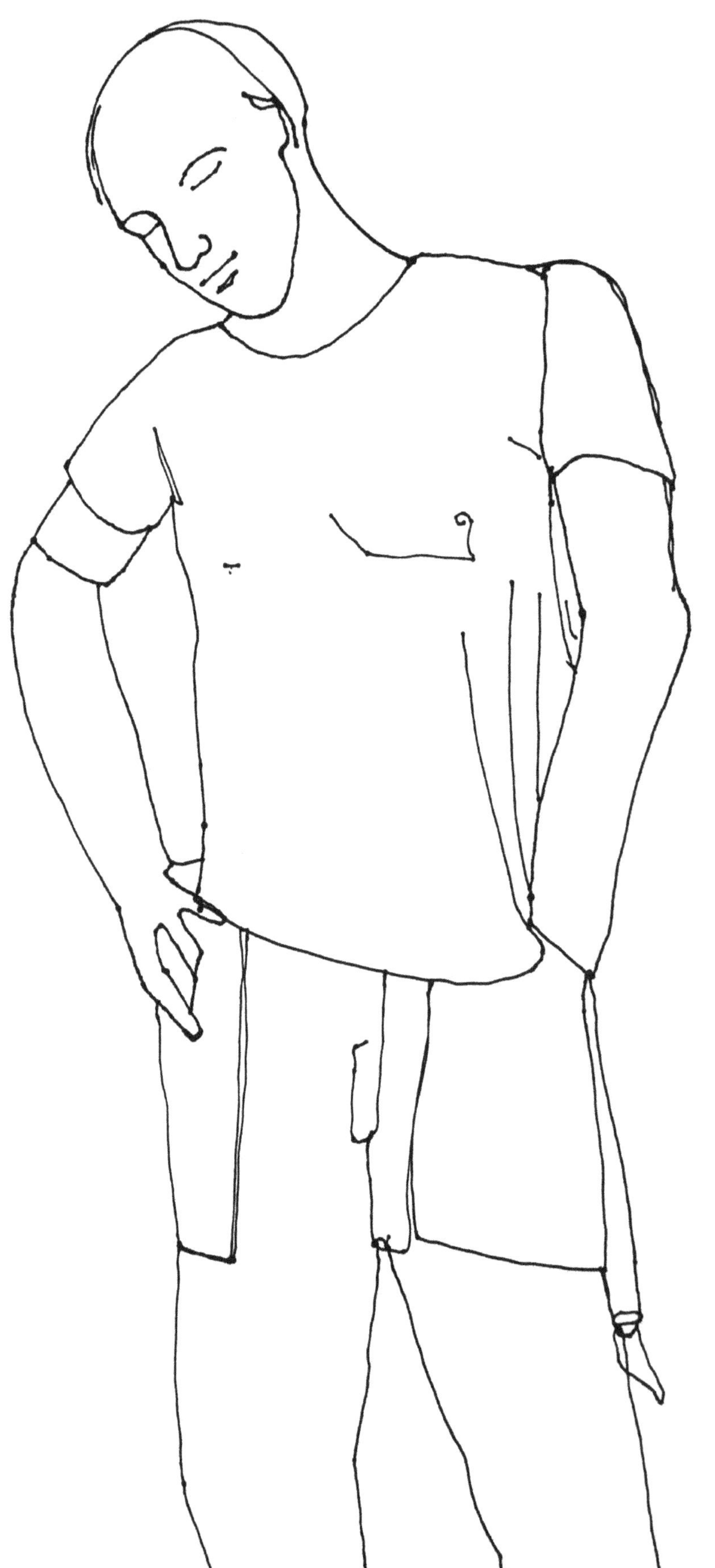

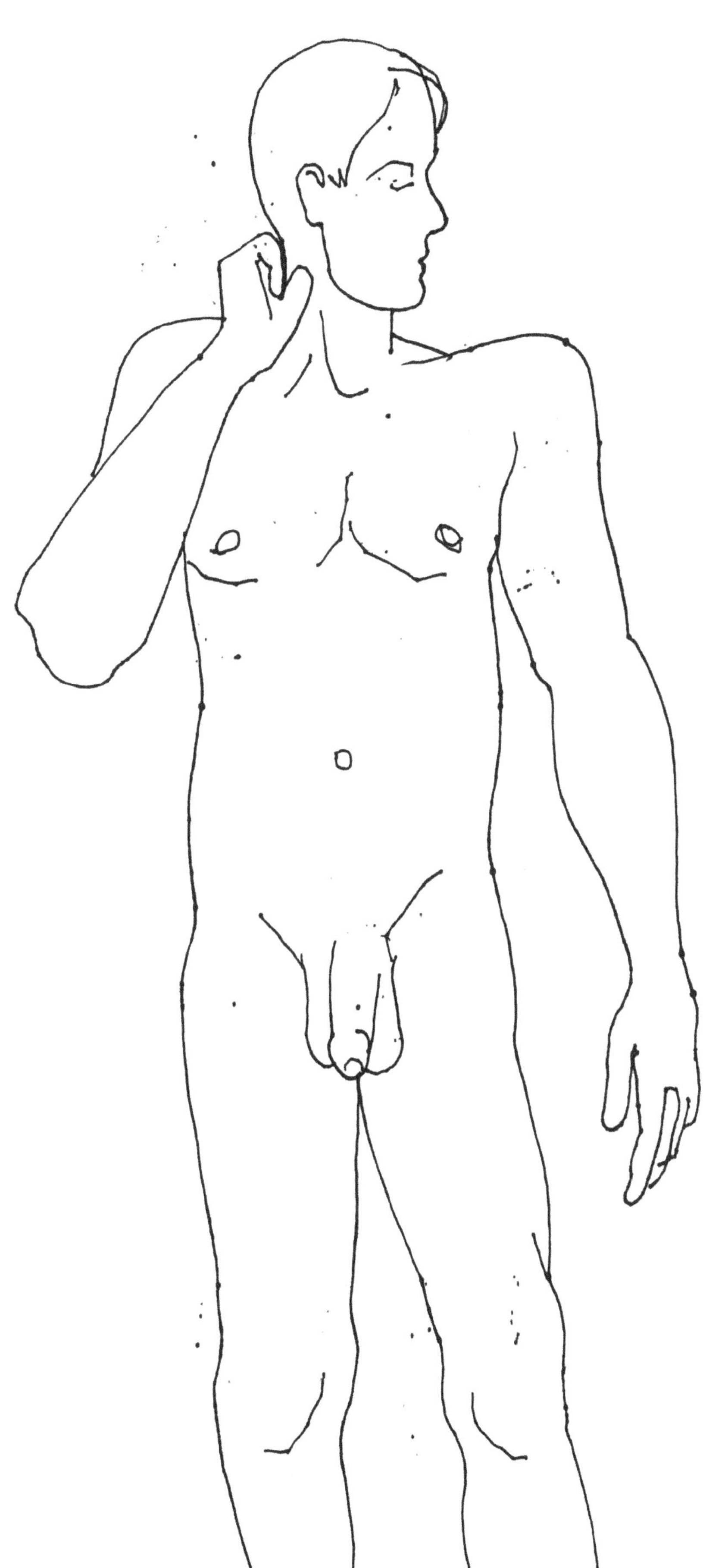

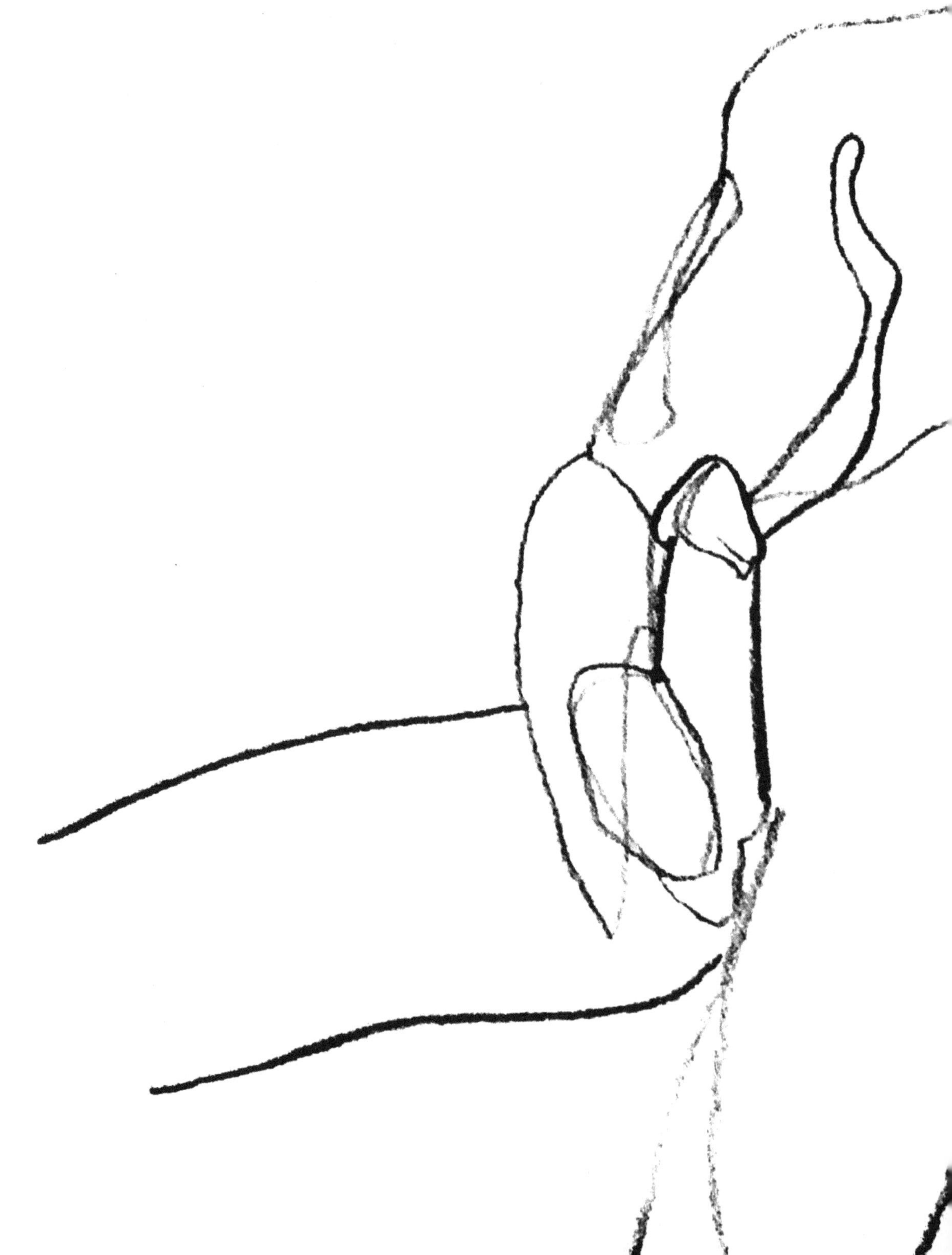

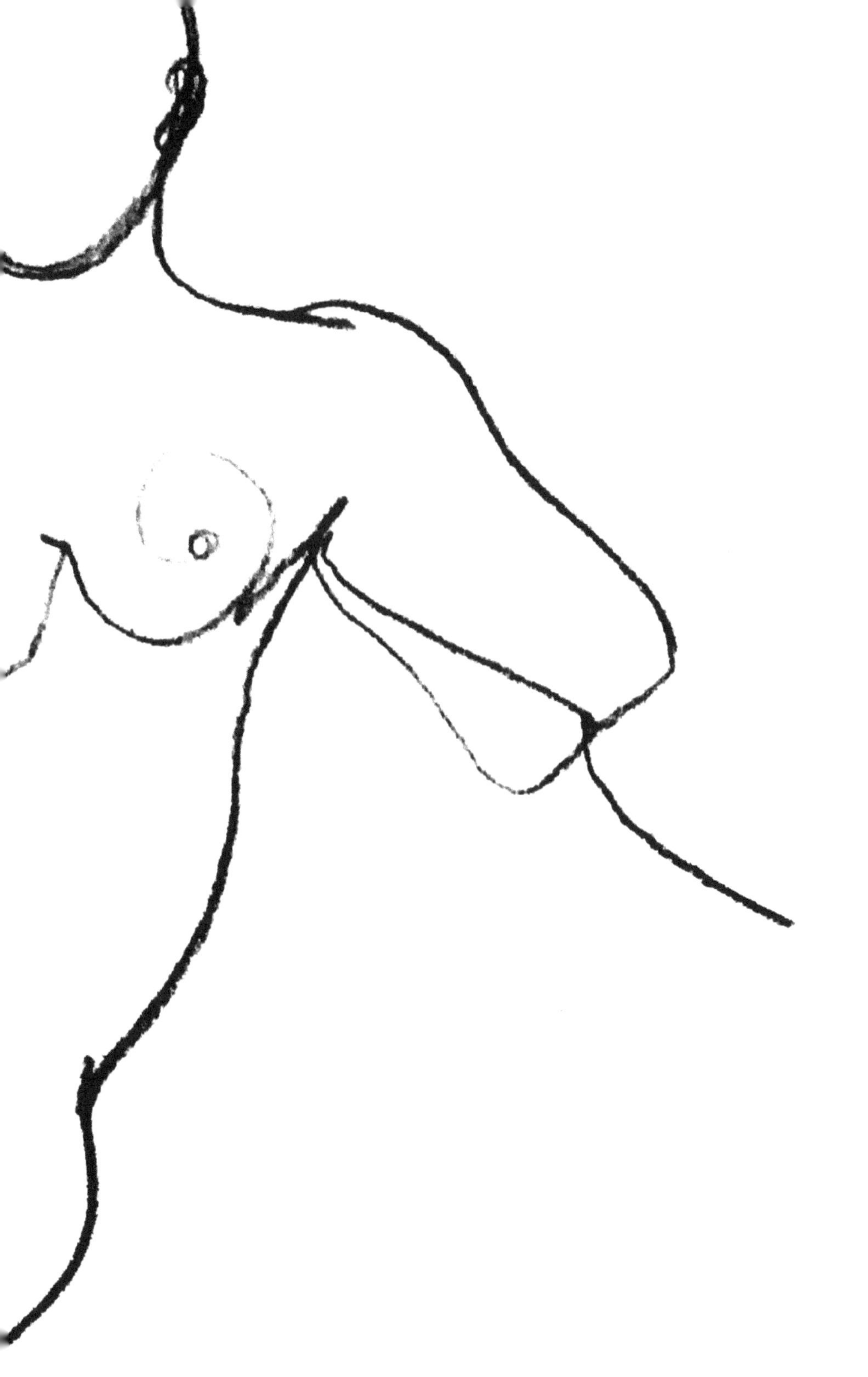

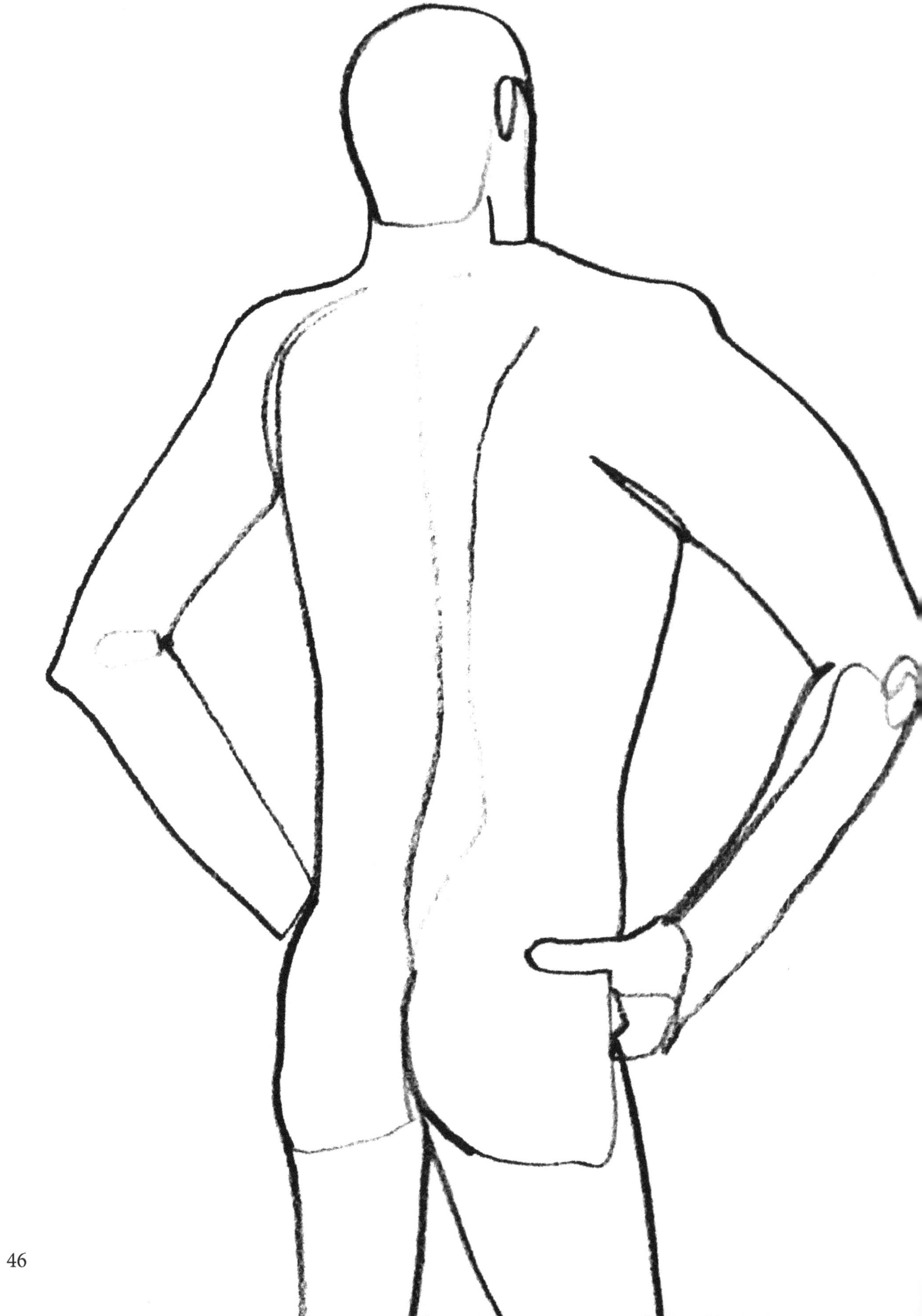

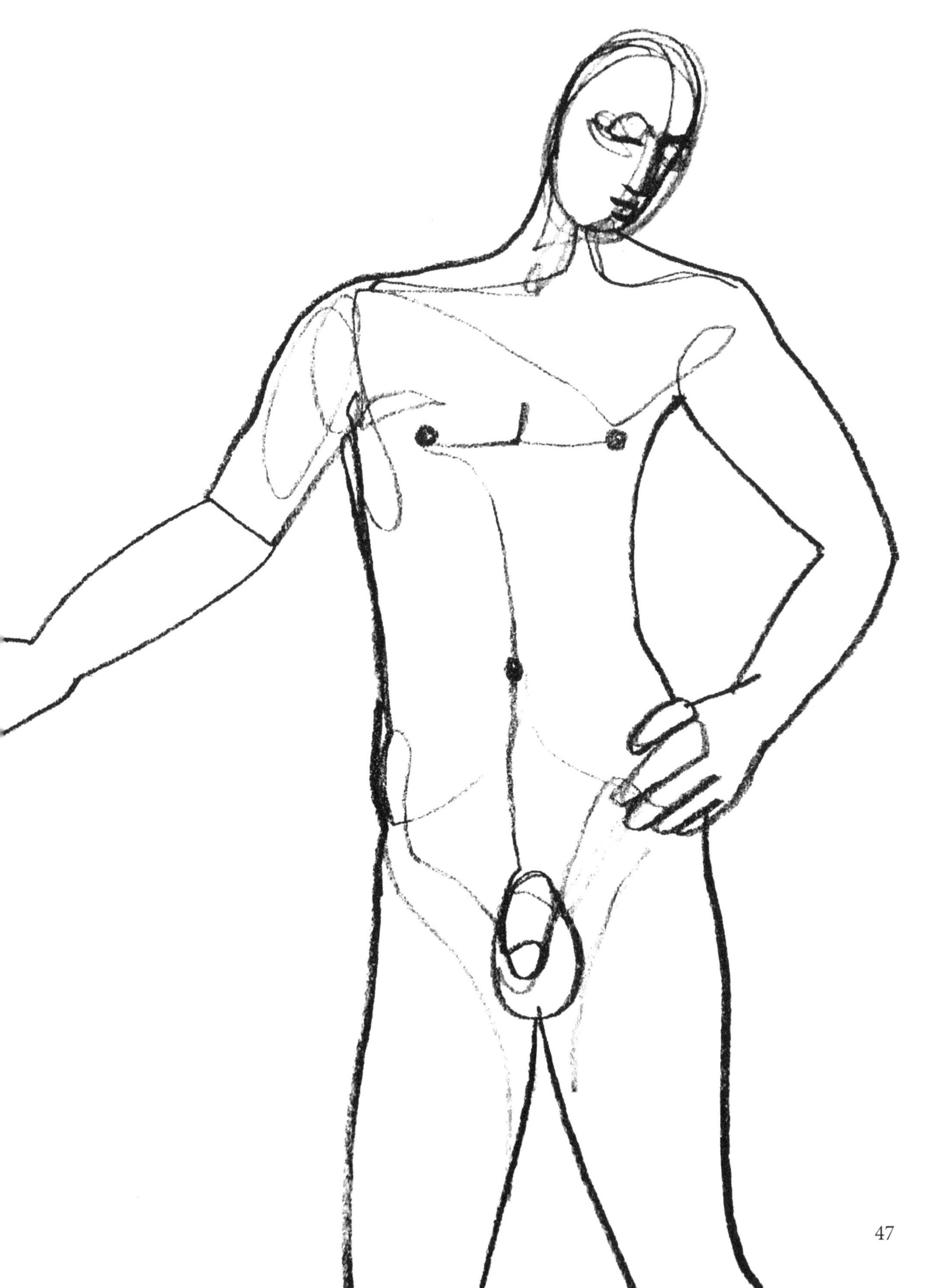

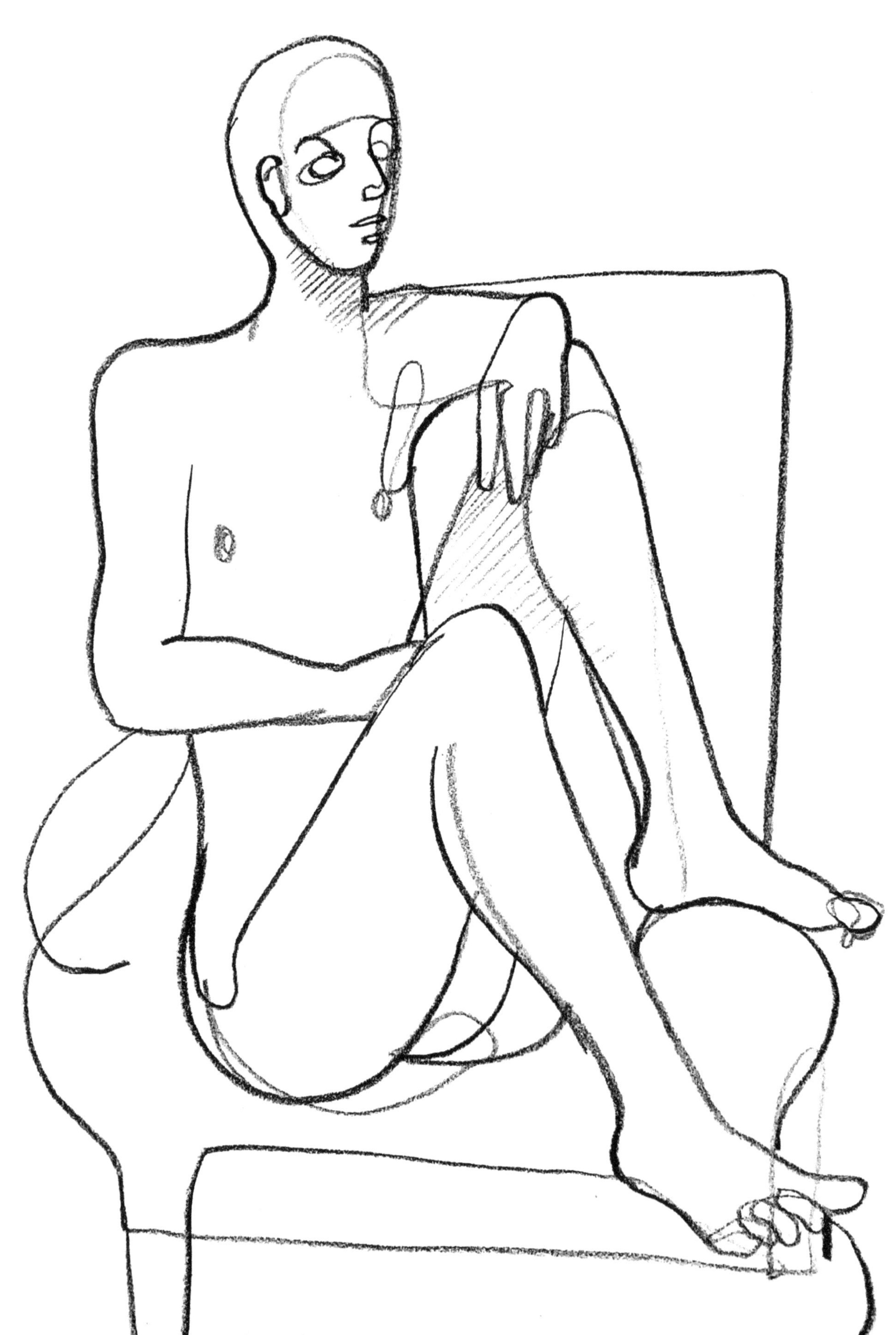

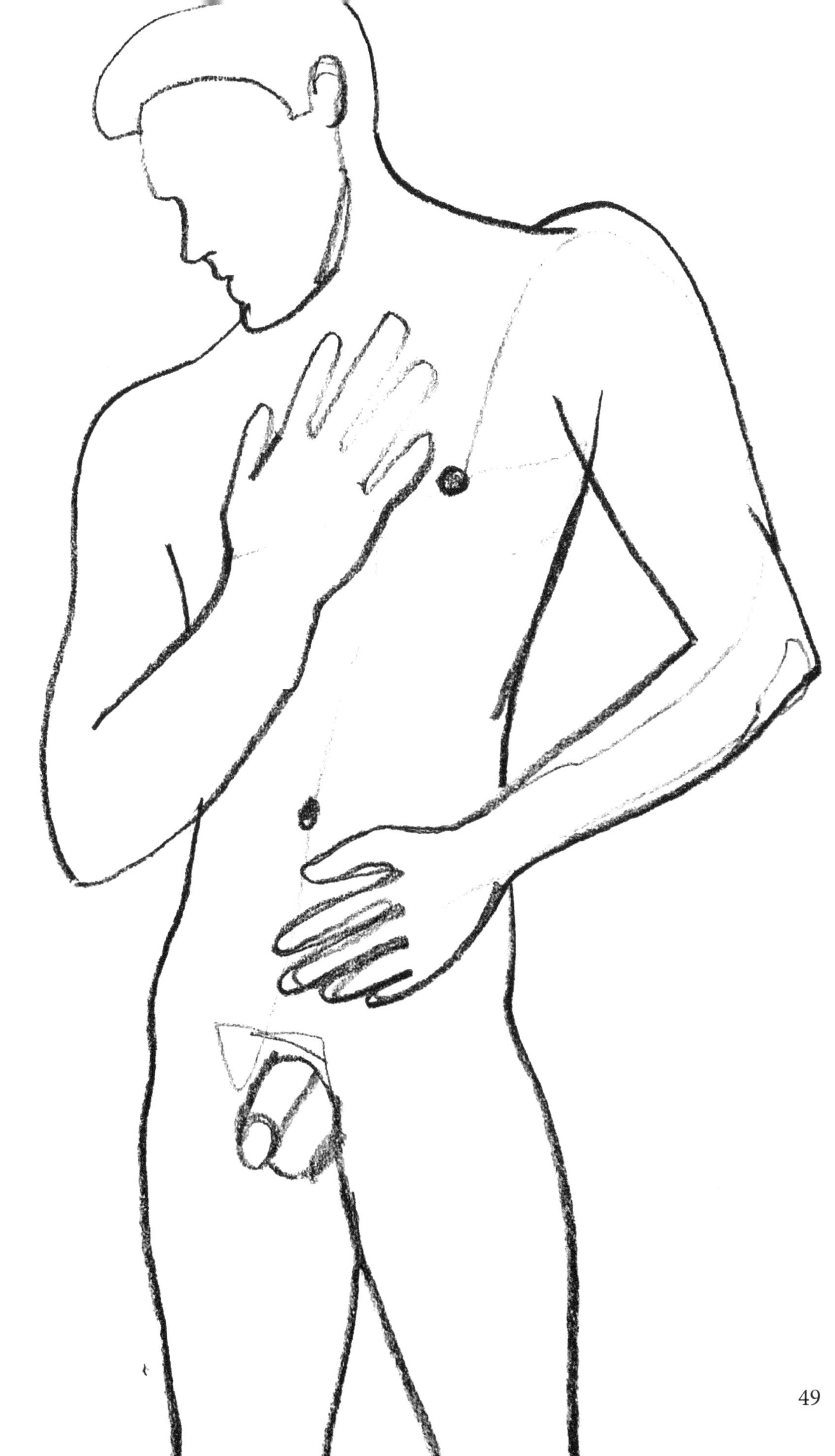

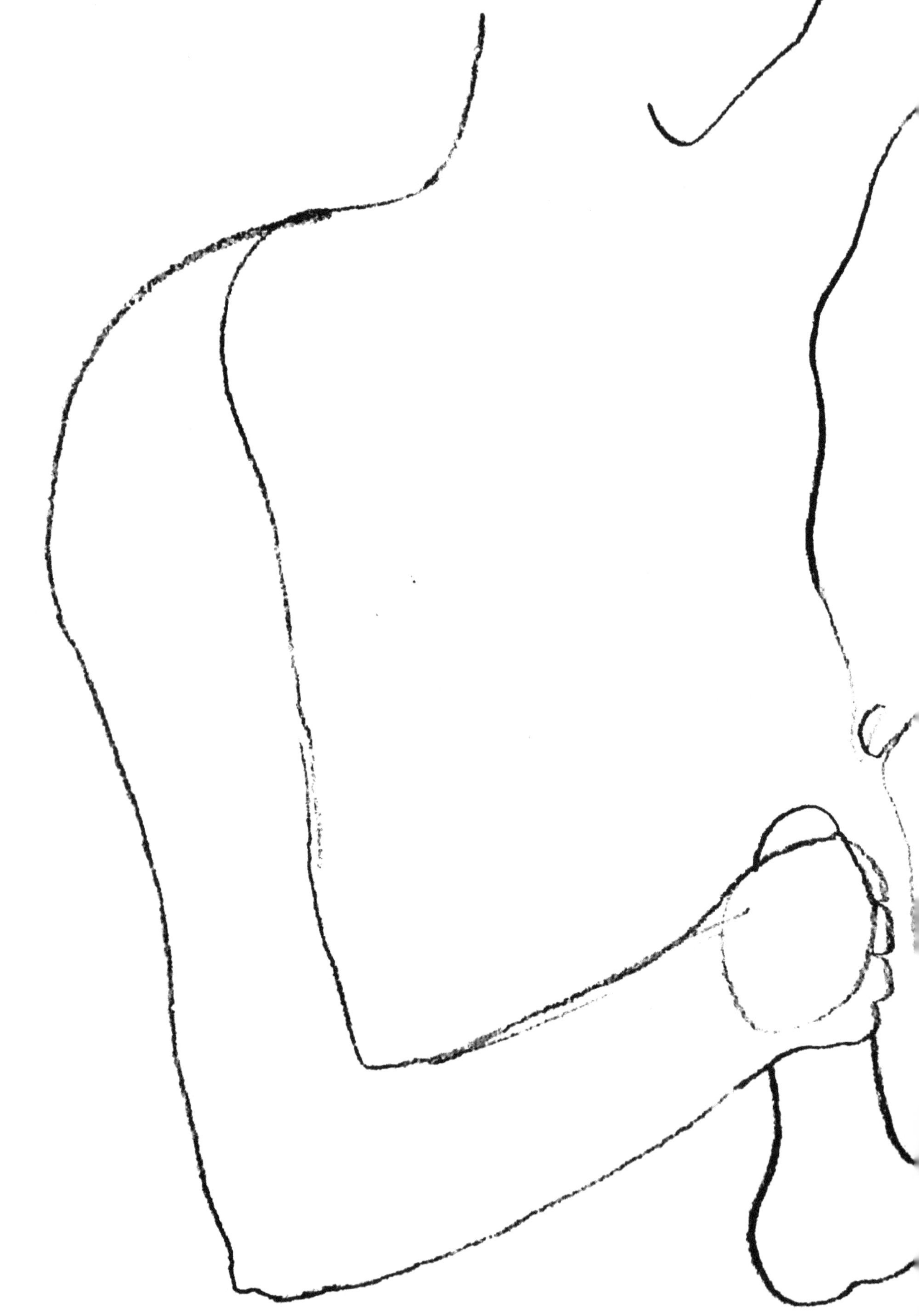

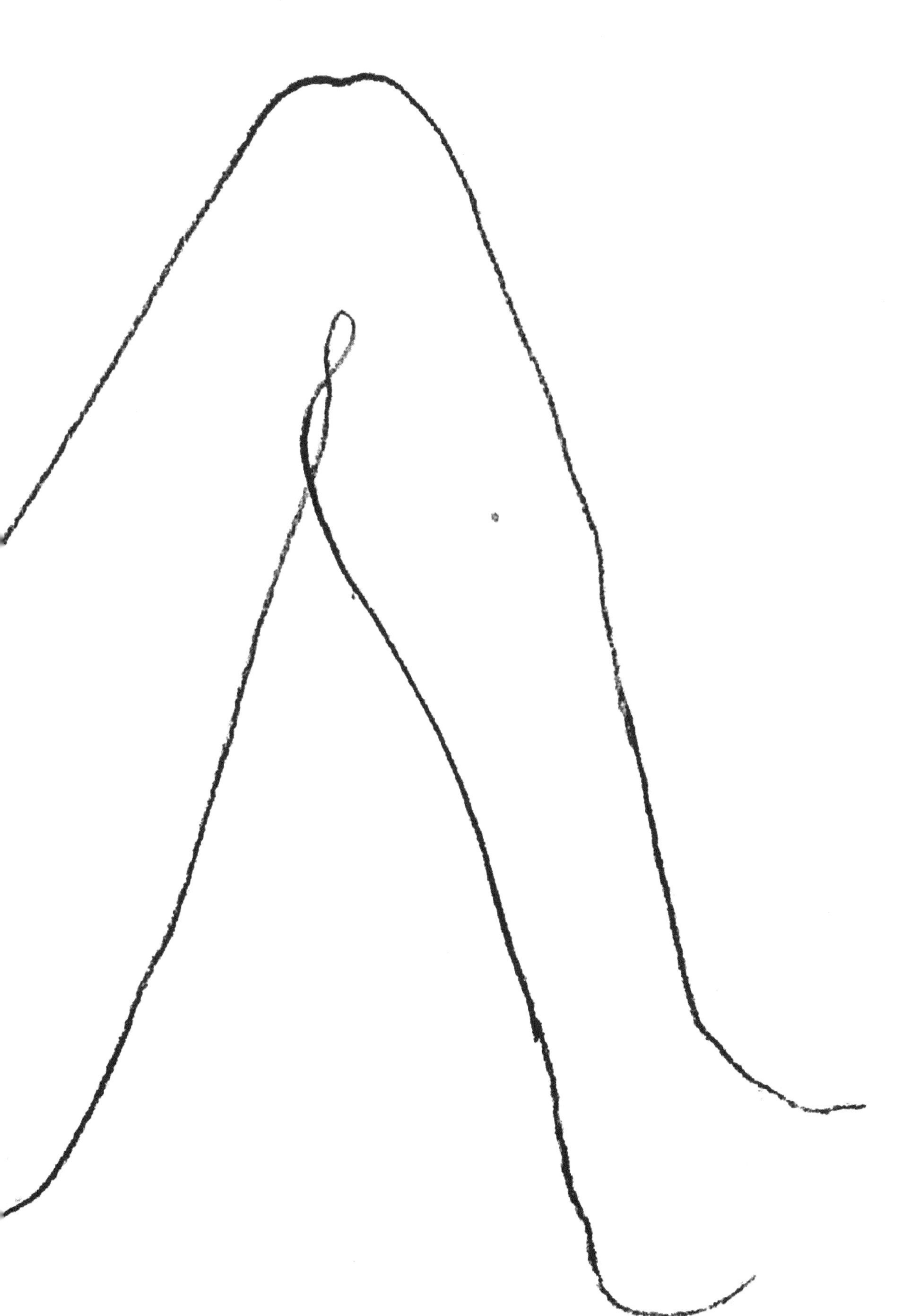

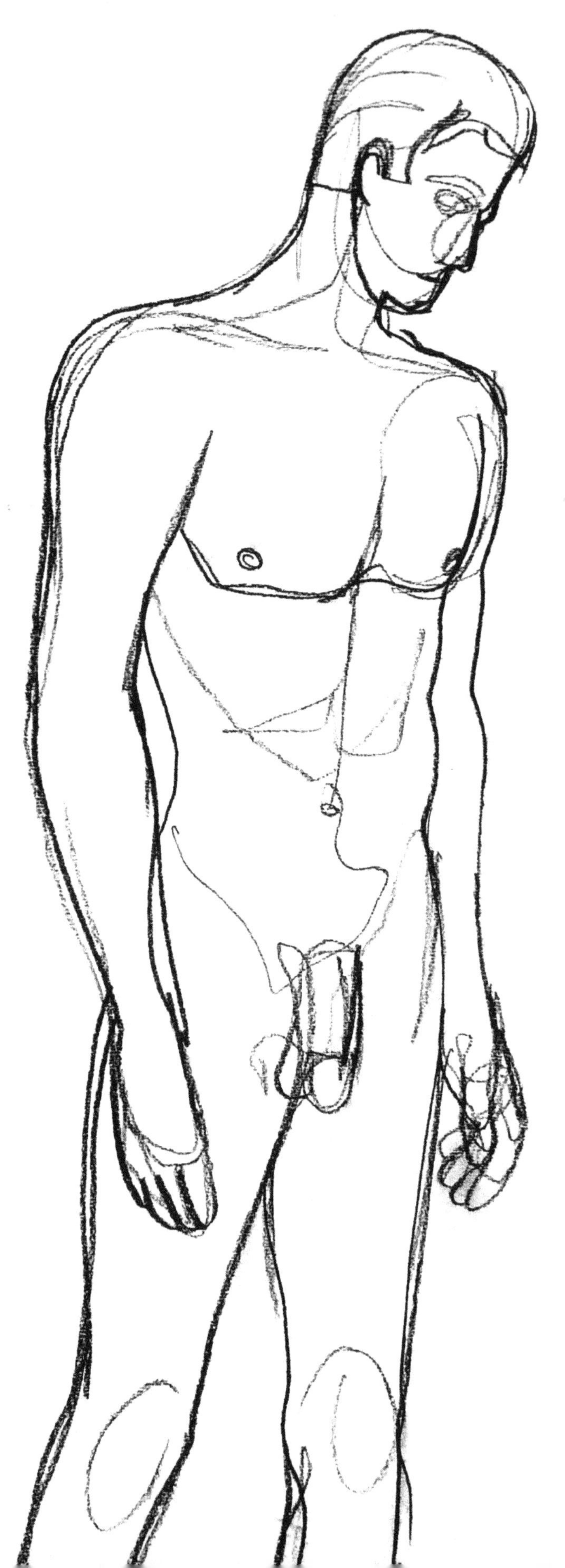

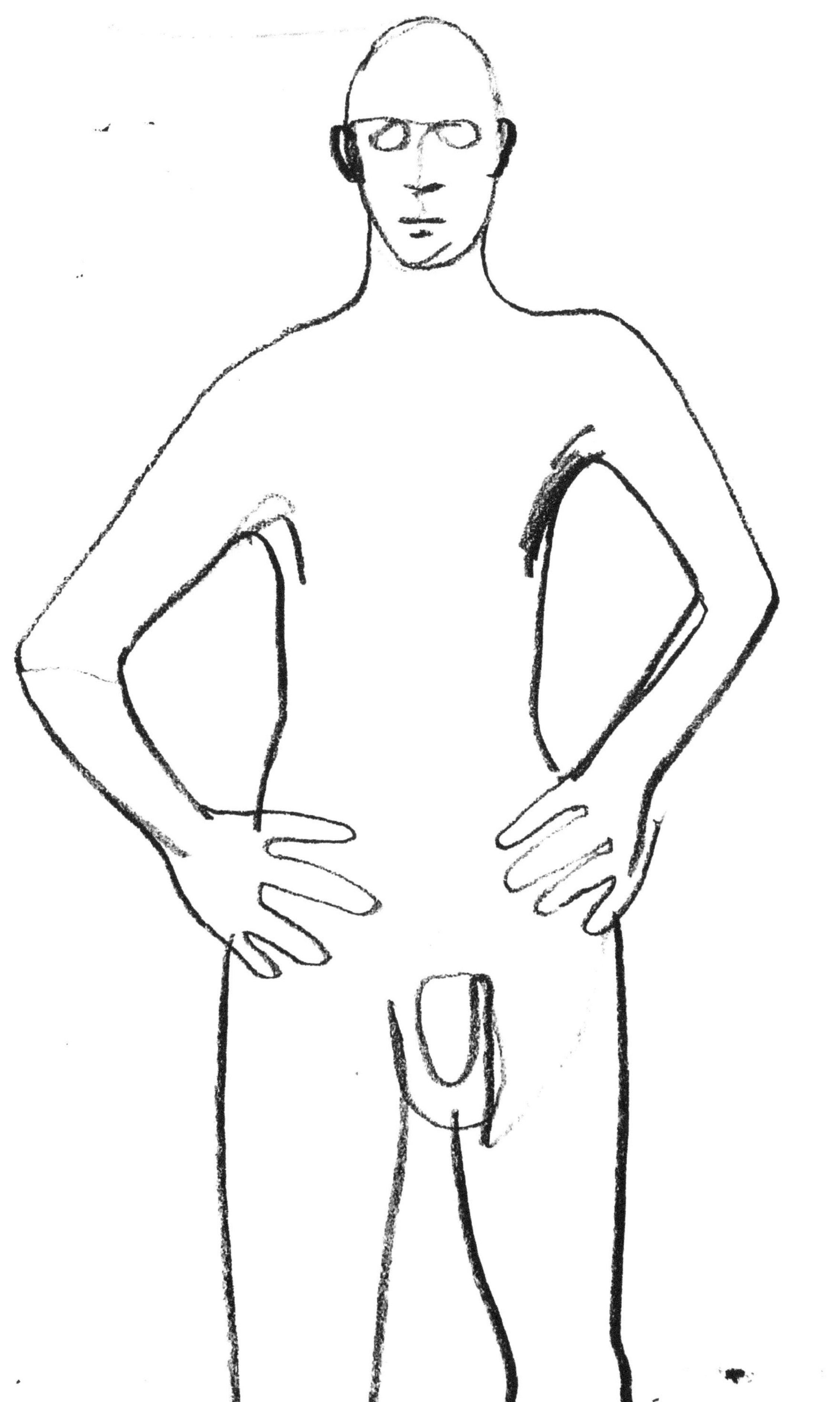

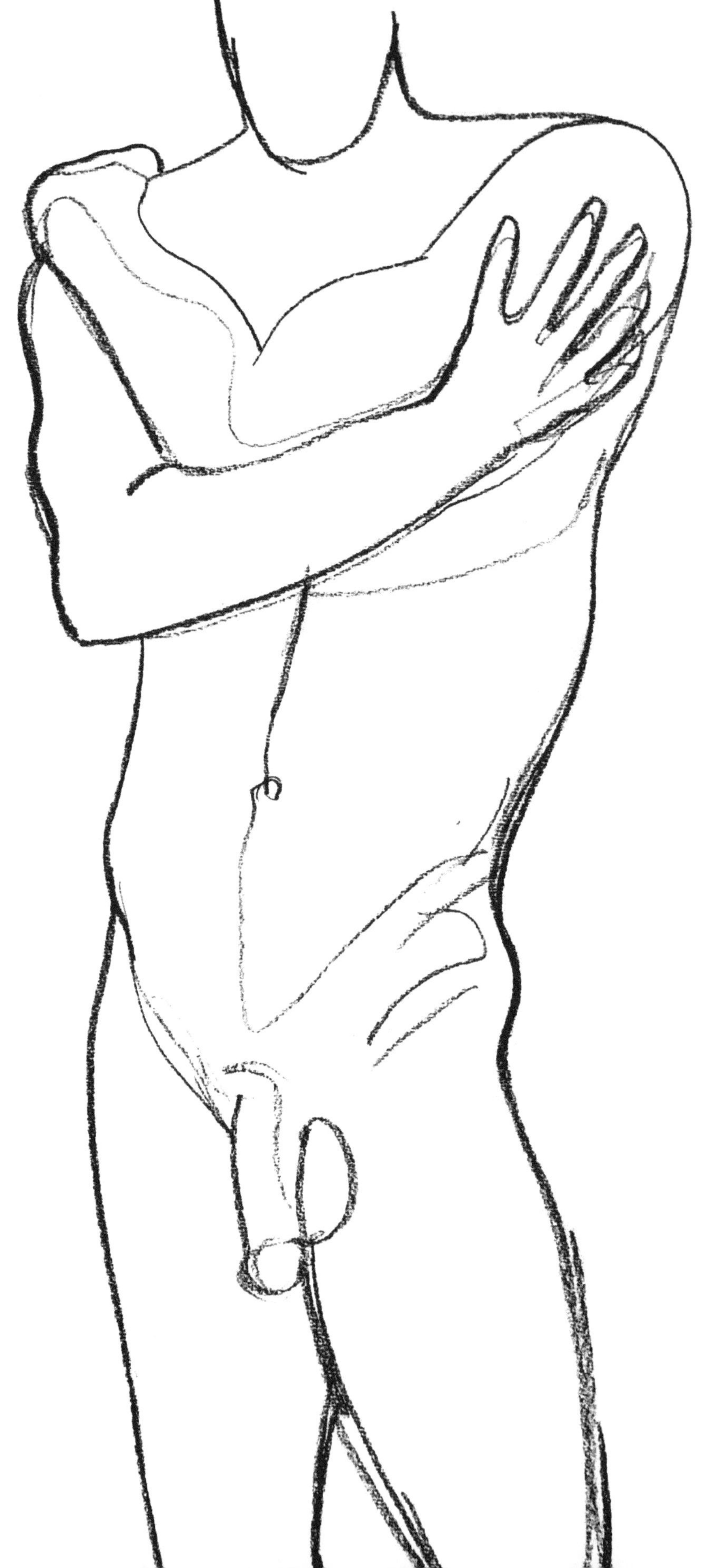

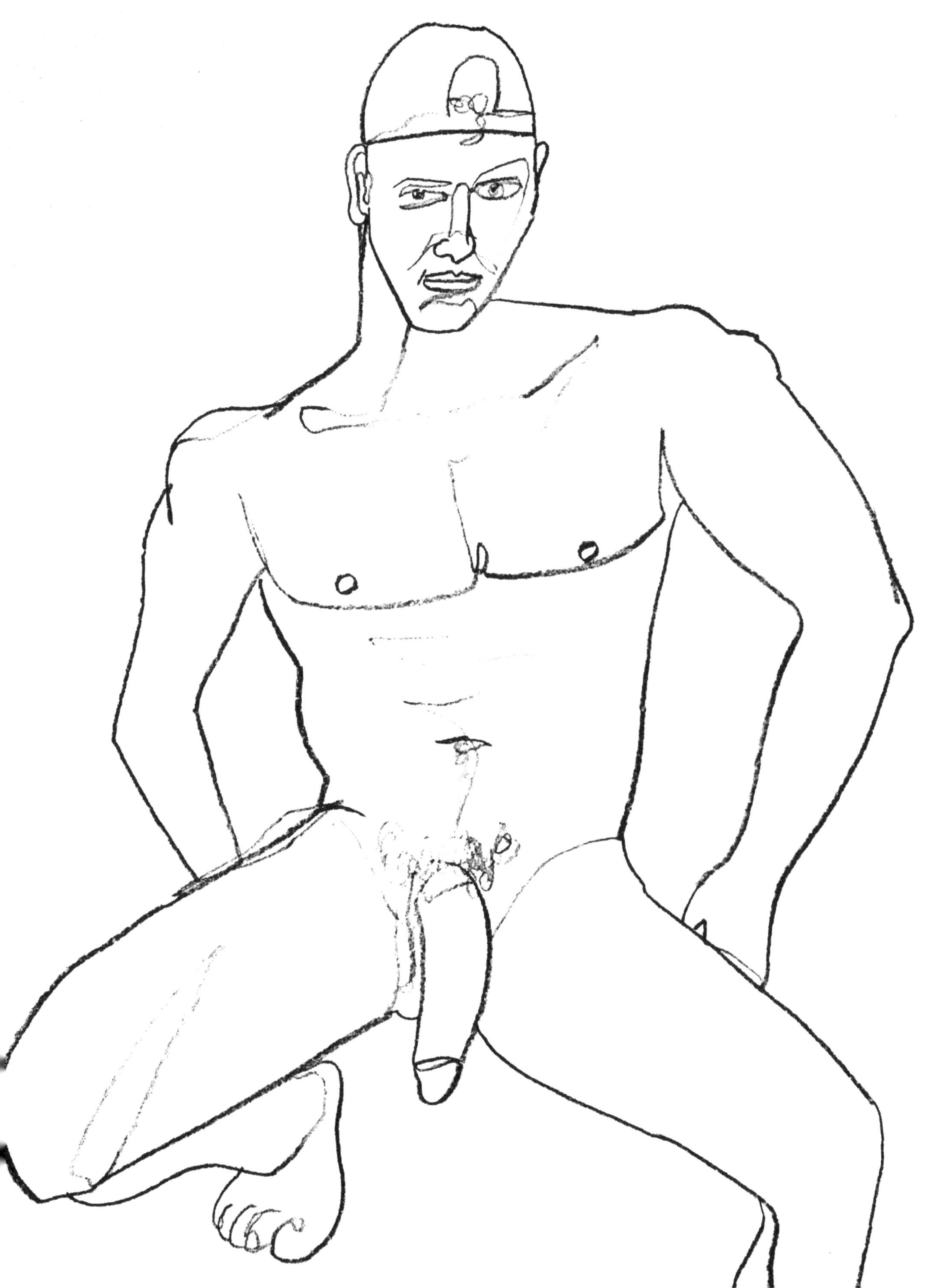

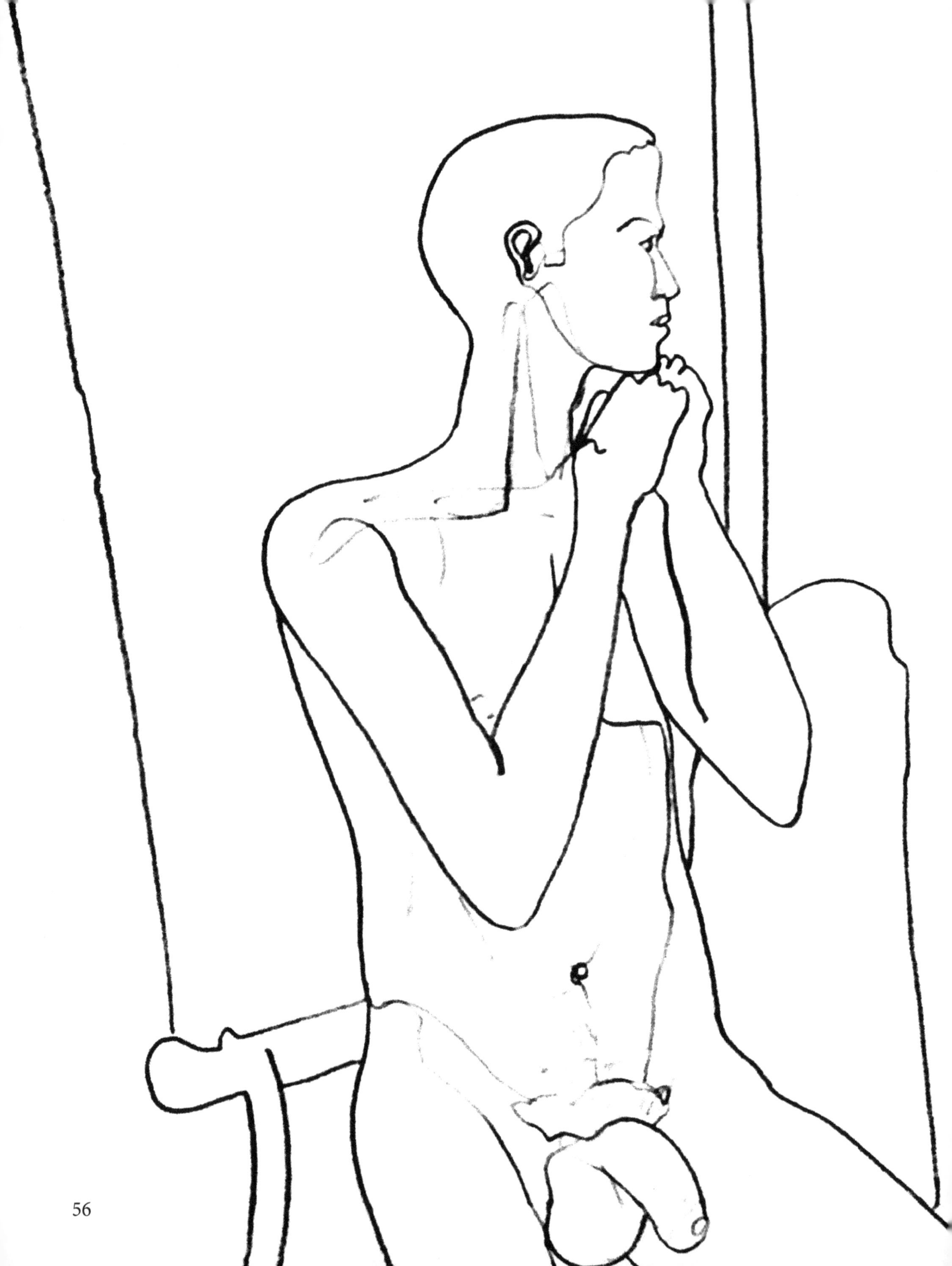

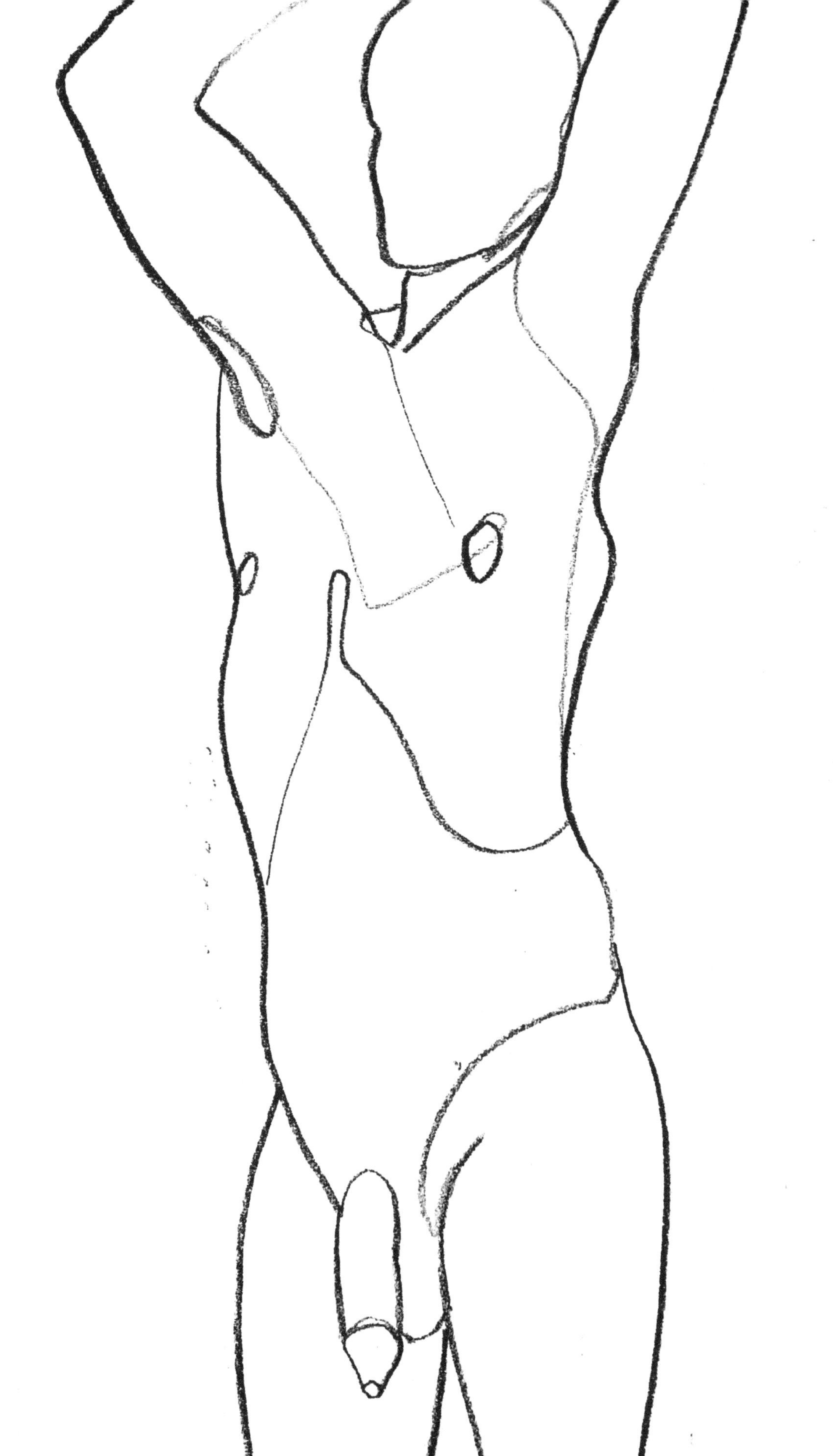

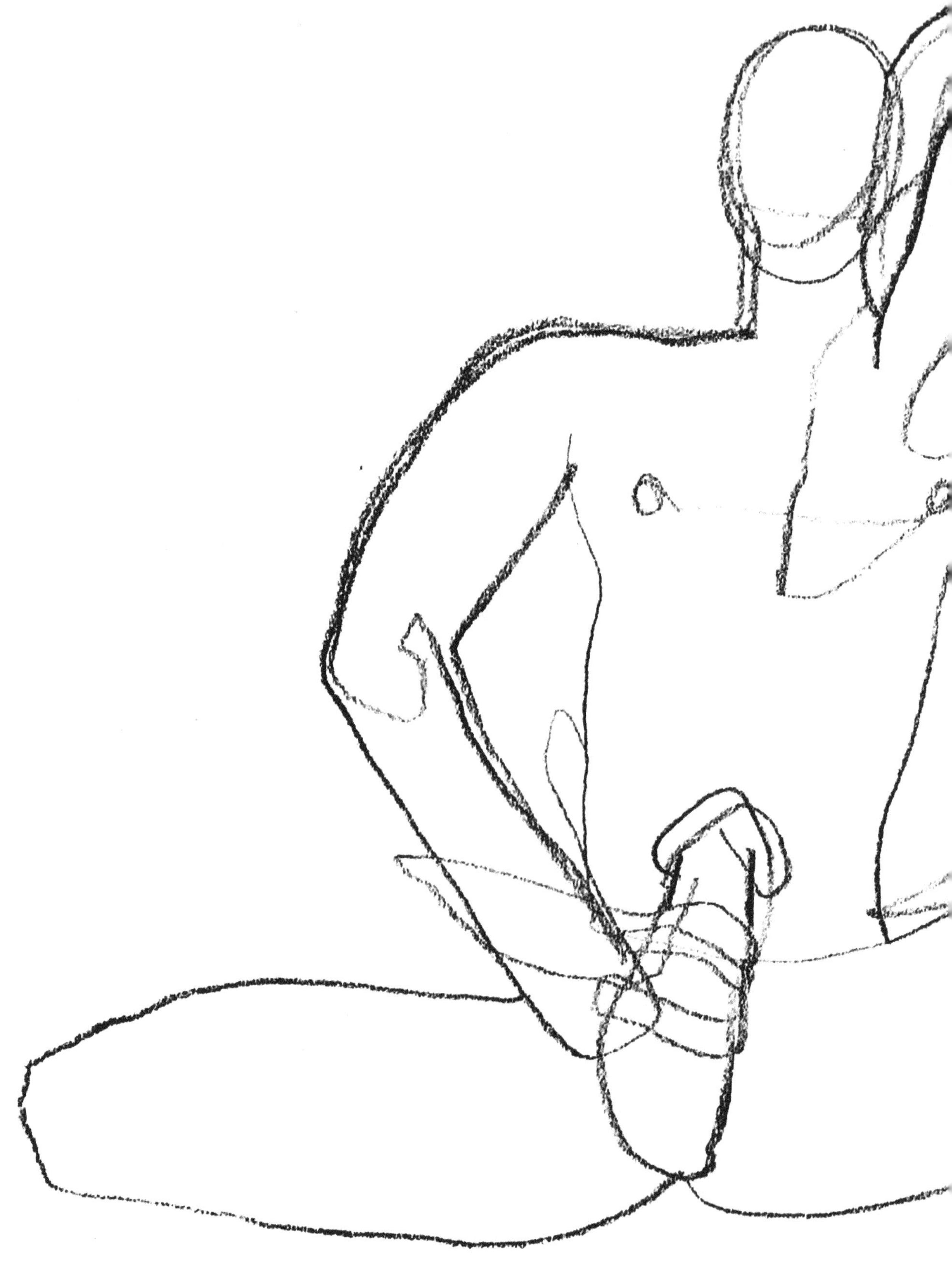

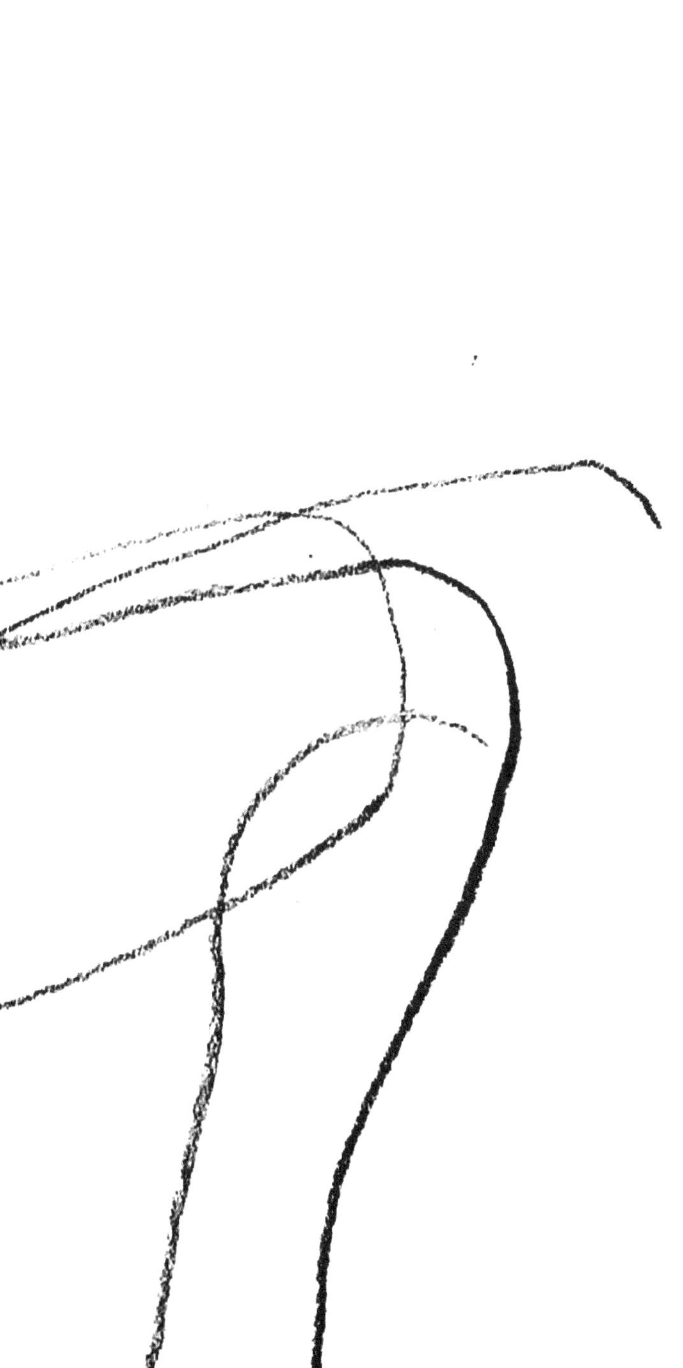

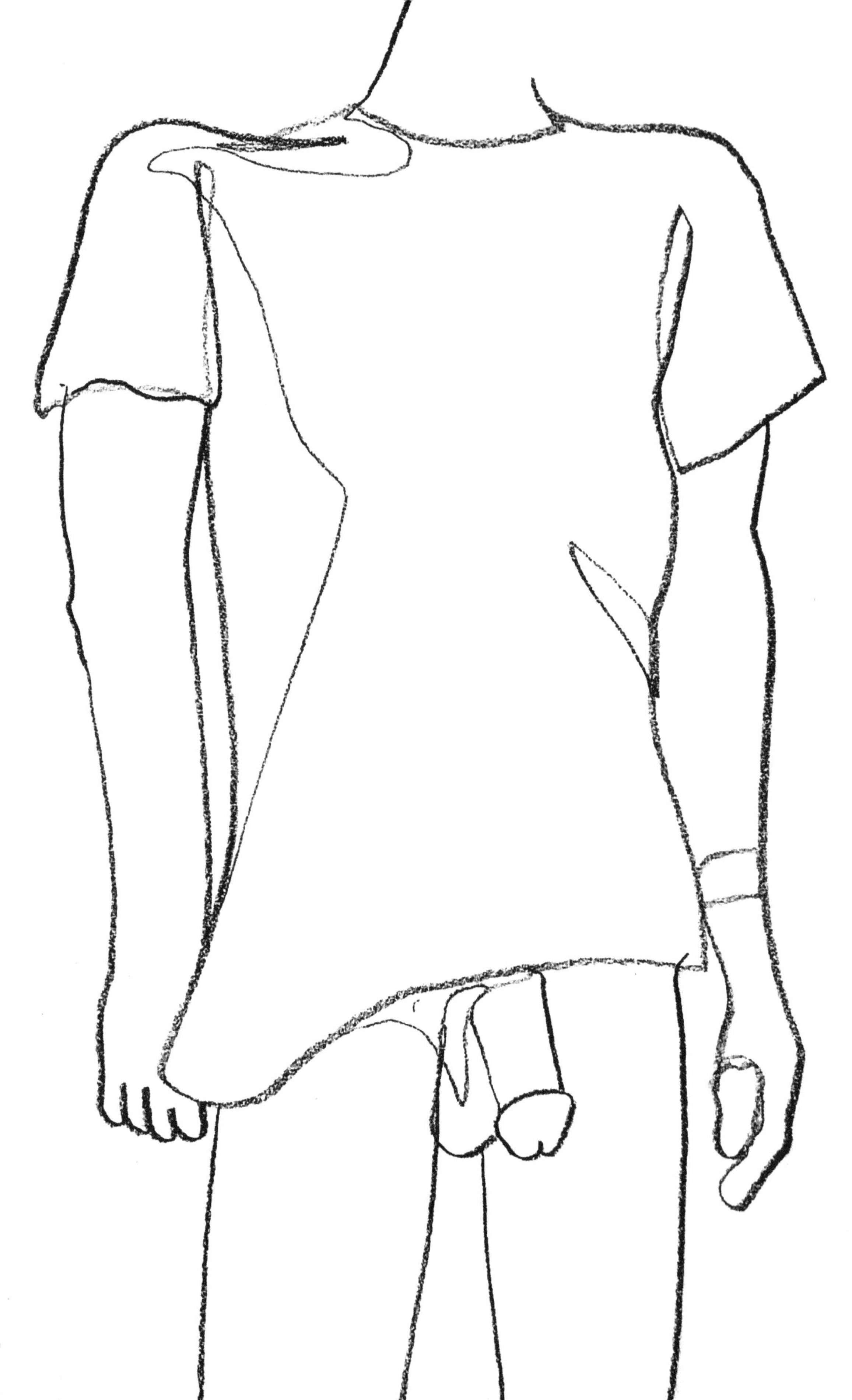

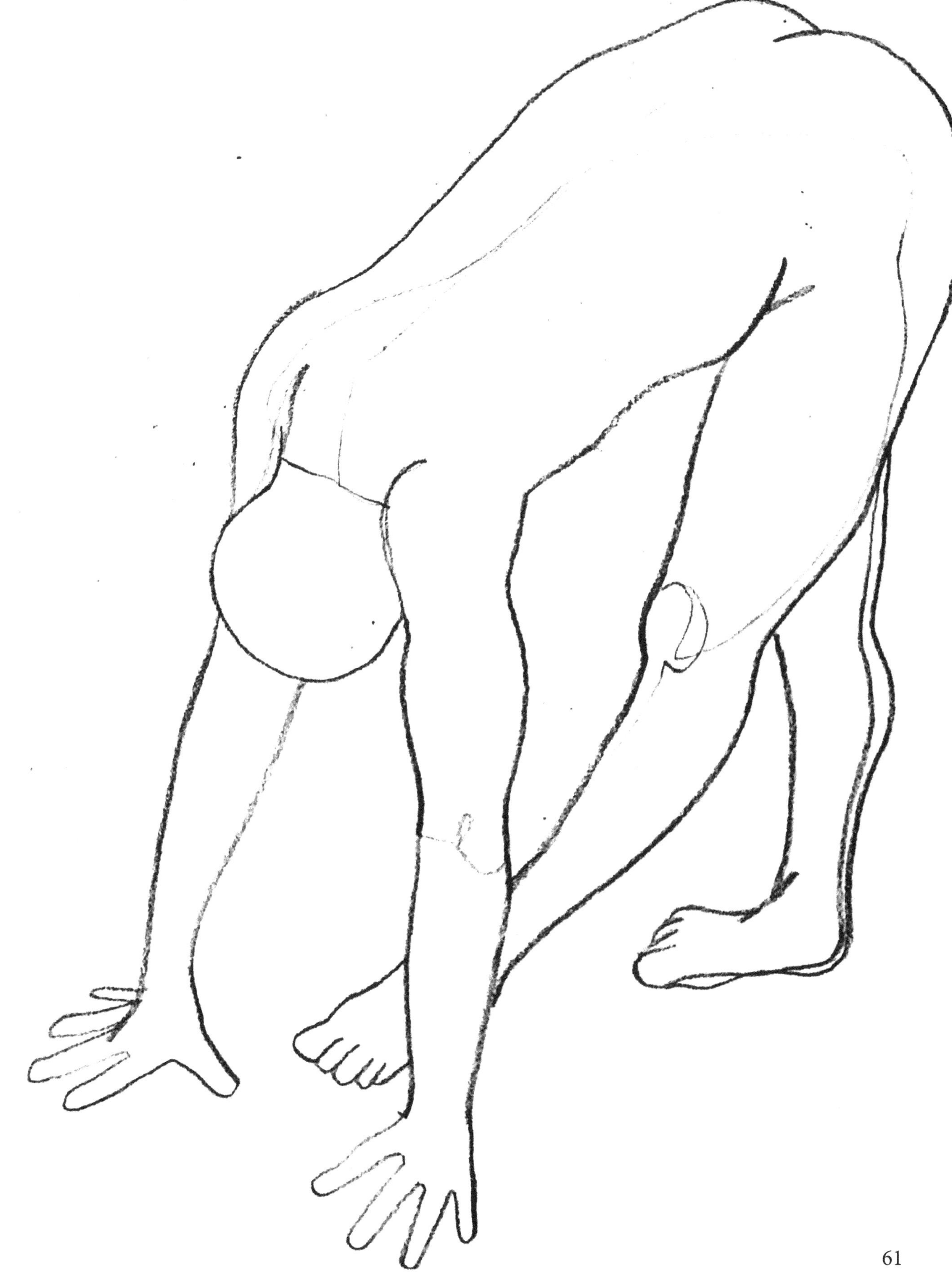

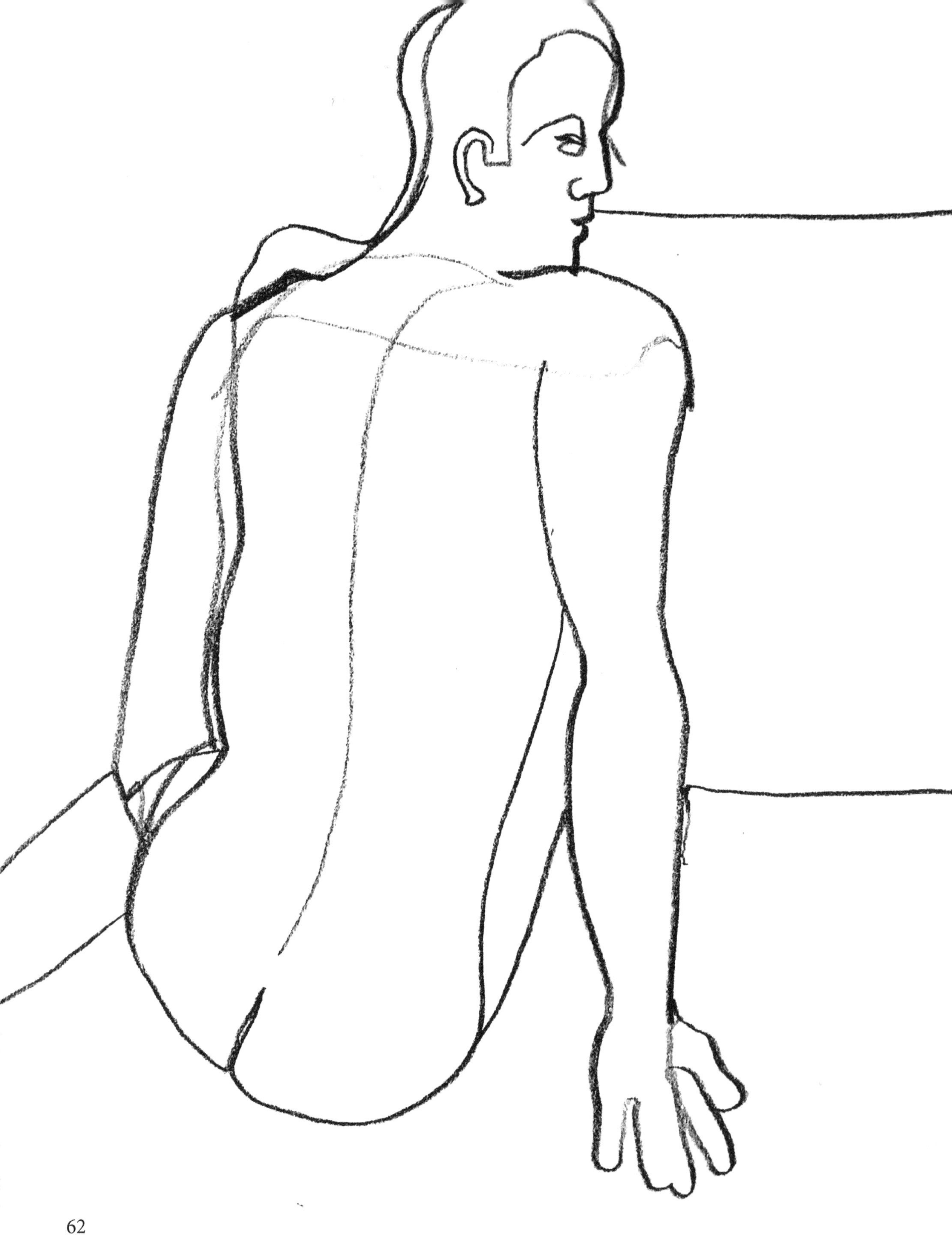

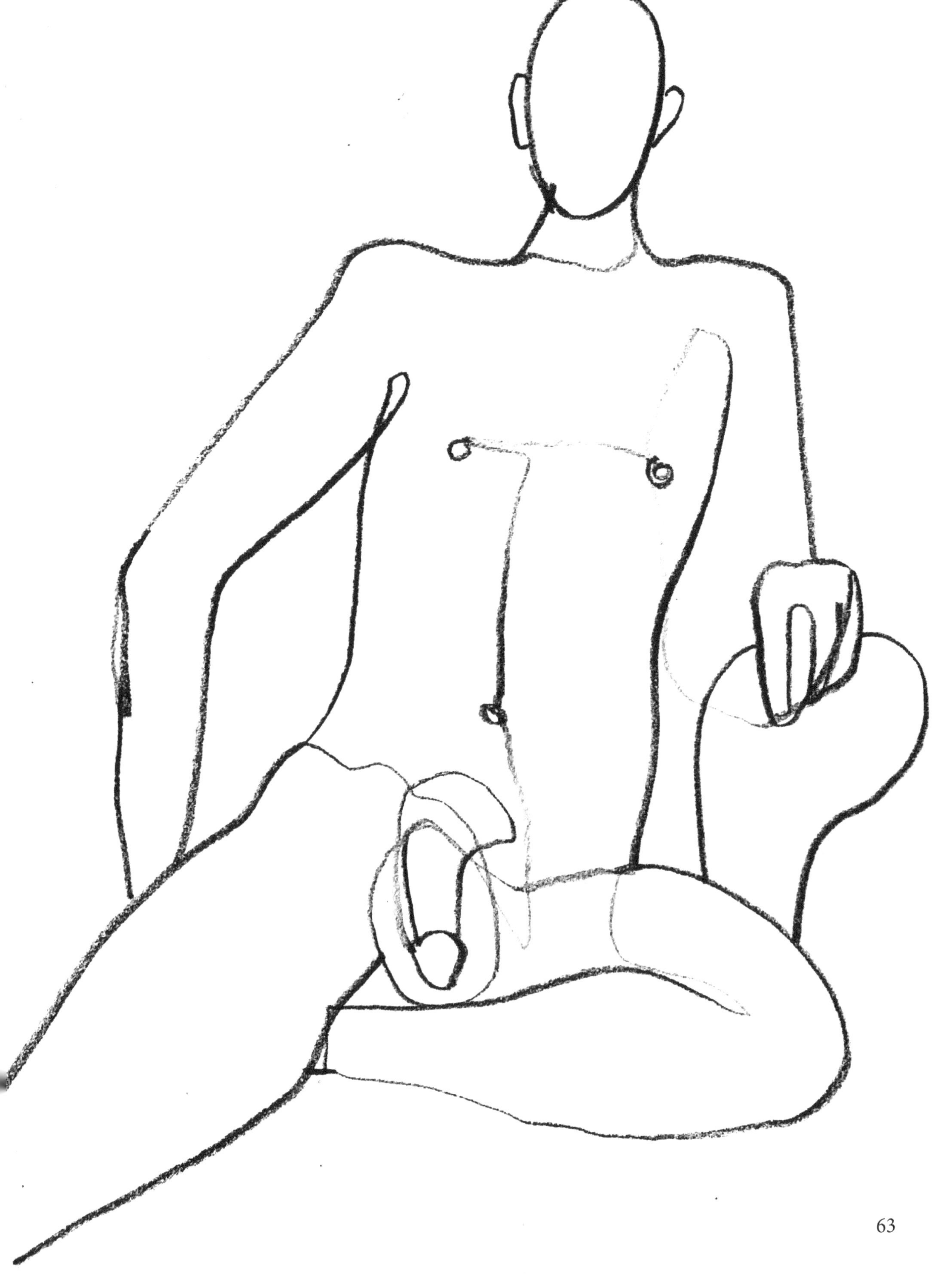

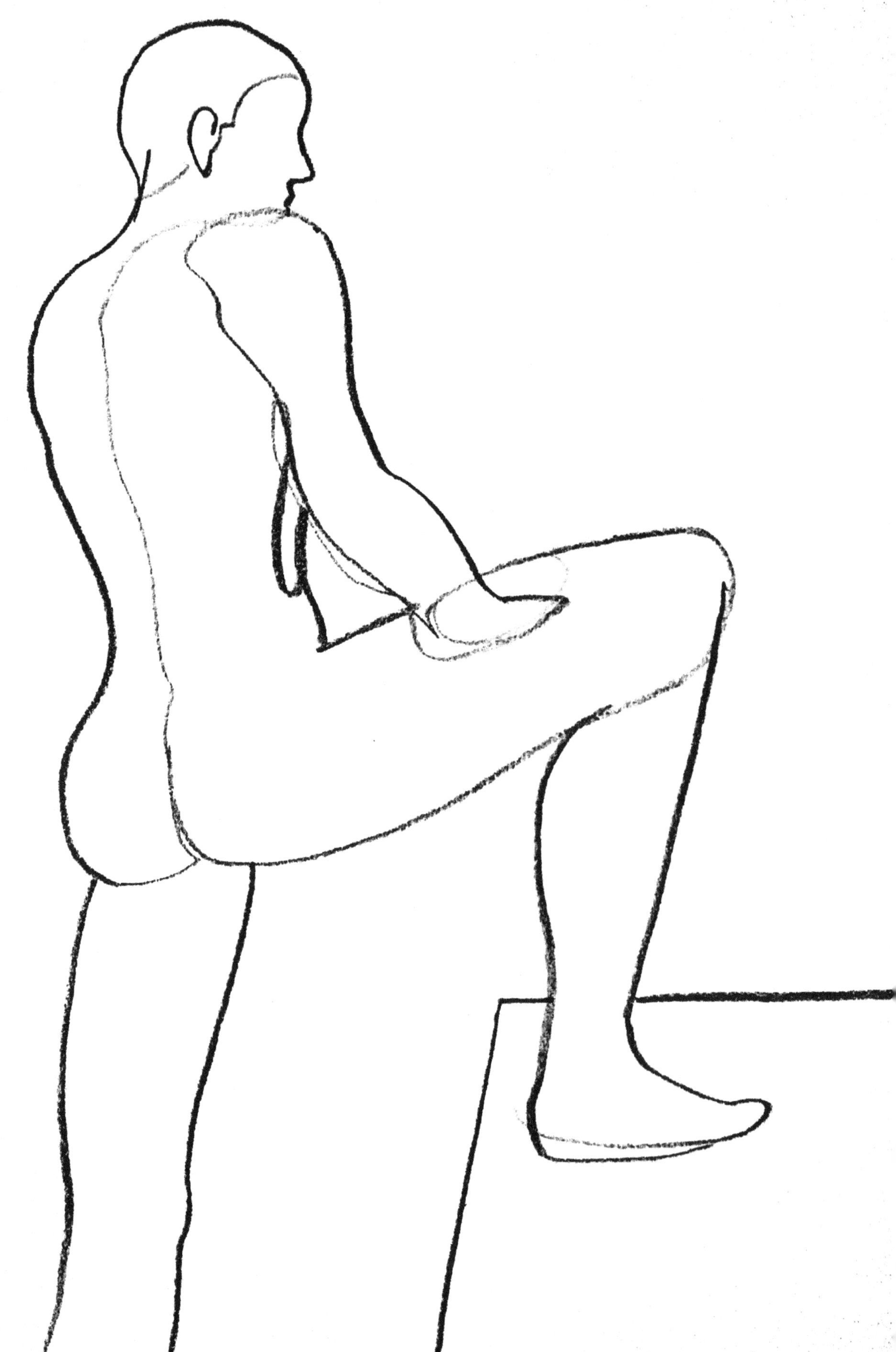

64

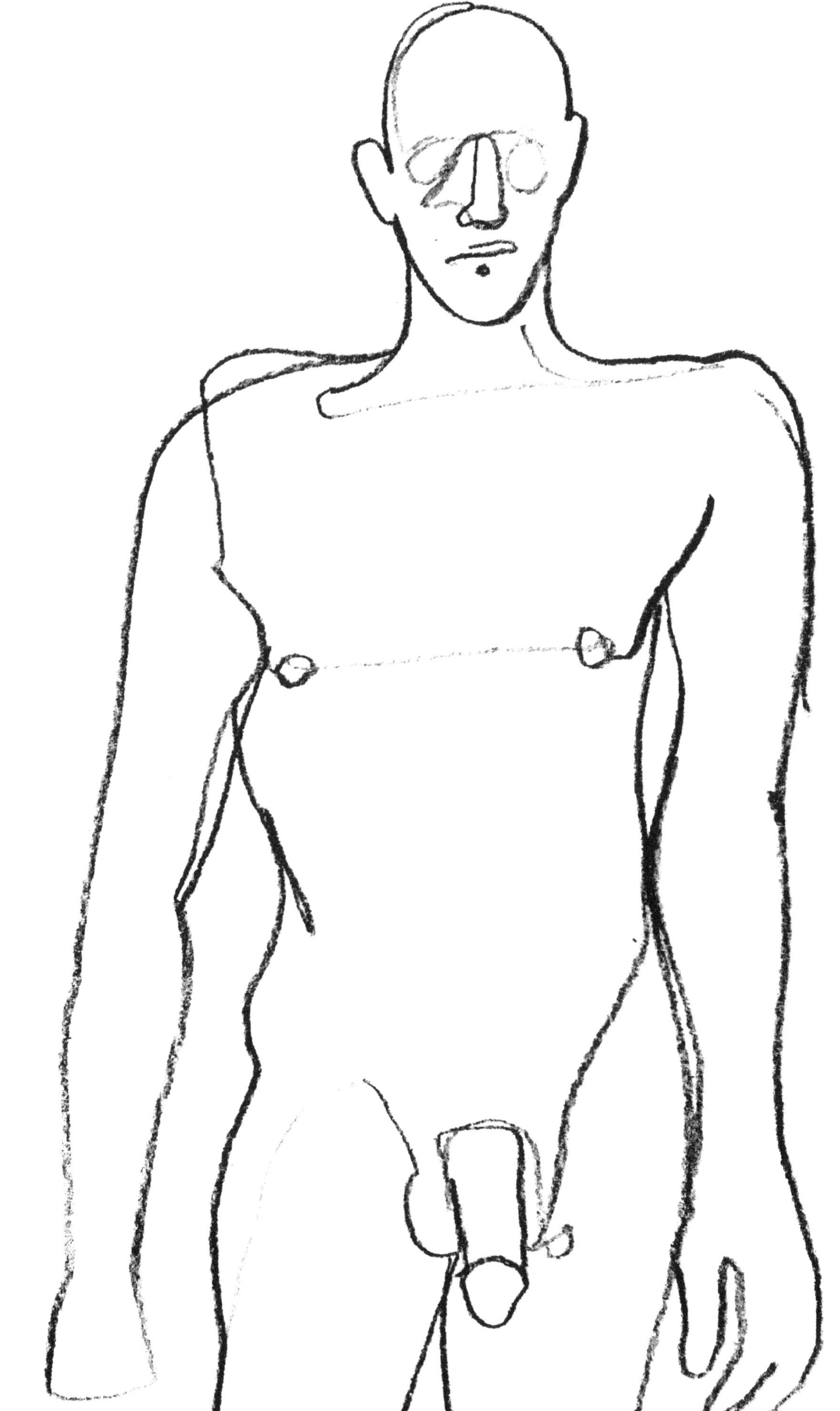

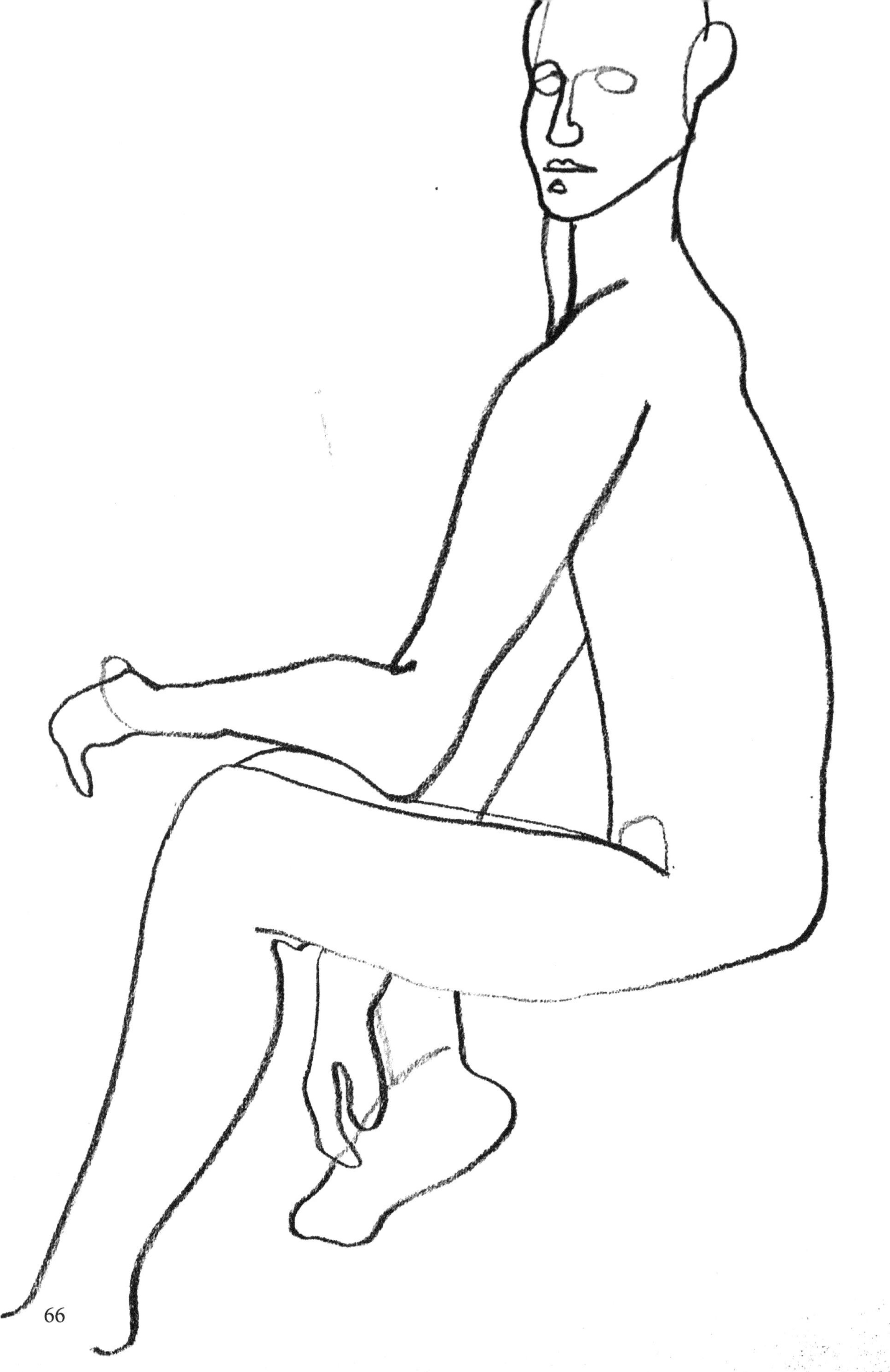

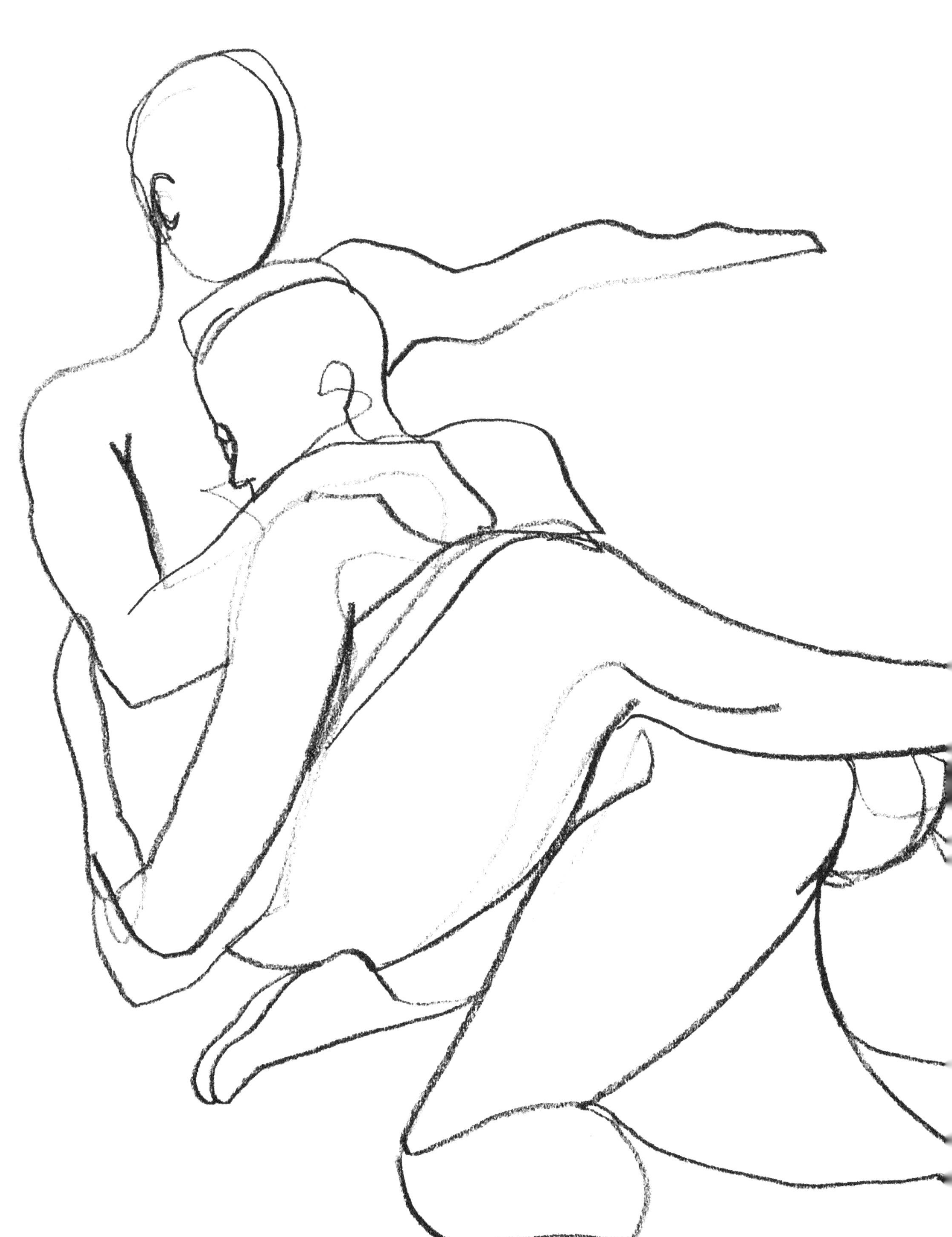

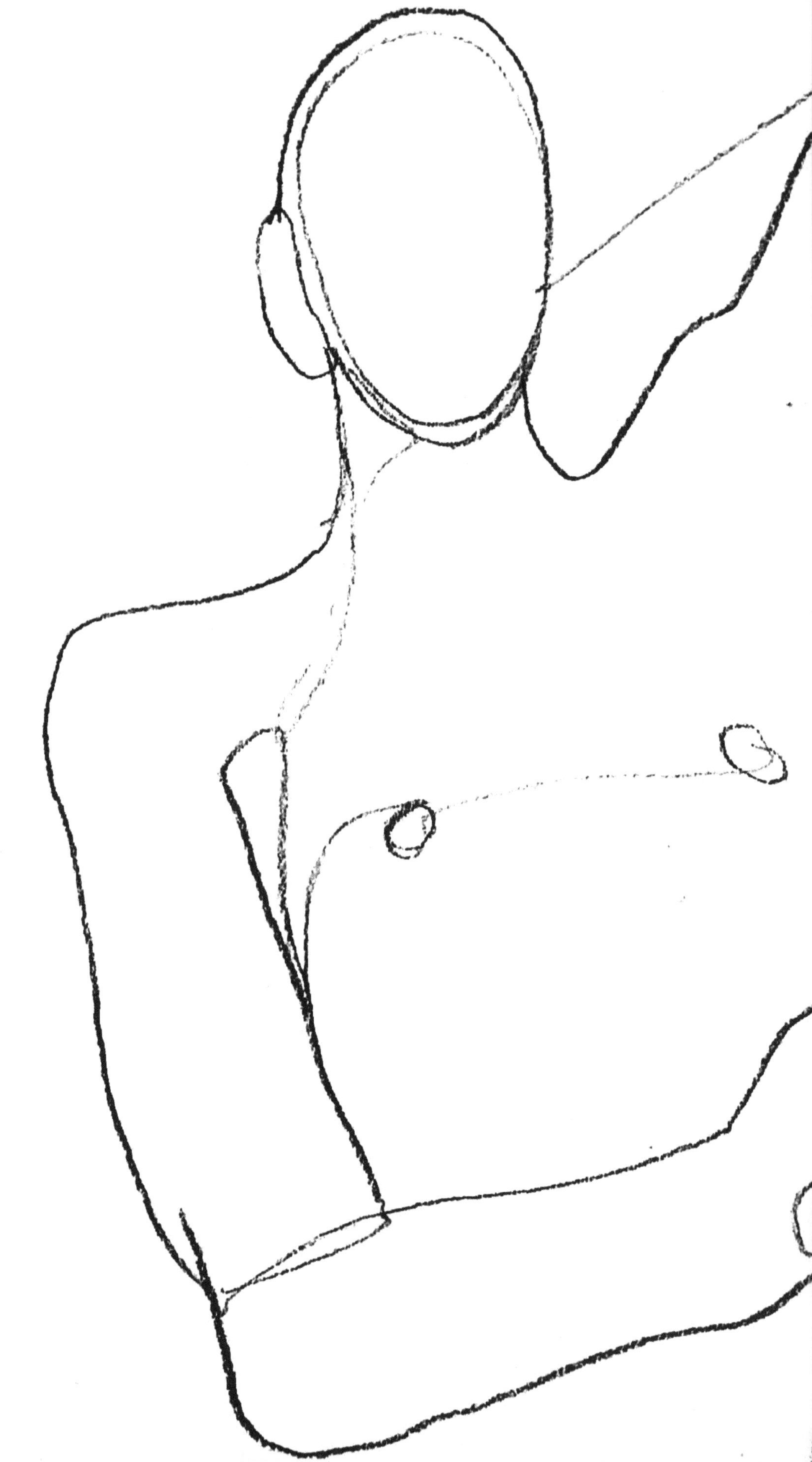

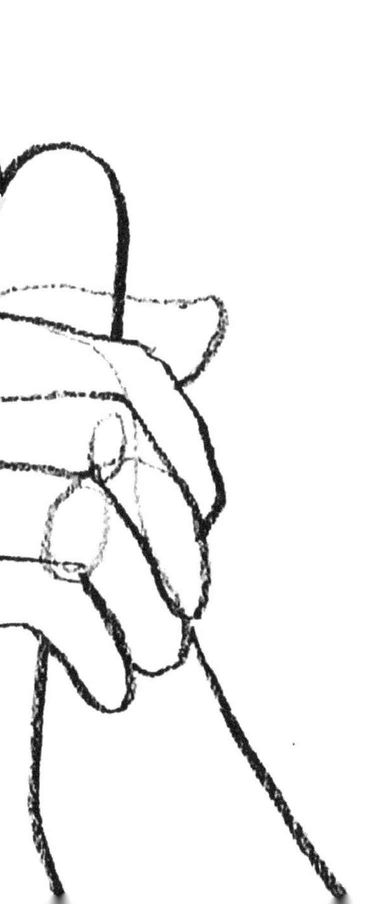

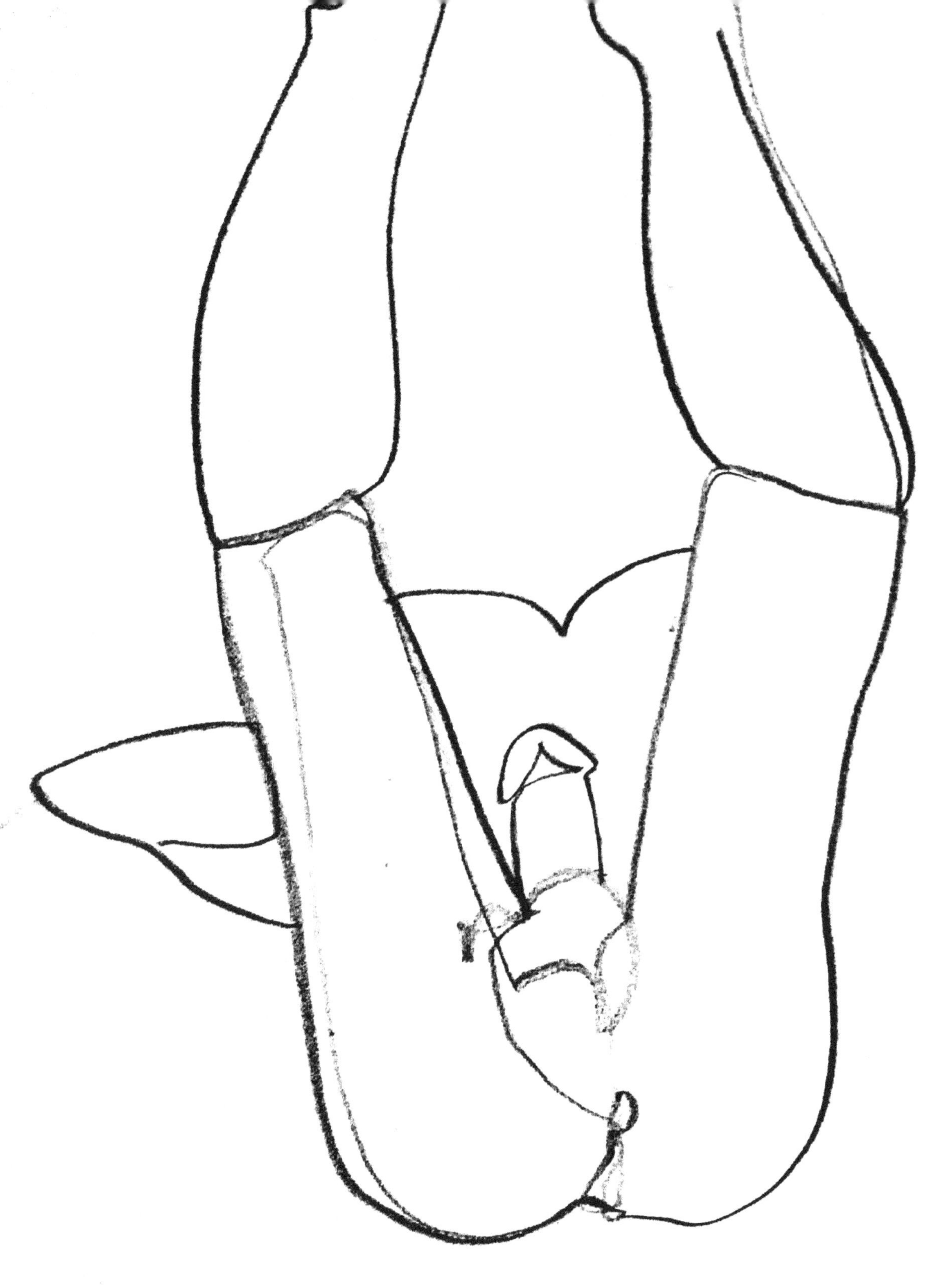

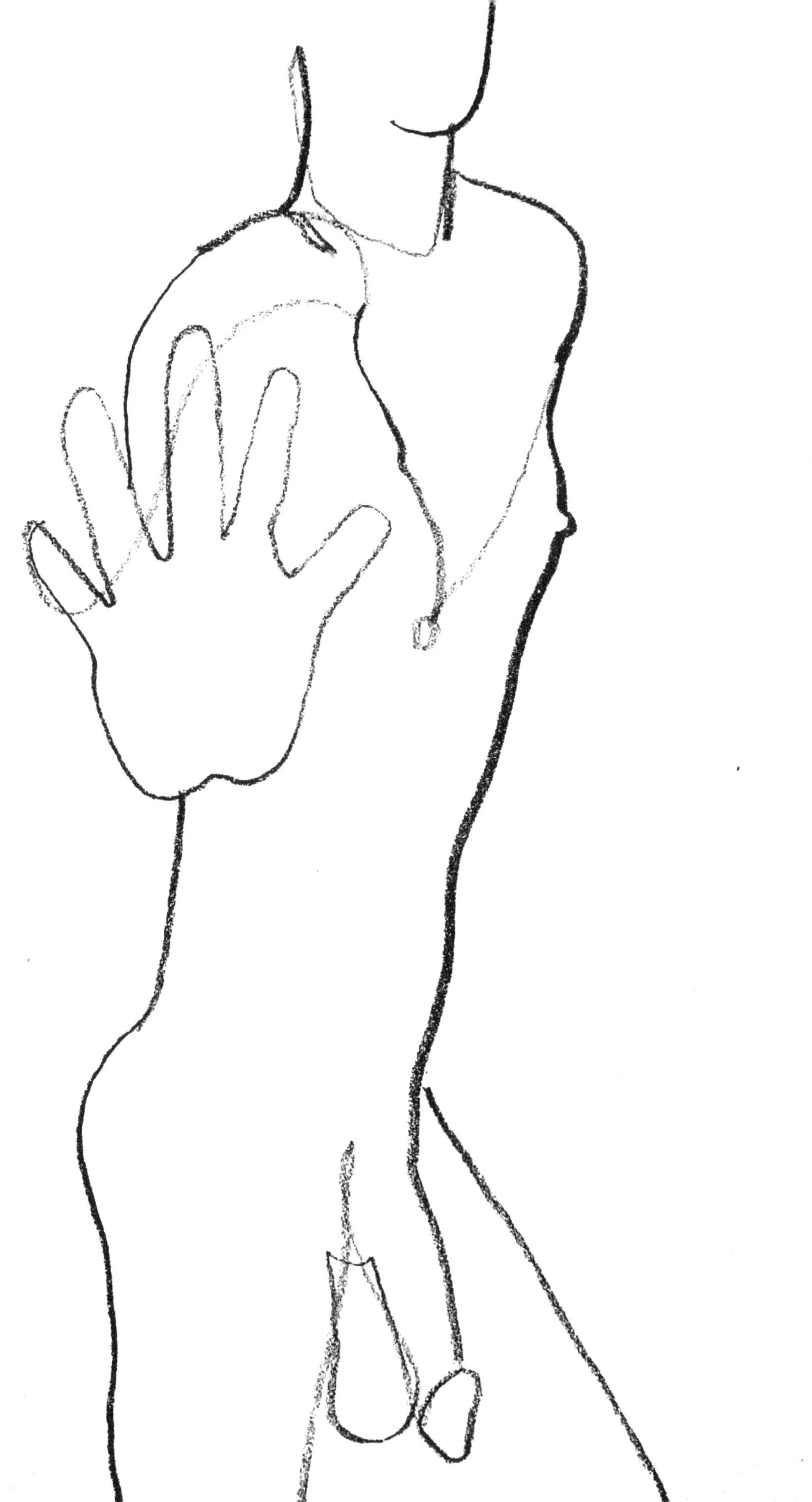

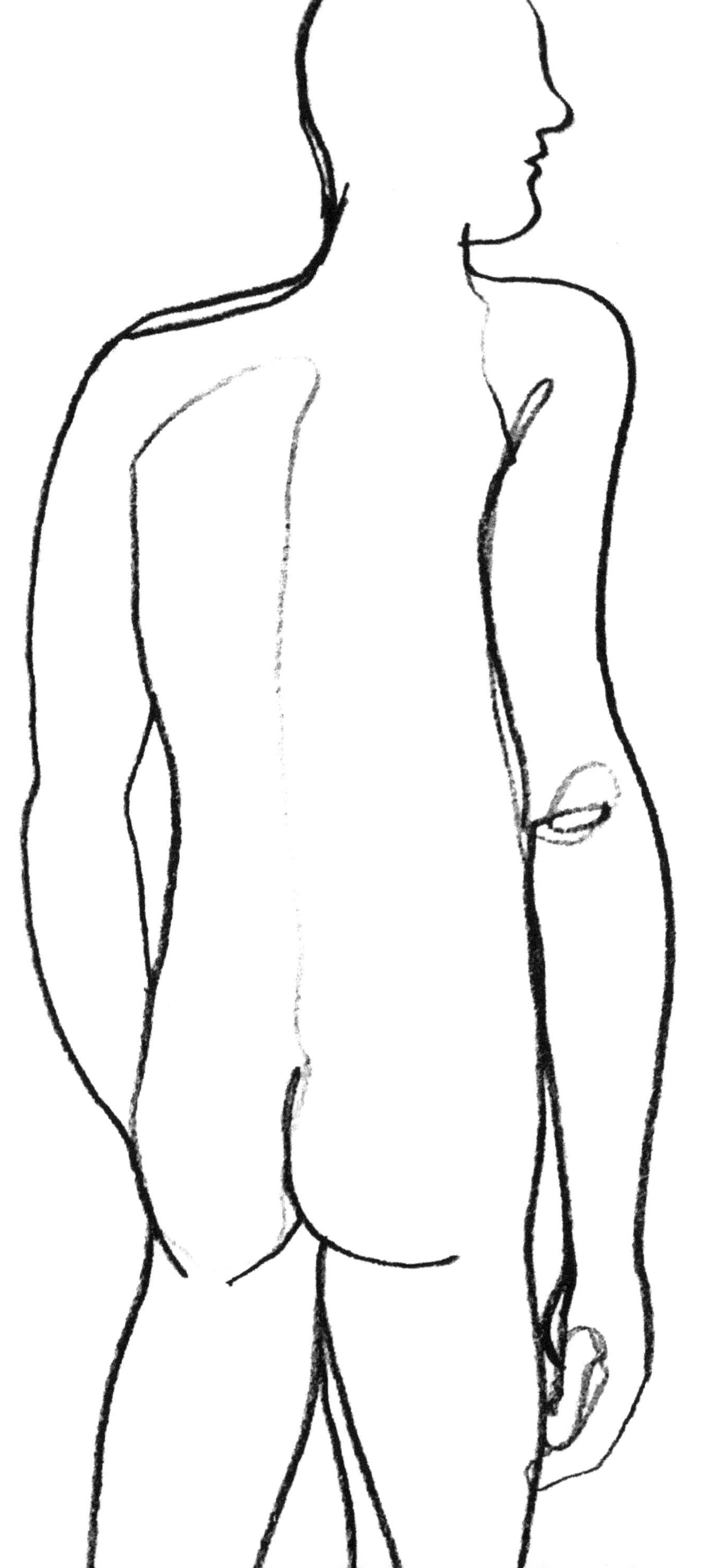

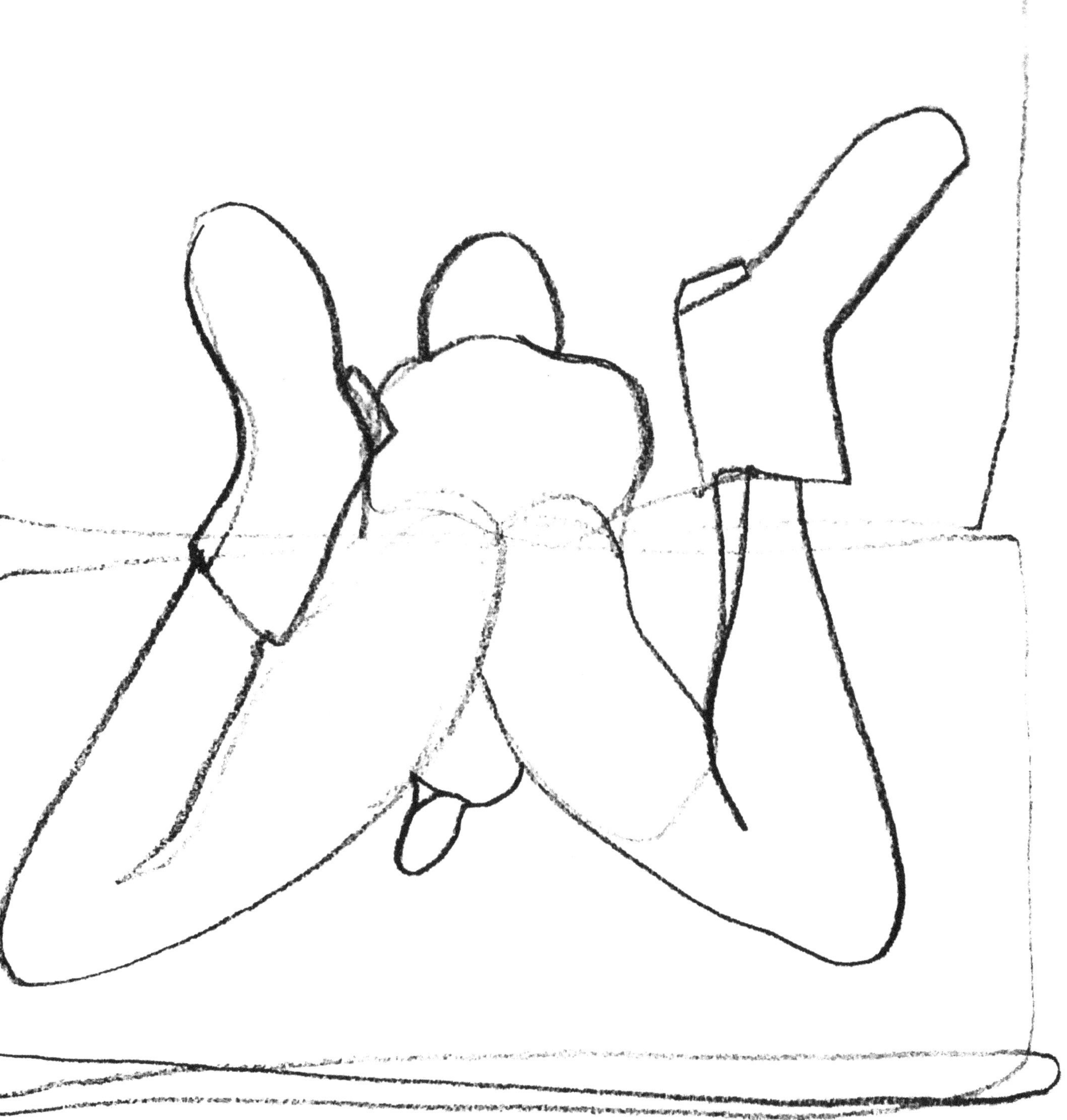

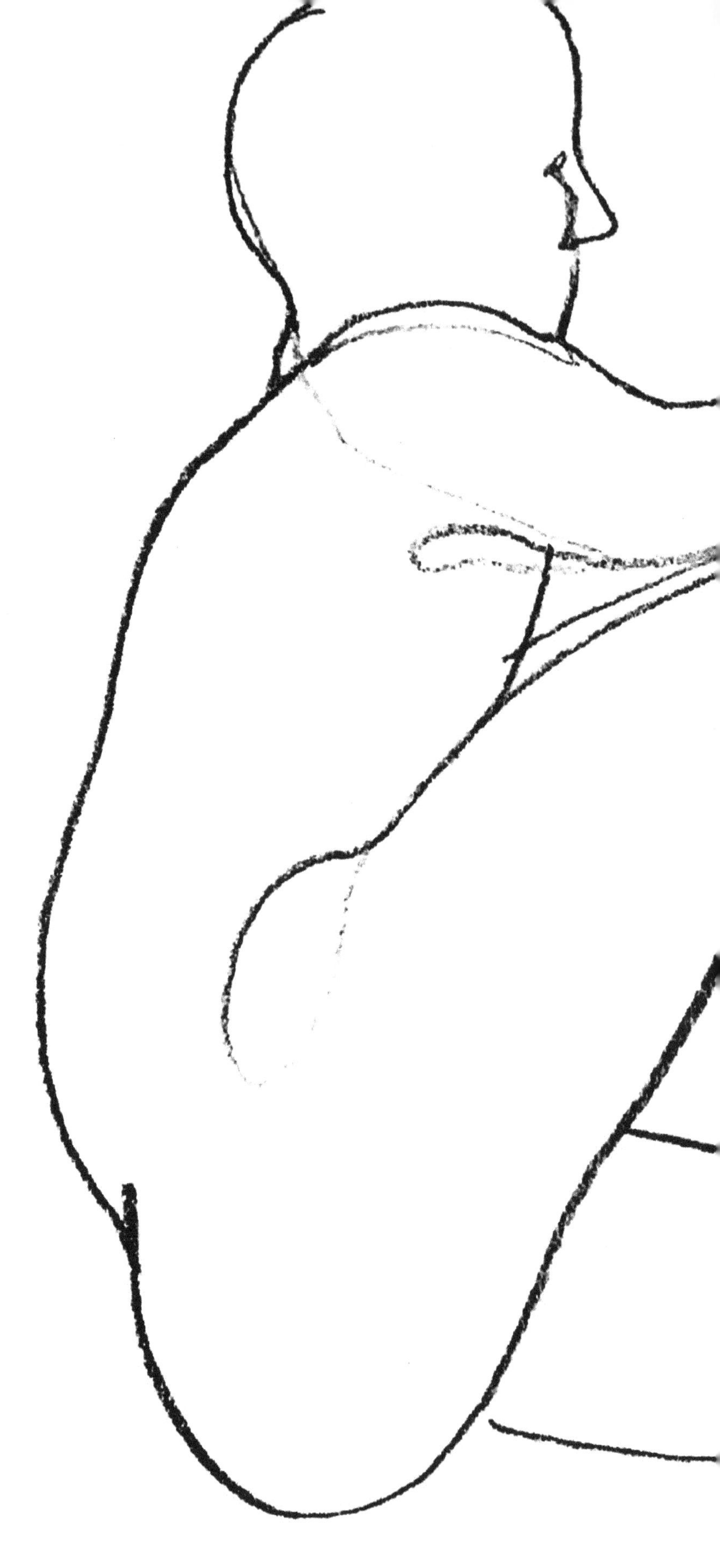

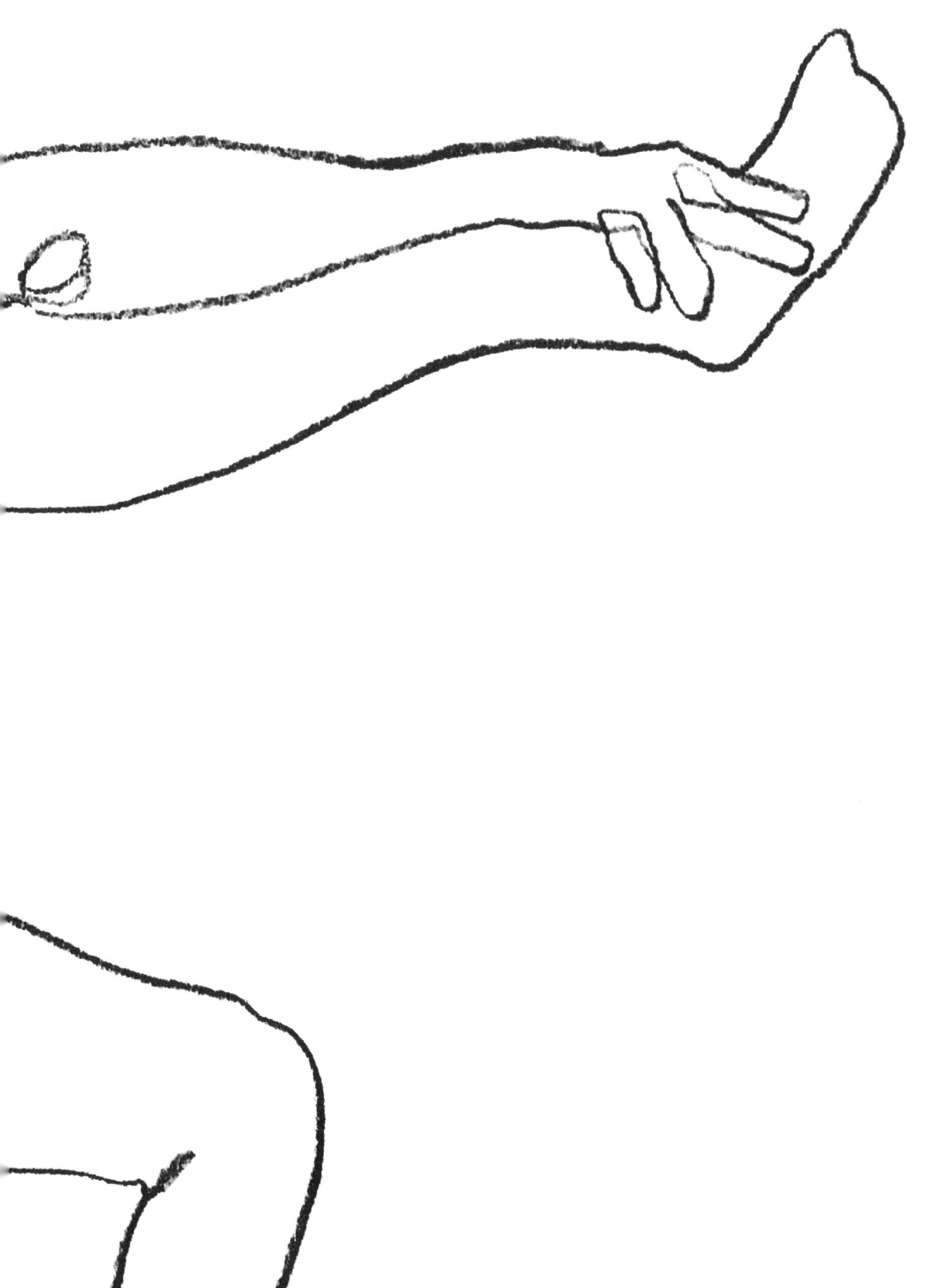

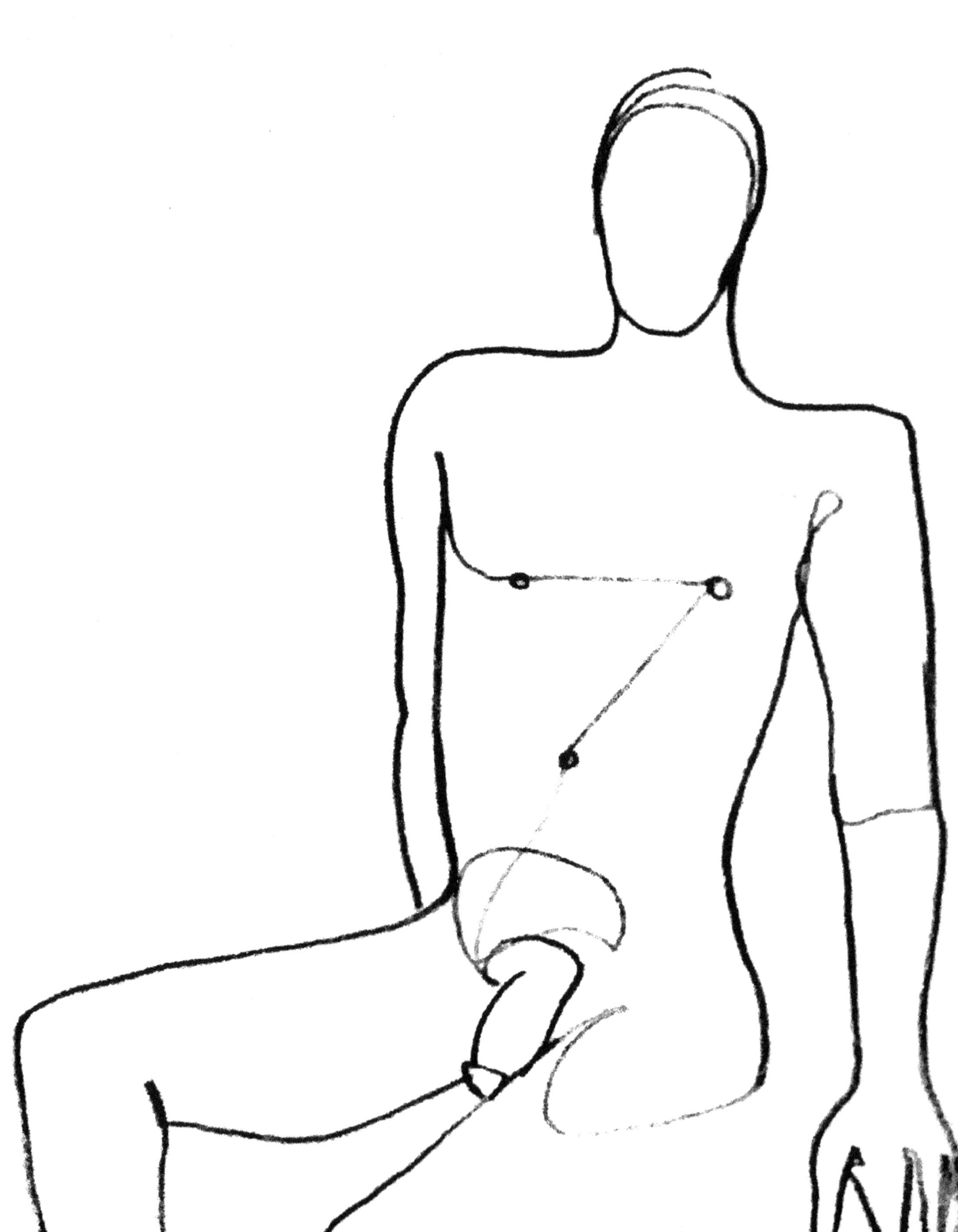

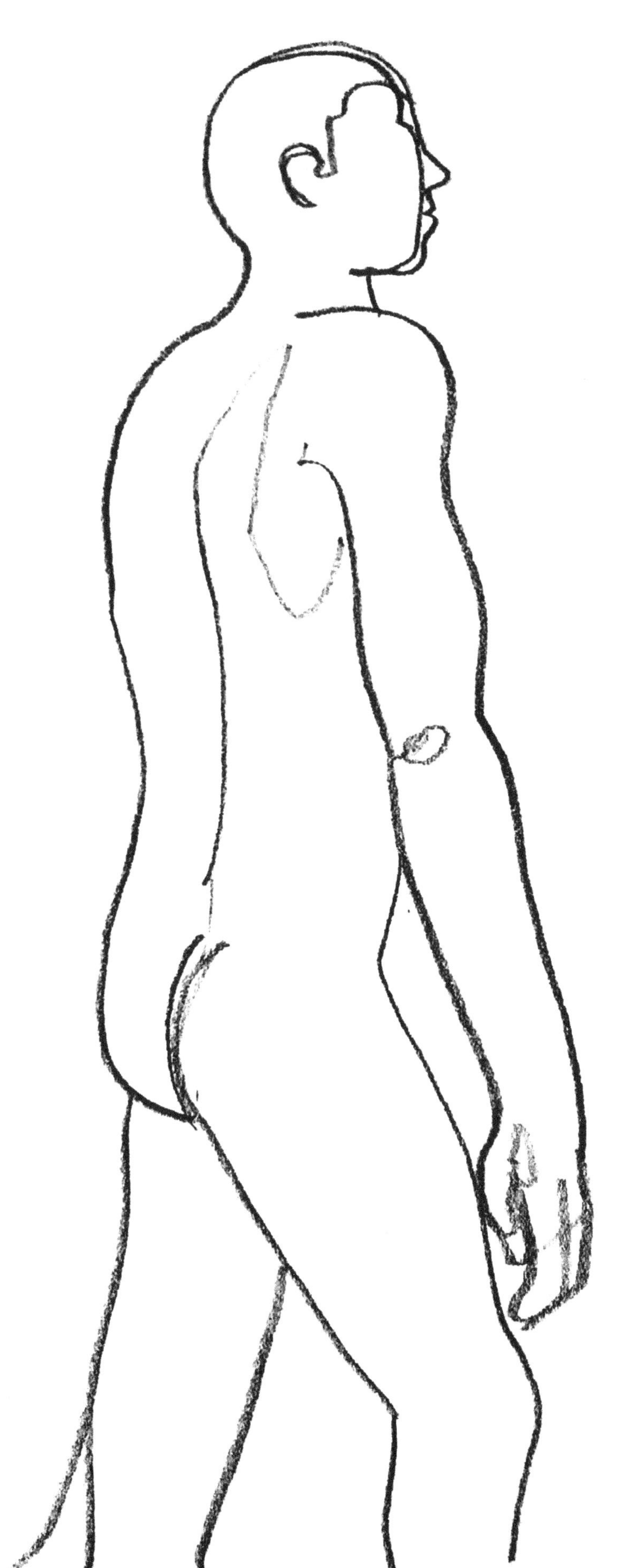

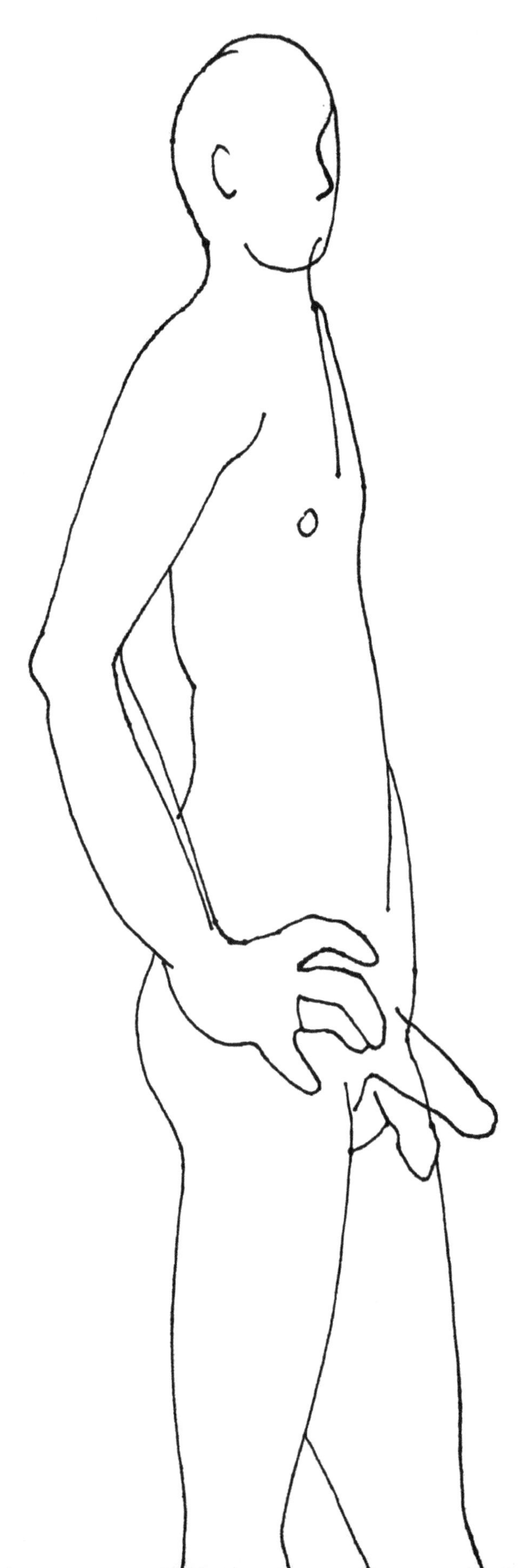

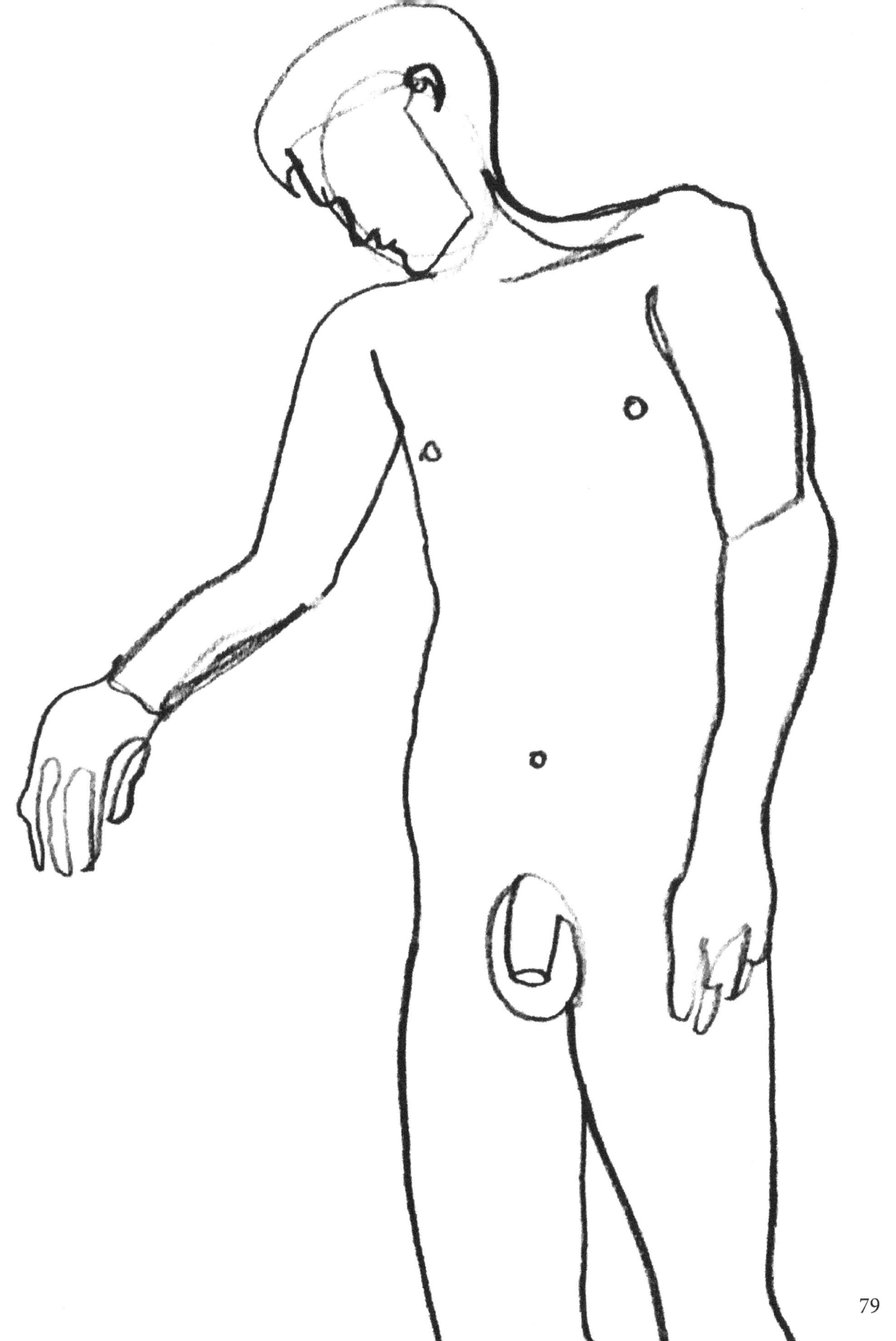

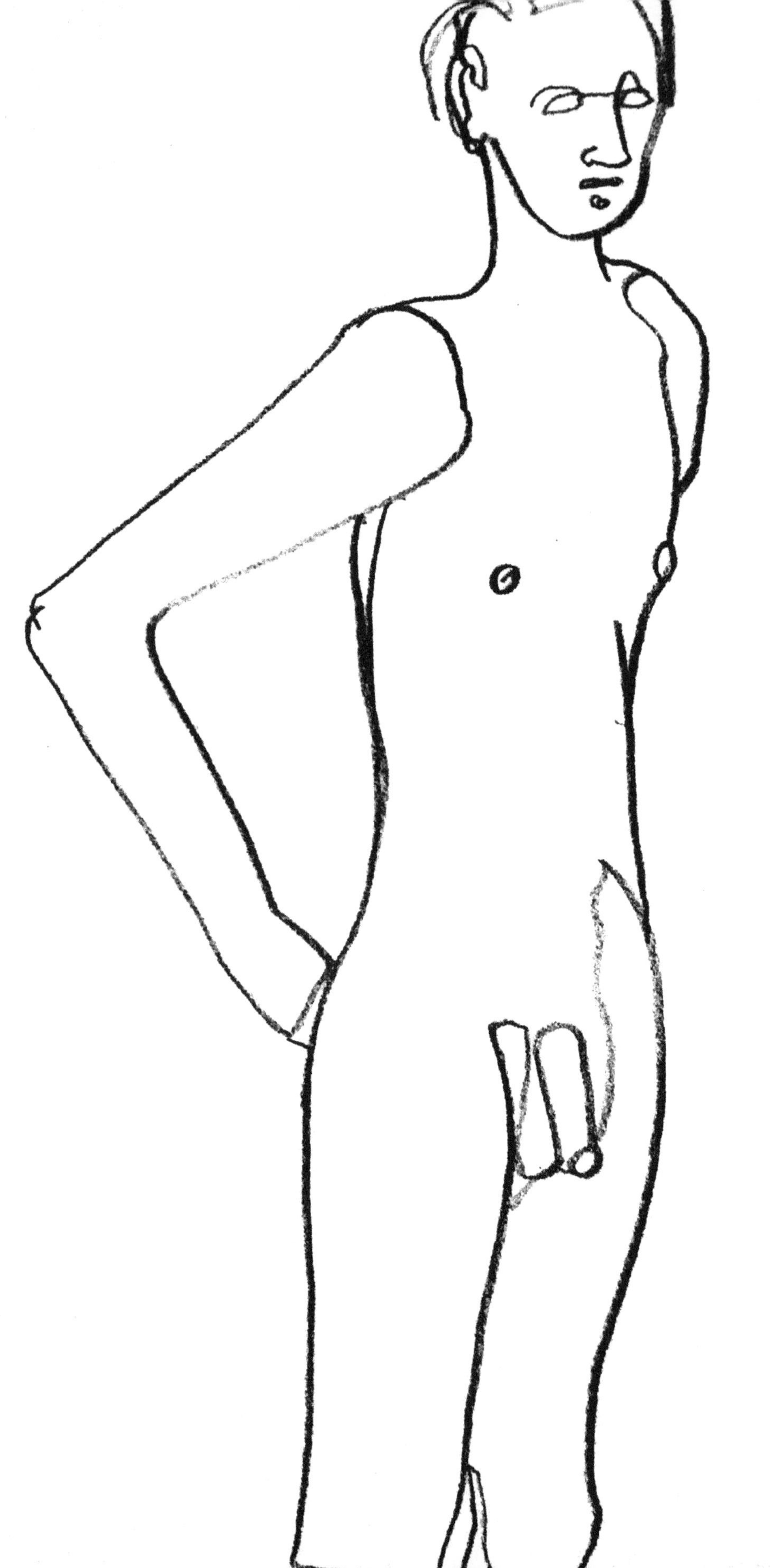

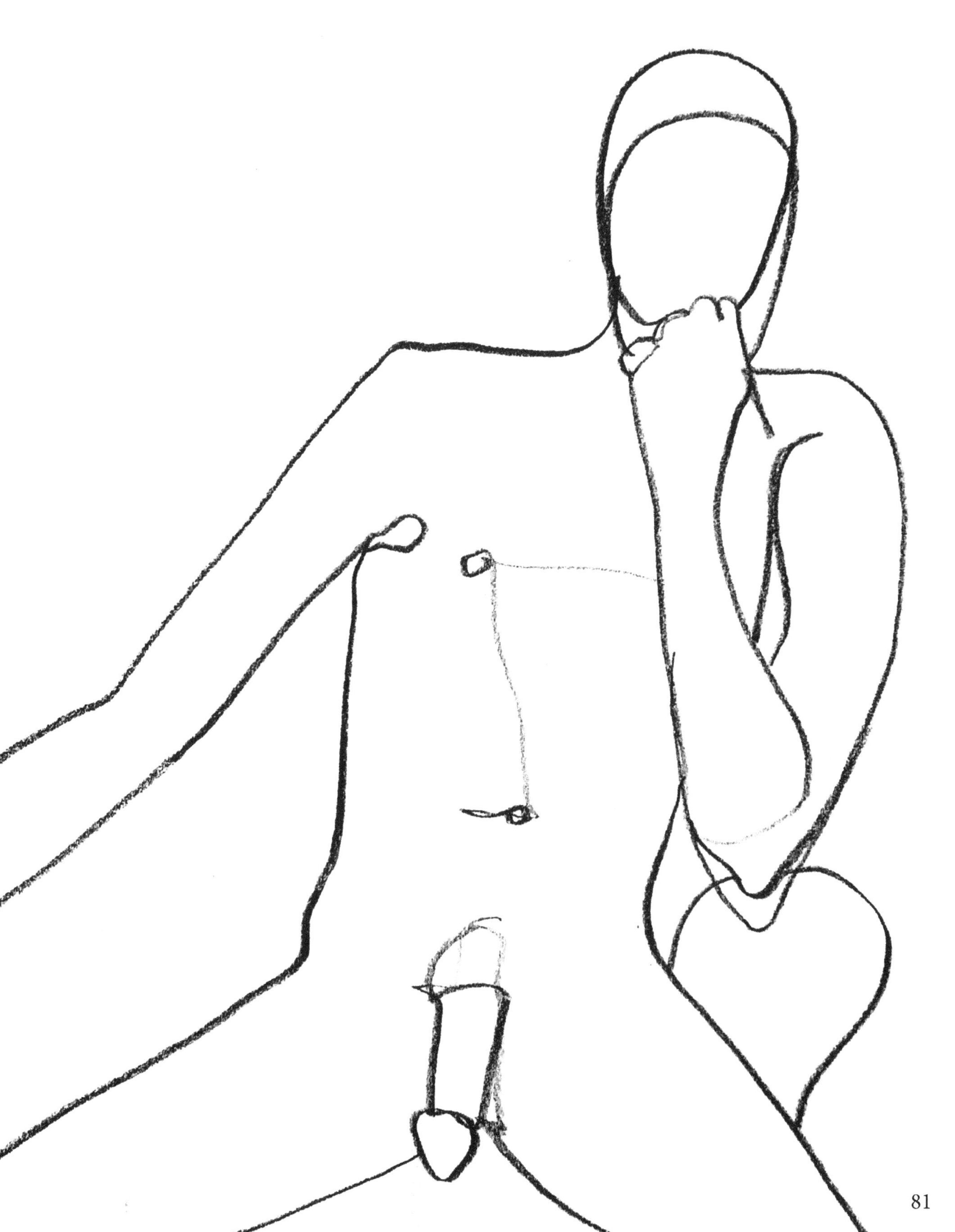

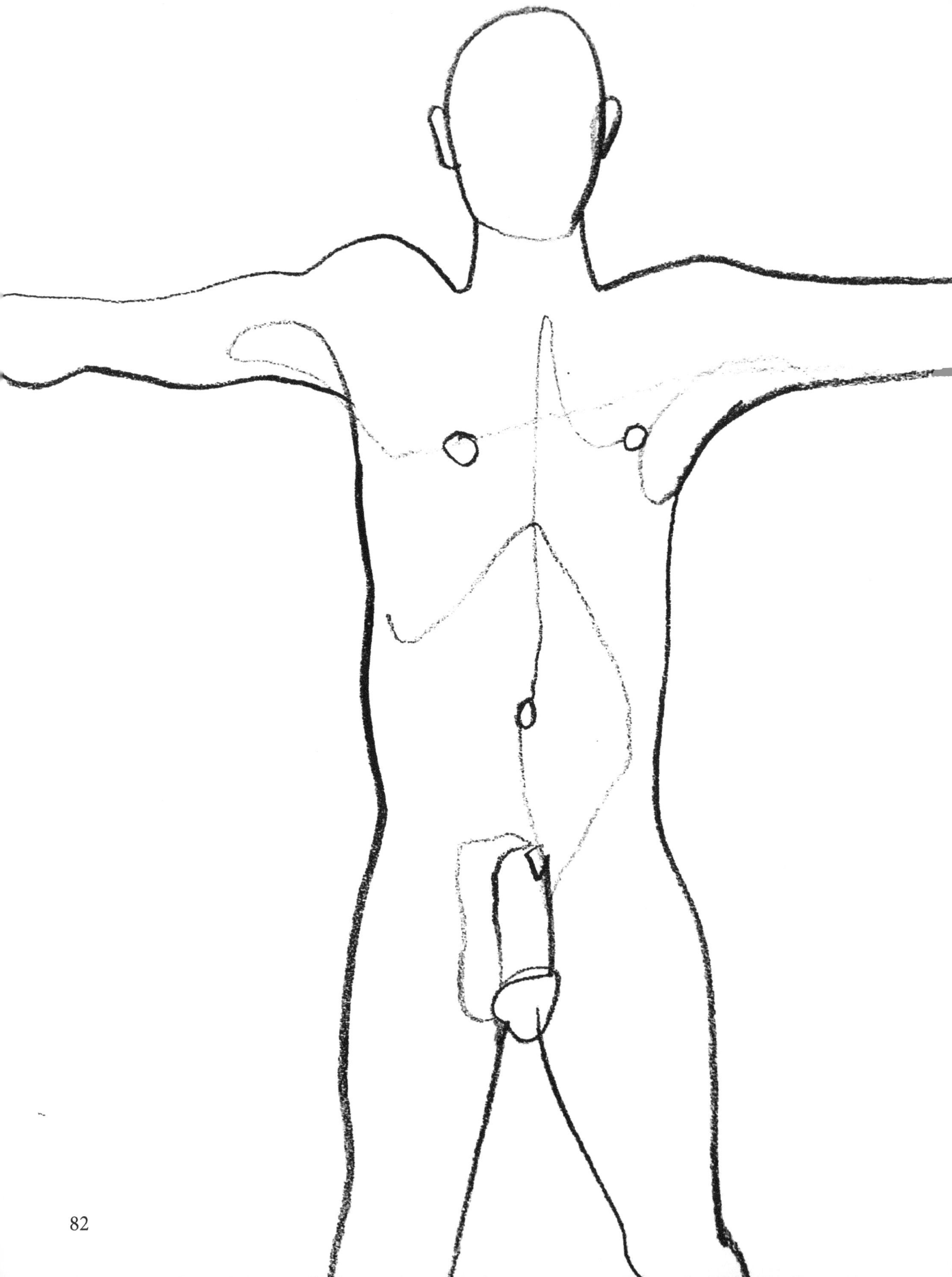

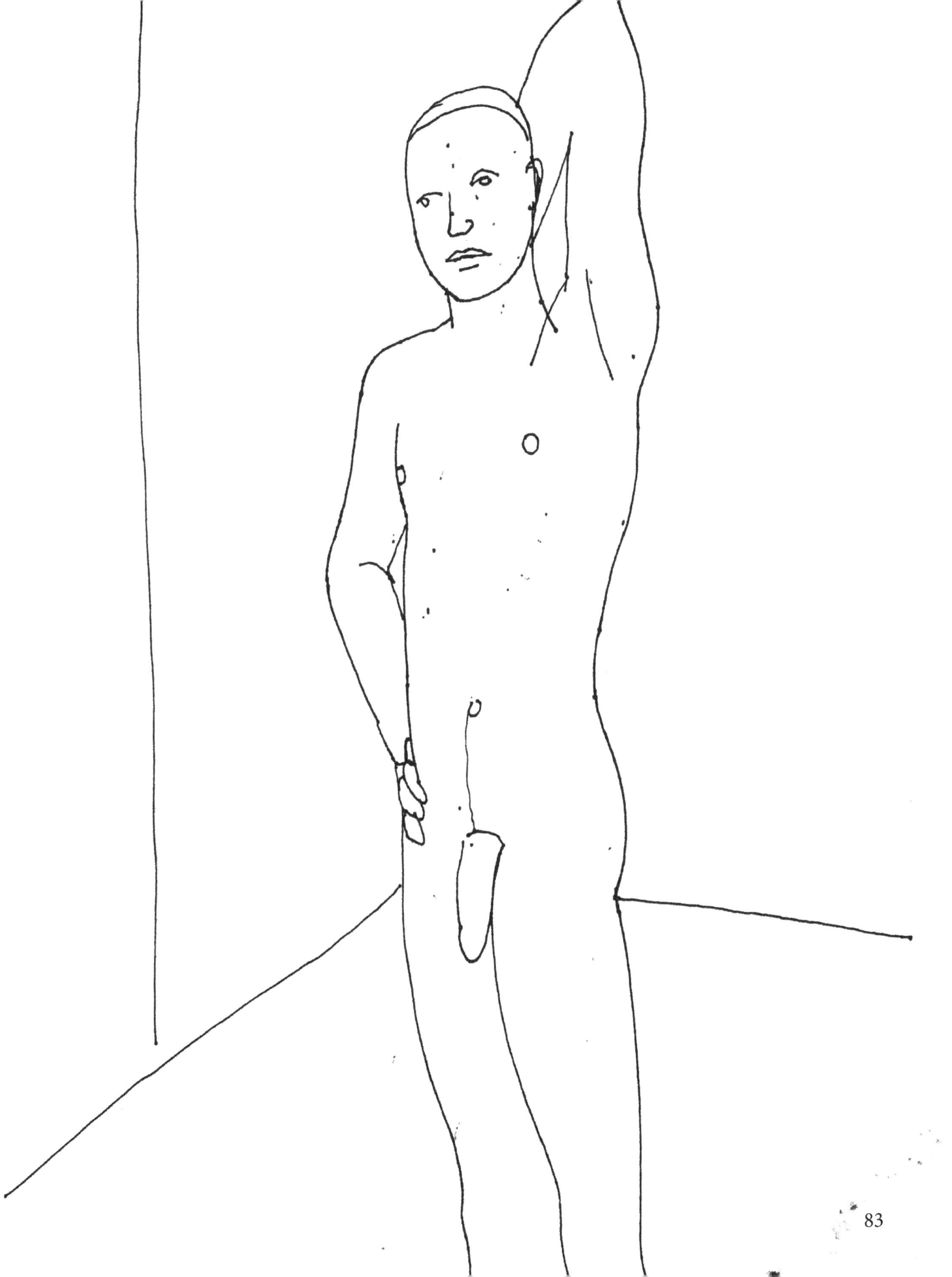

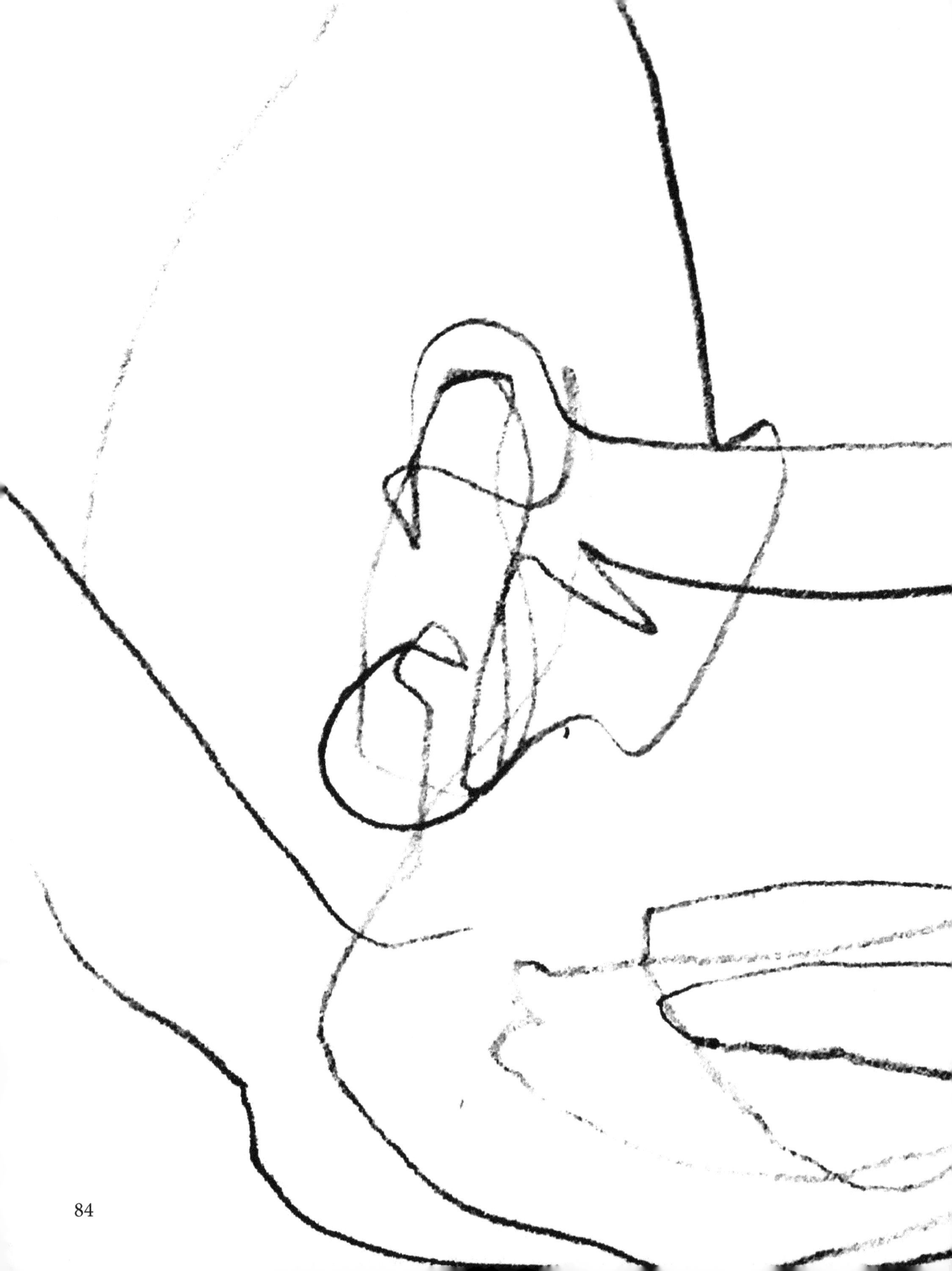

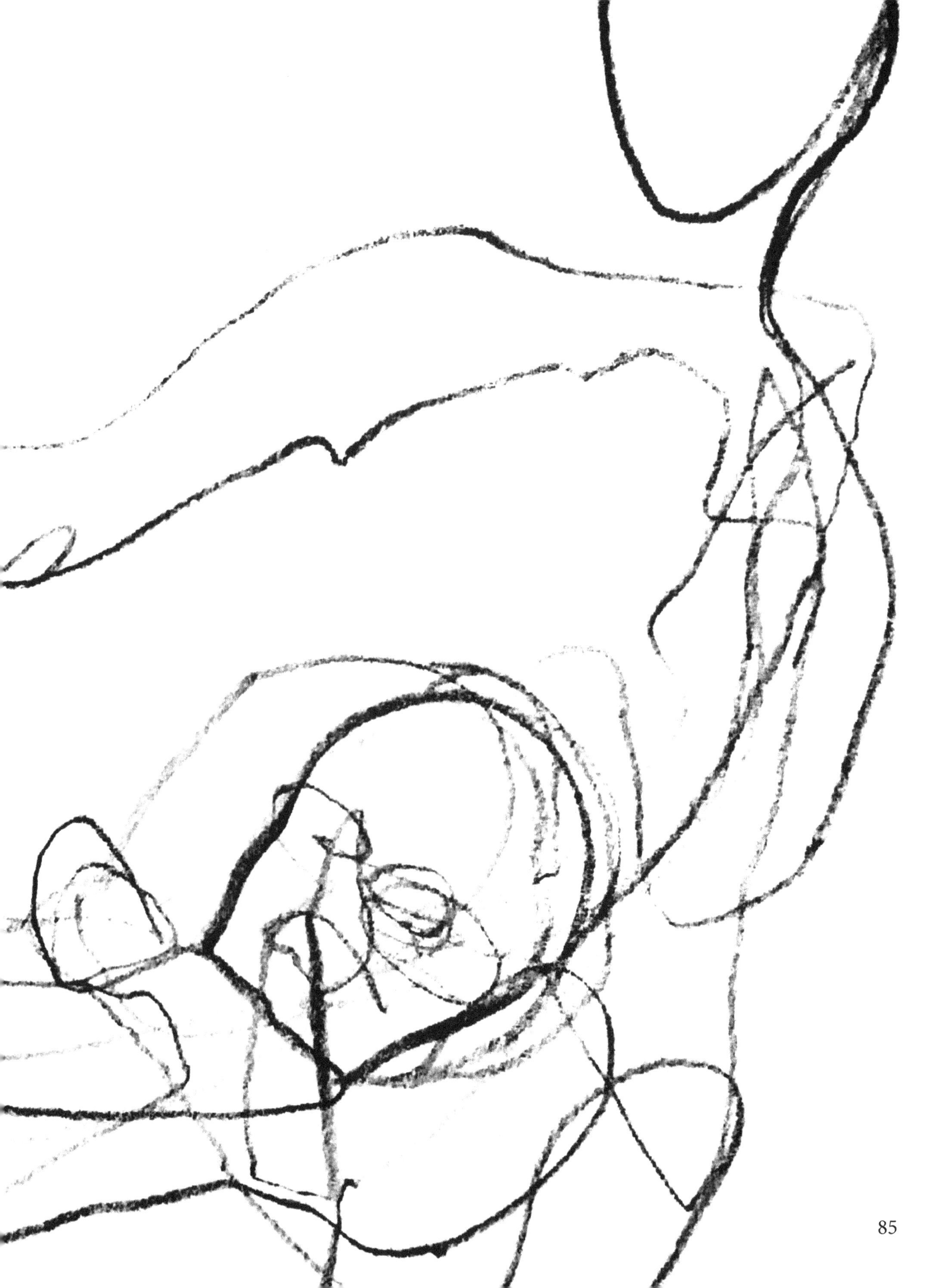

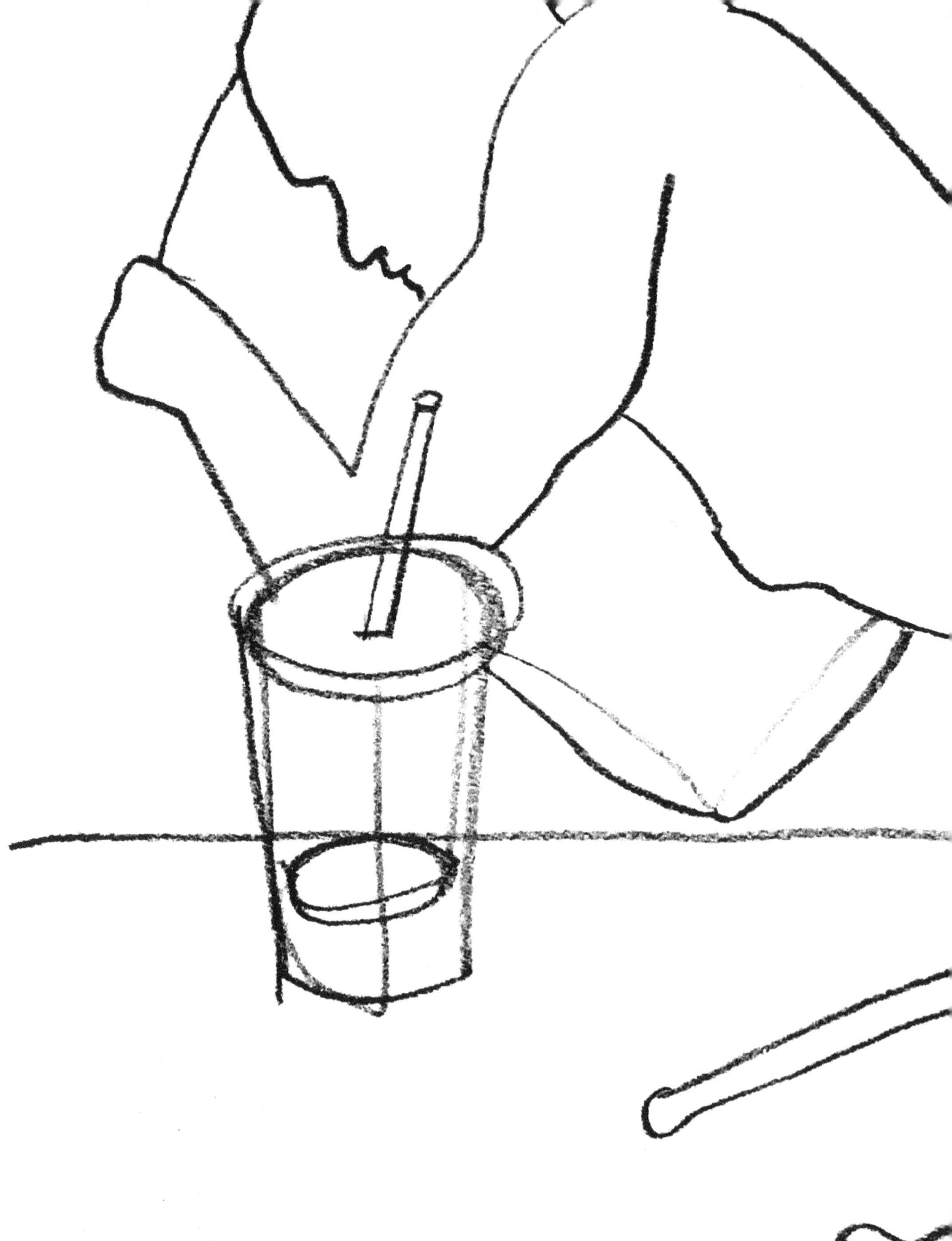

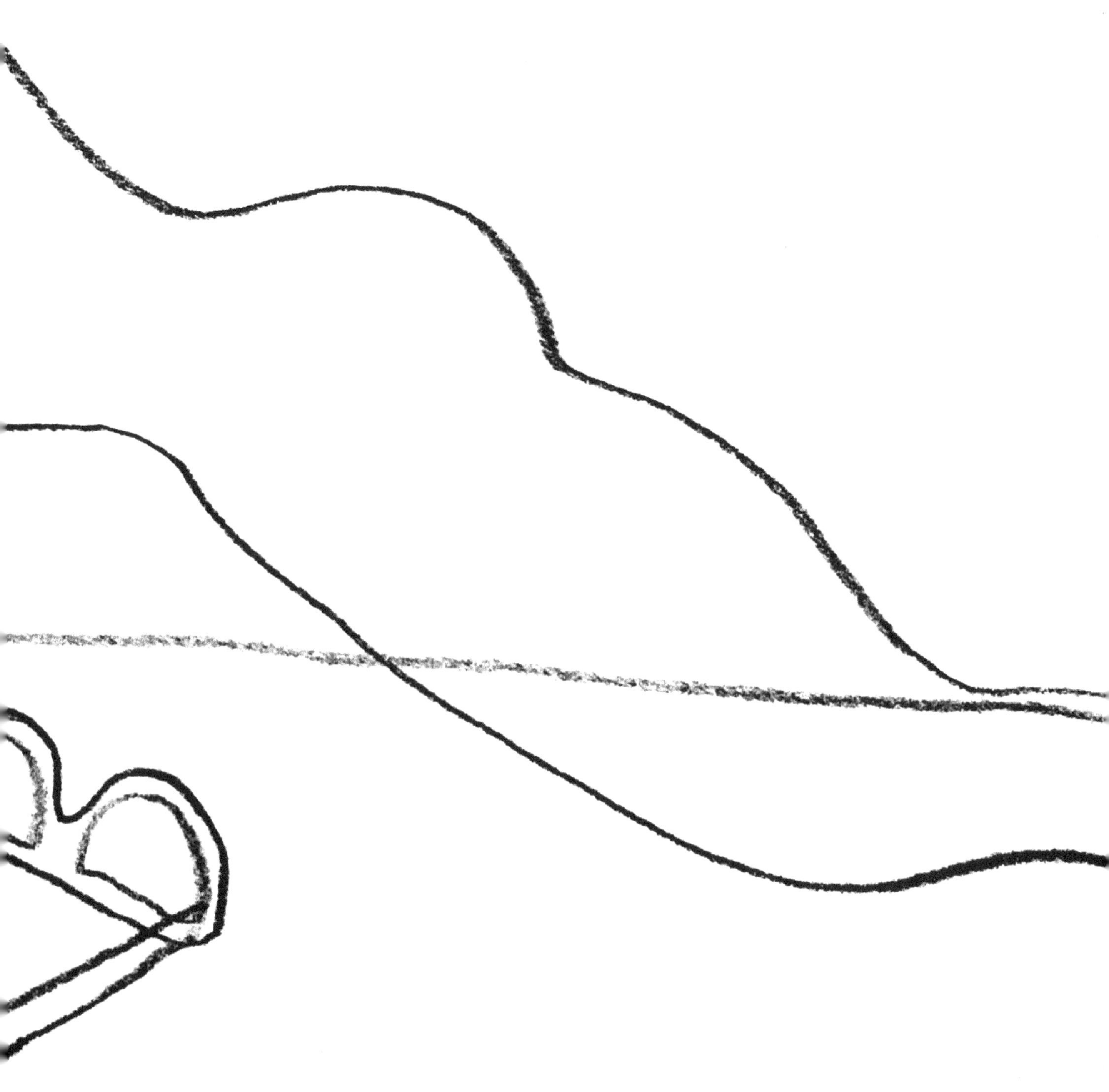

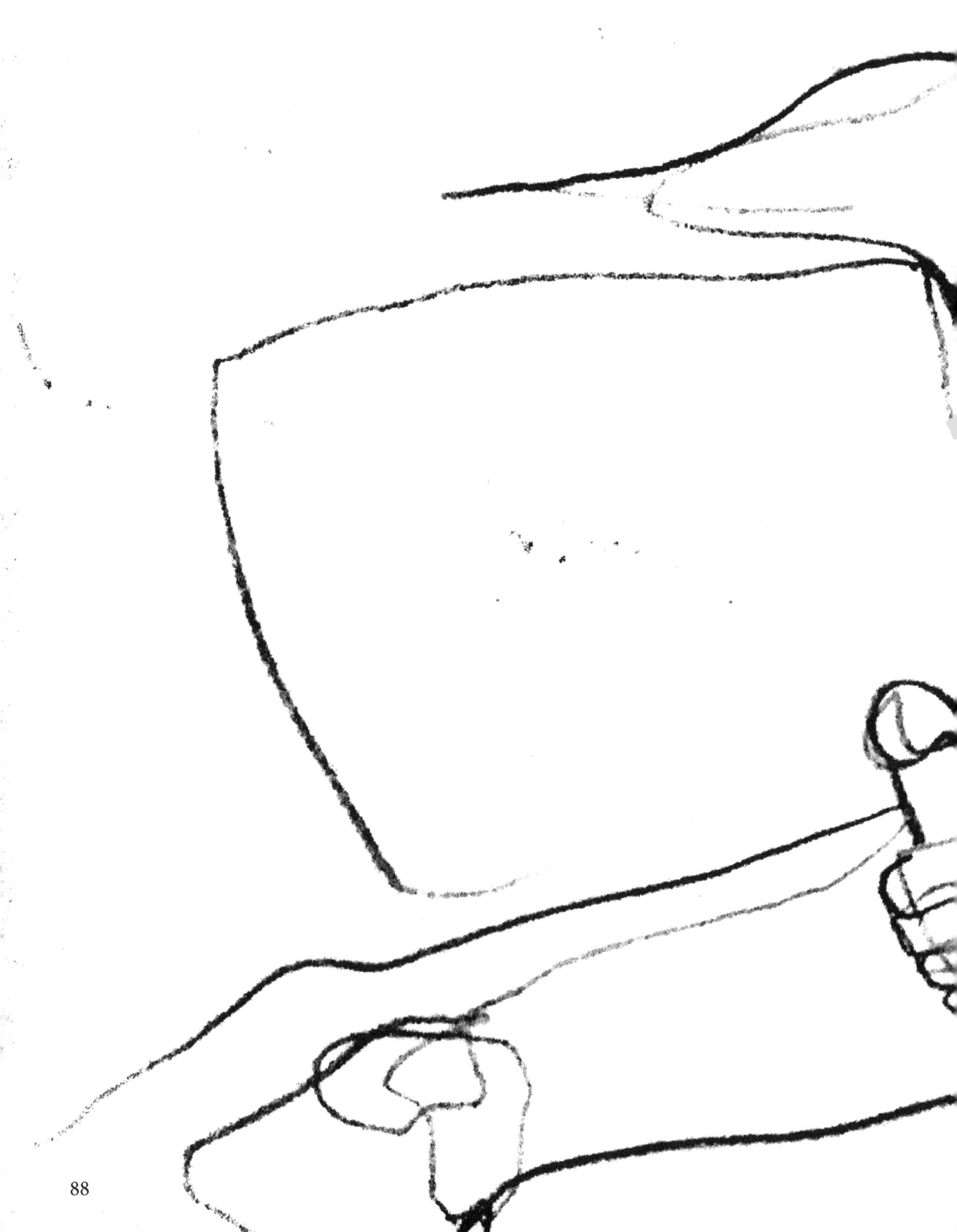

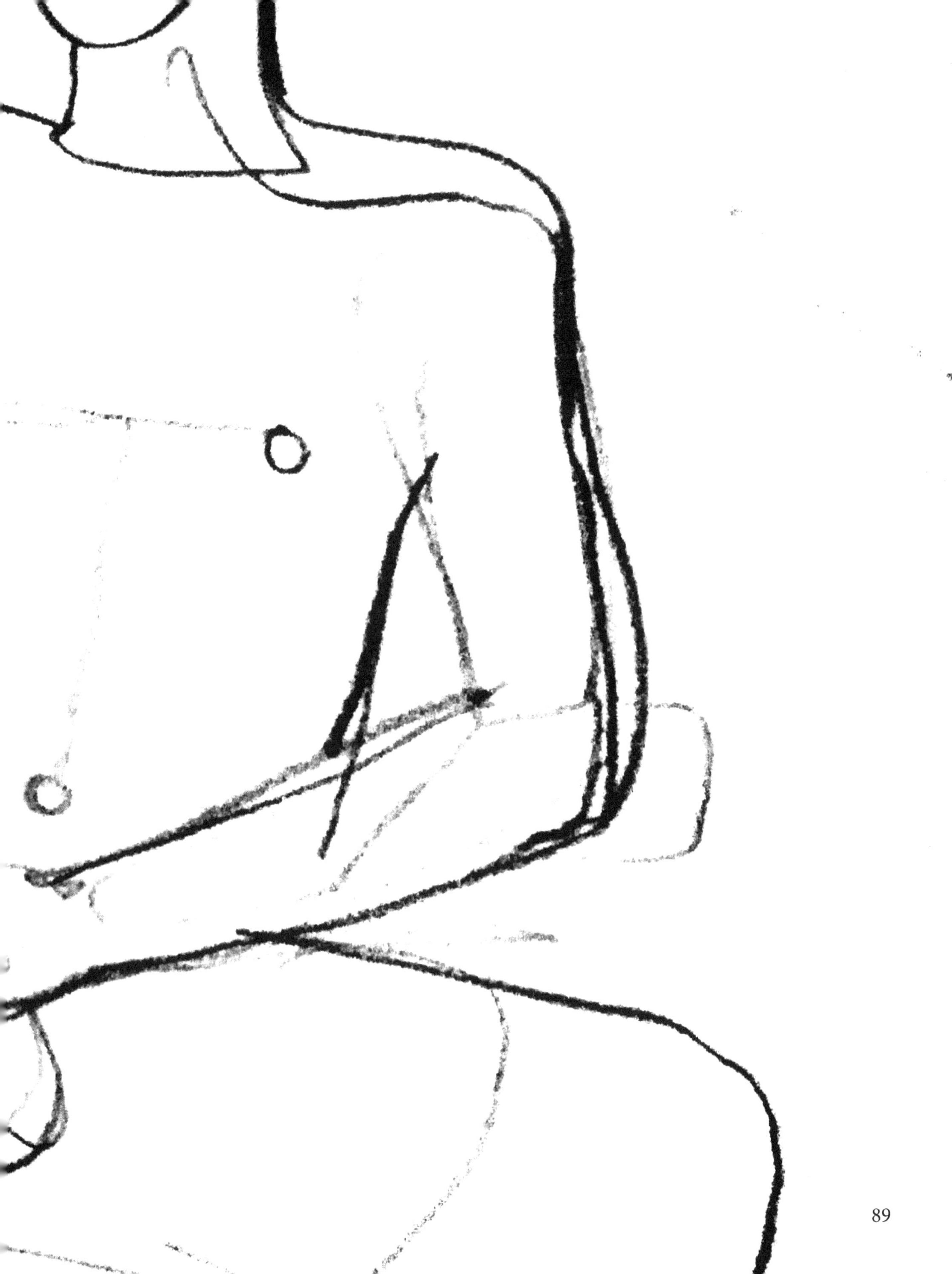

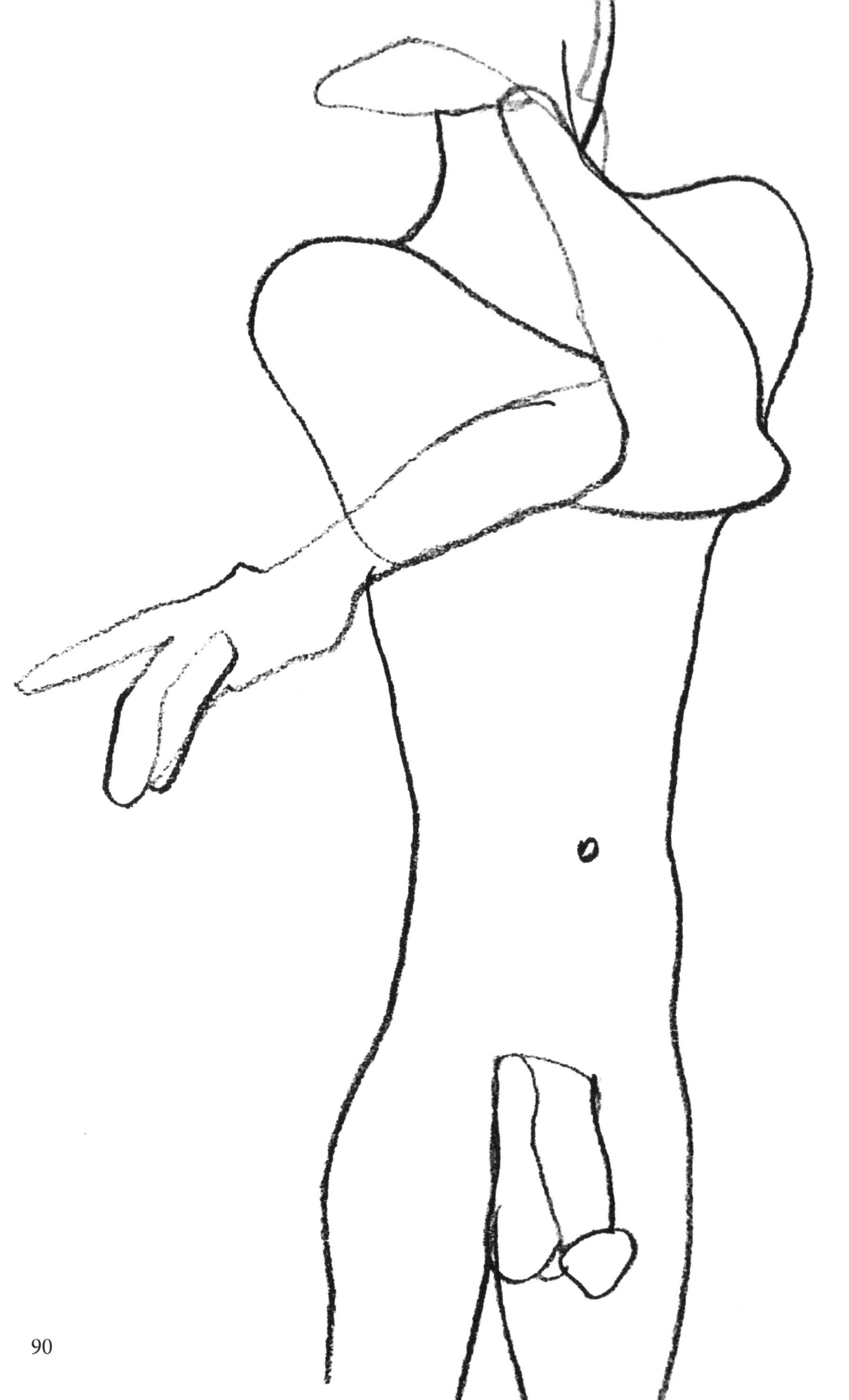

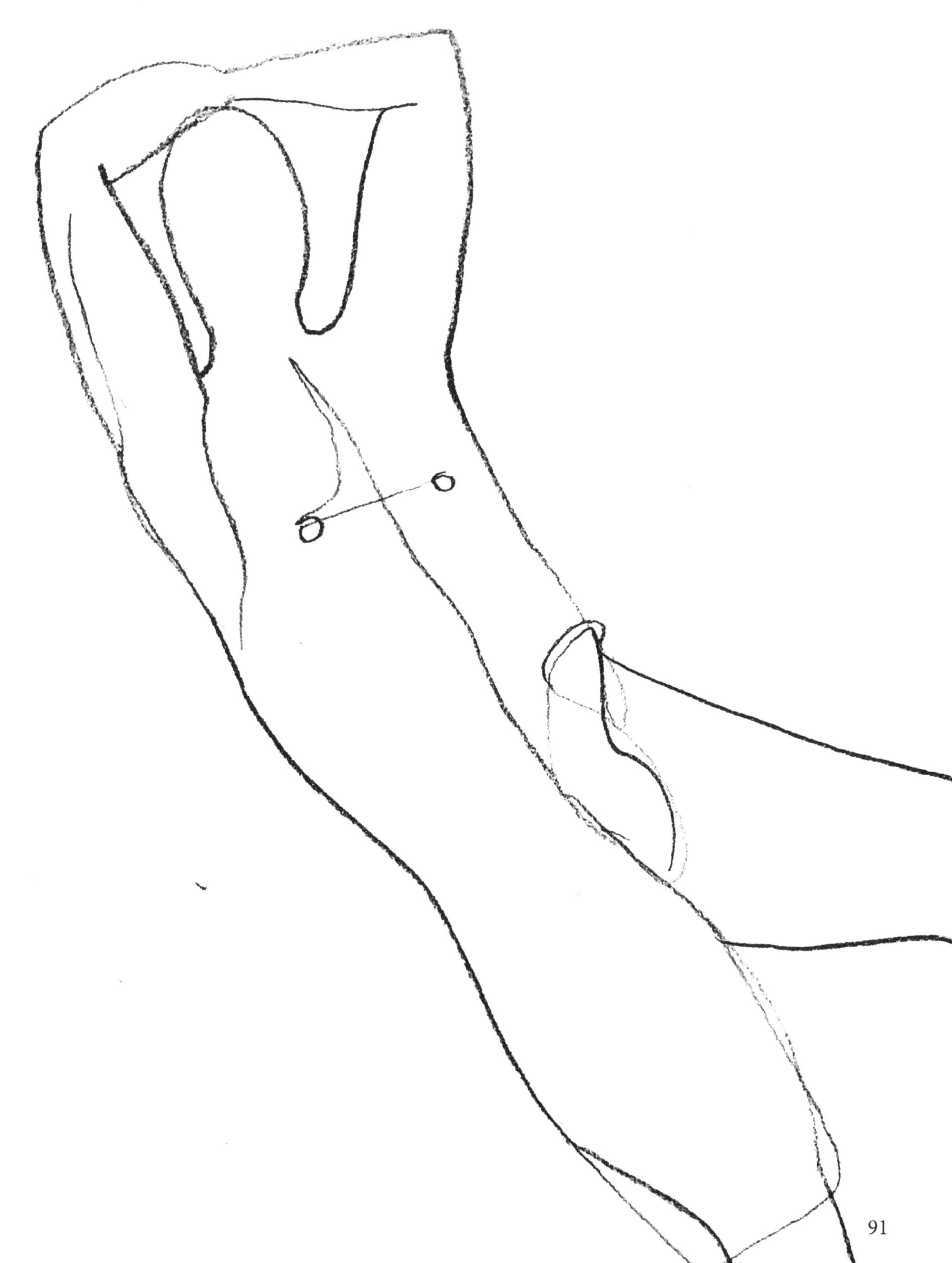

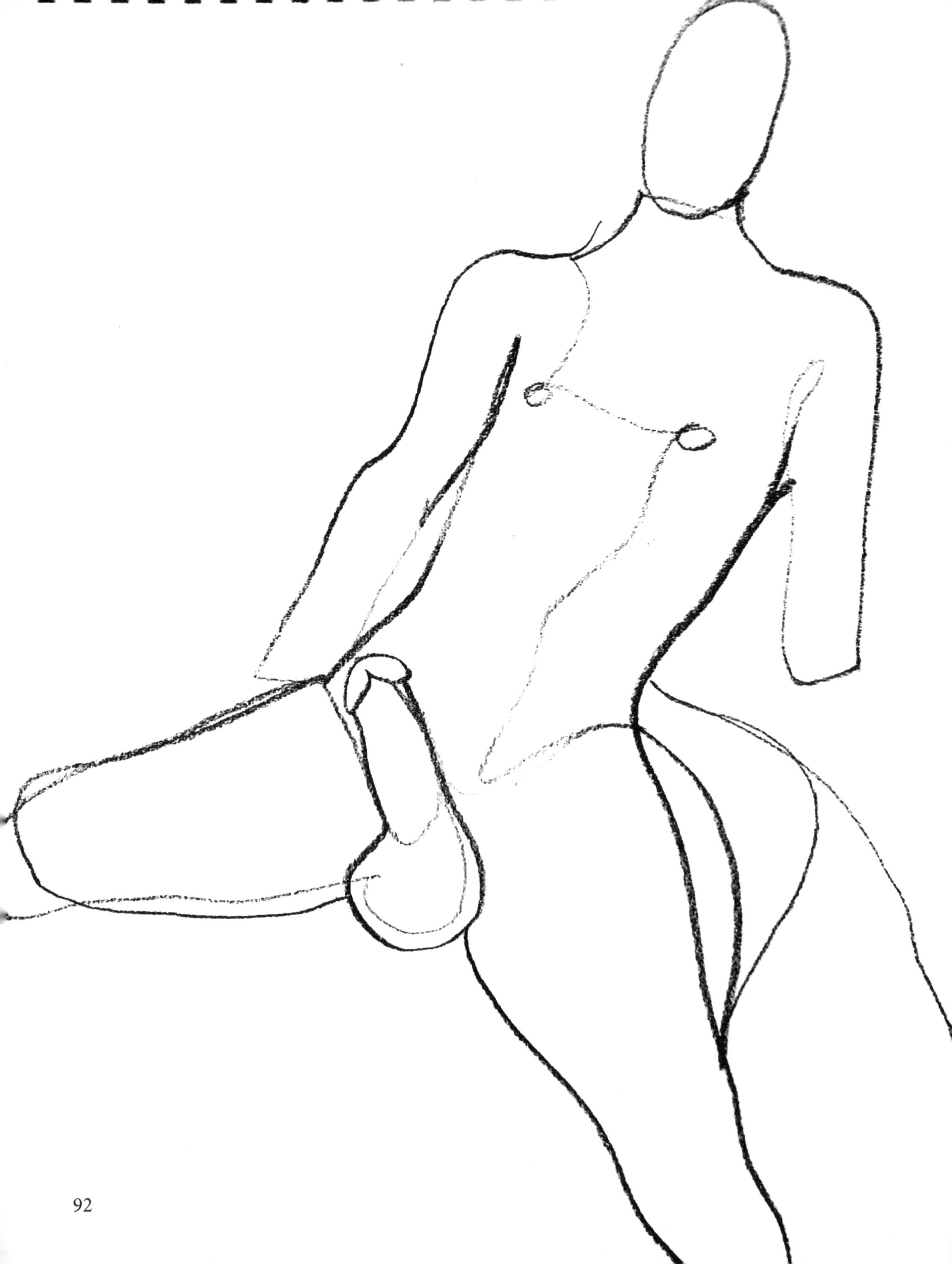

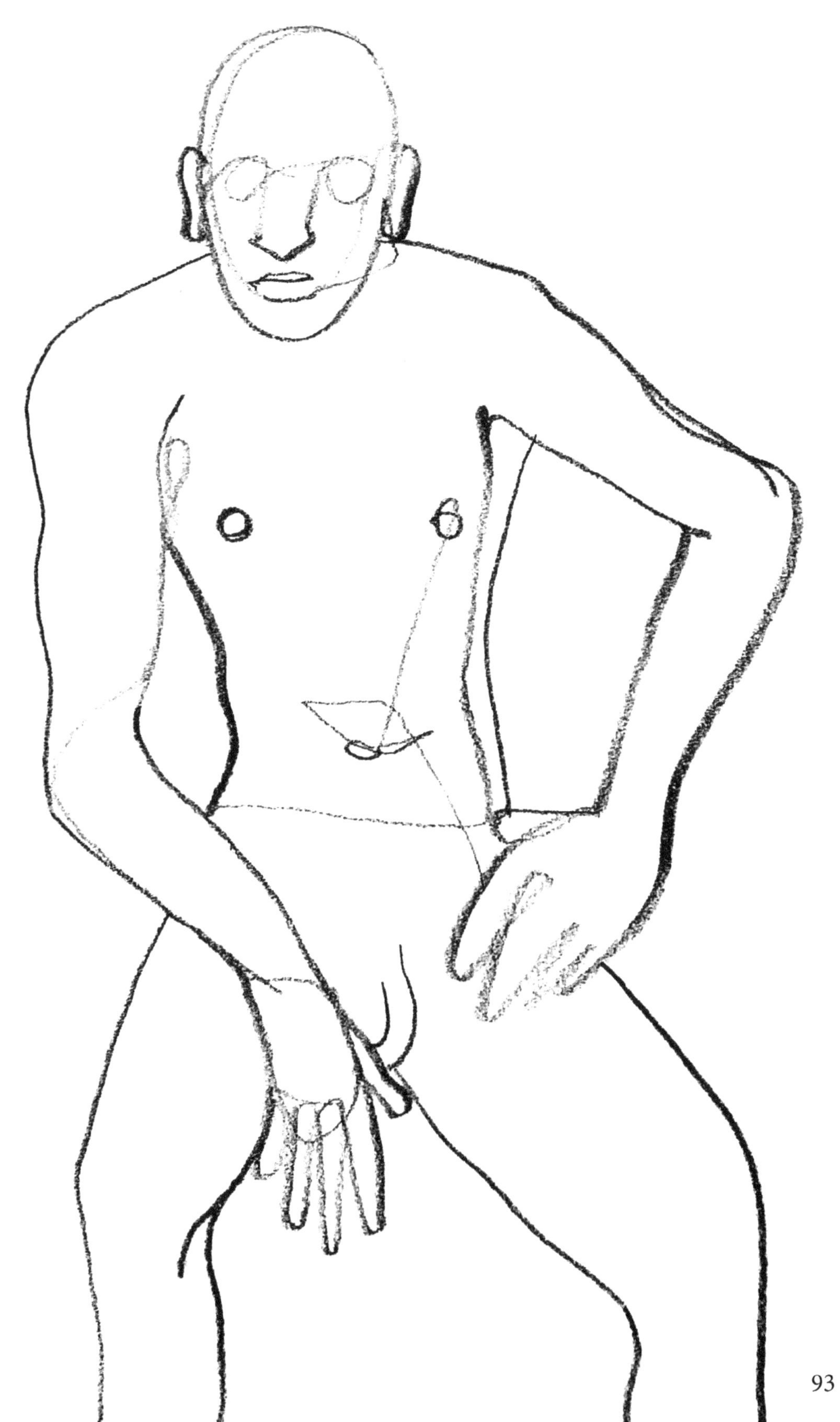

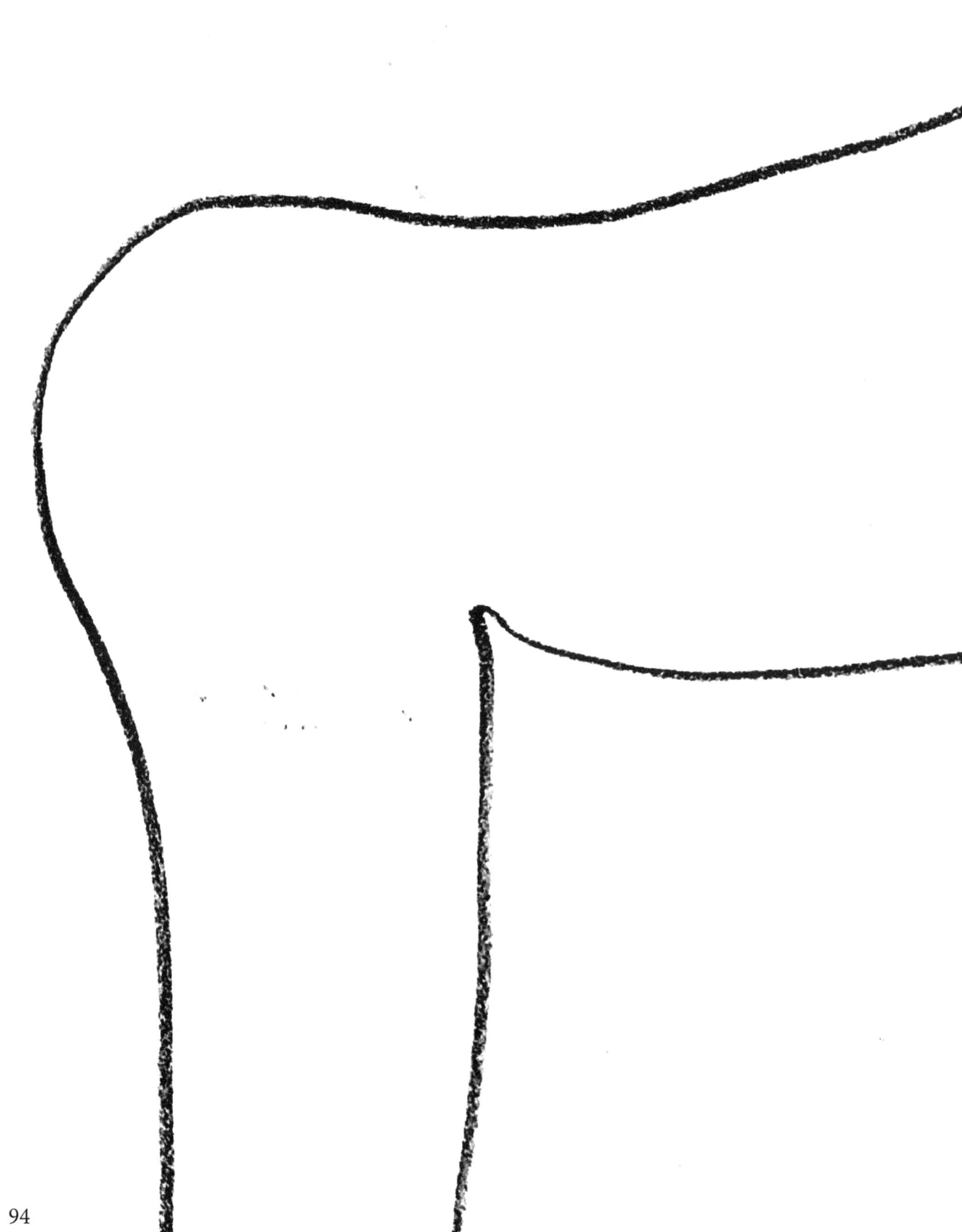

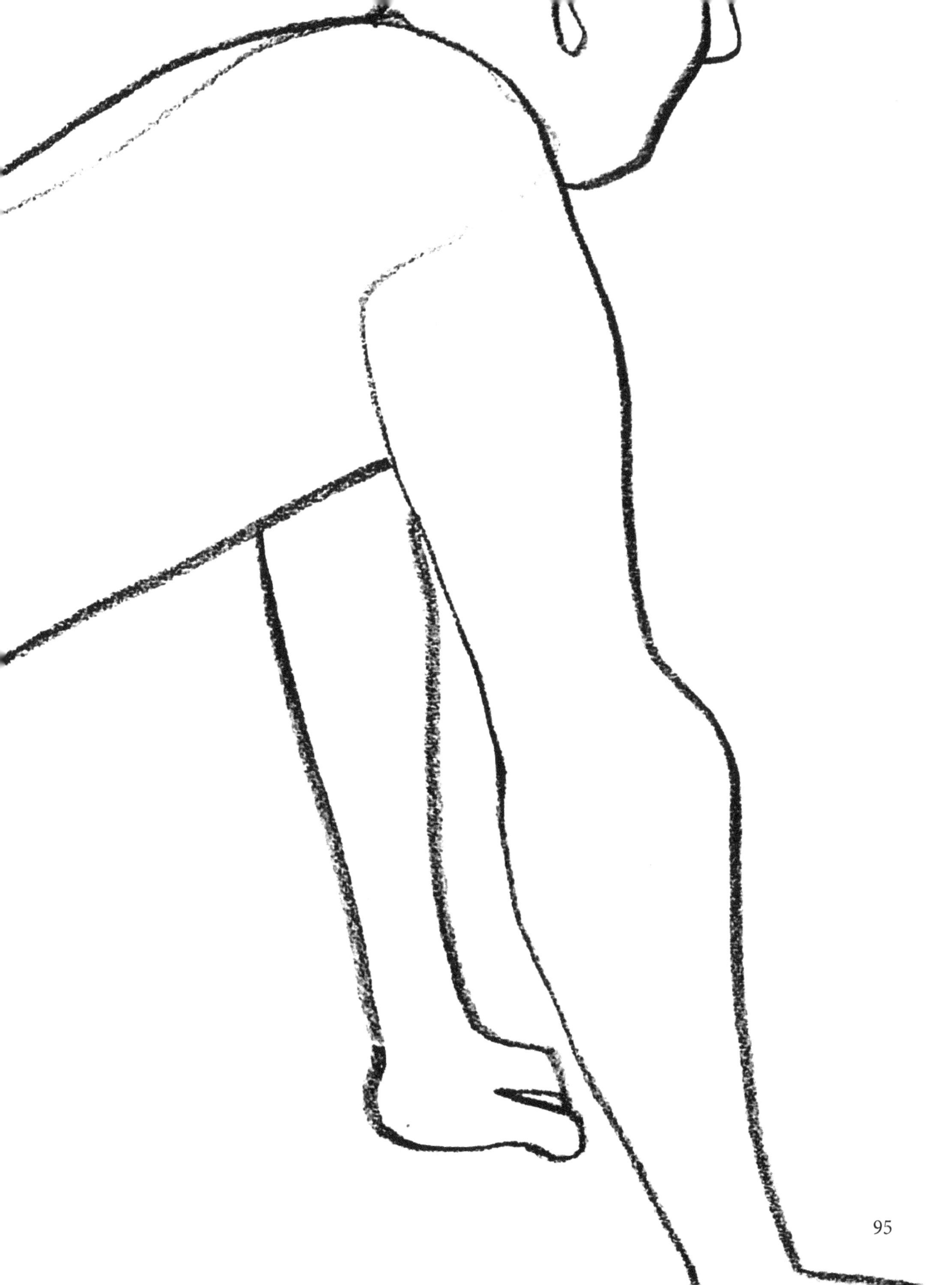

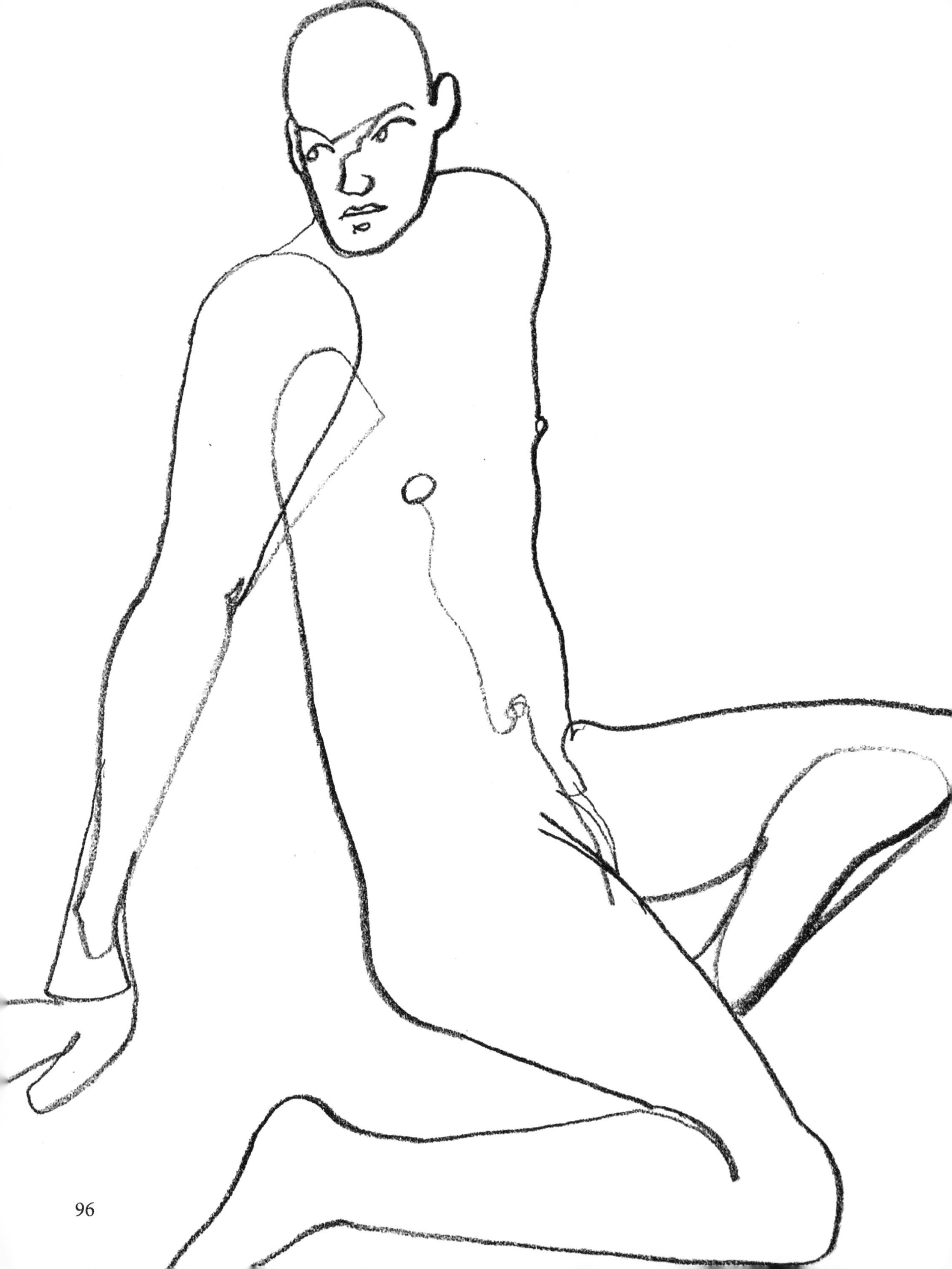

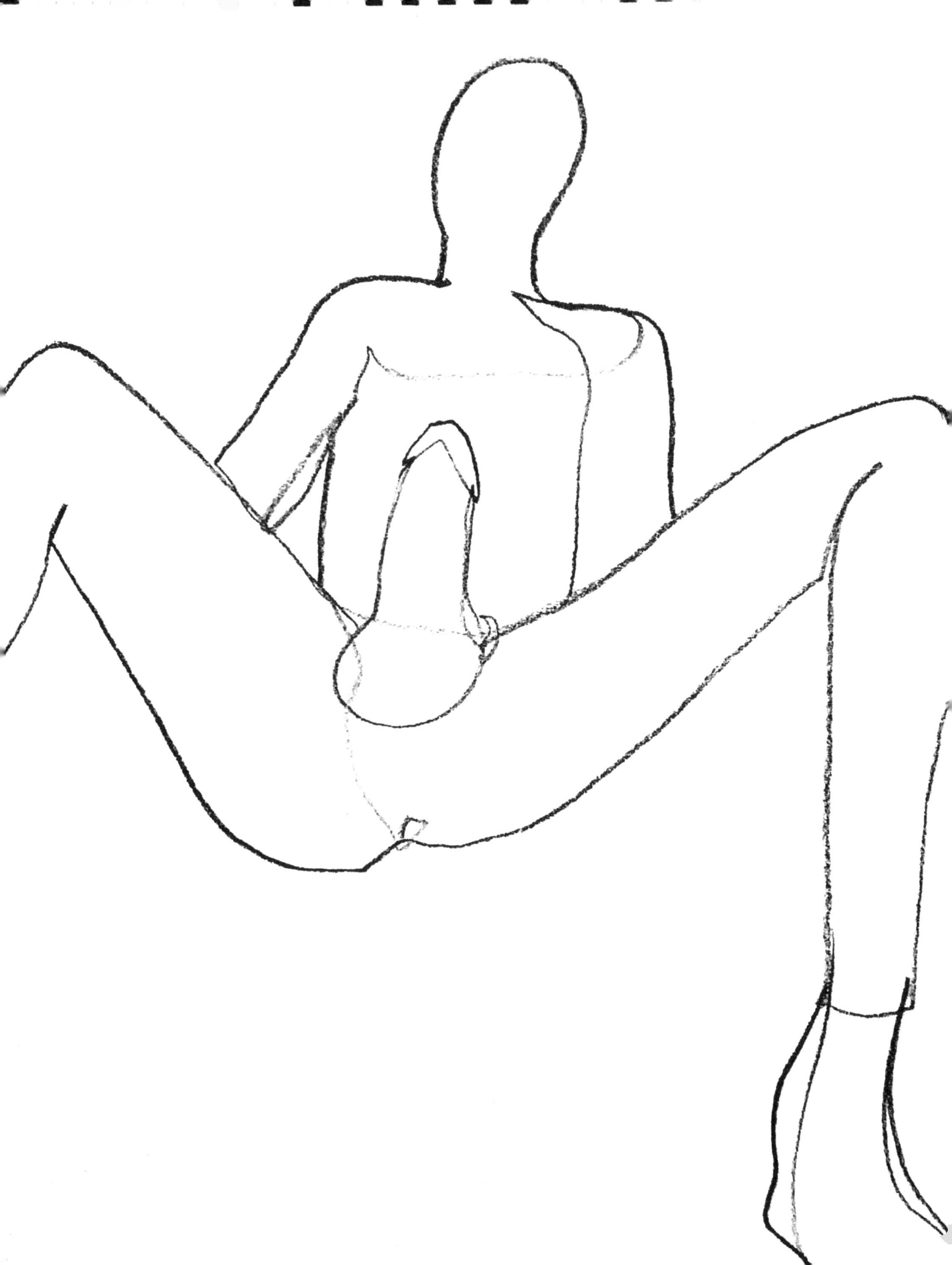

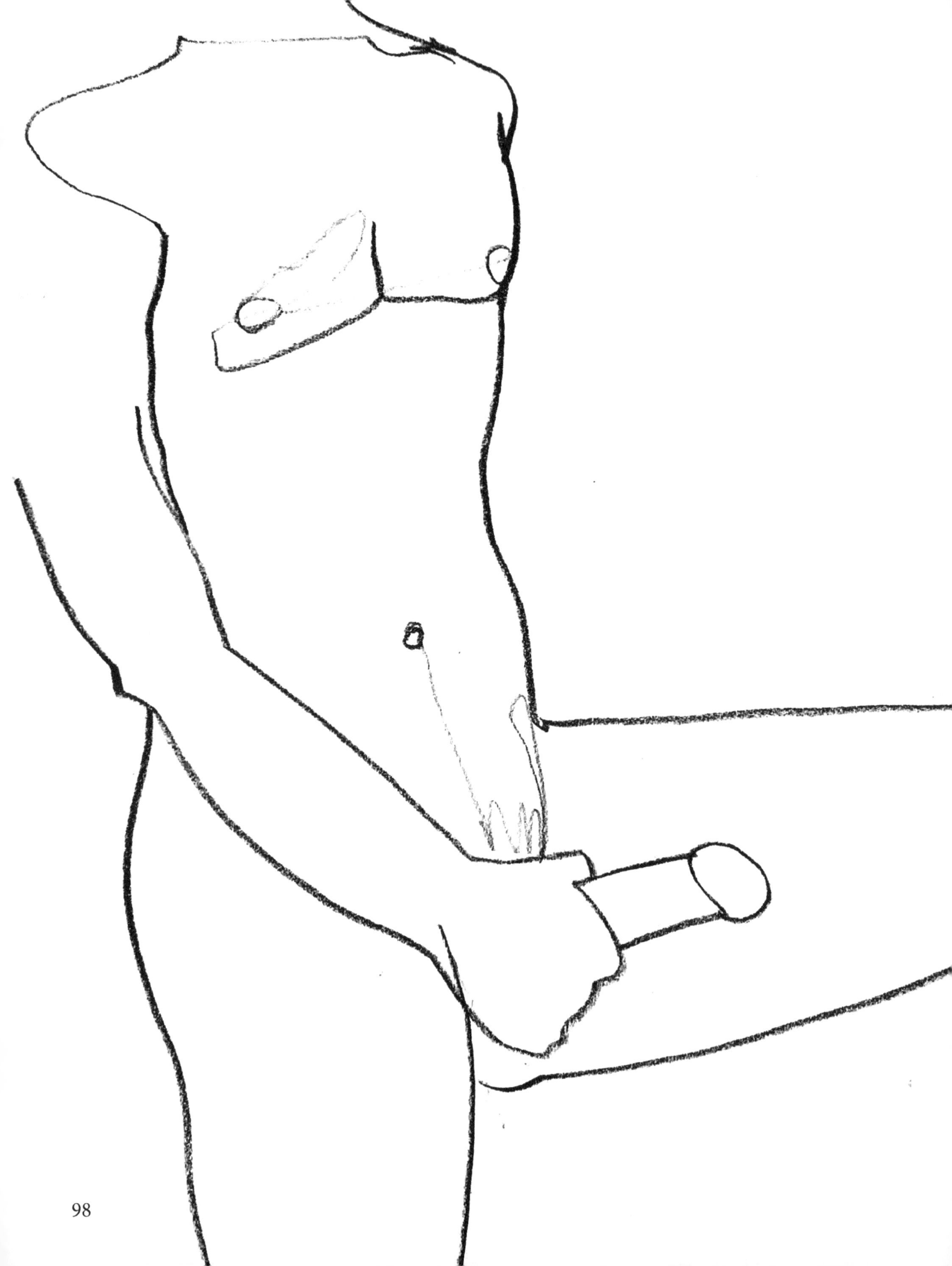

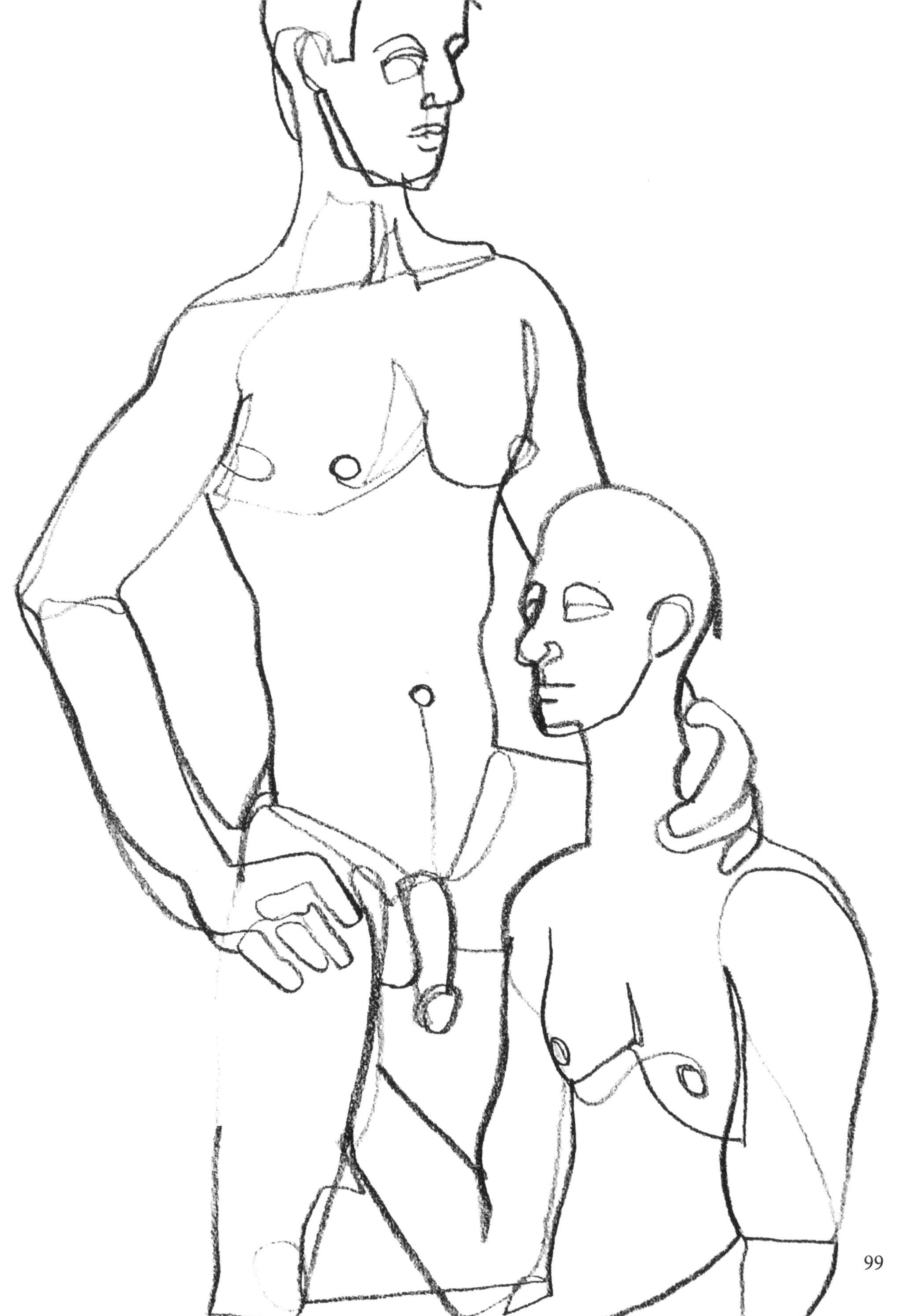

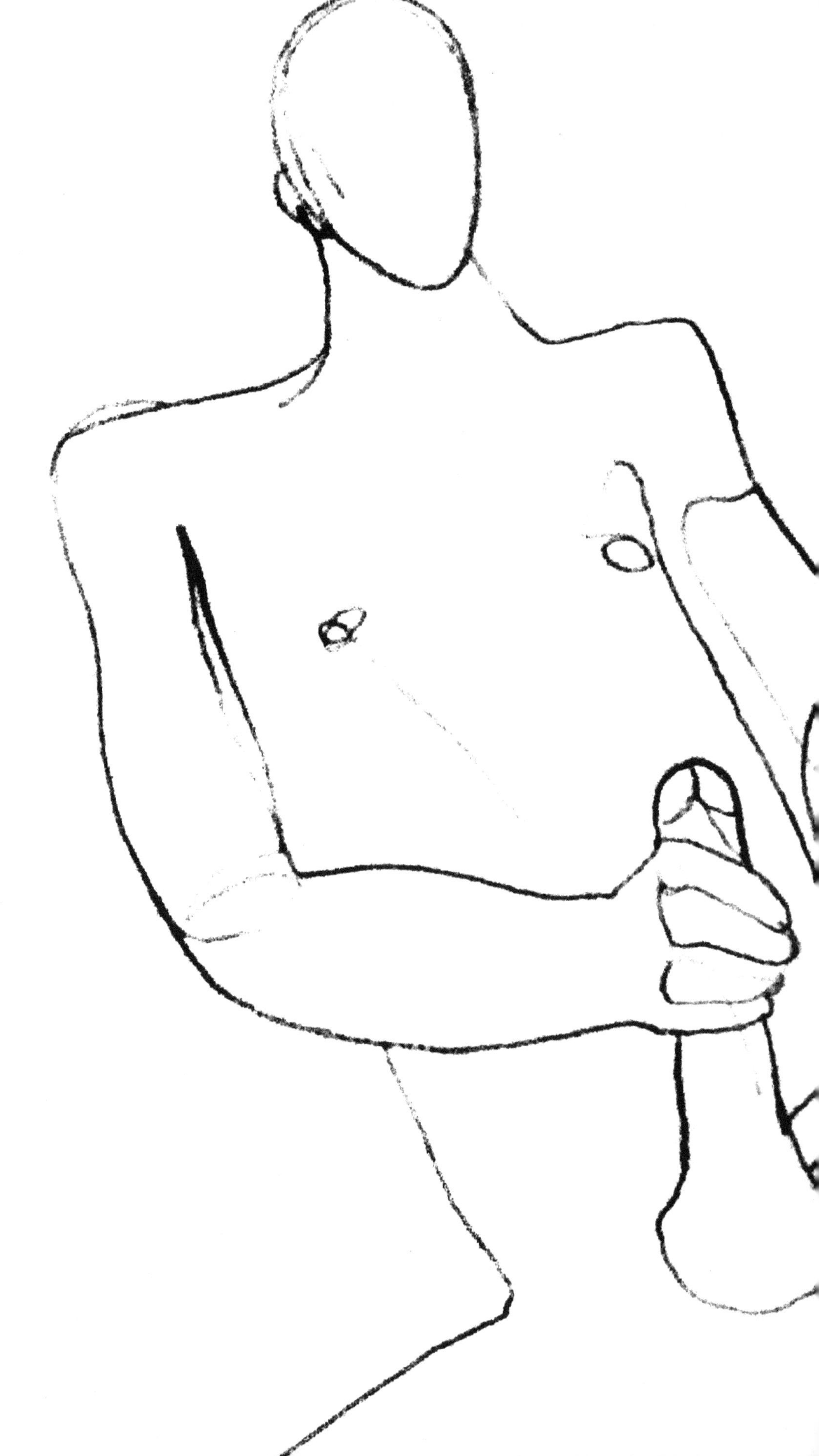

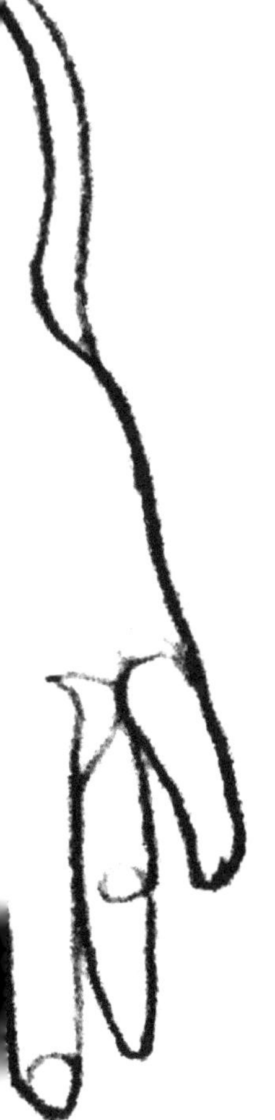

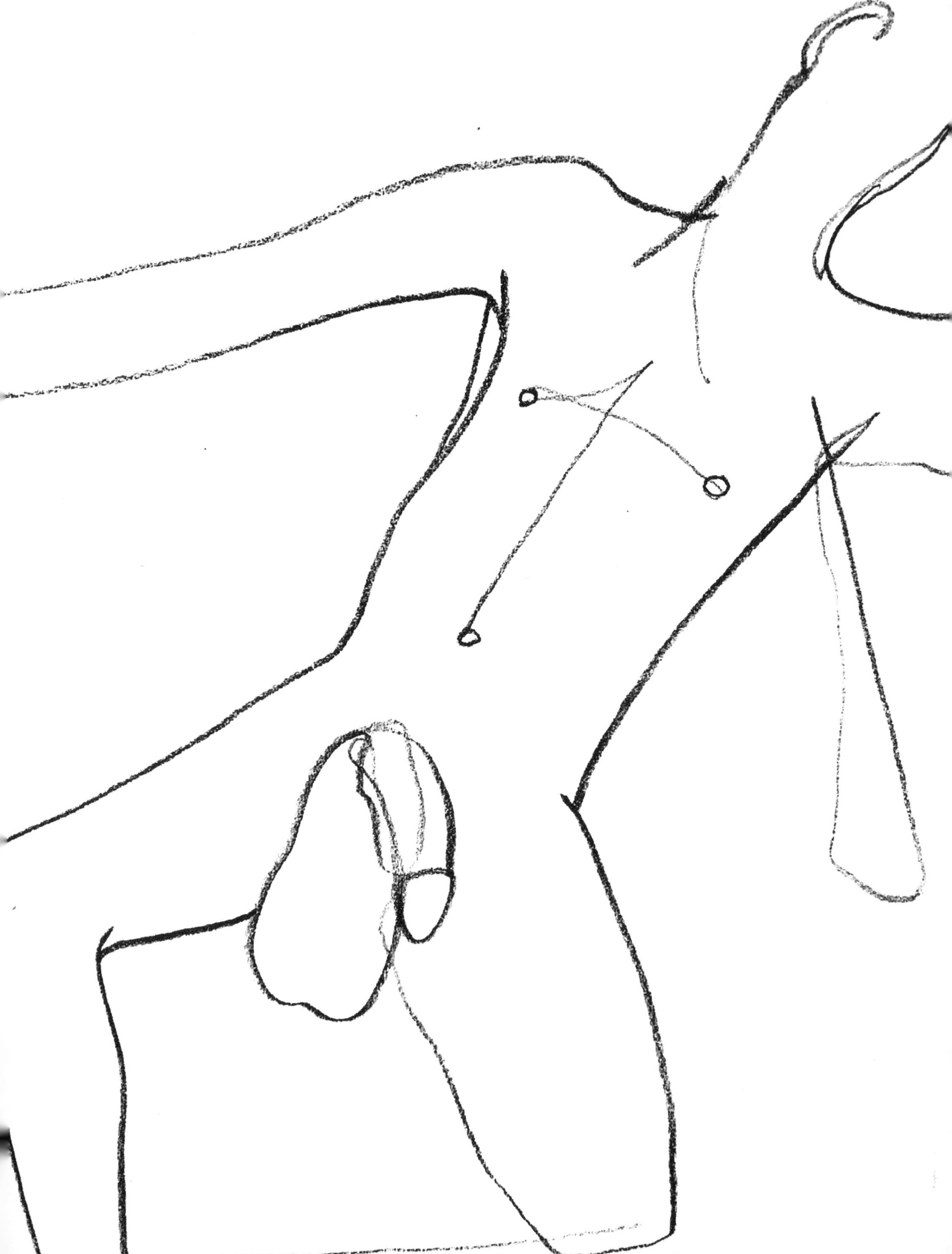

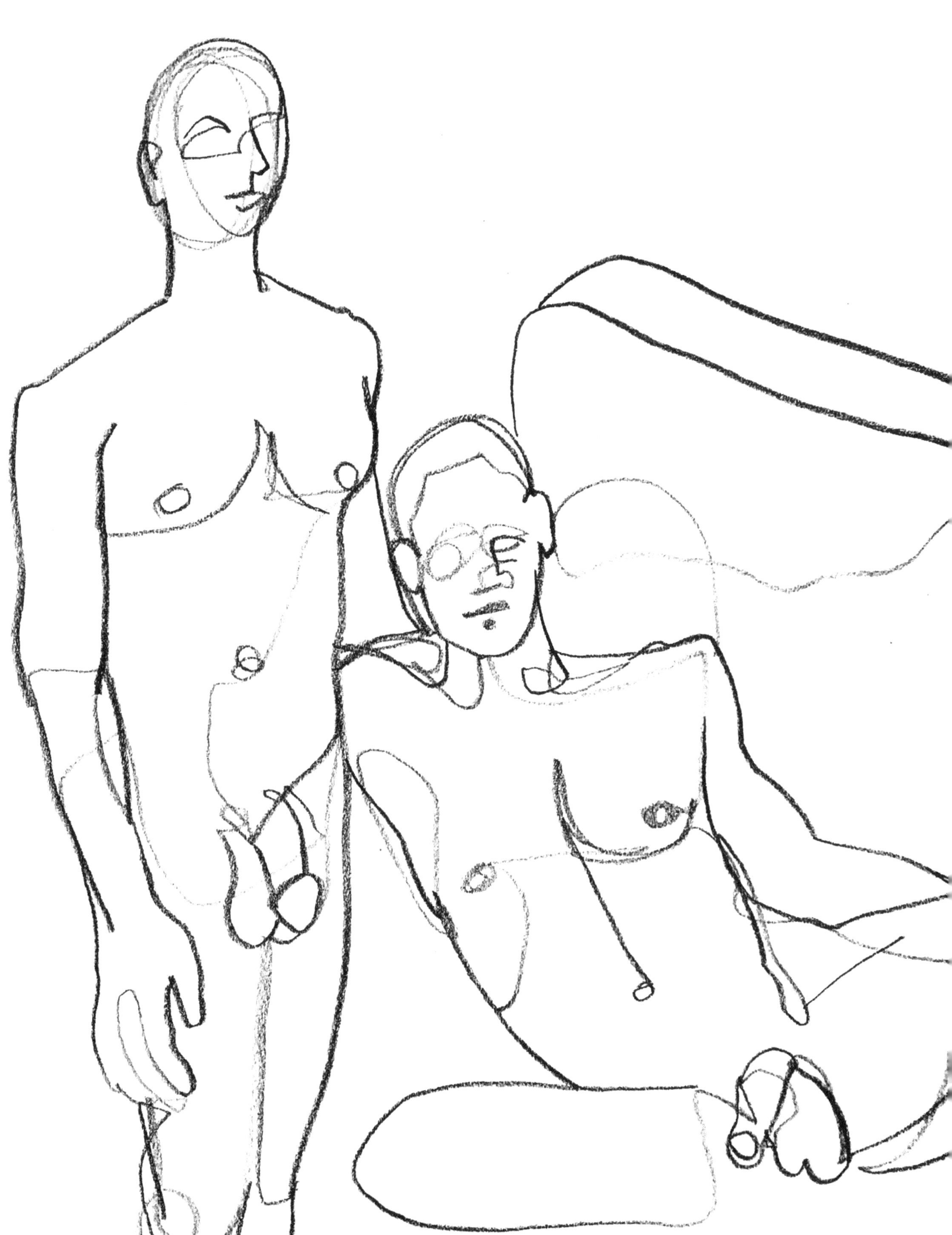

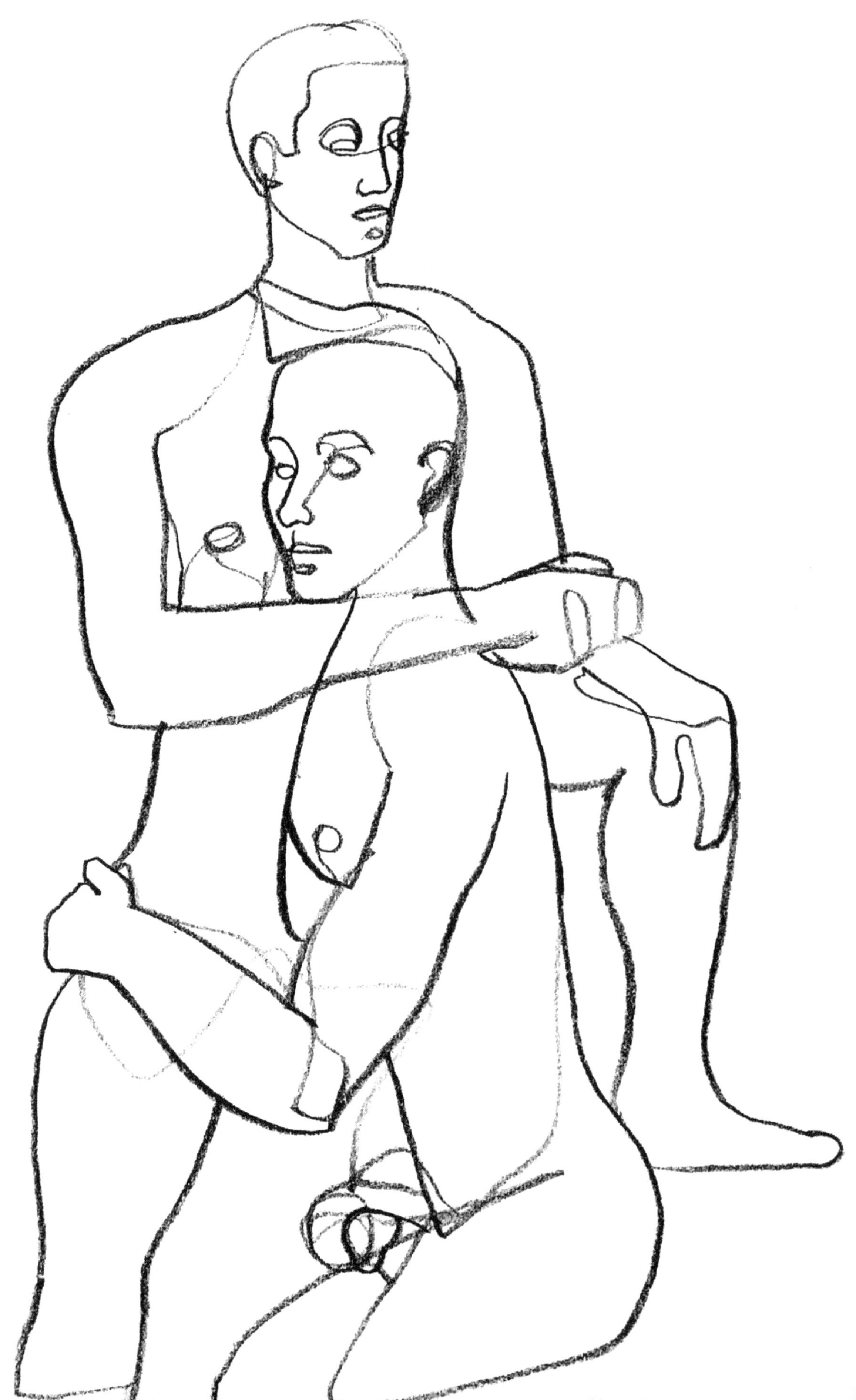

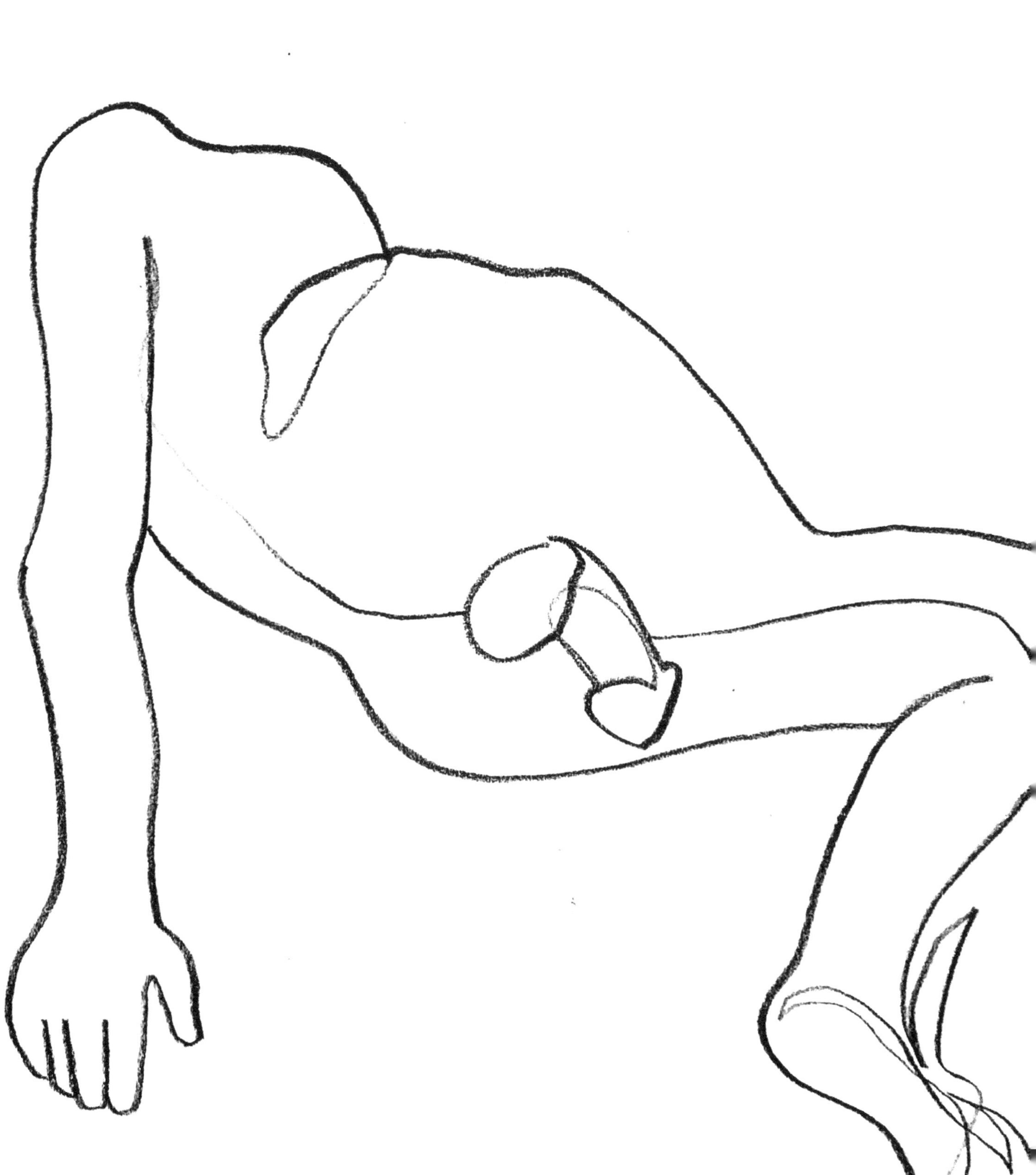

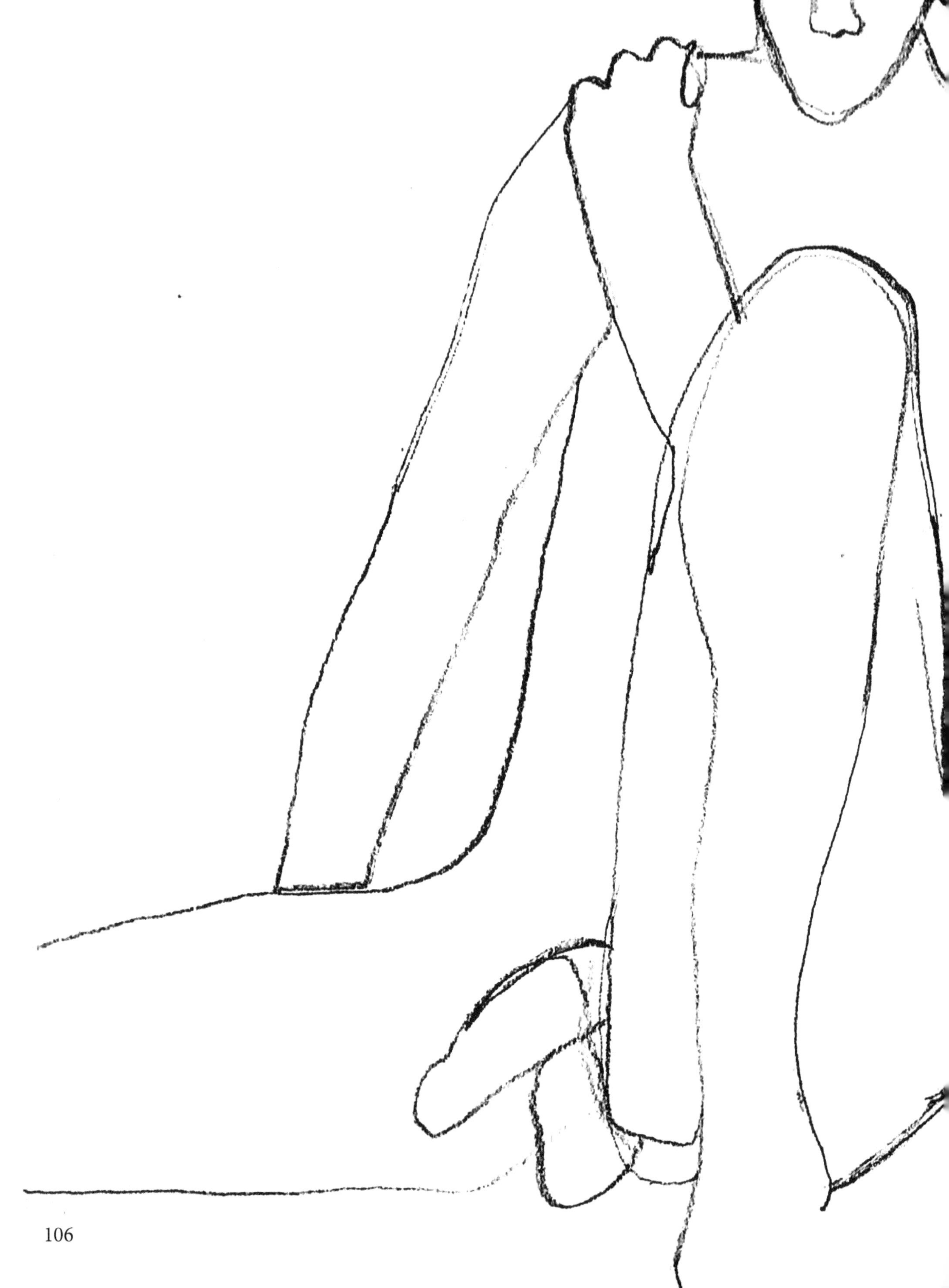

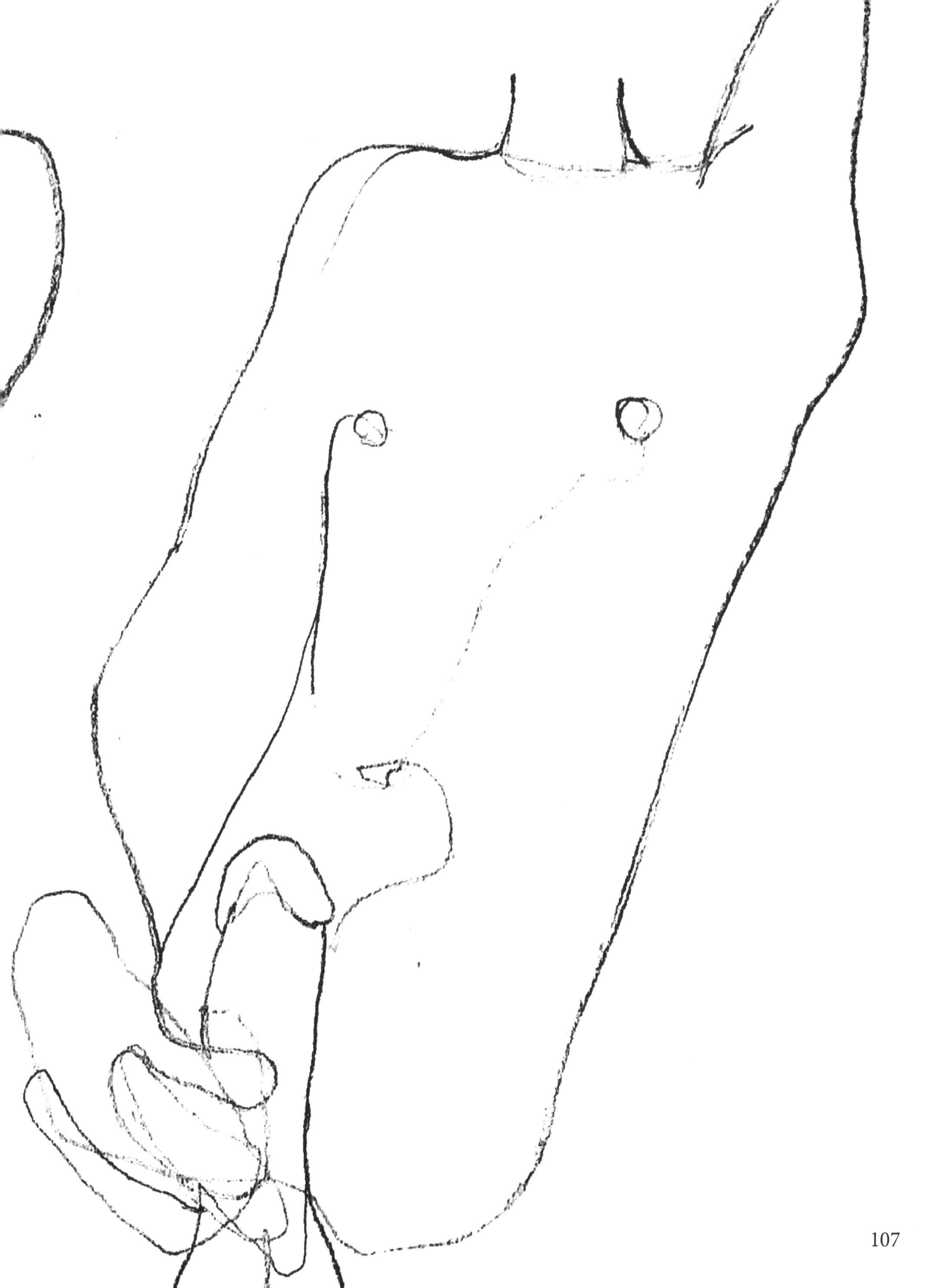

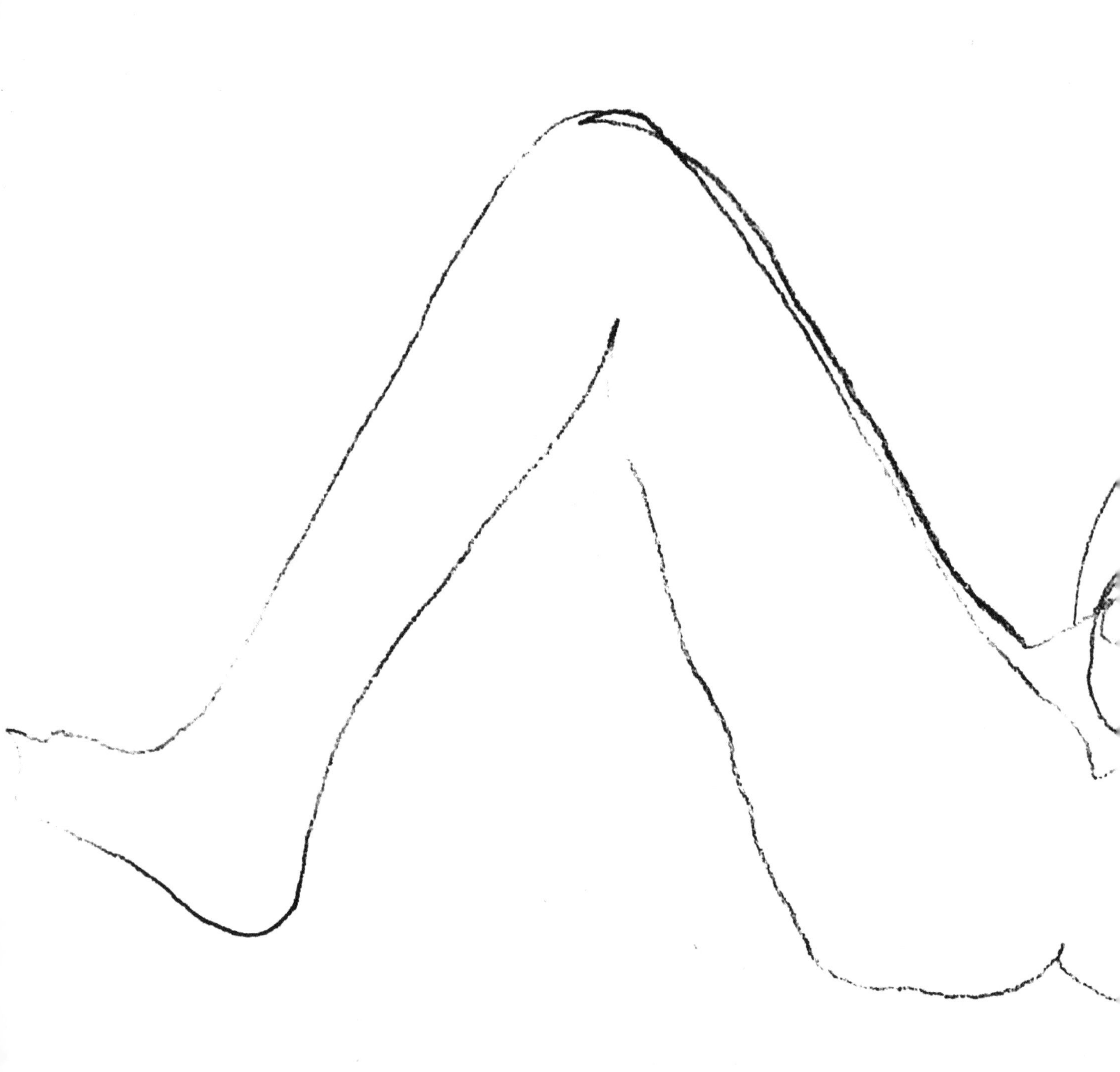

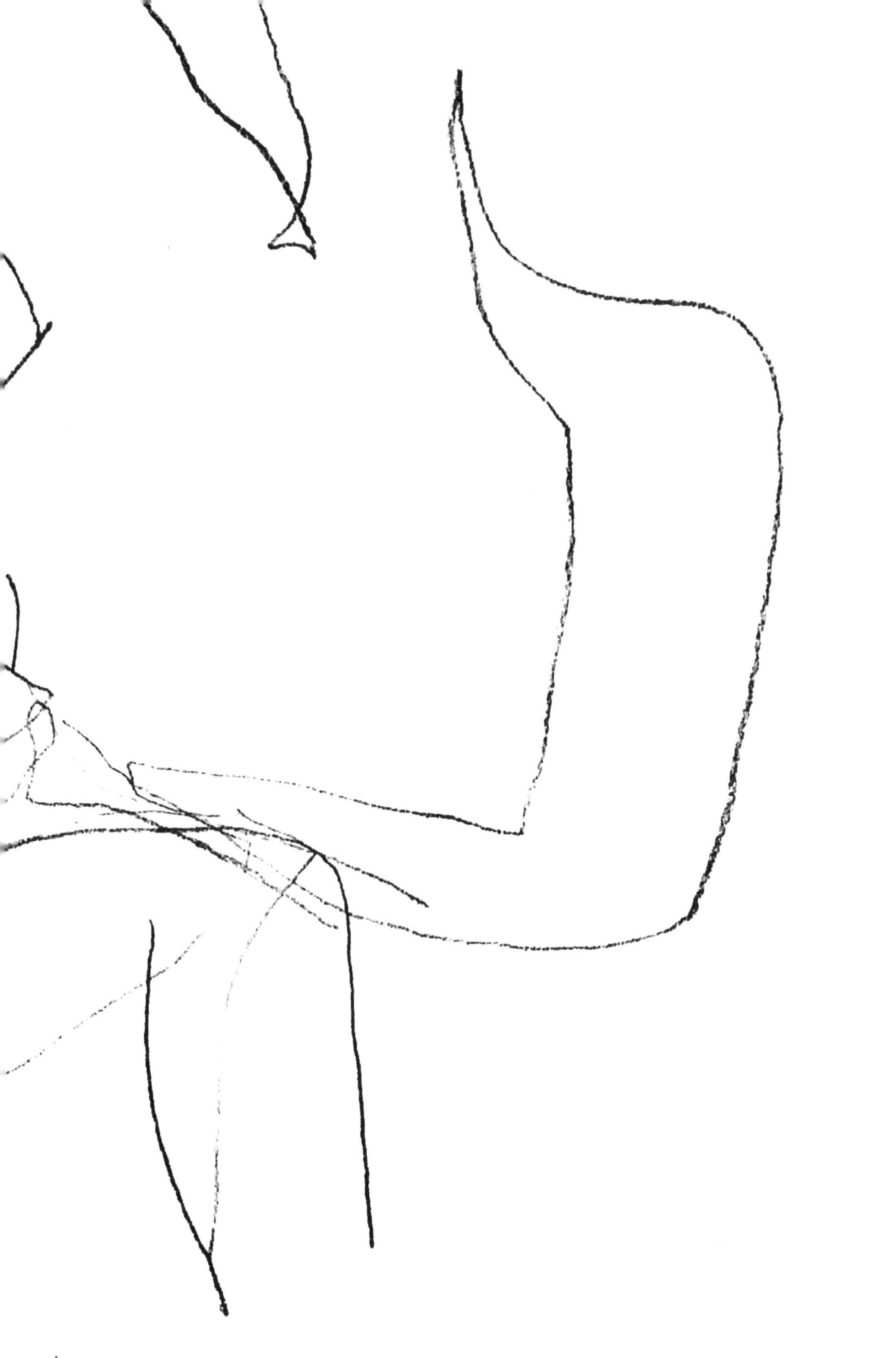

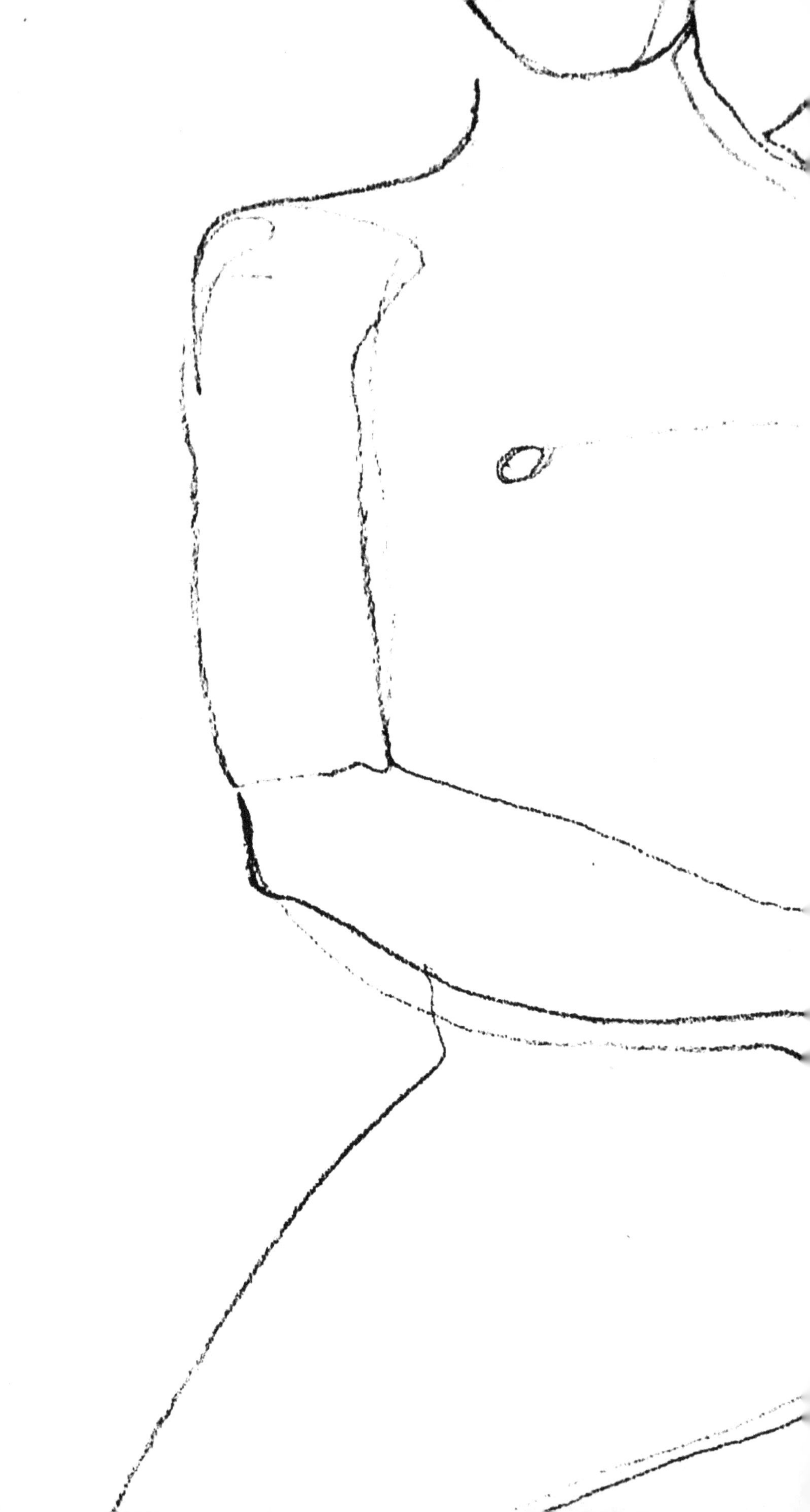

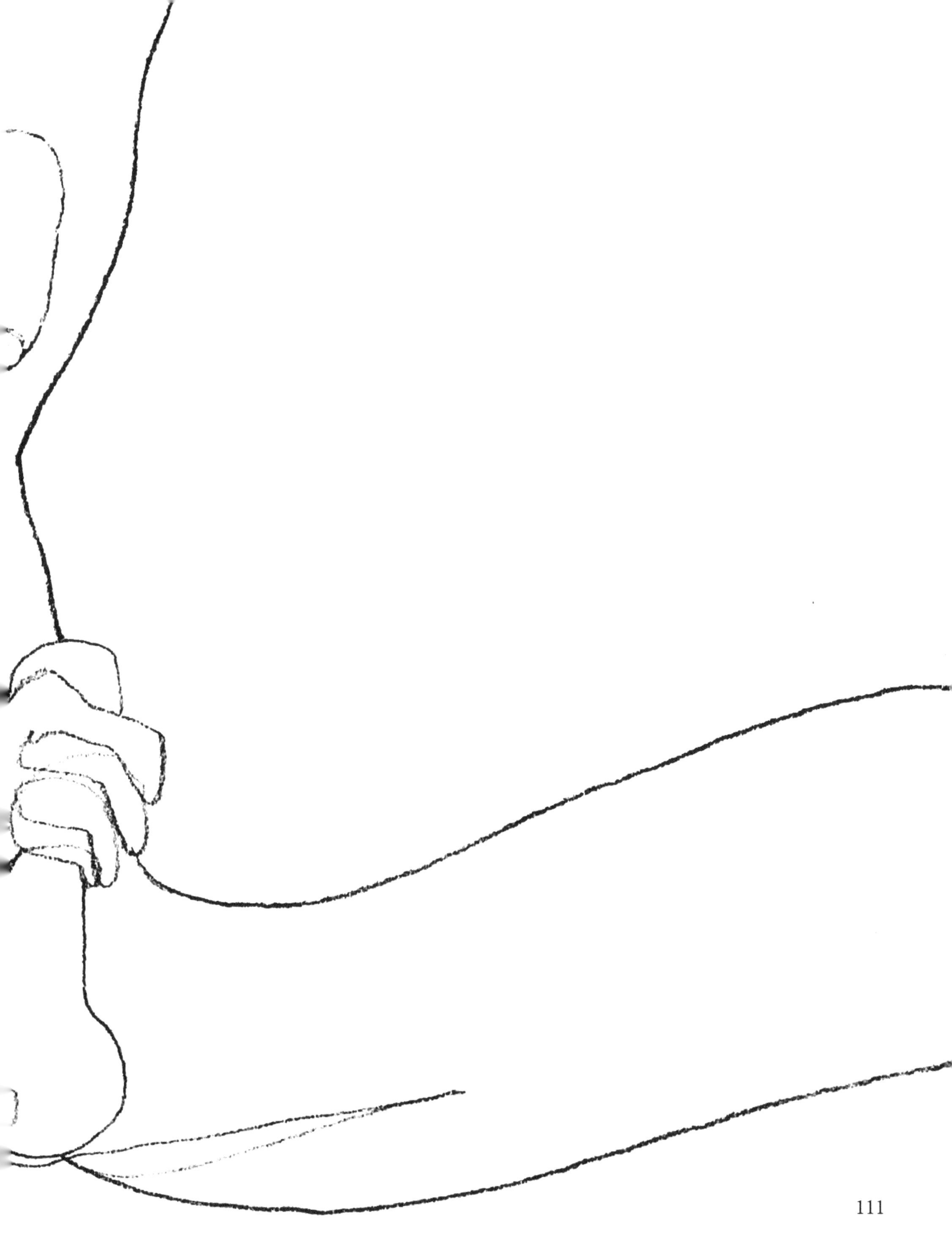

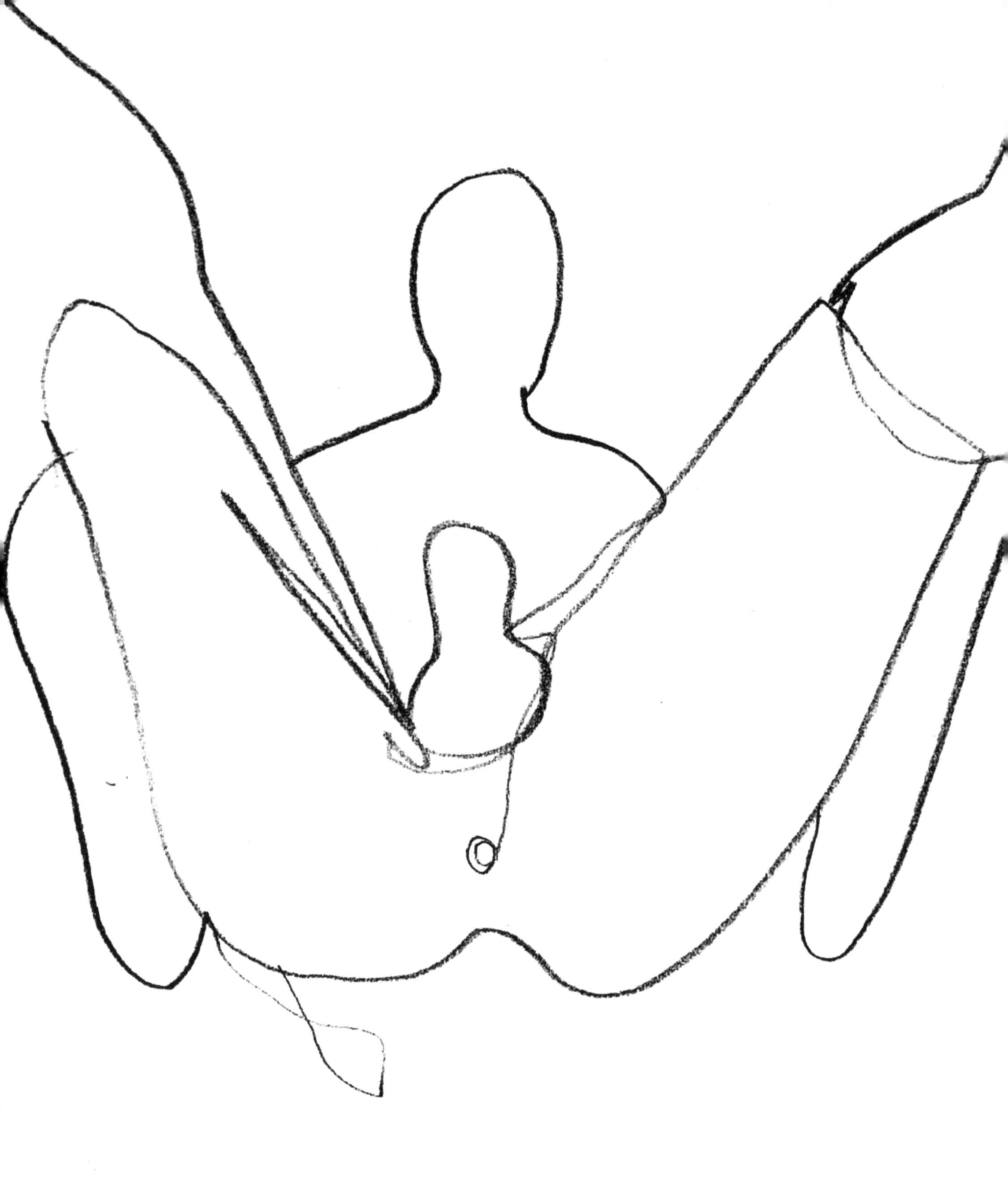

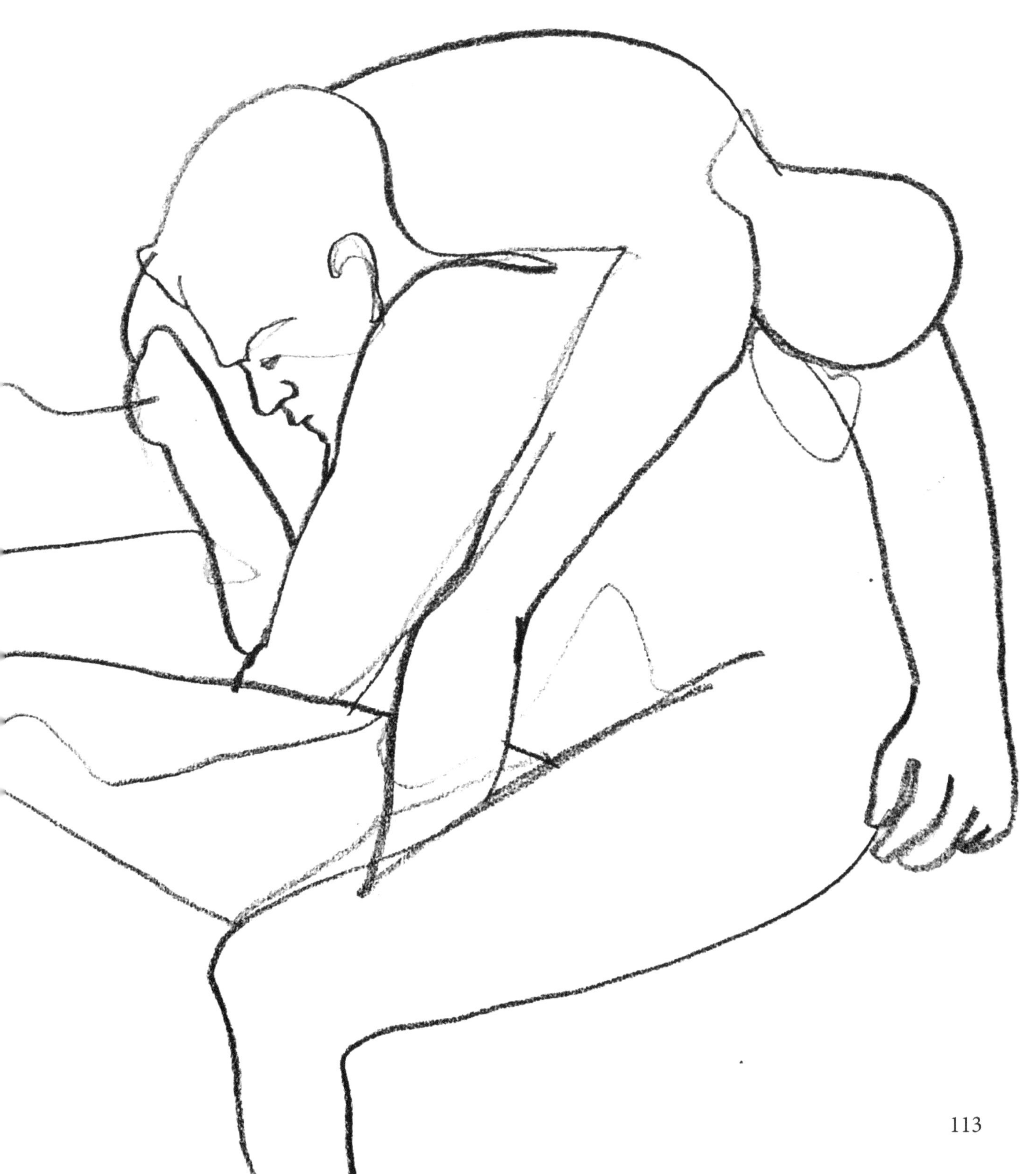

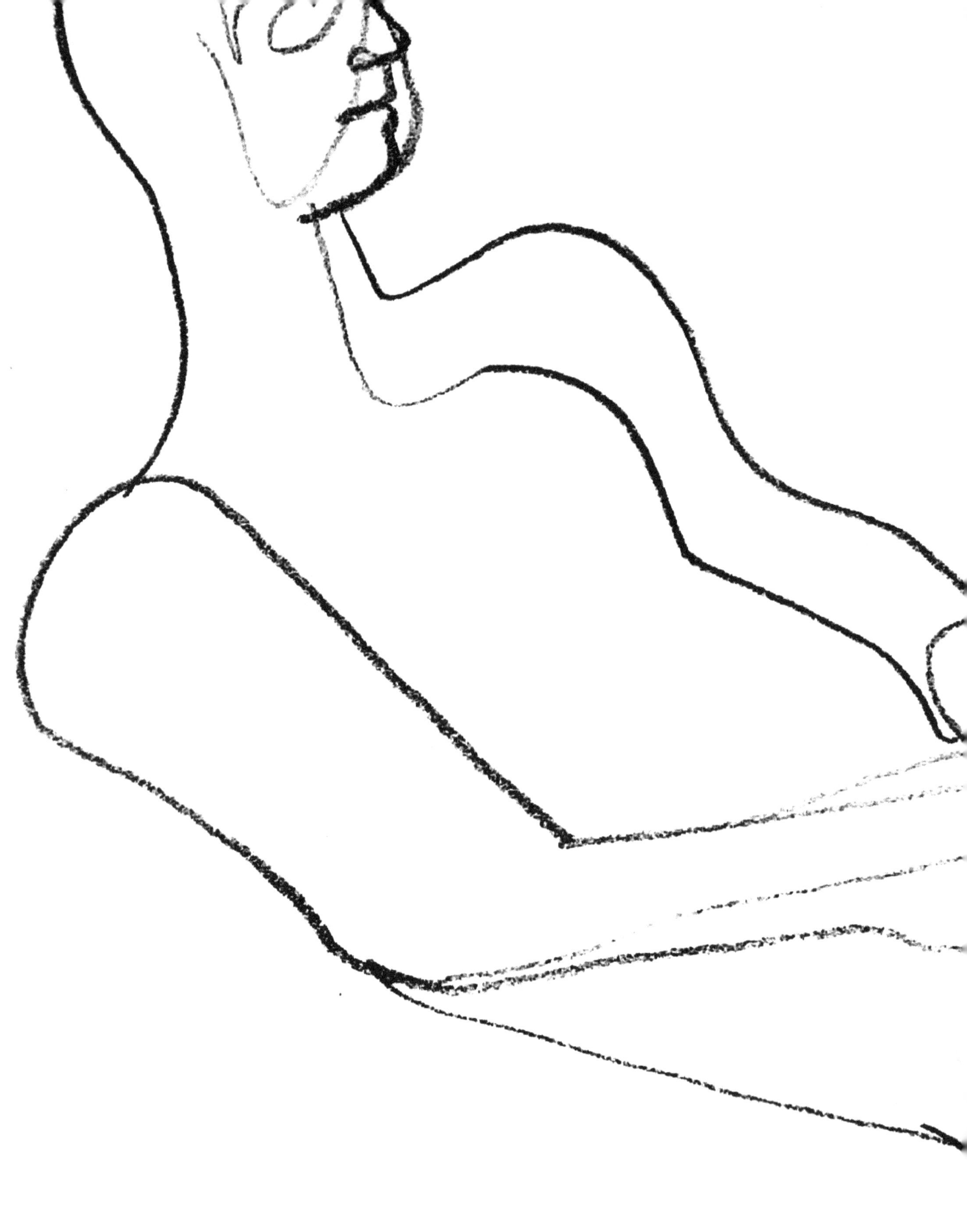

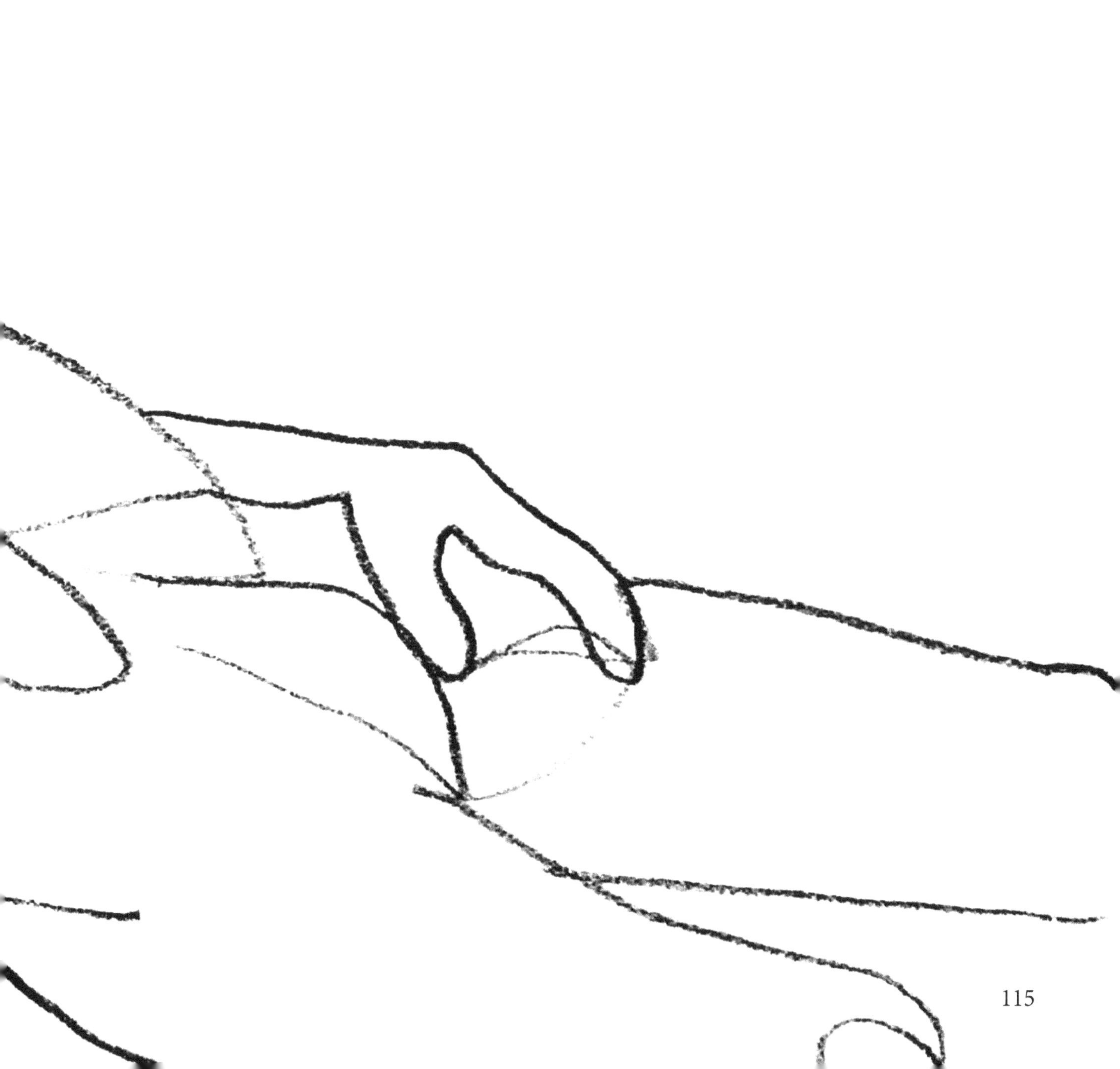

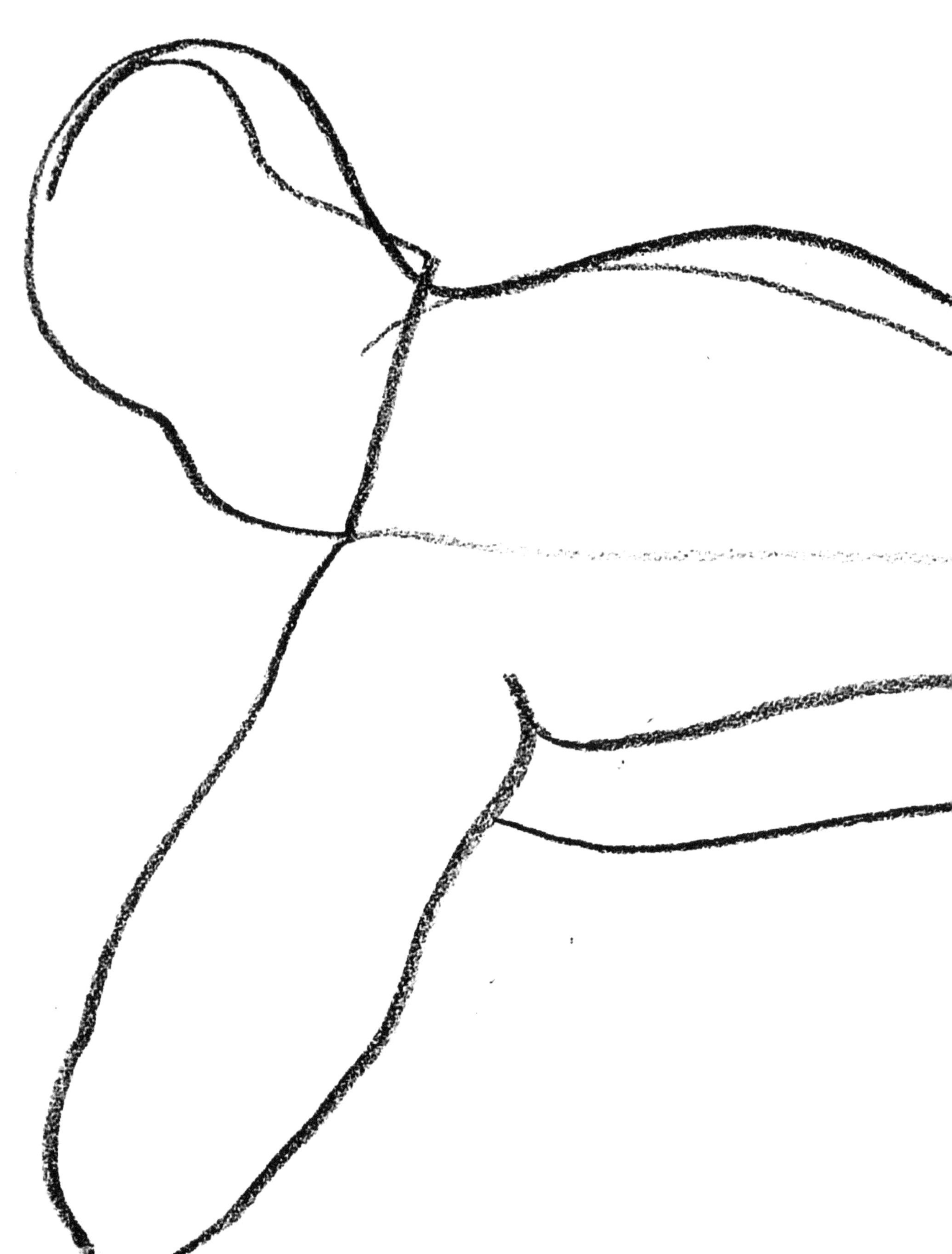

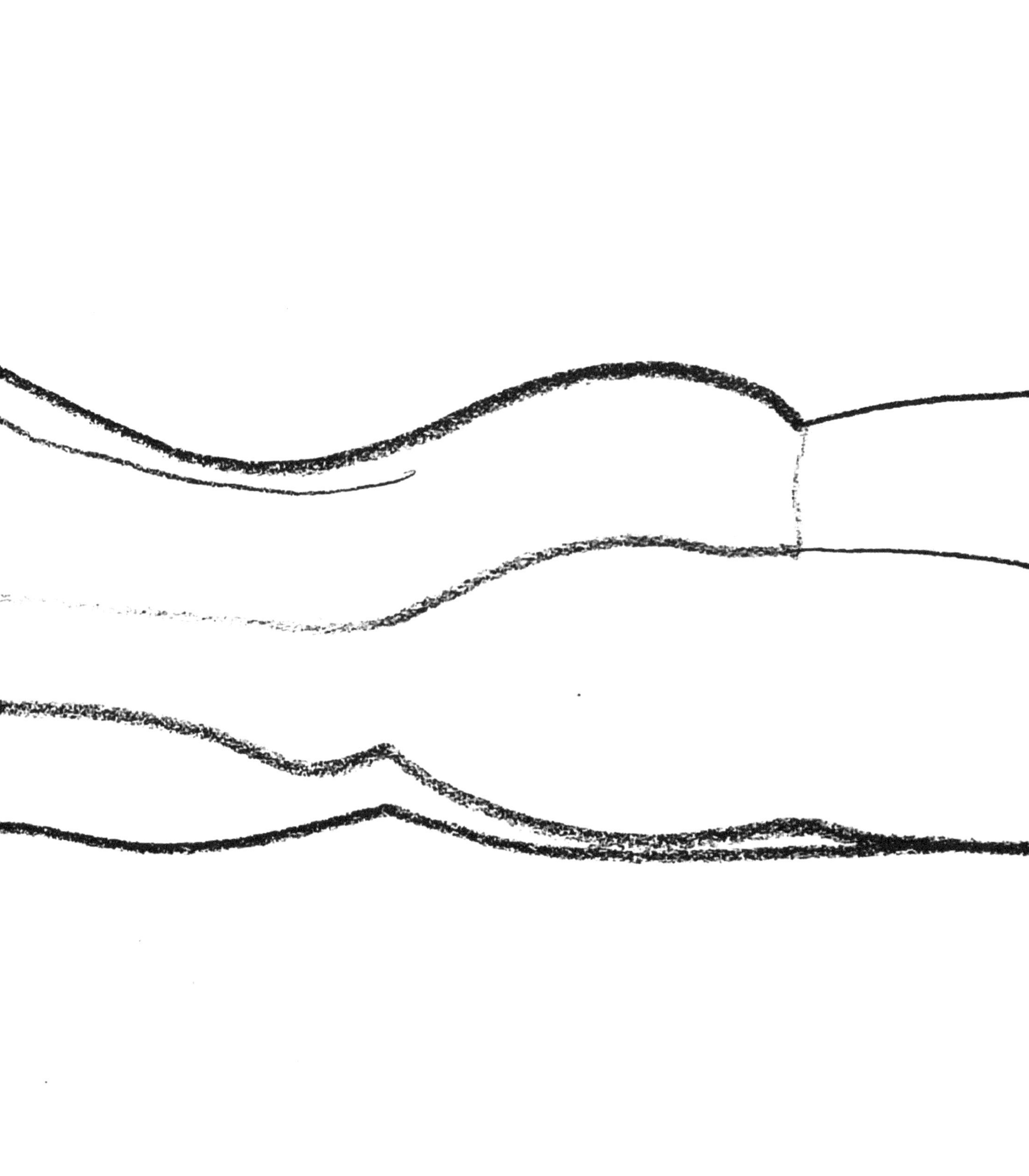

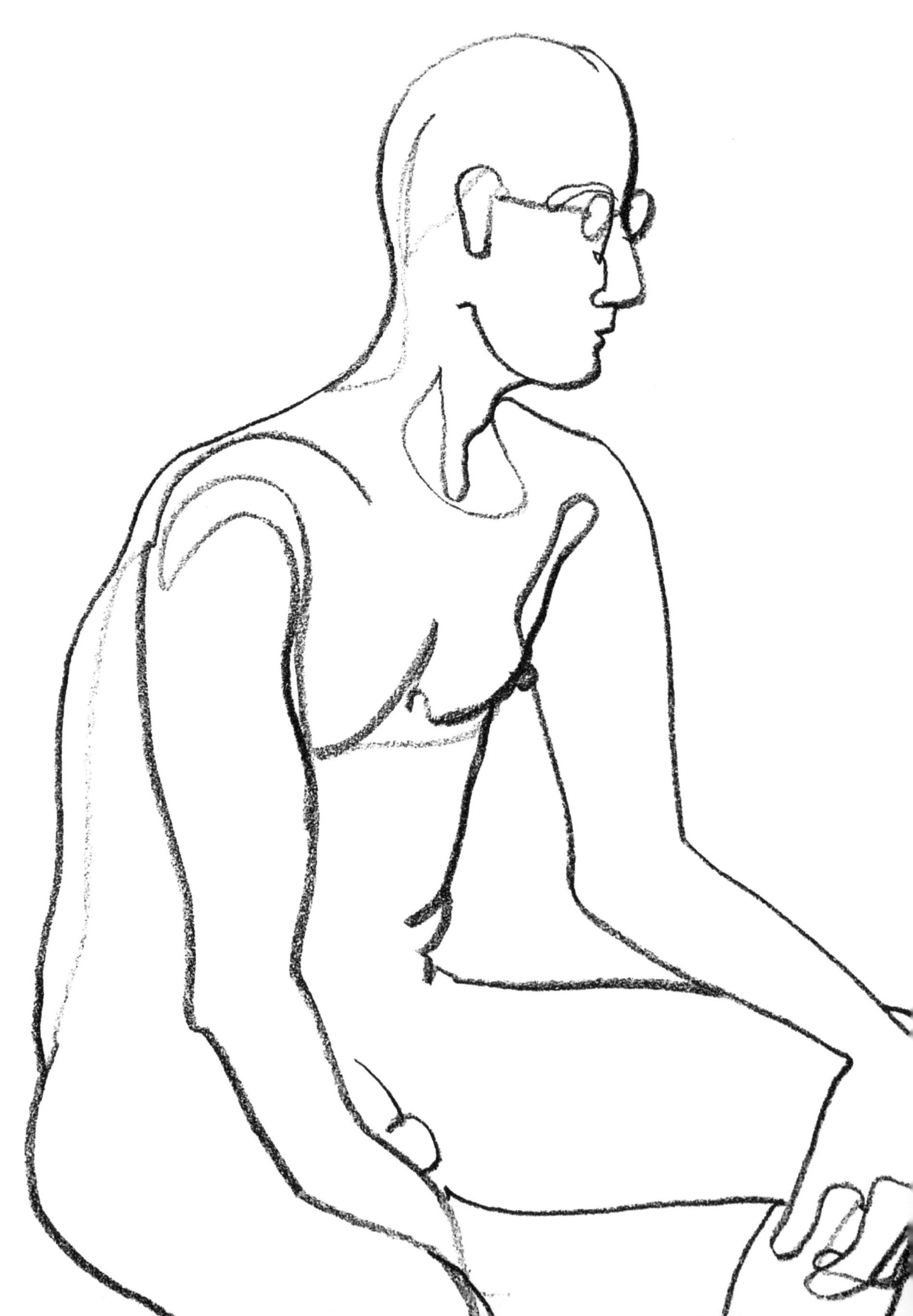

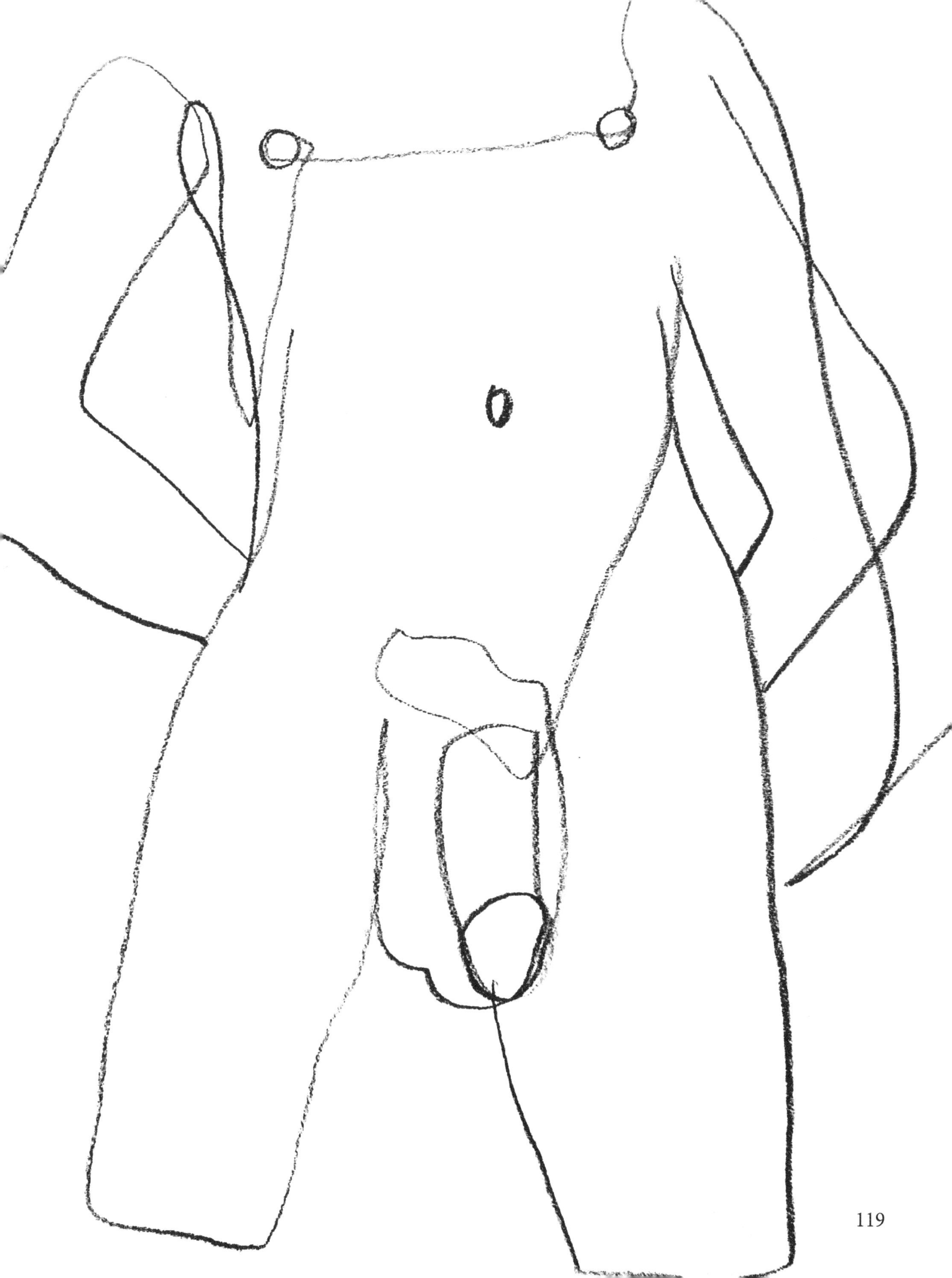

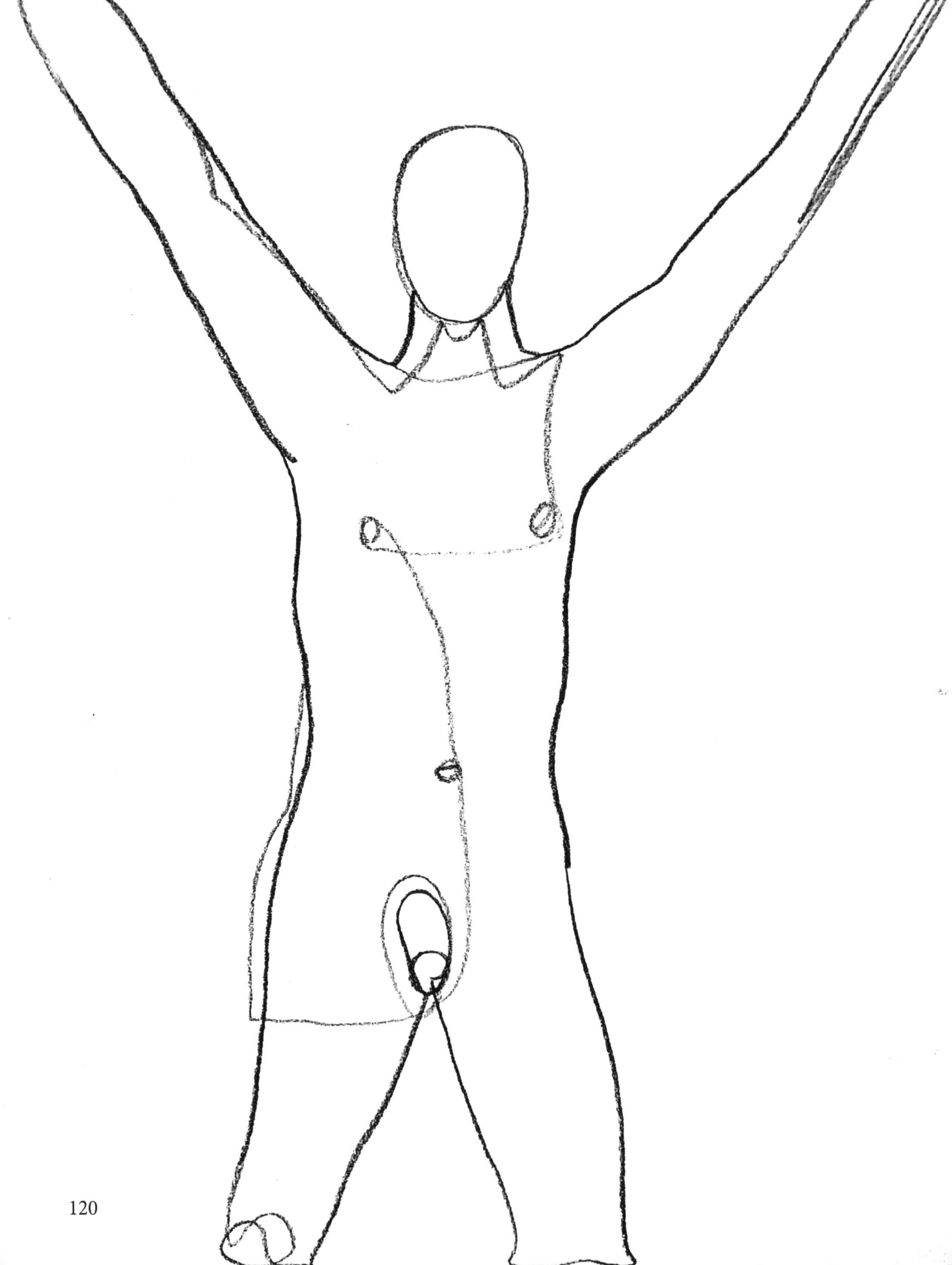

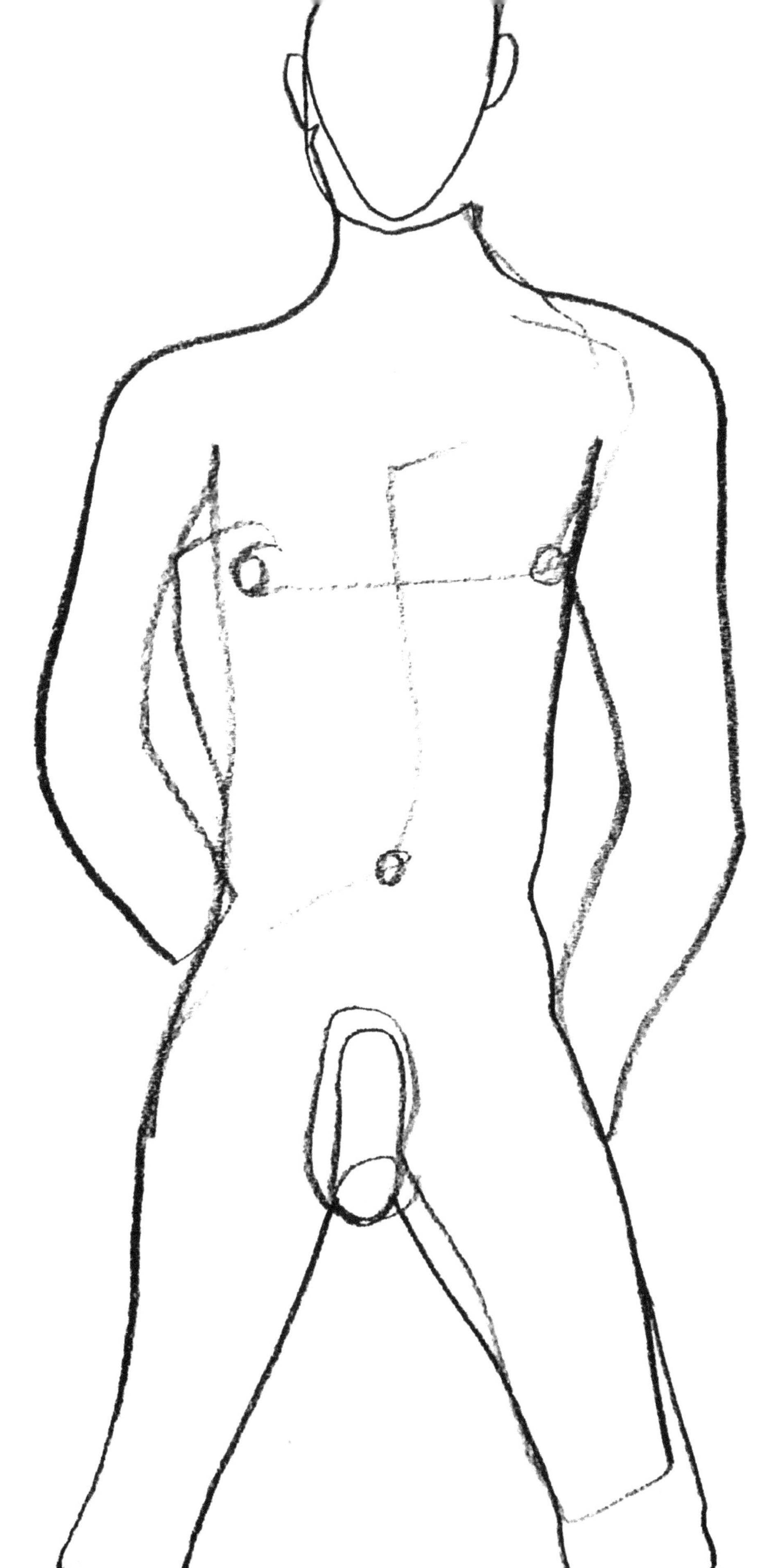

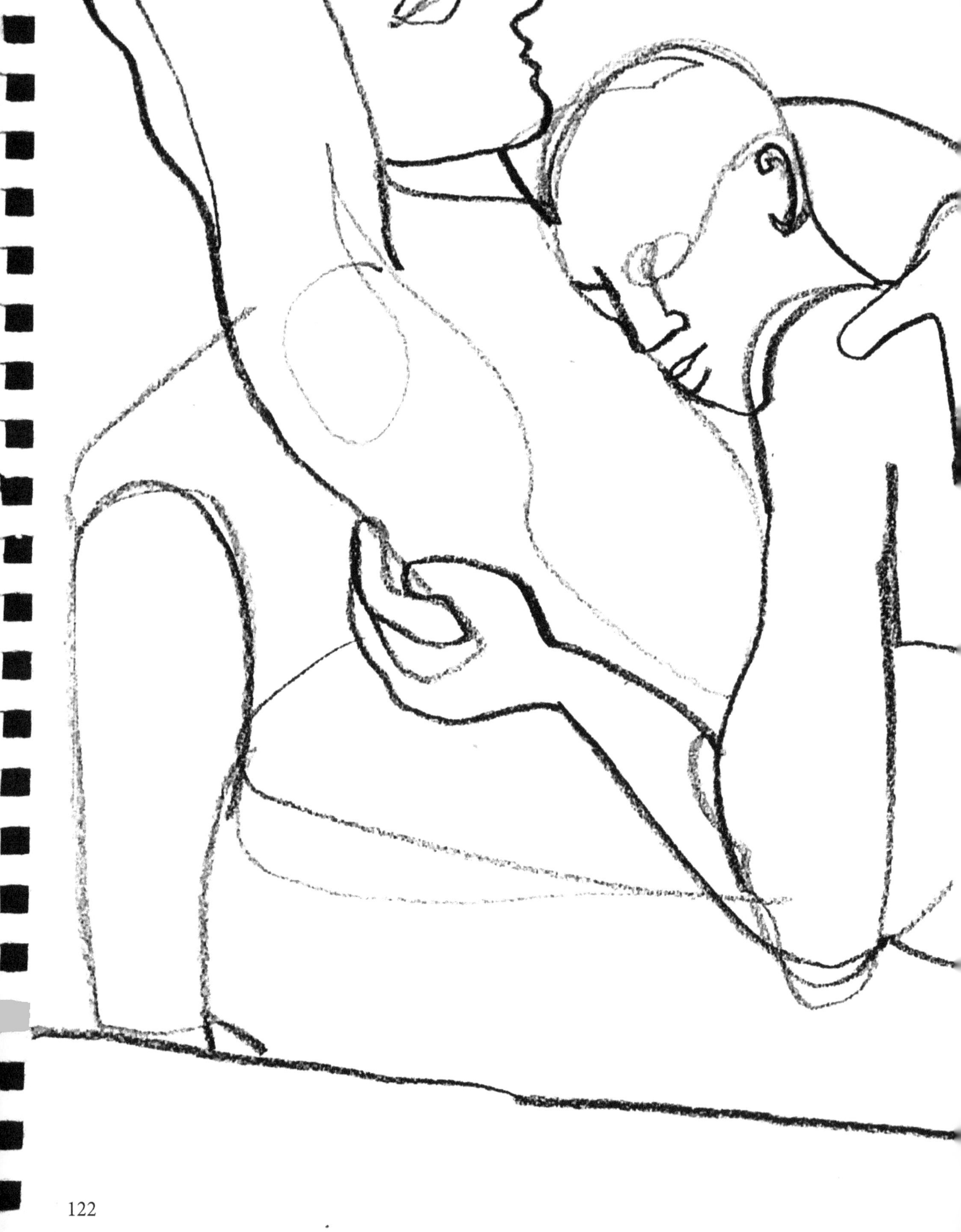

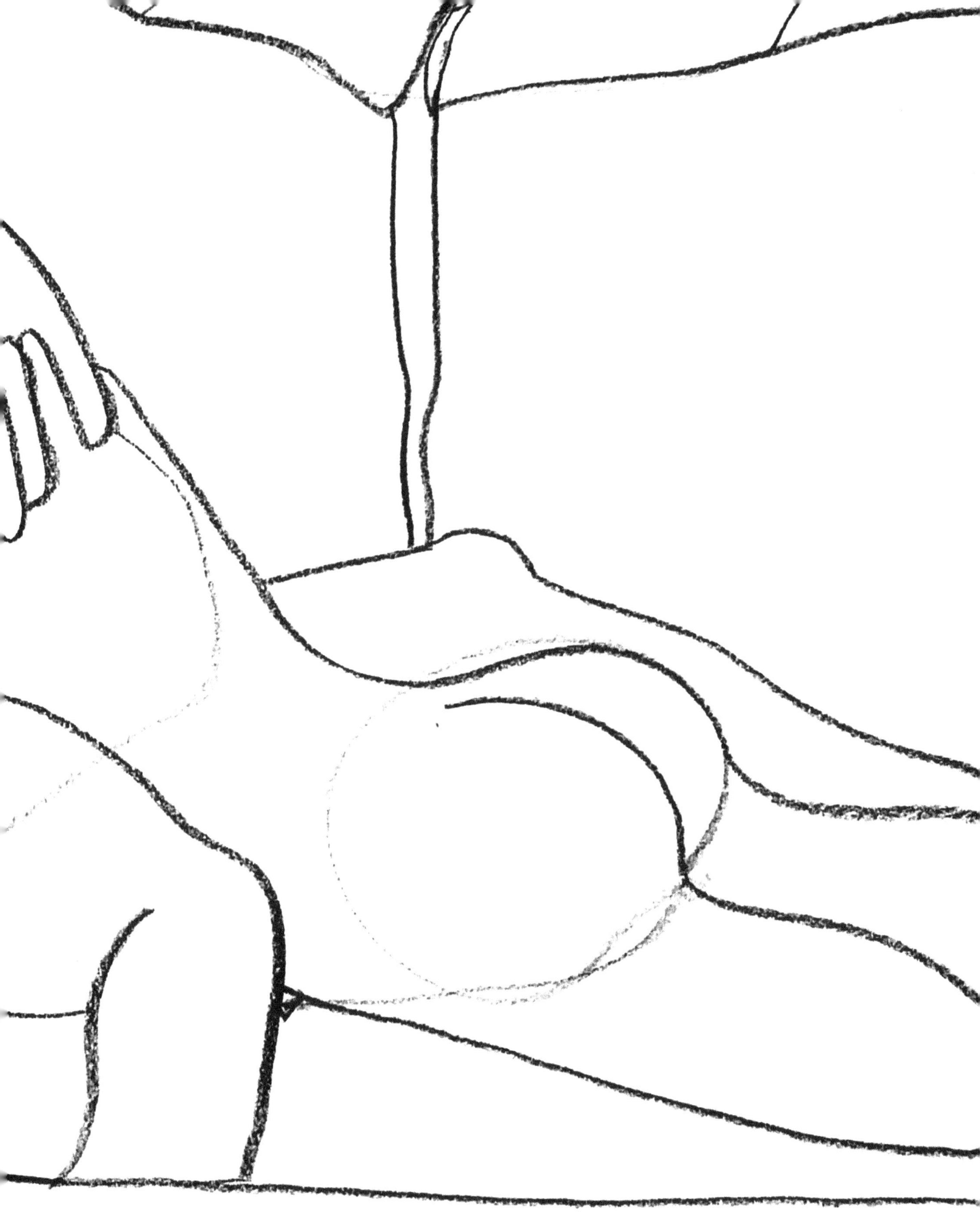

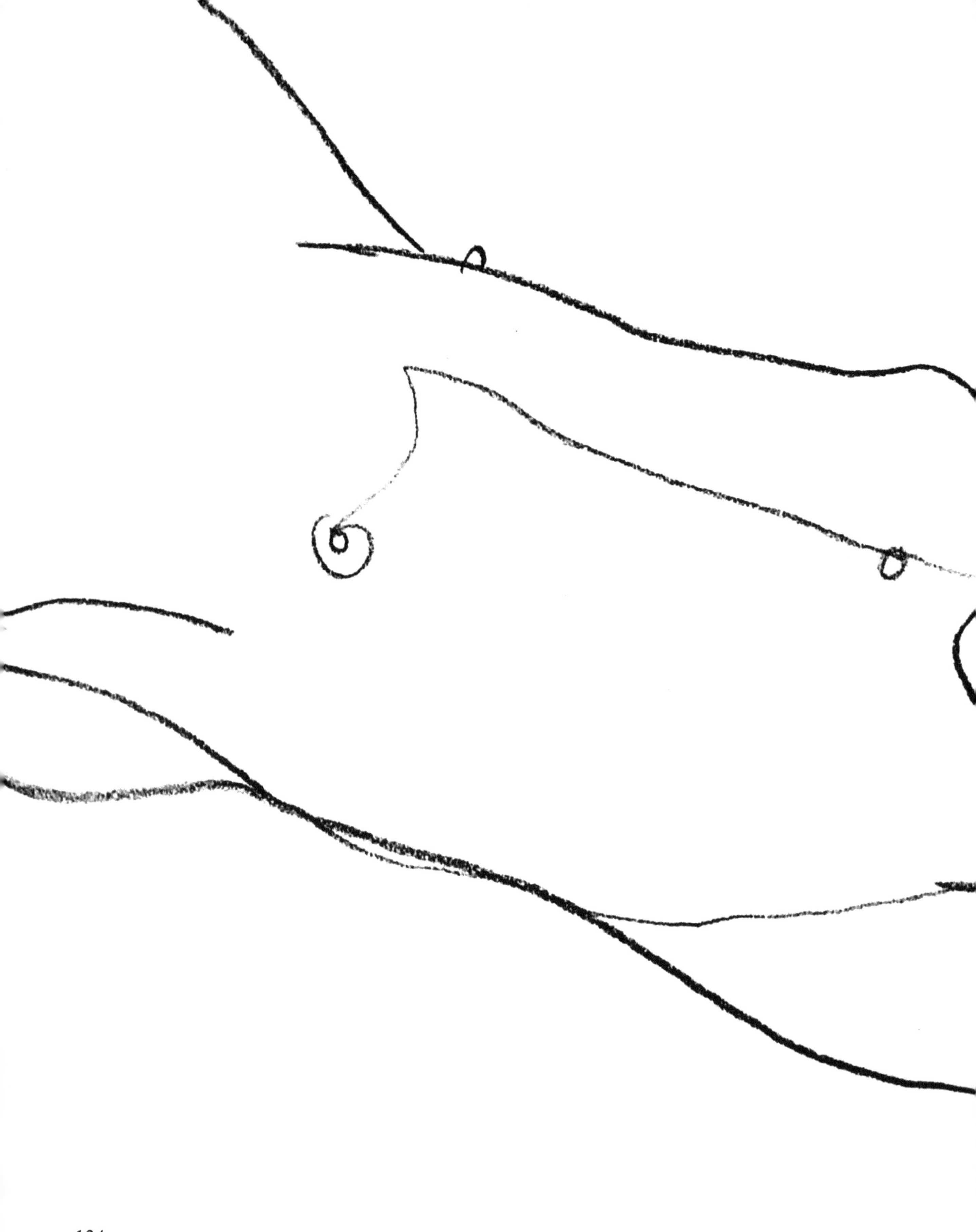

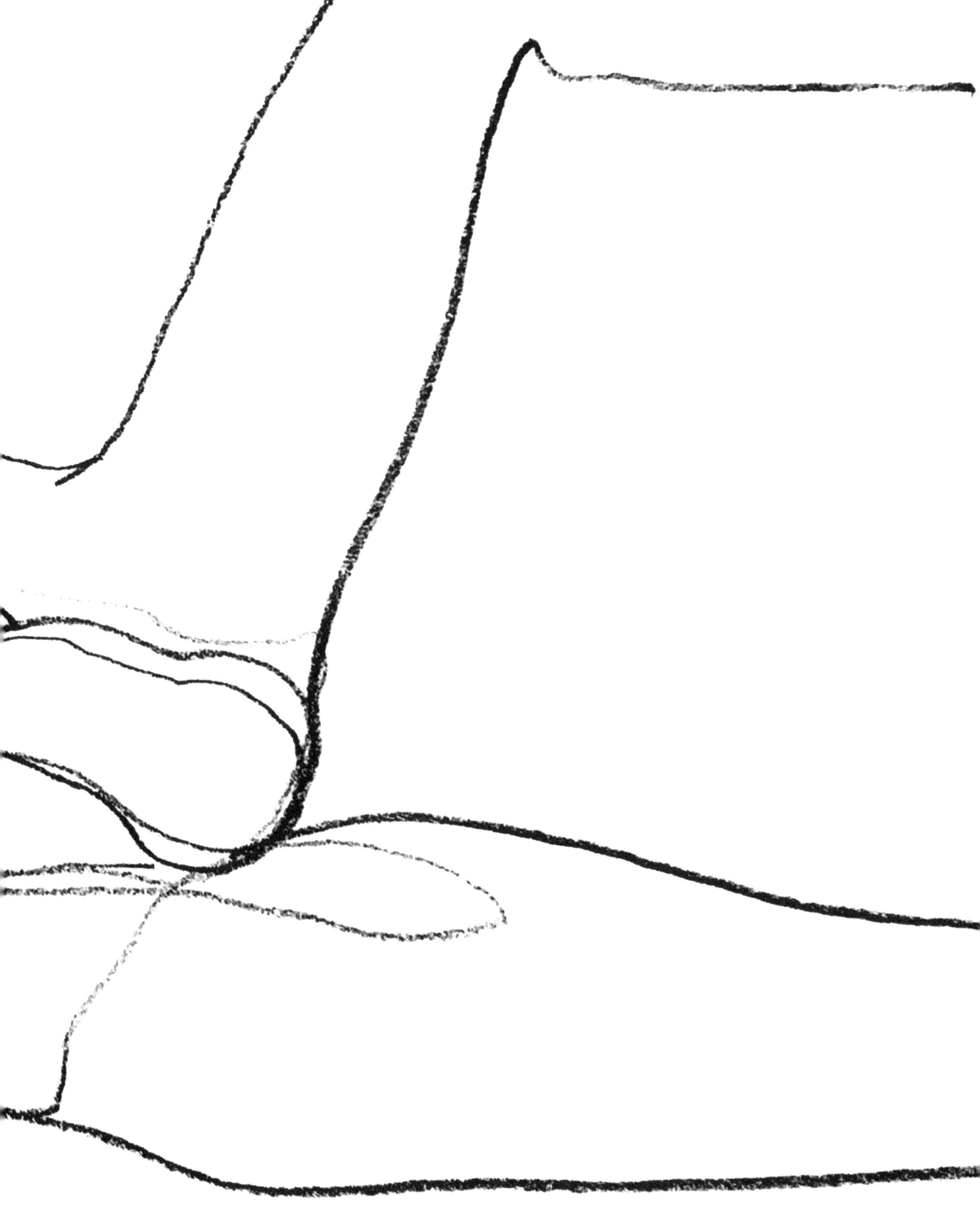

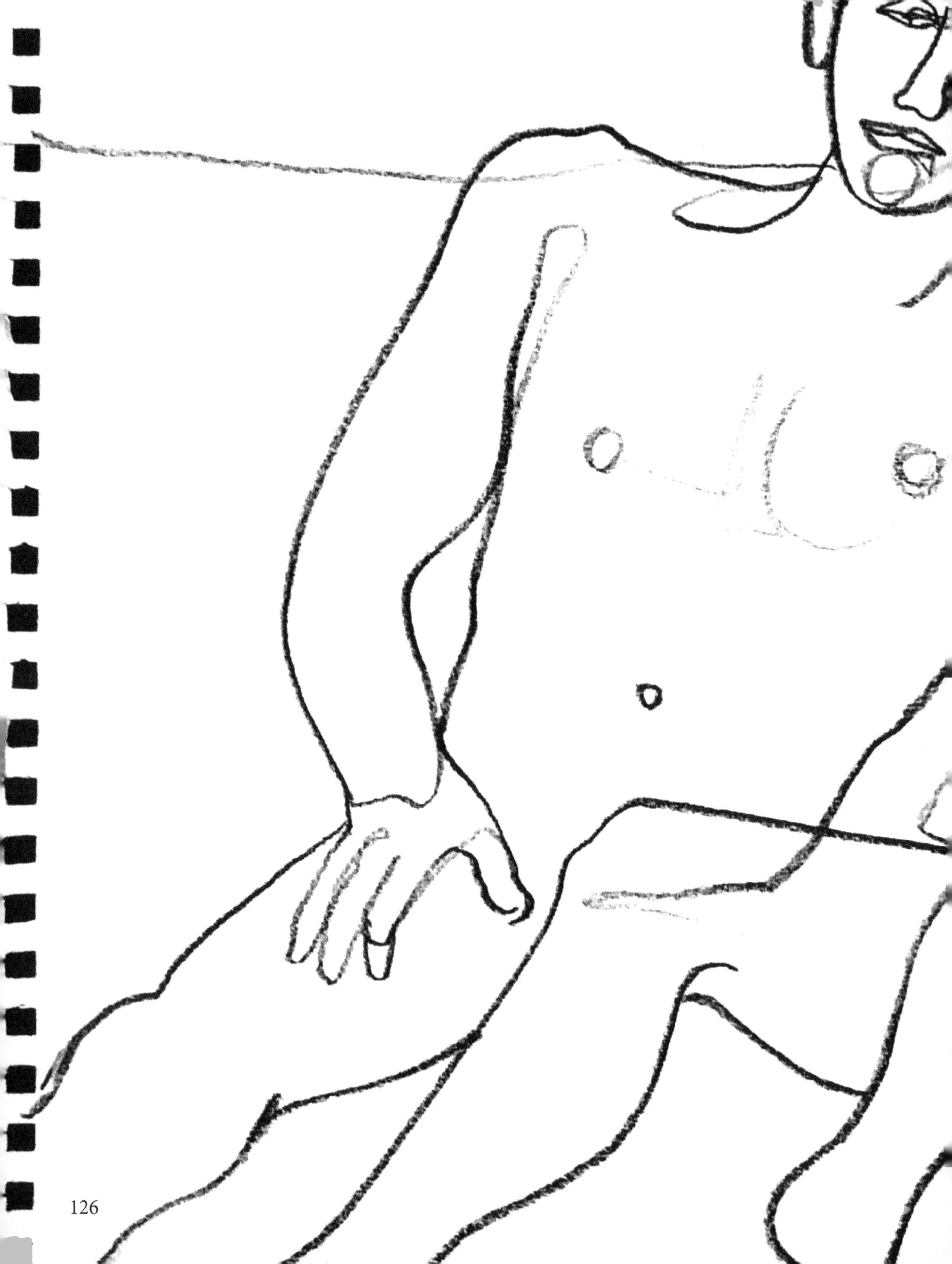

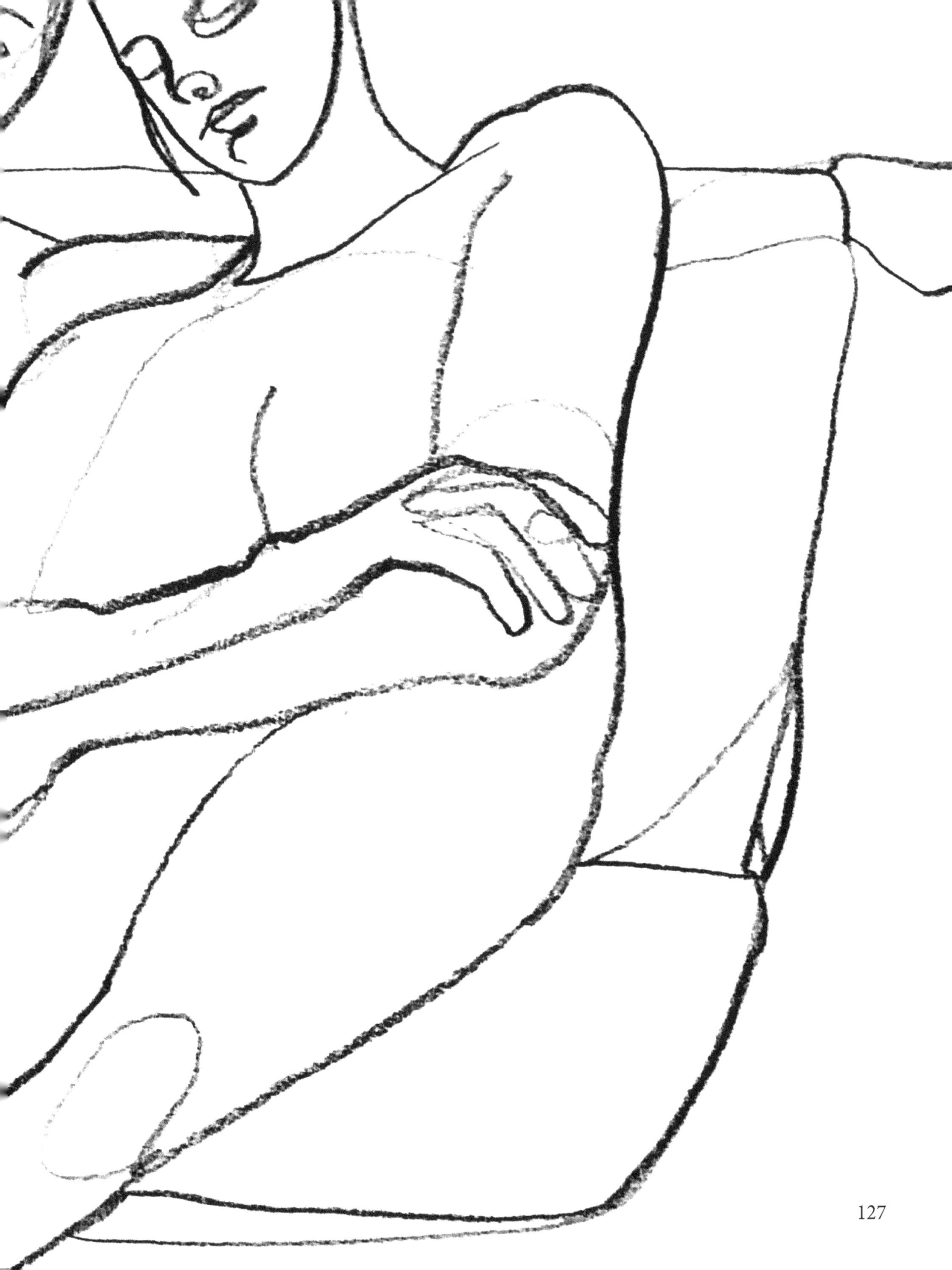

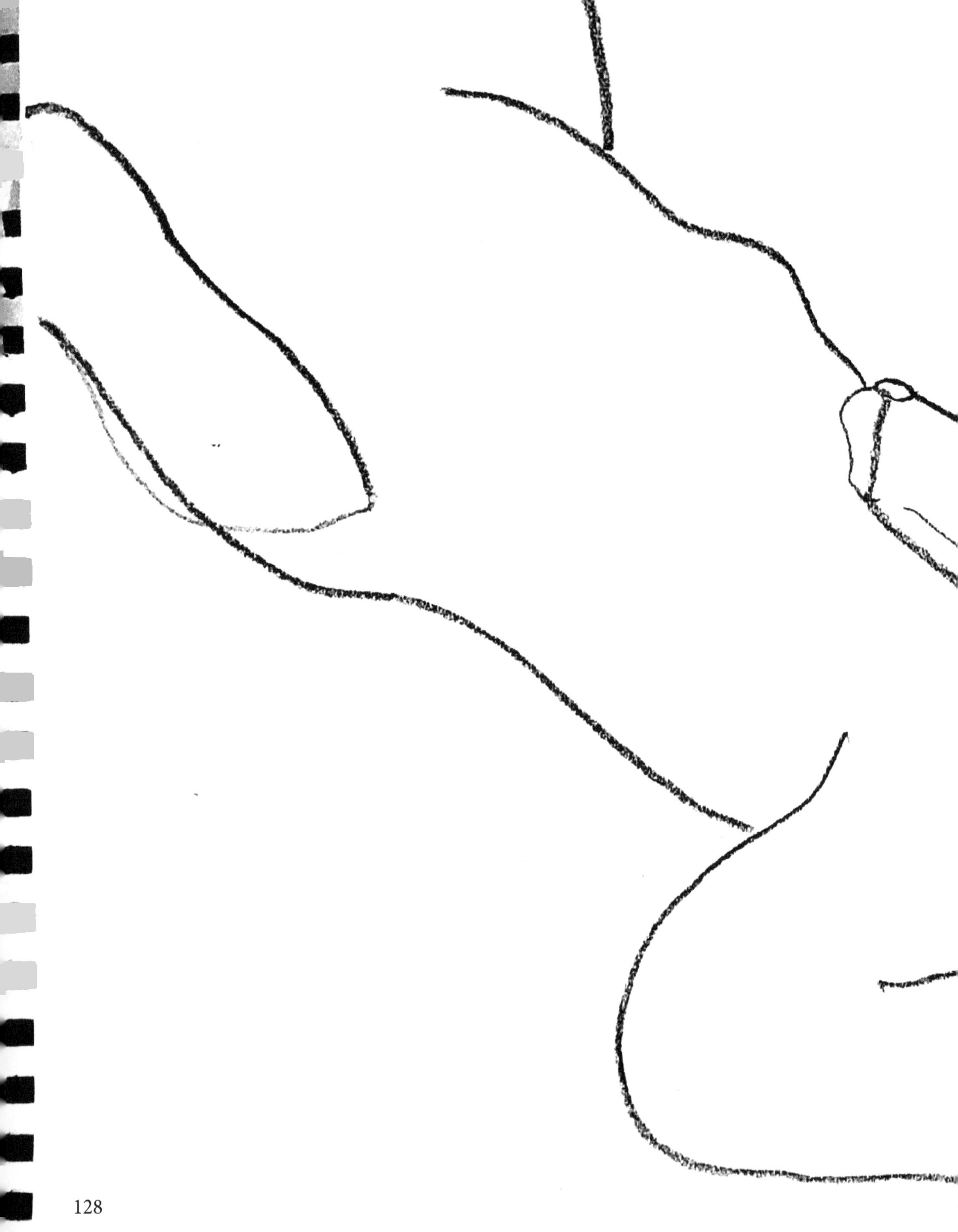

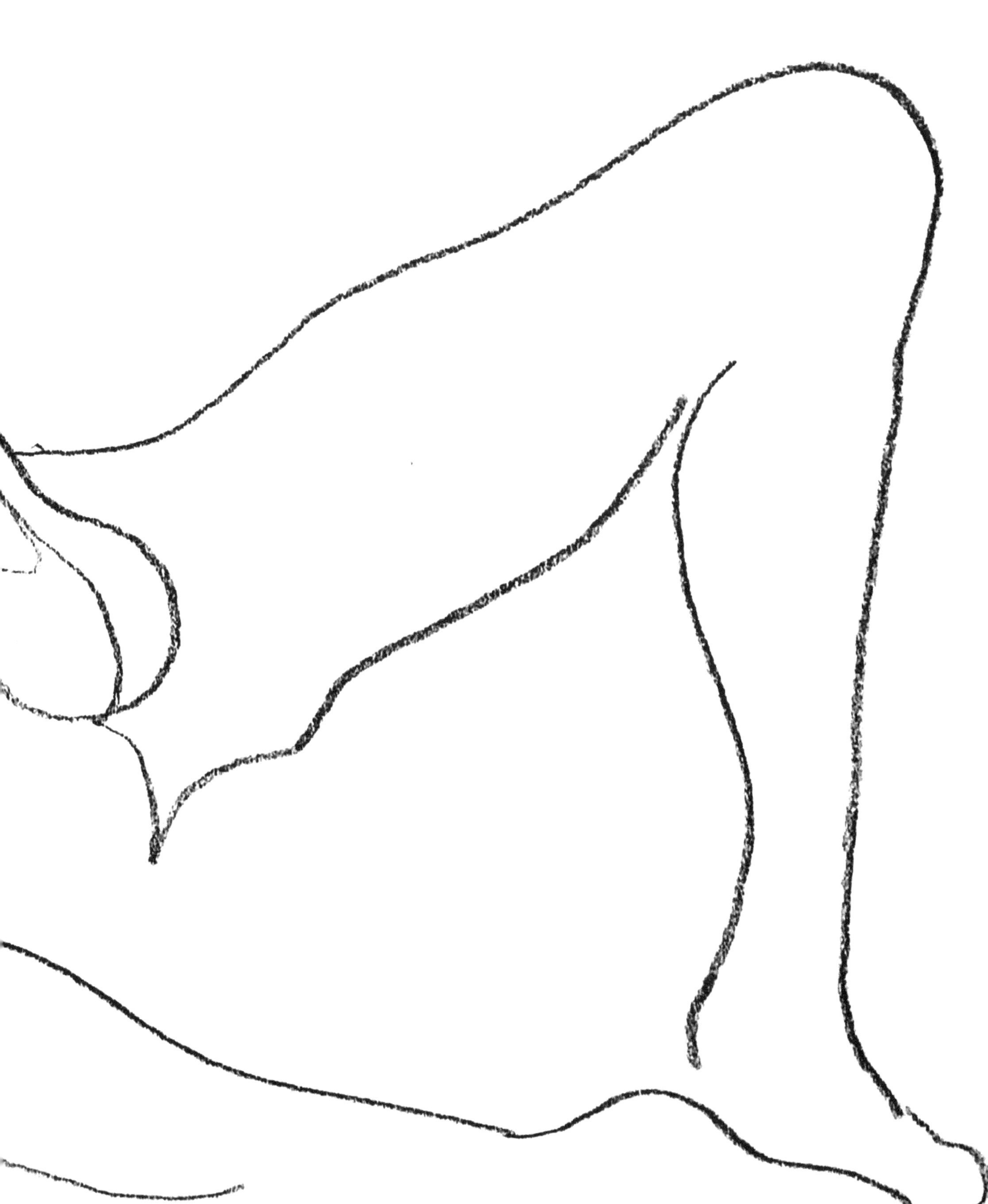

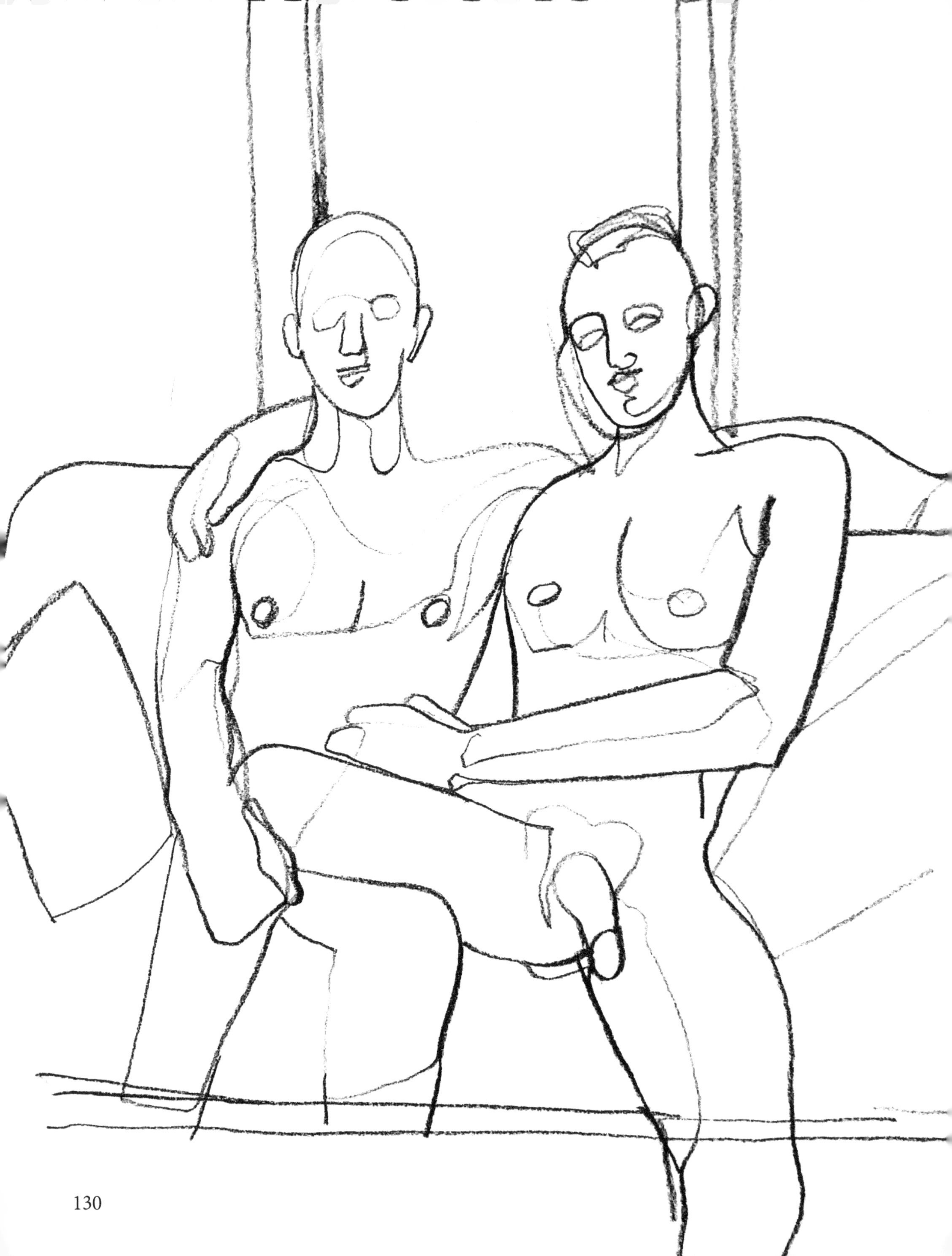

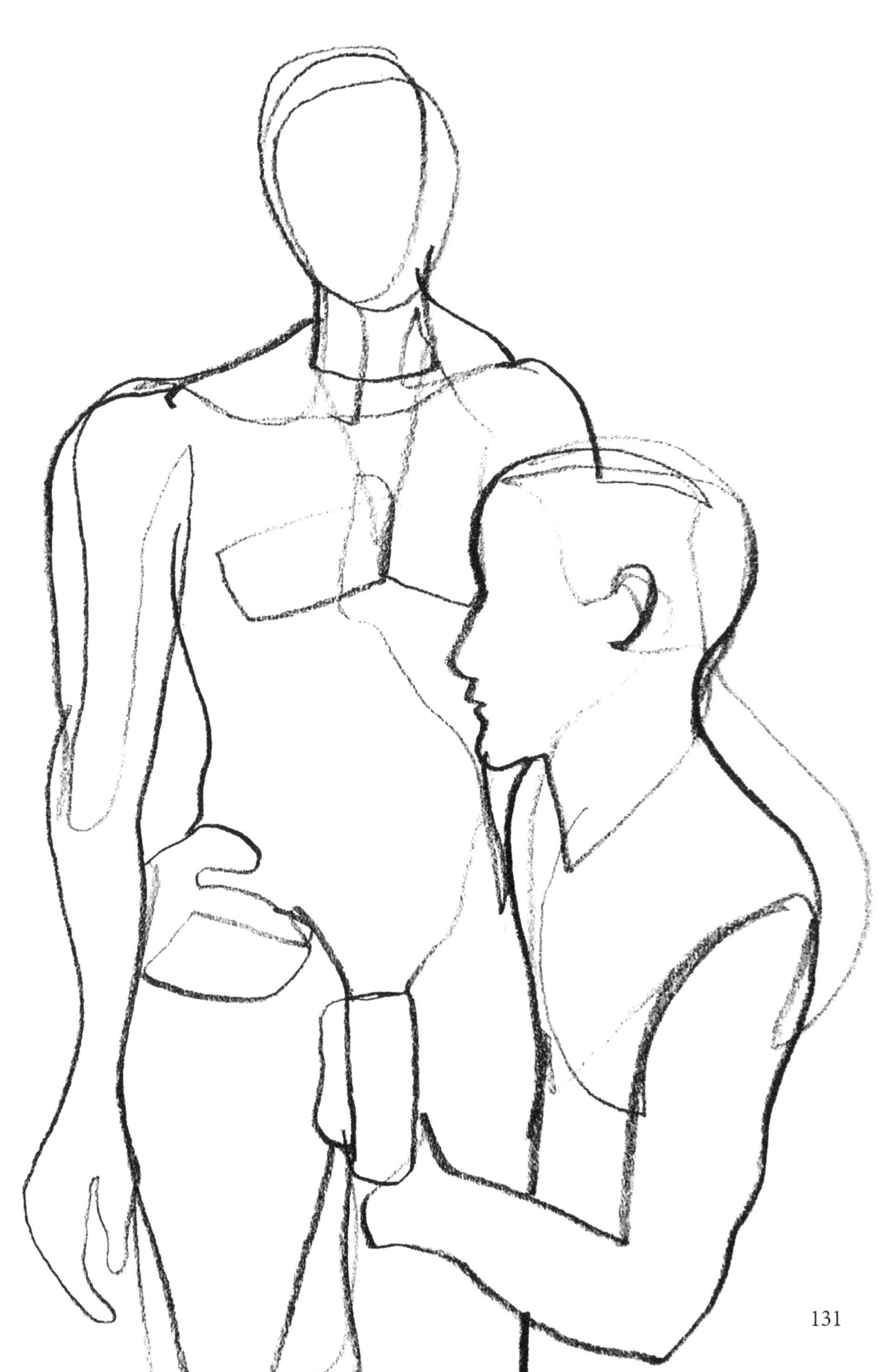

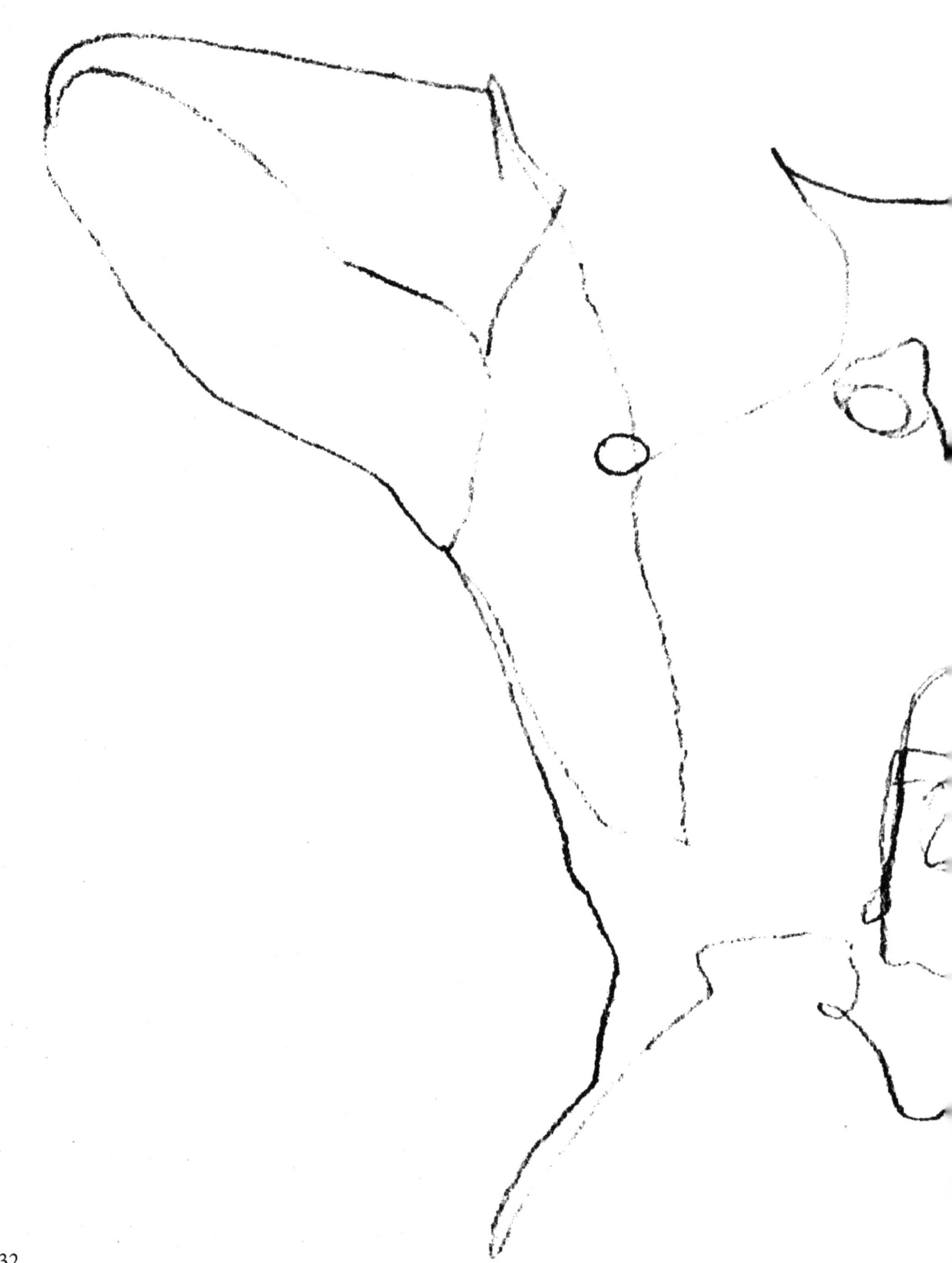

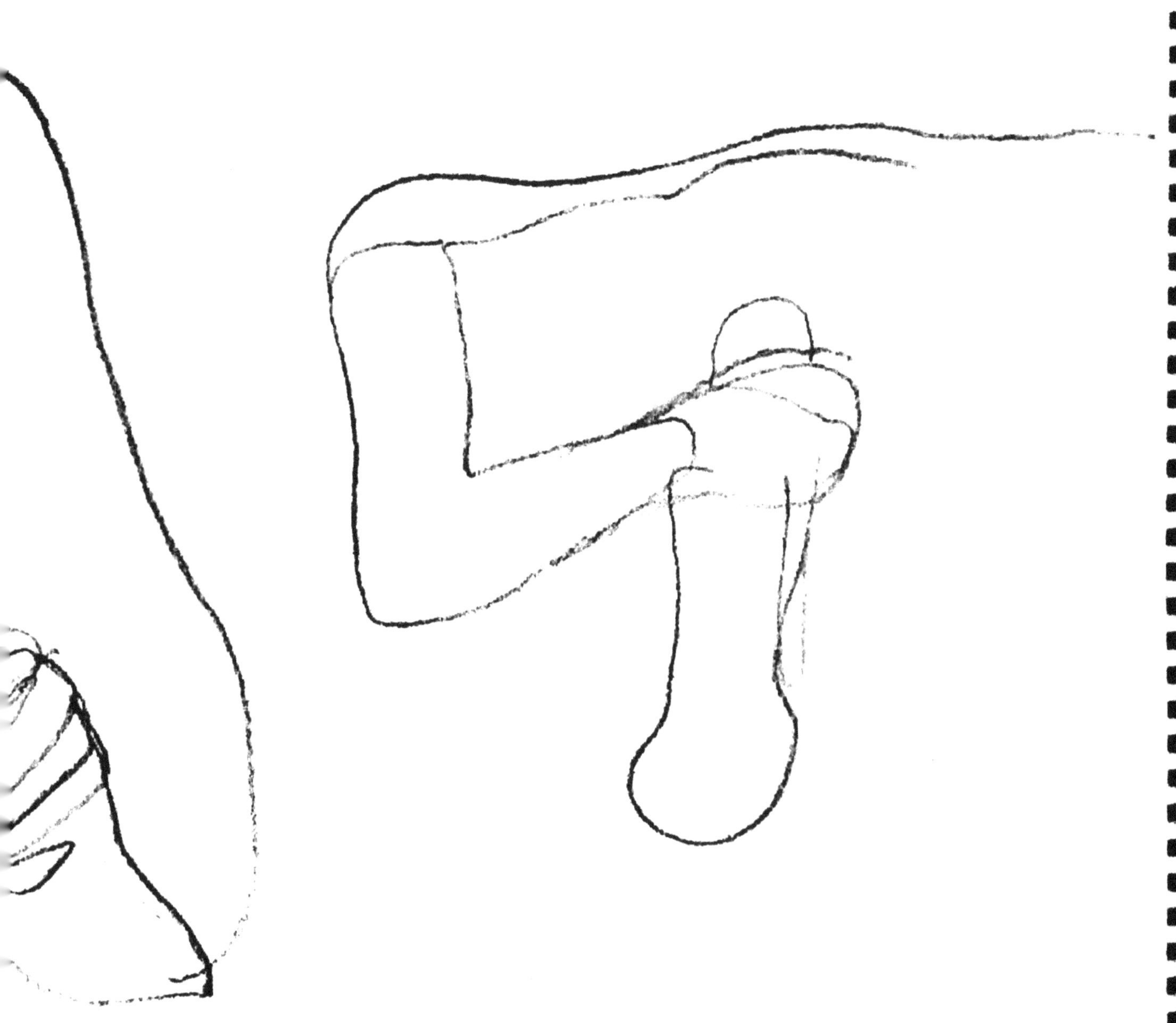

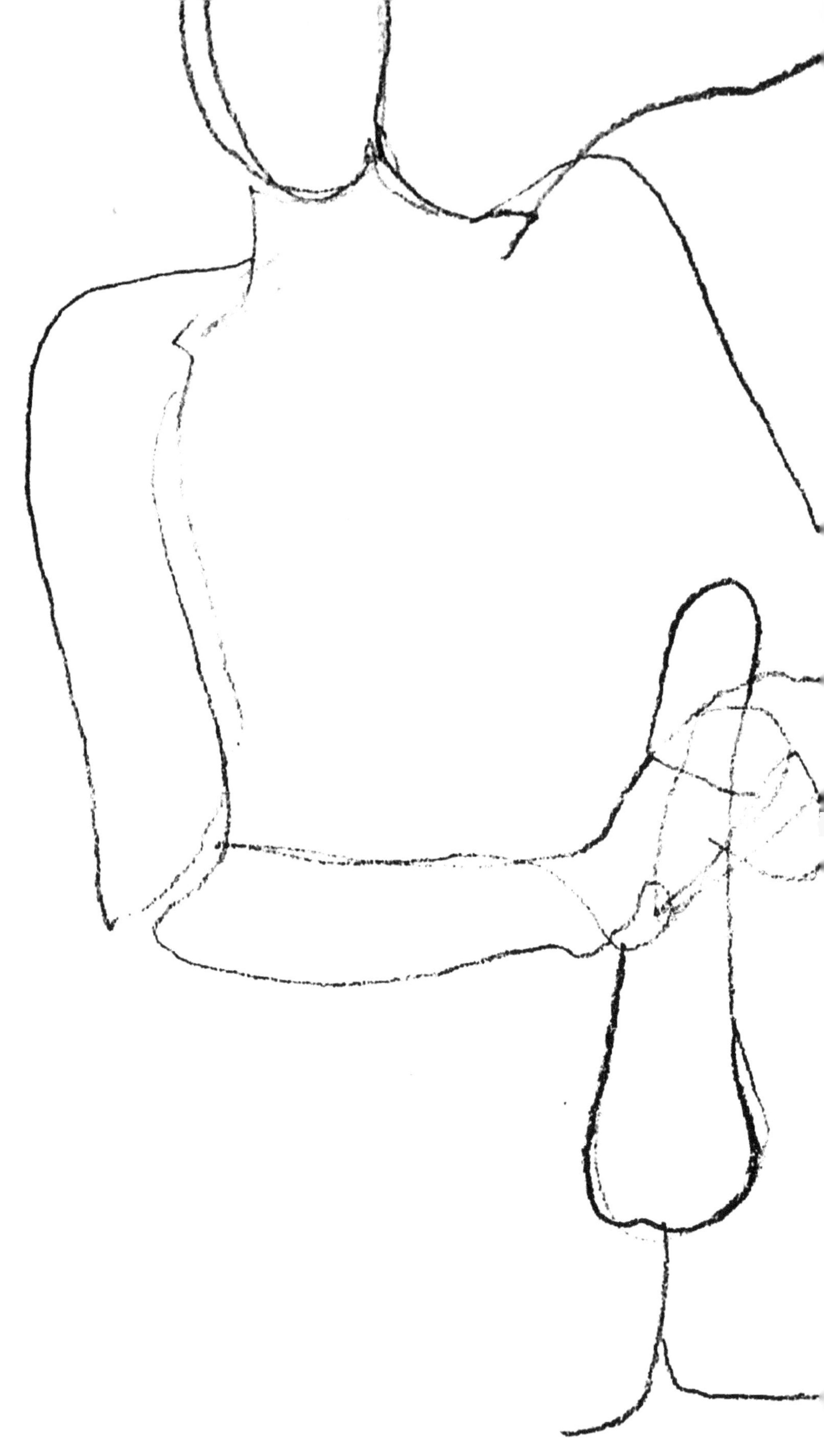

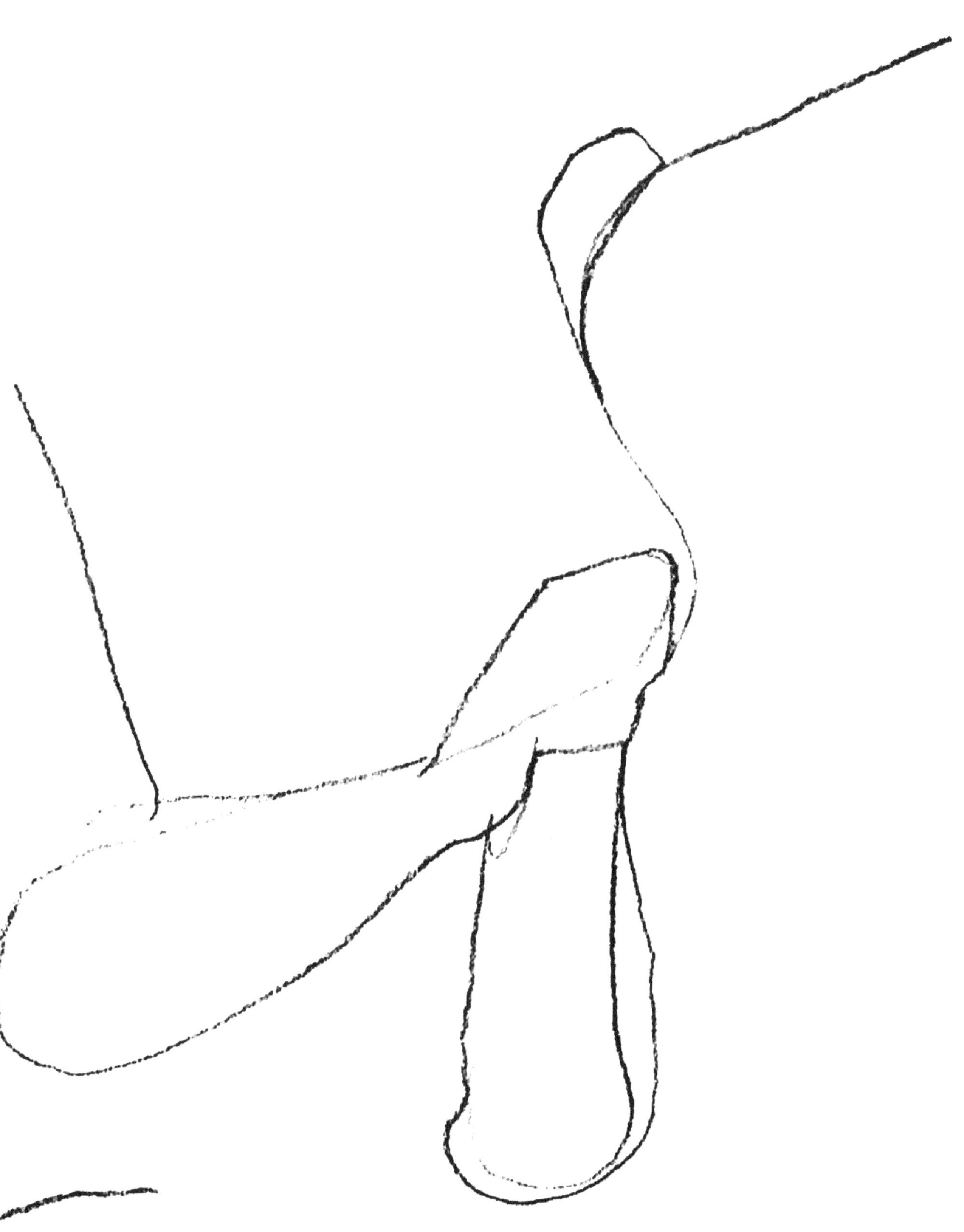

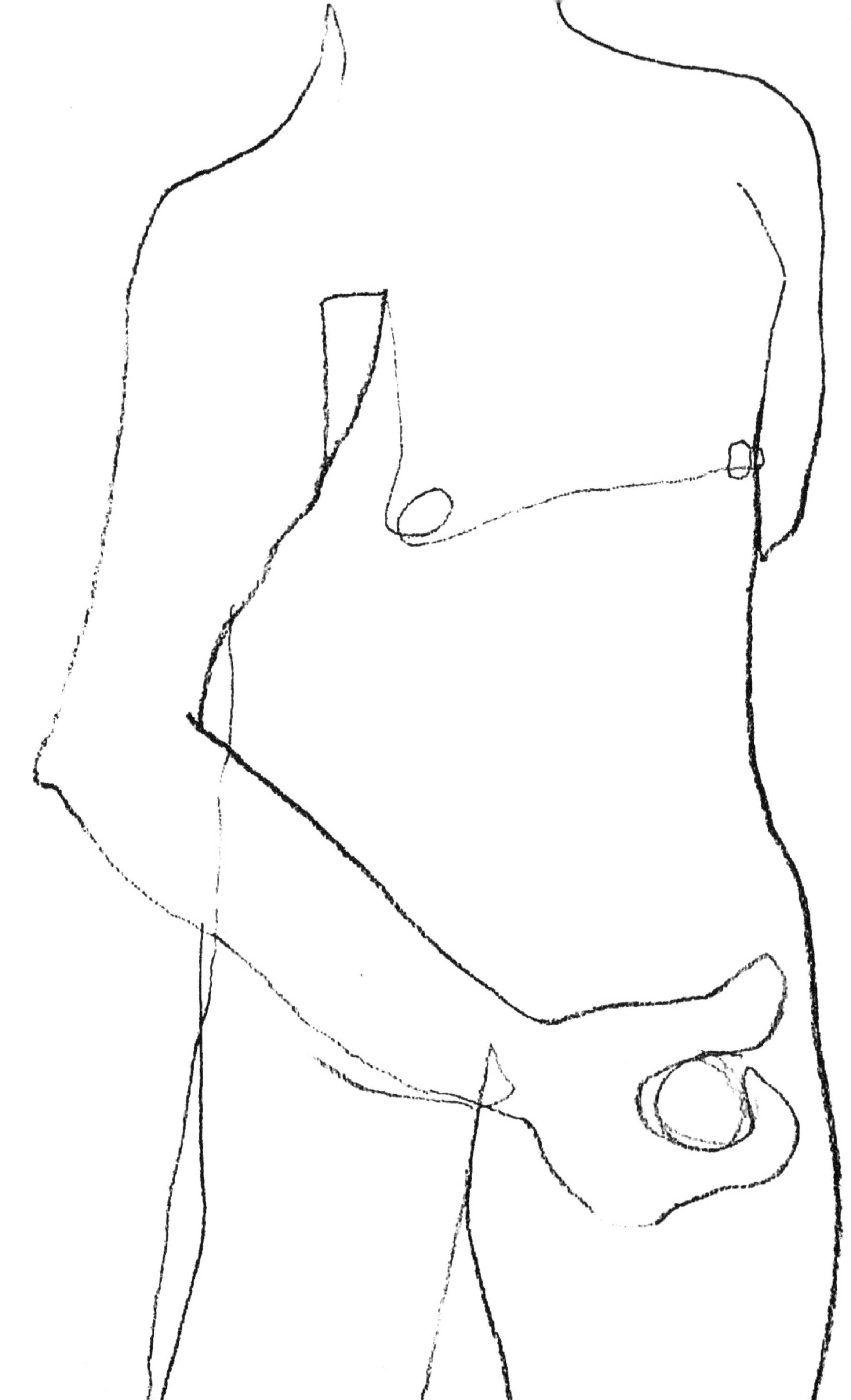

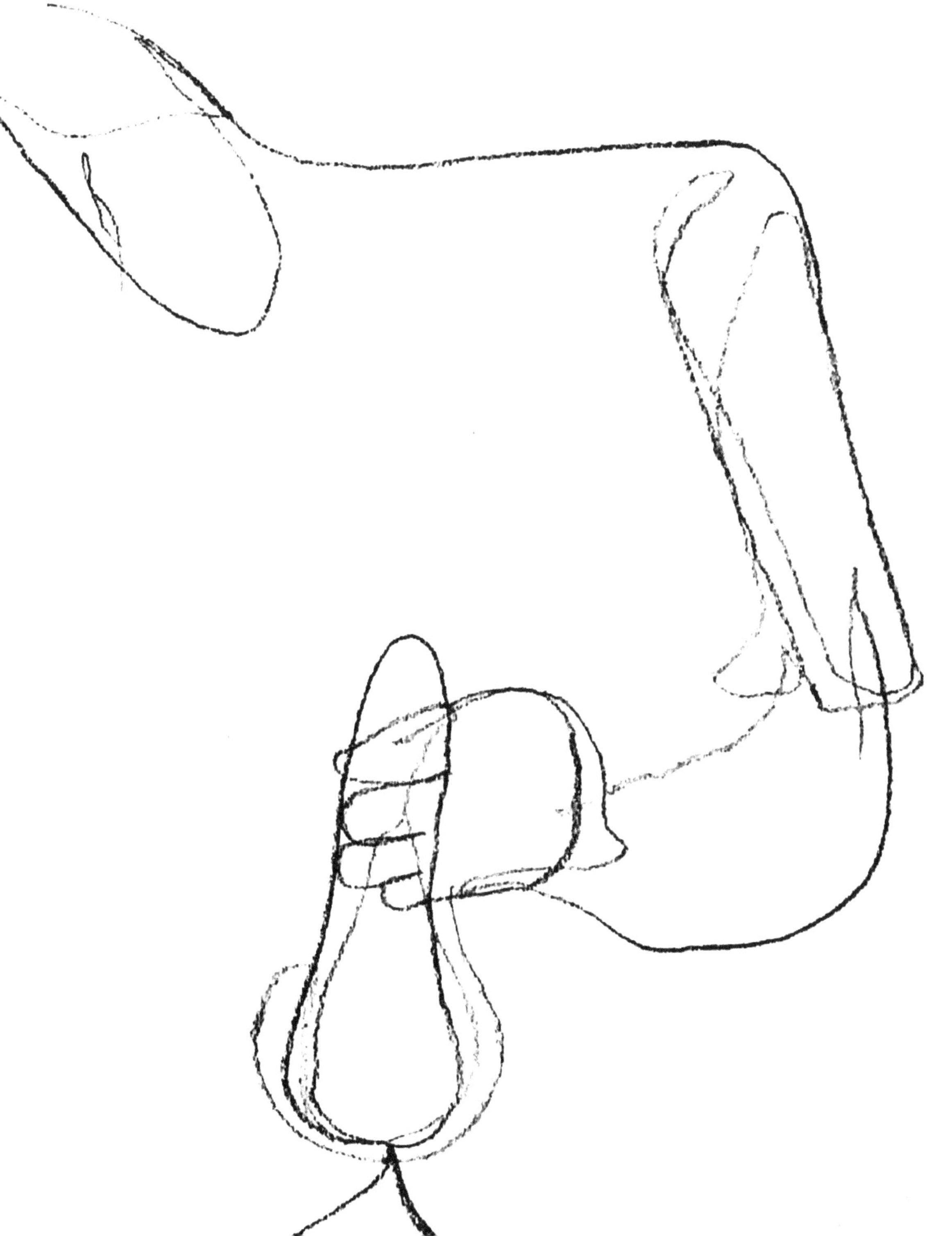

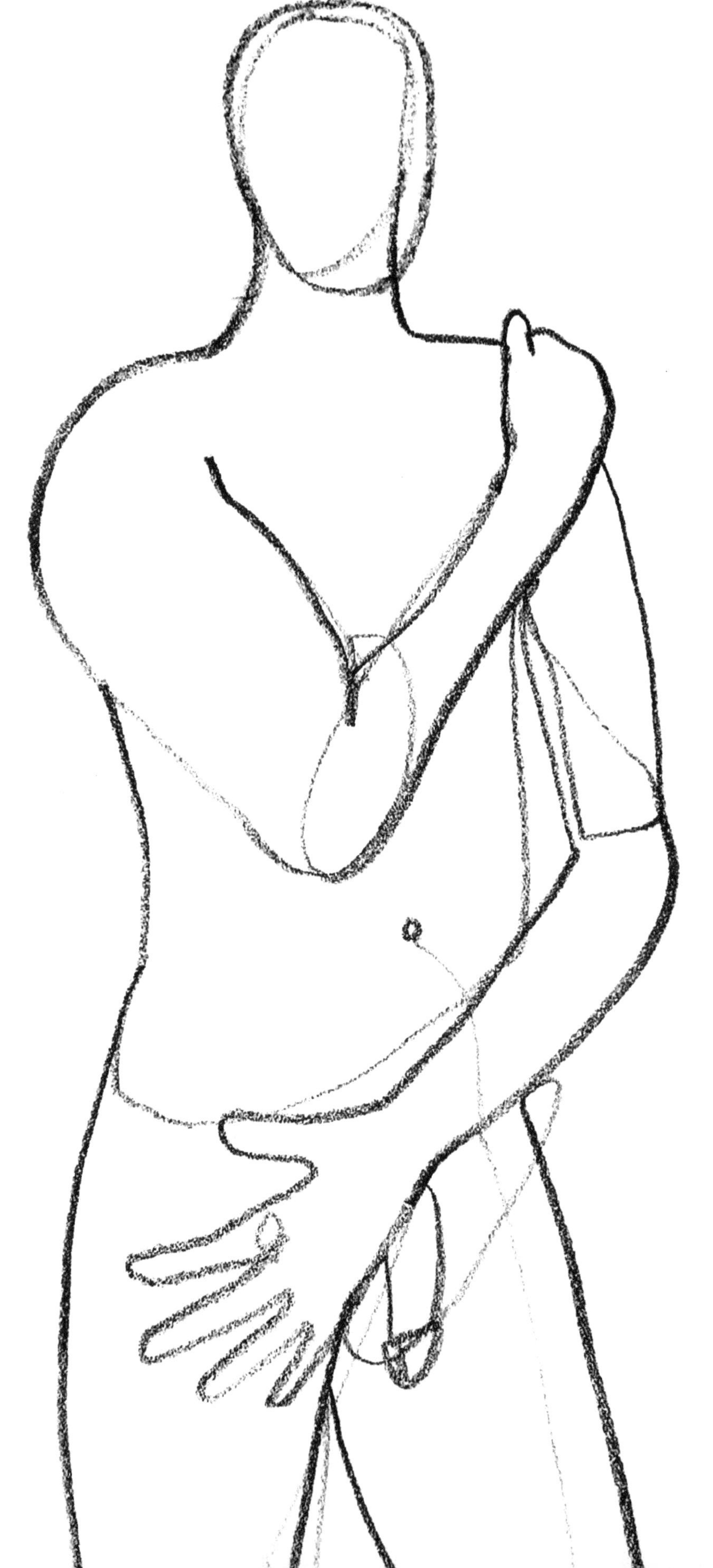

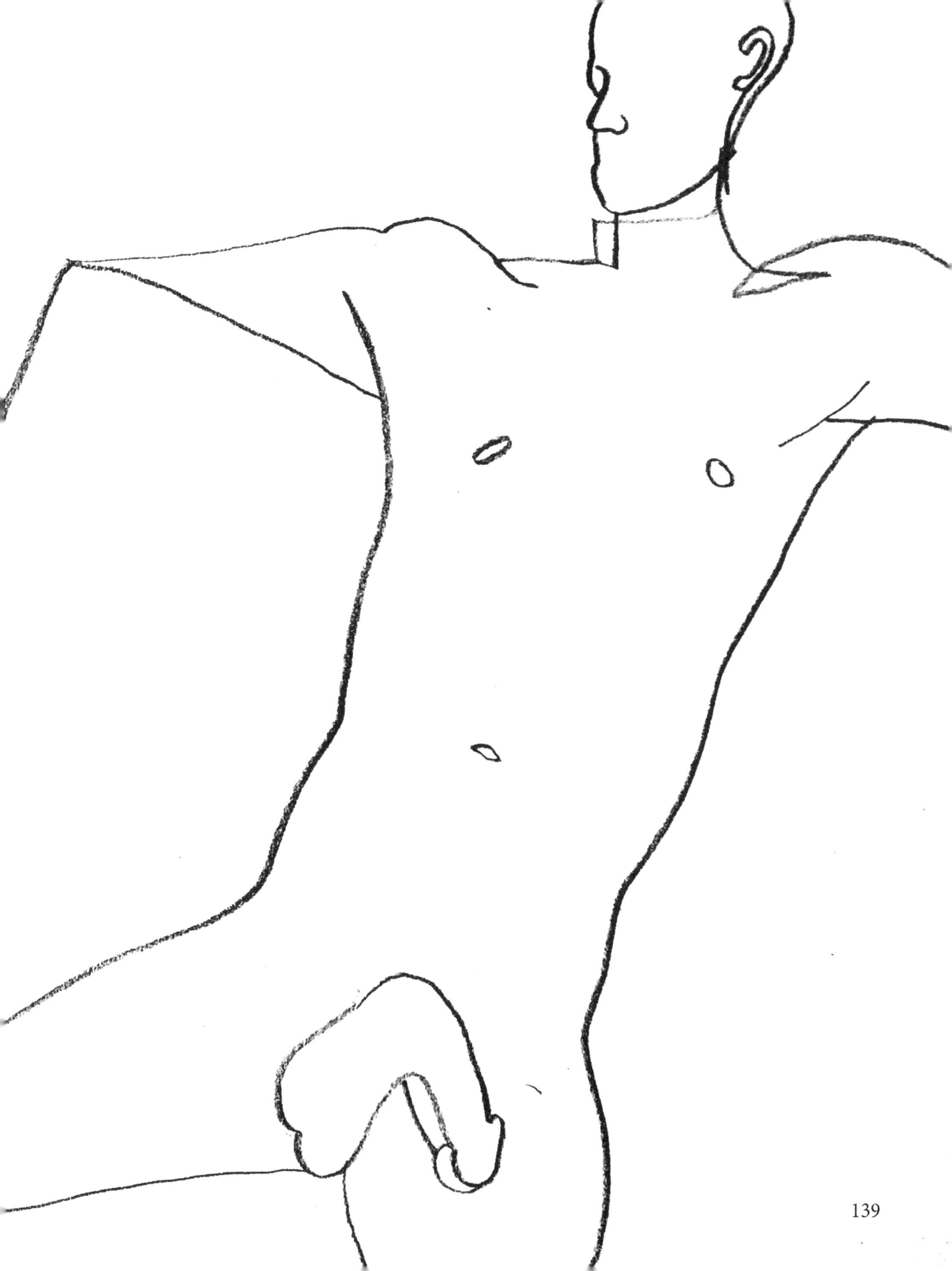

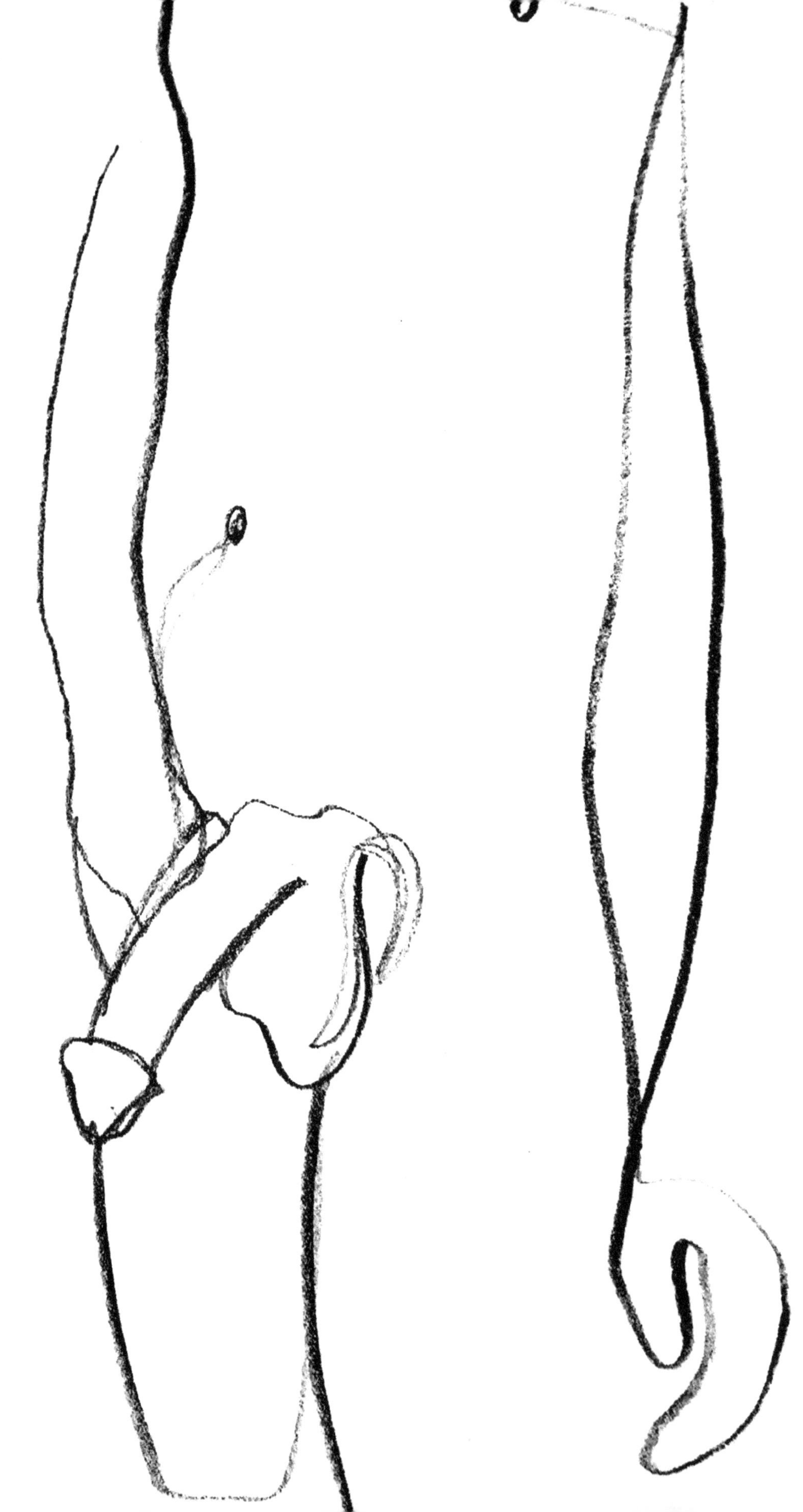

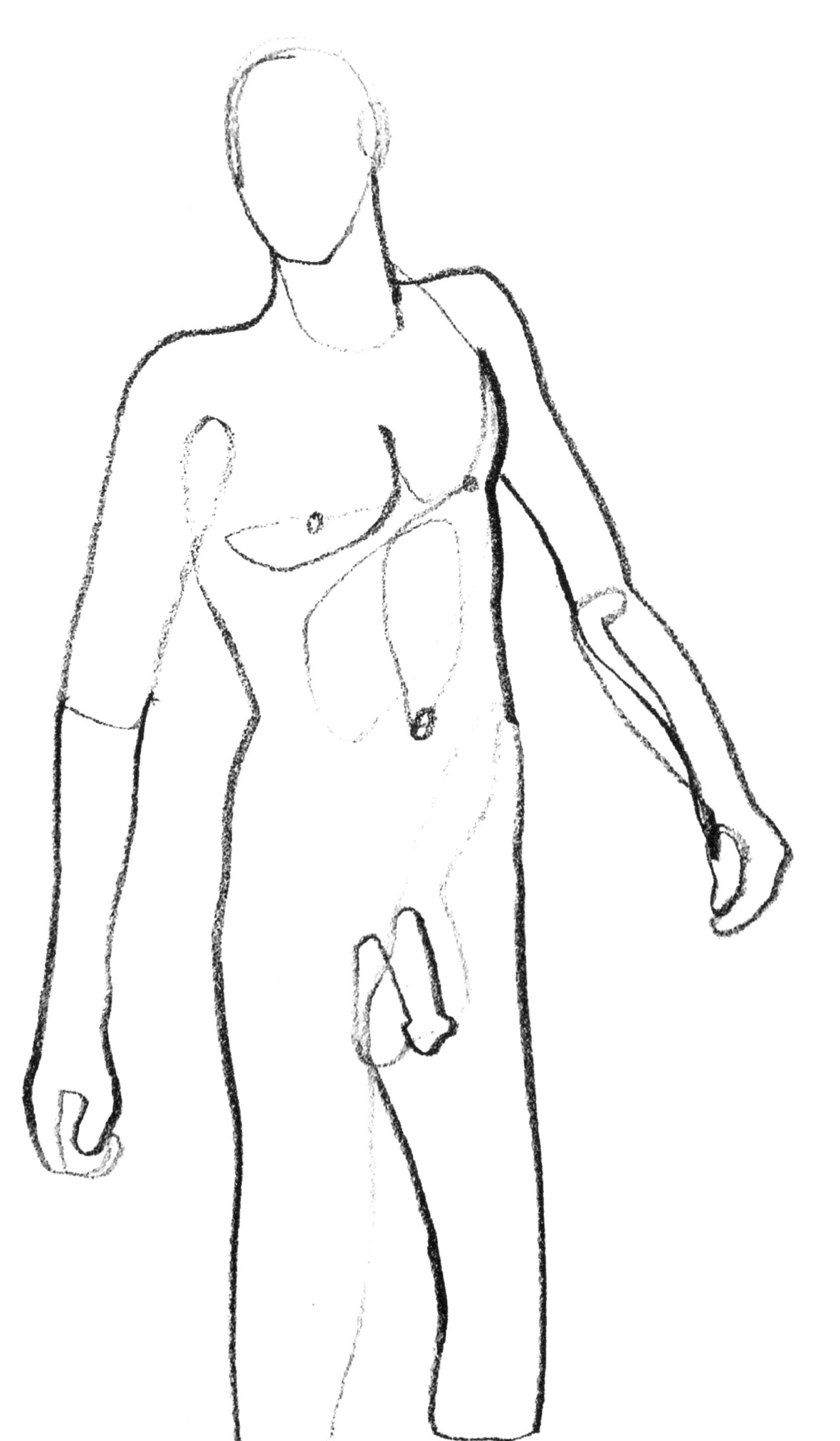

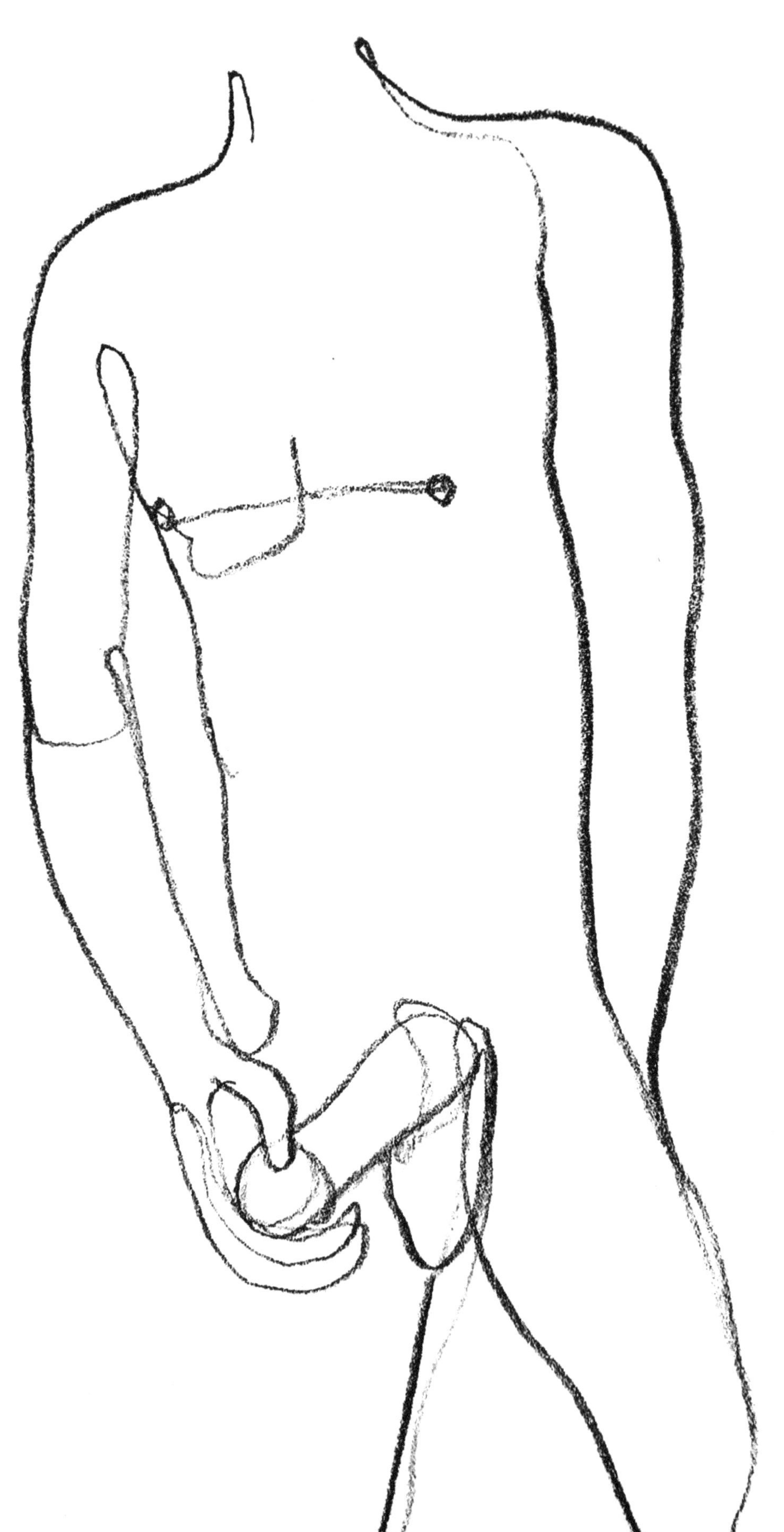

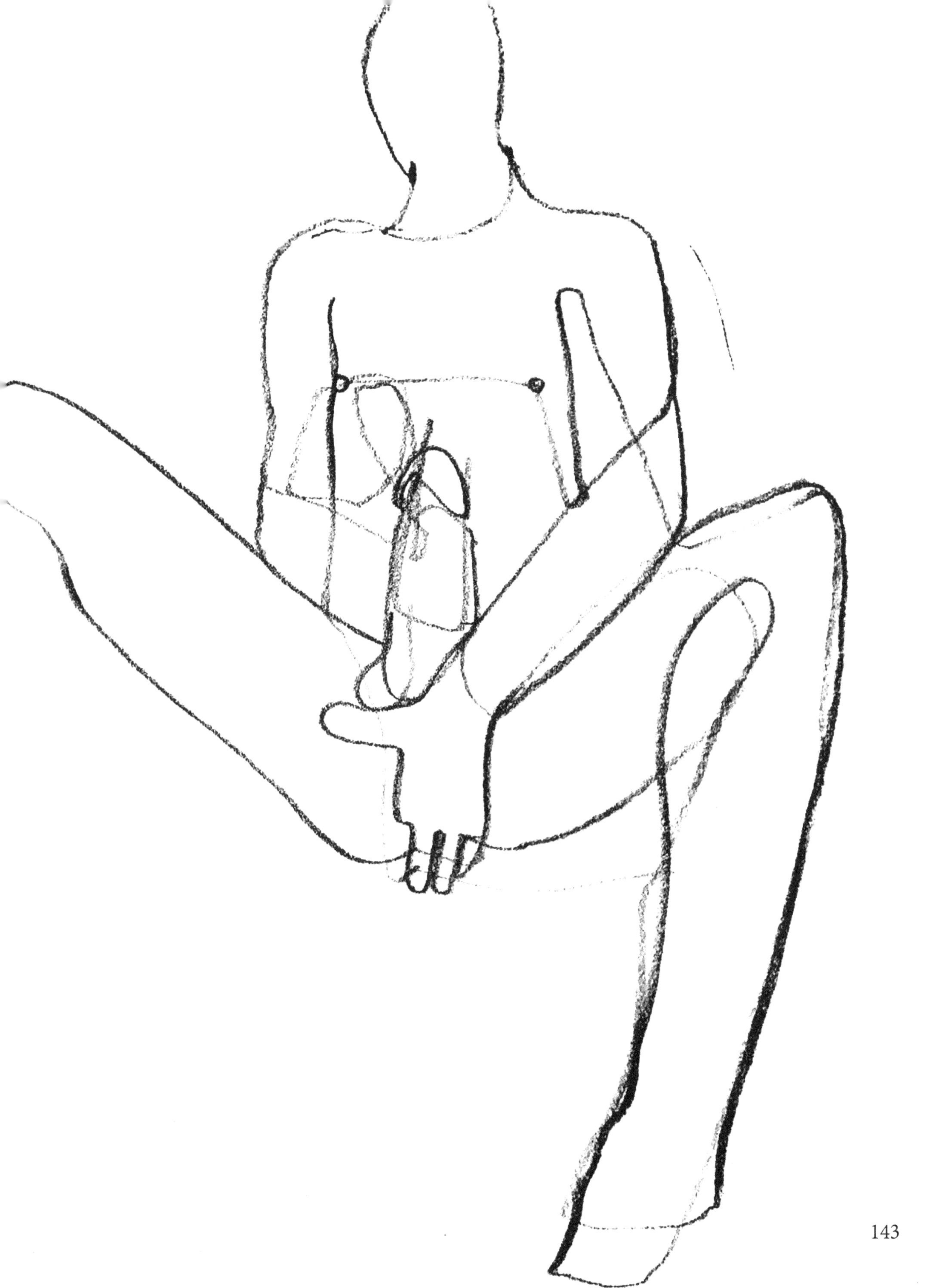

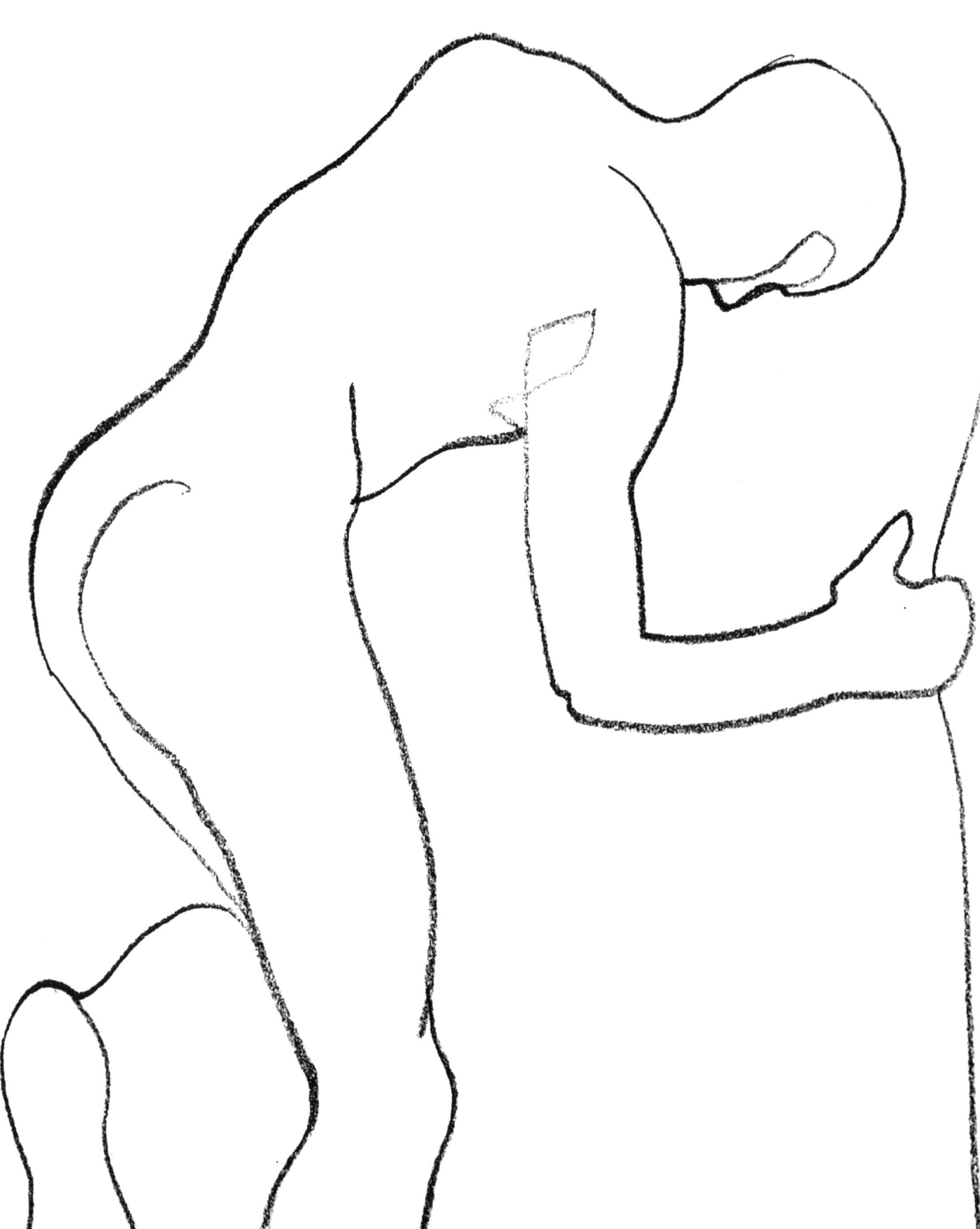

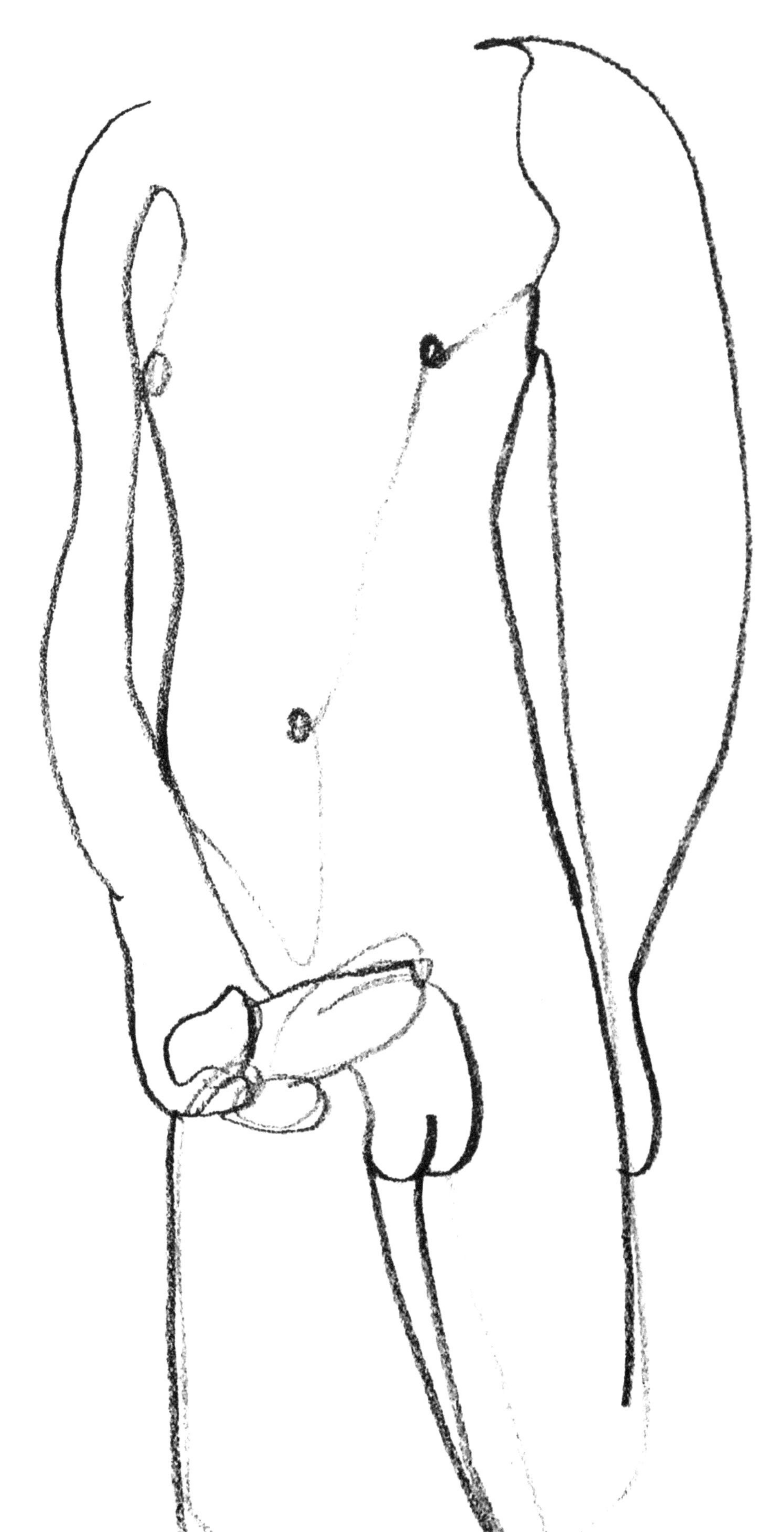

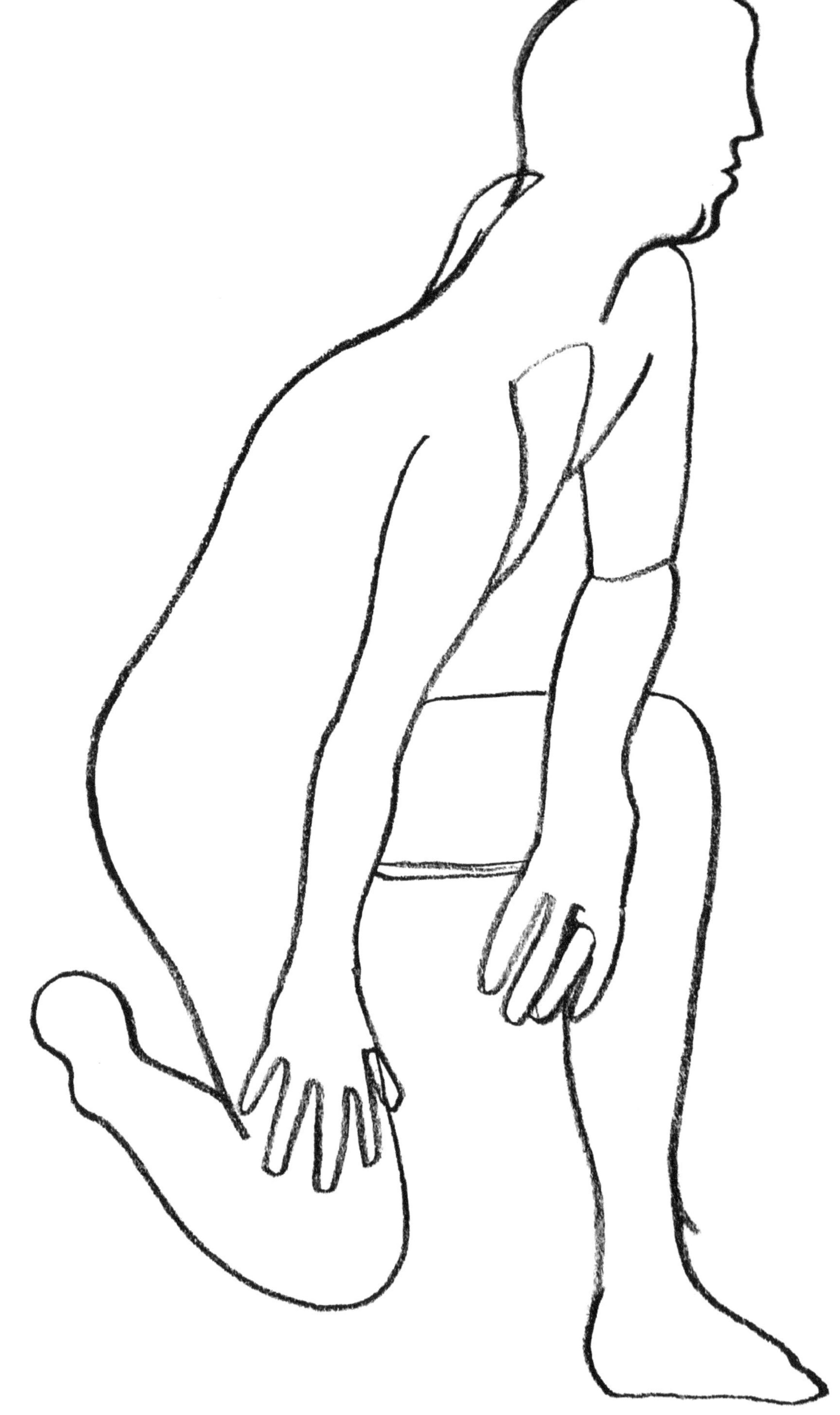

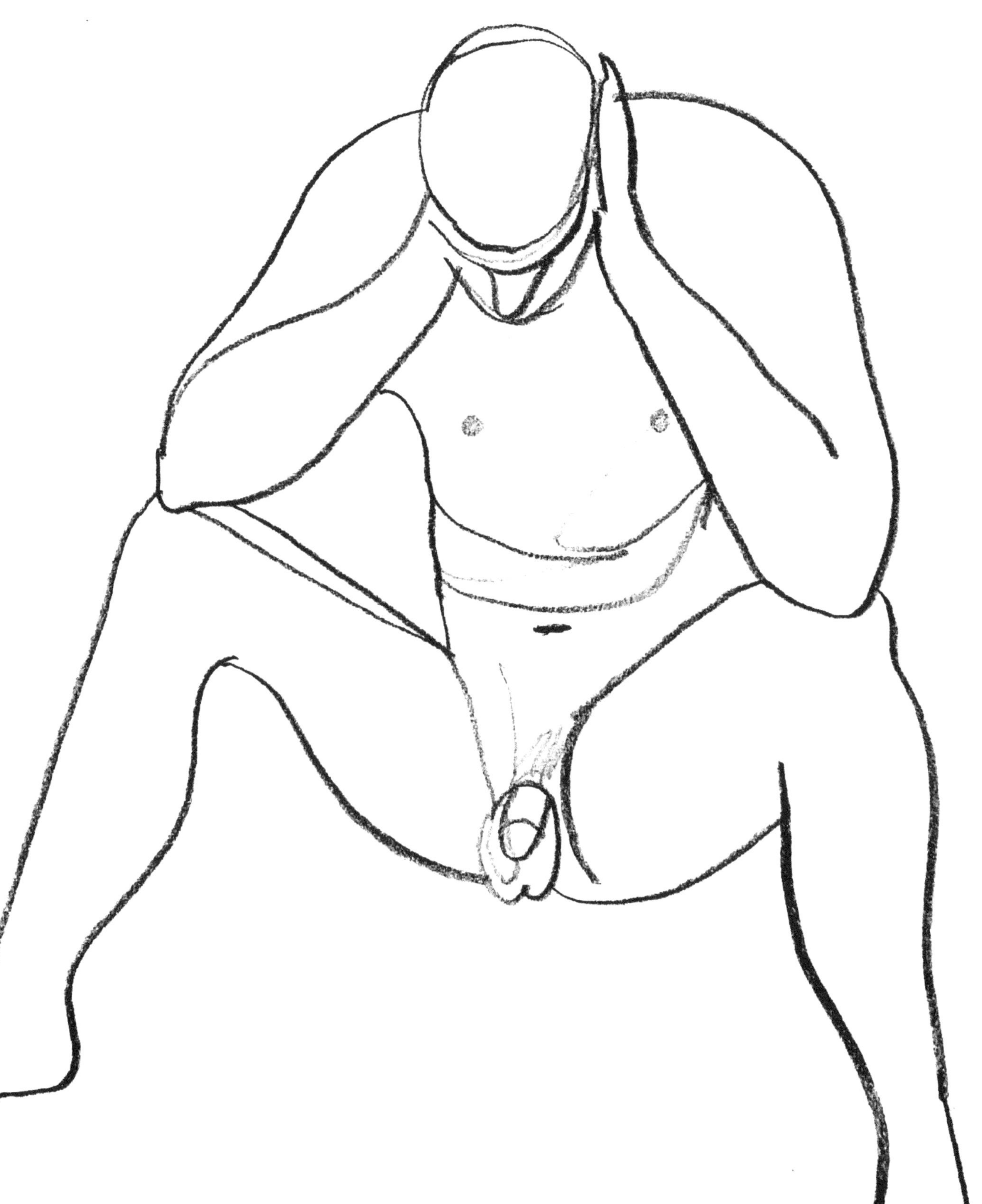

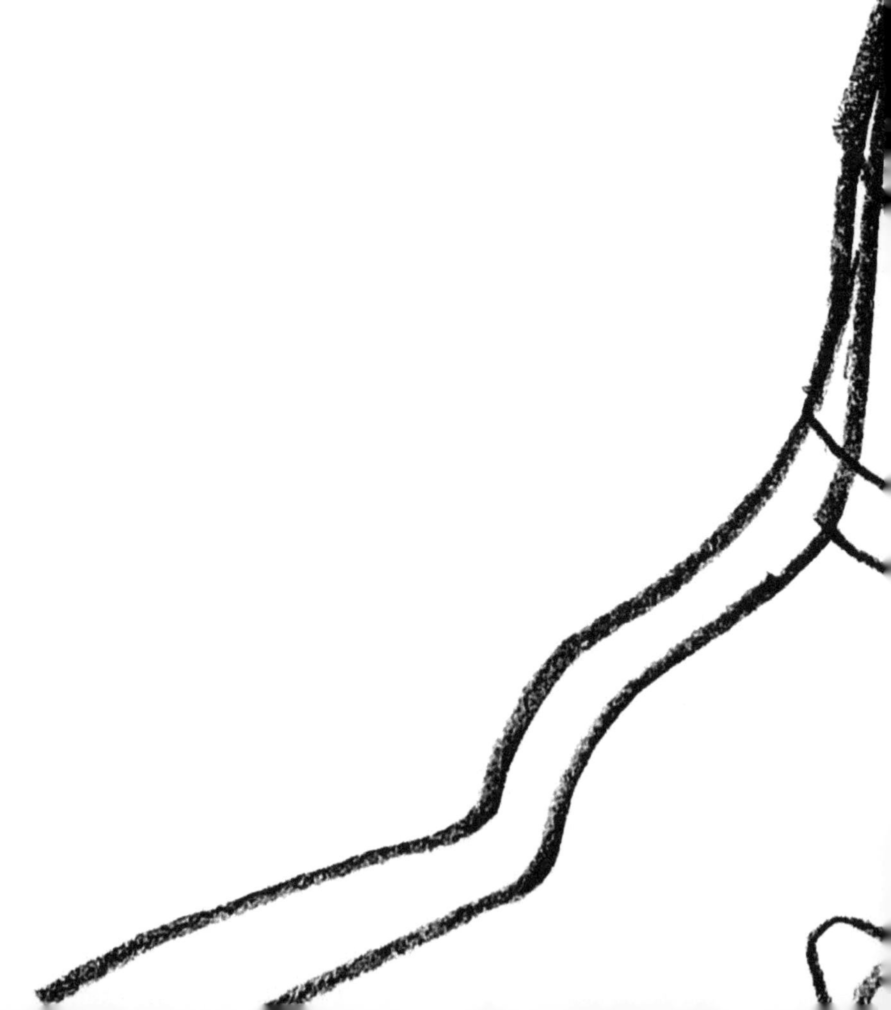

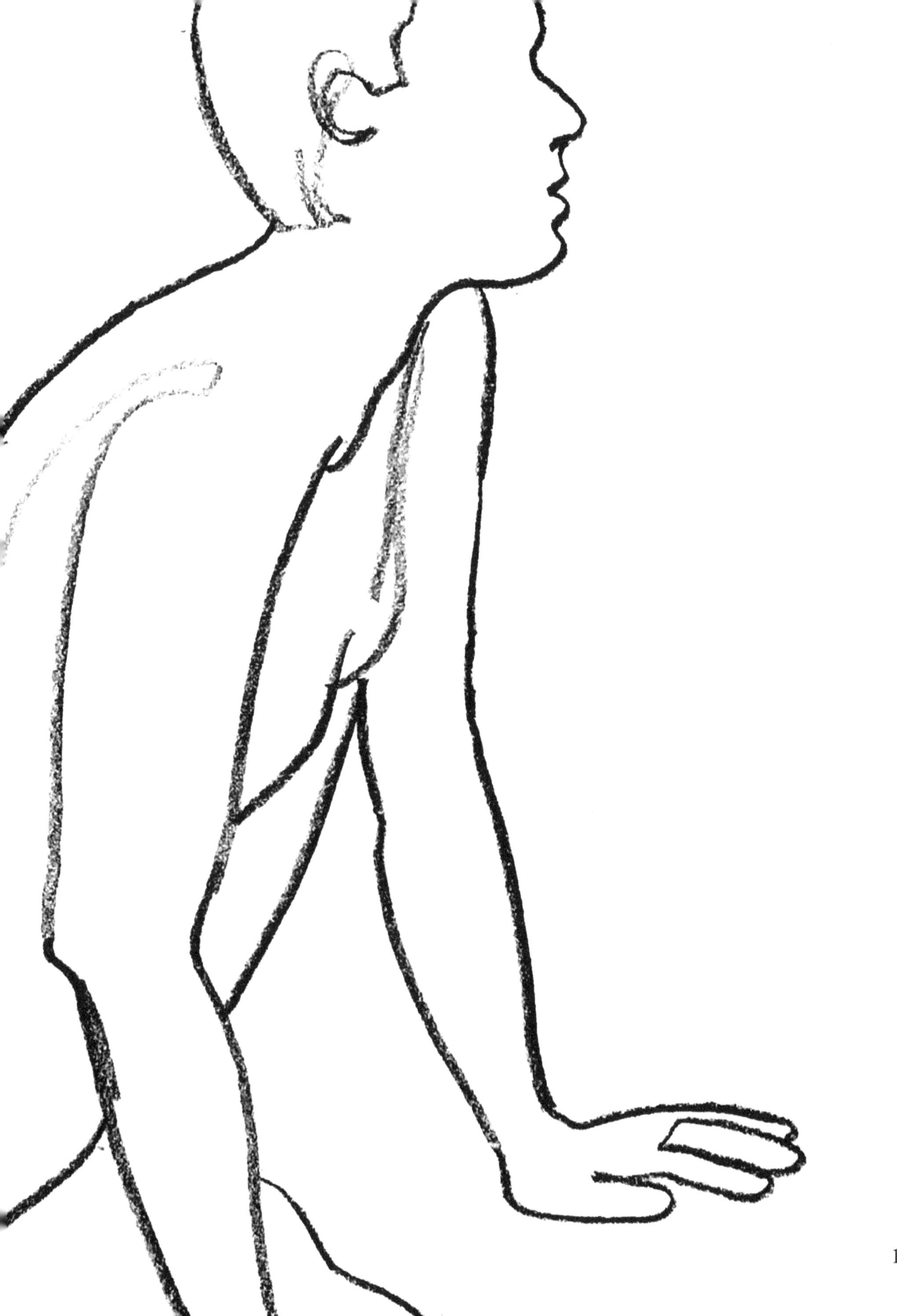

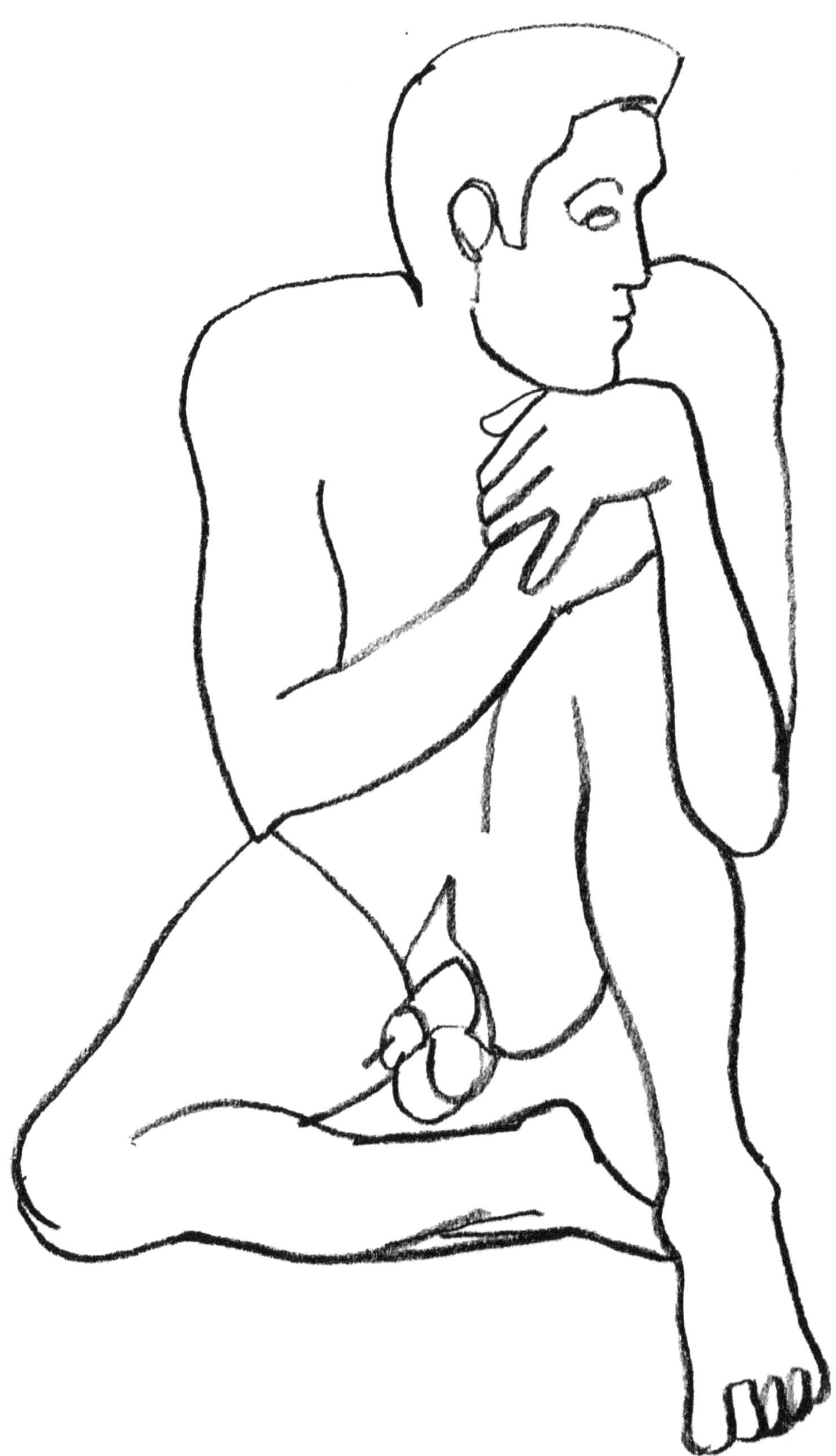

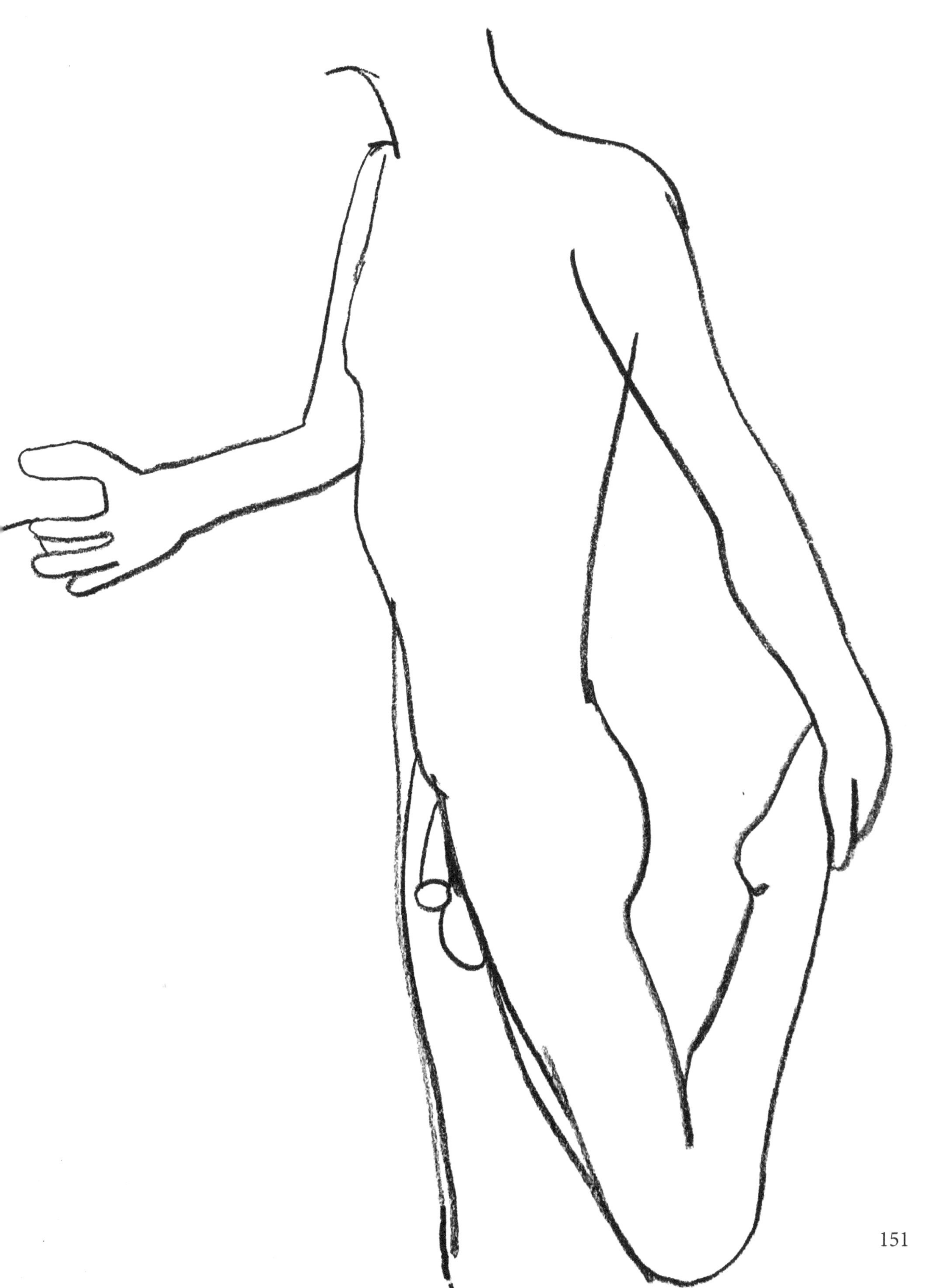

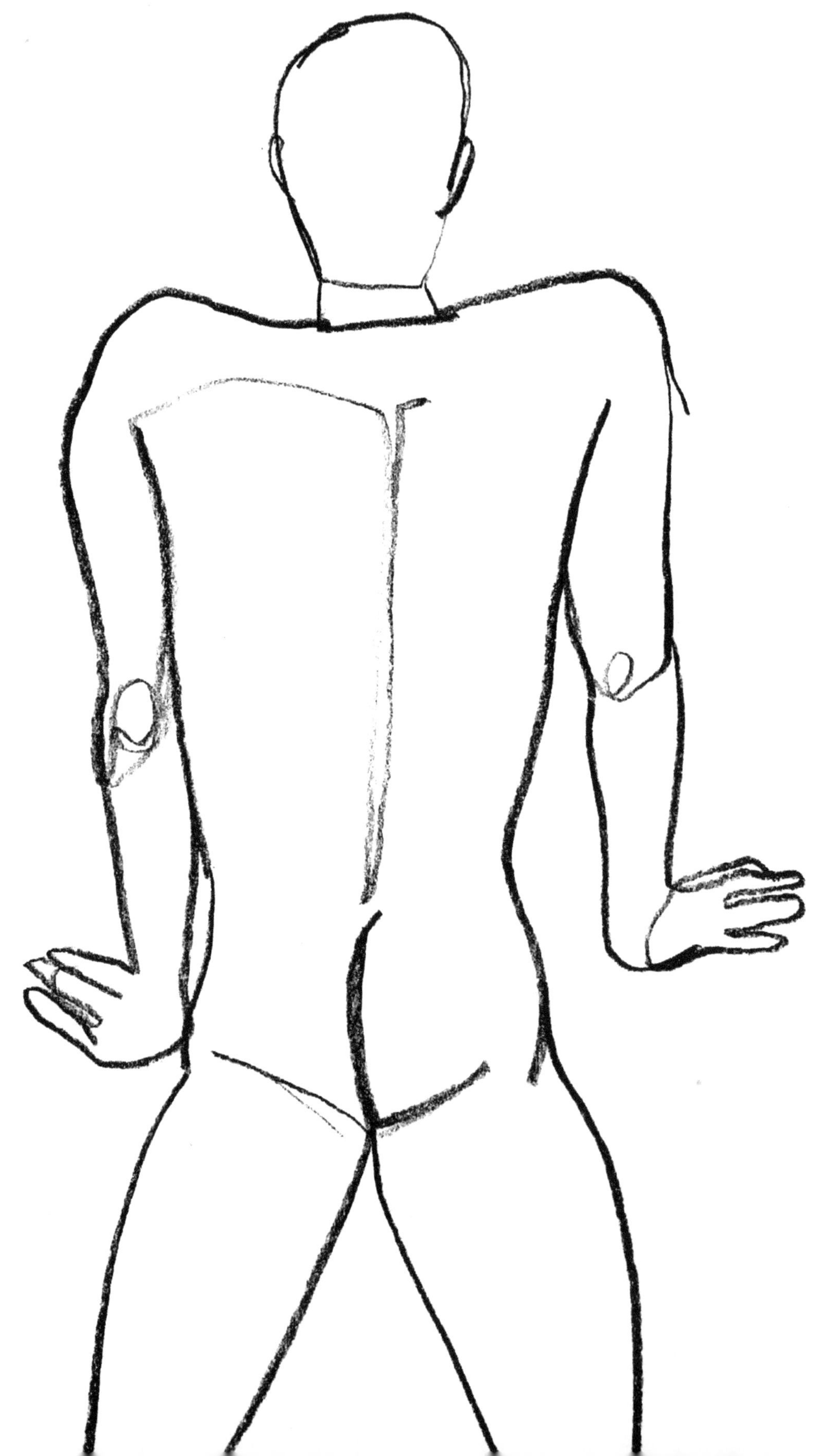

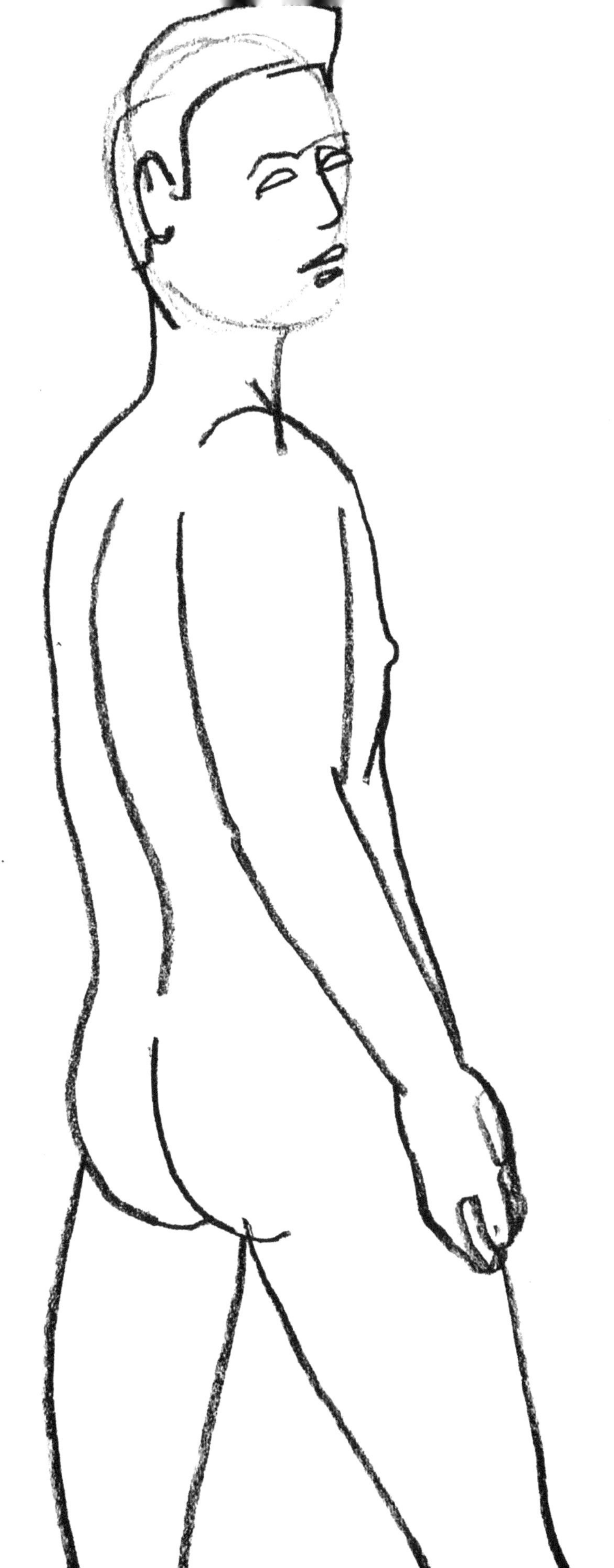

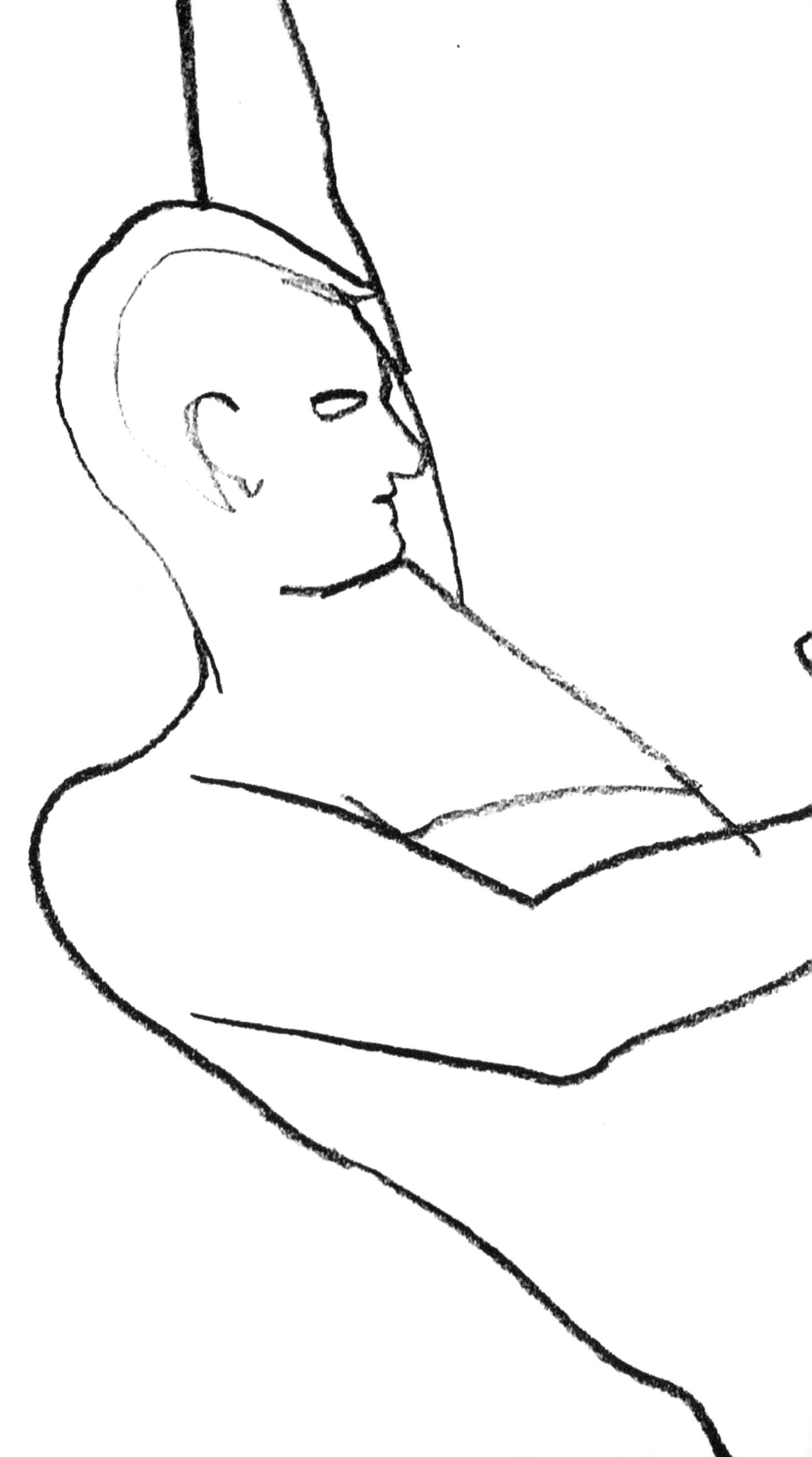

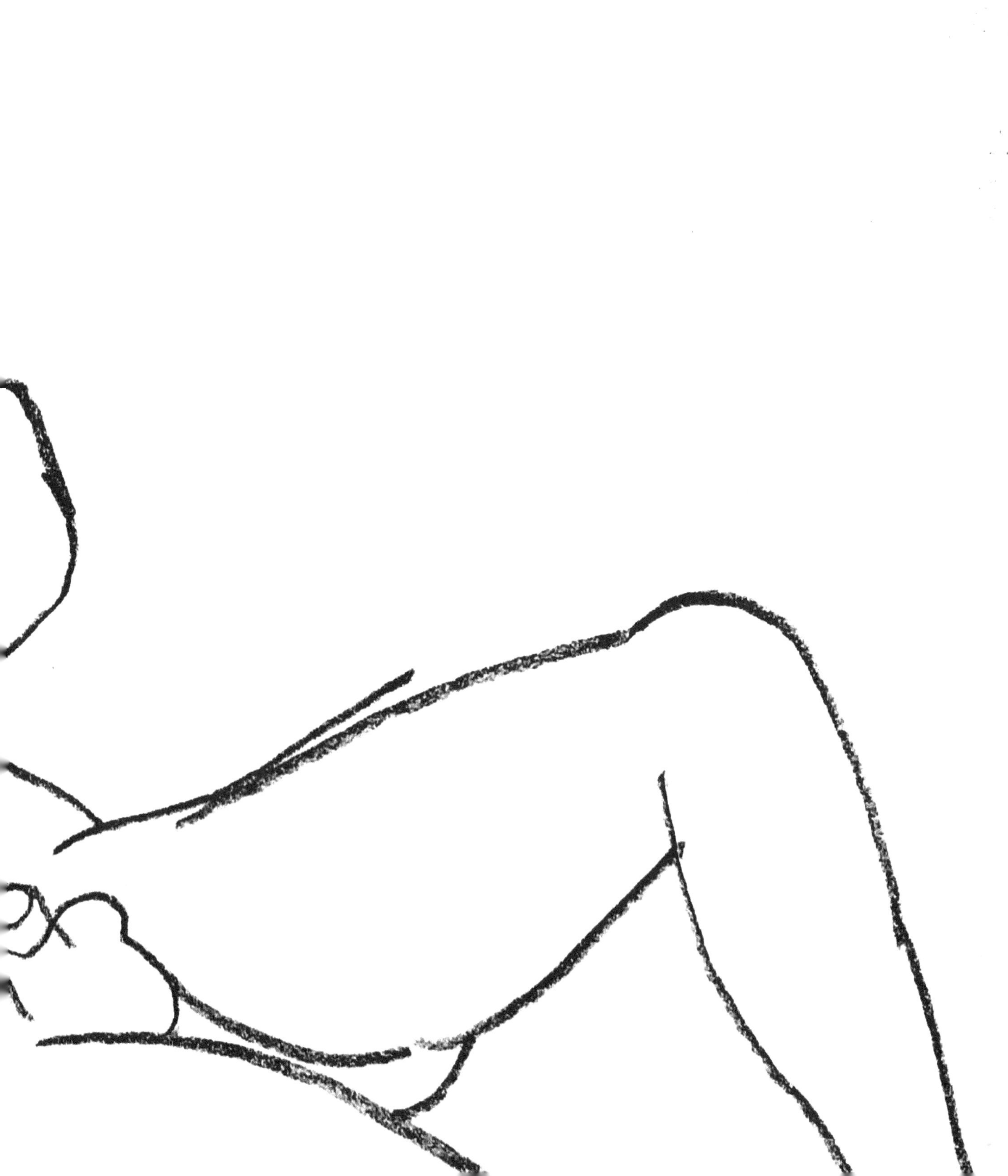

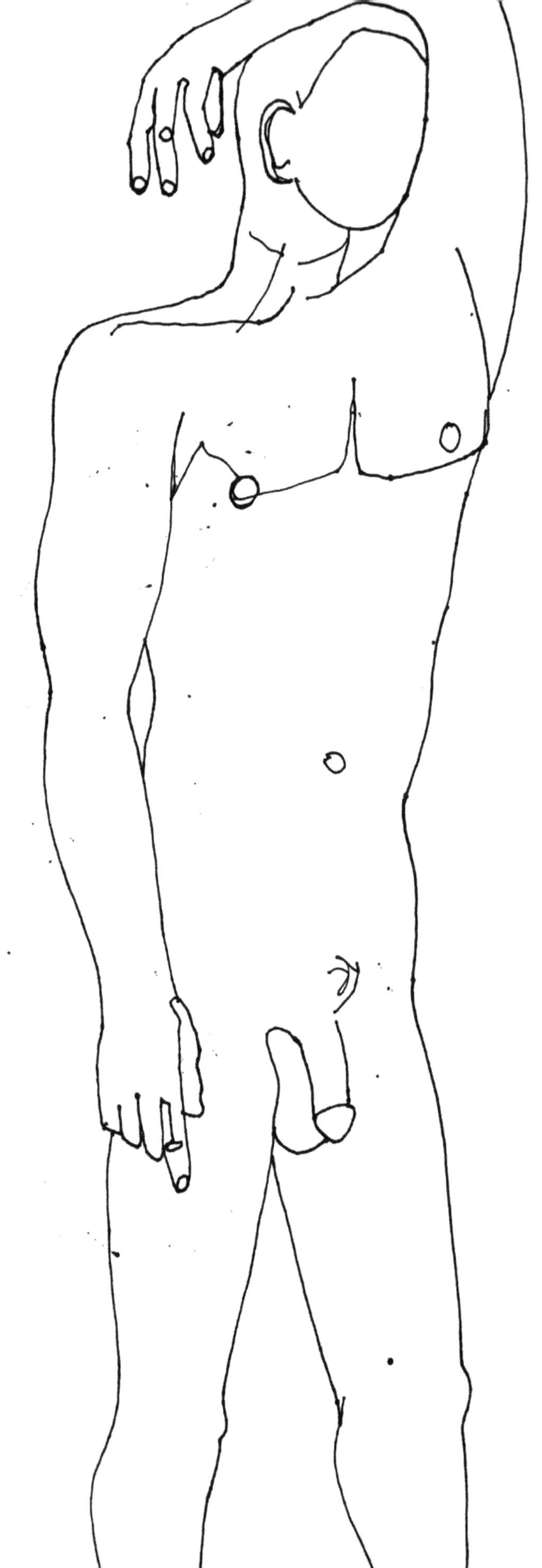

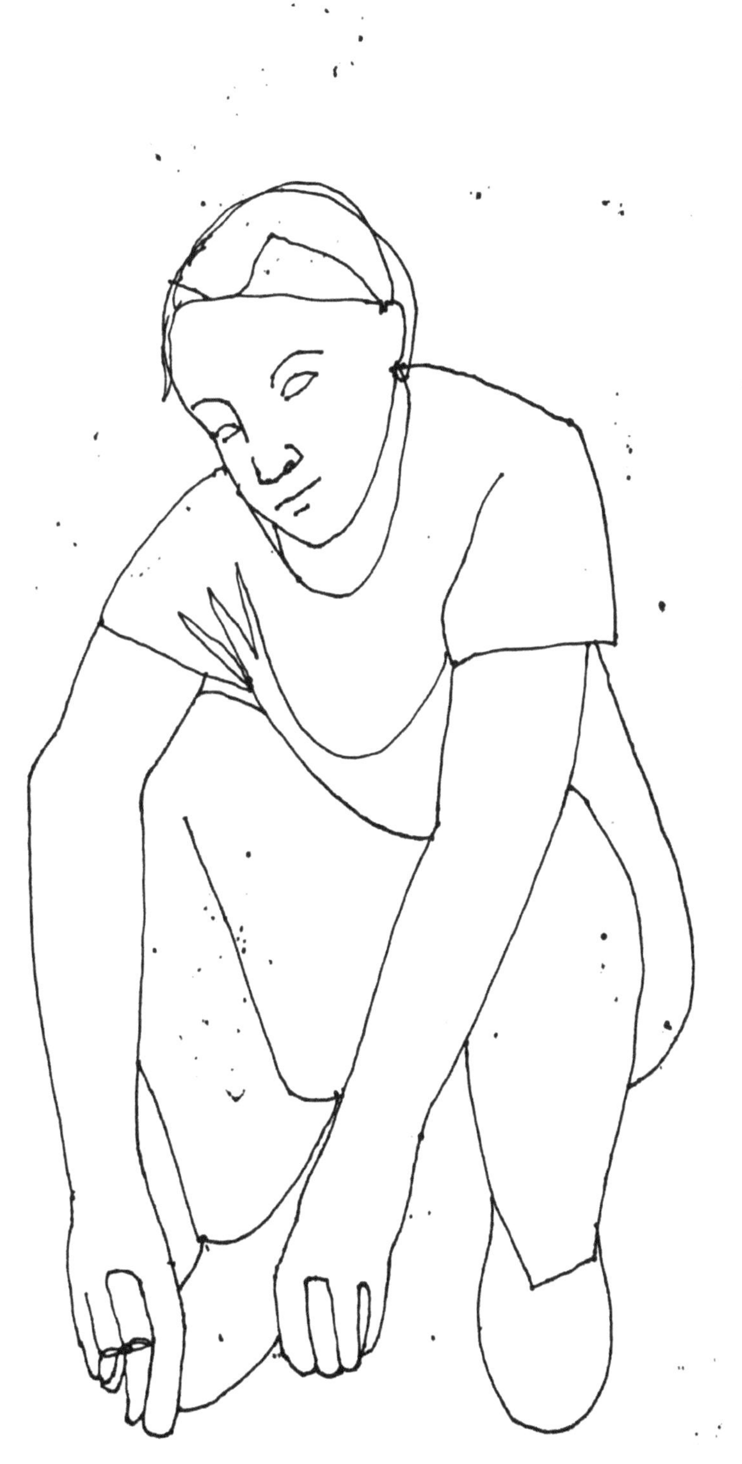

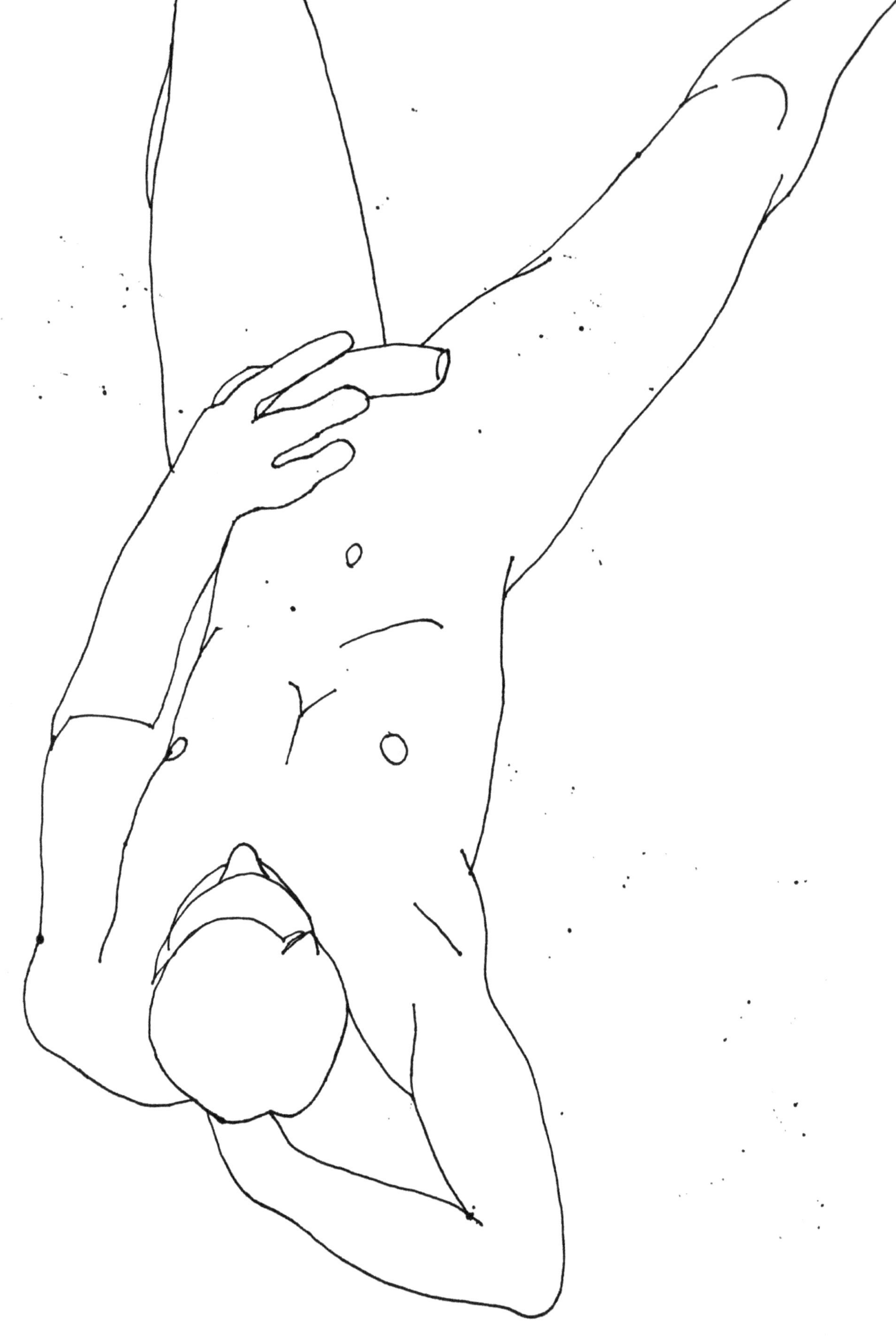

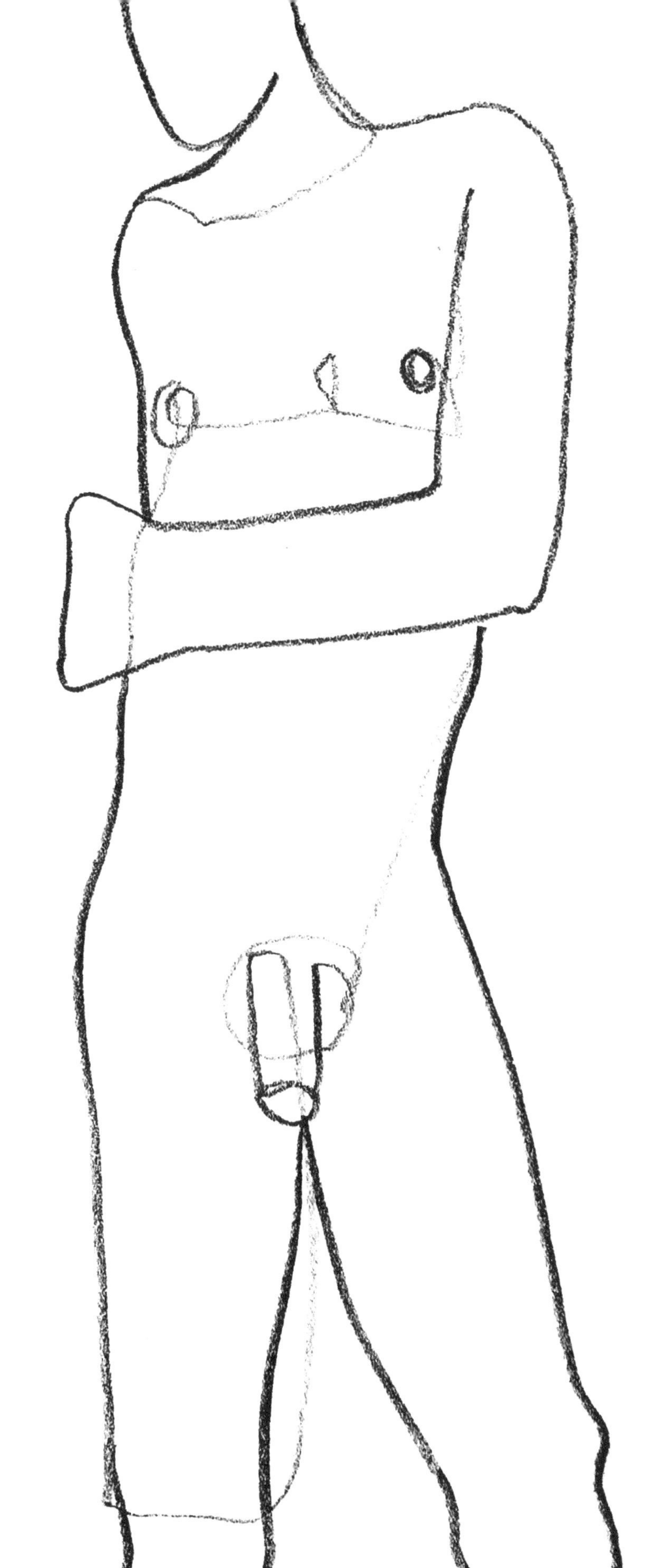

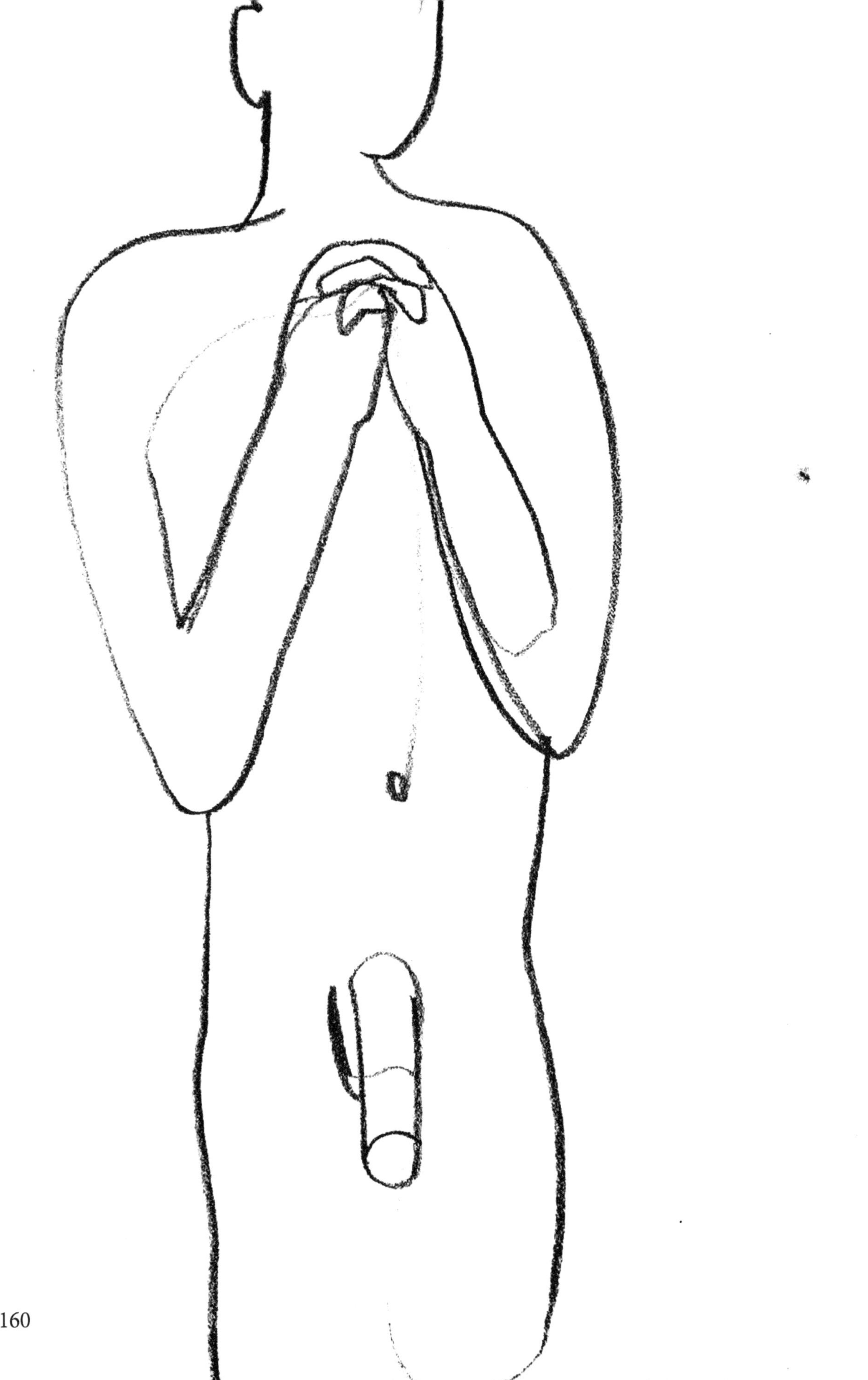

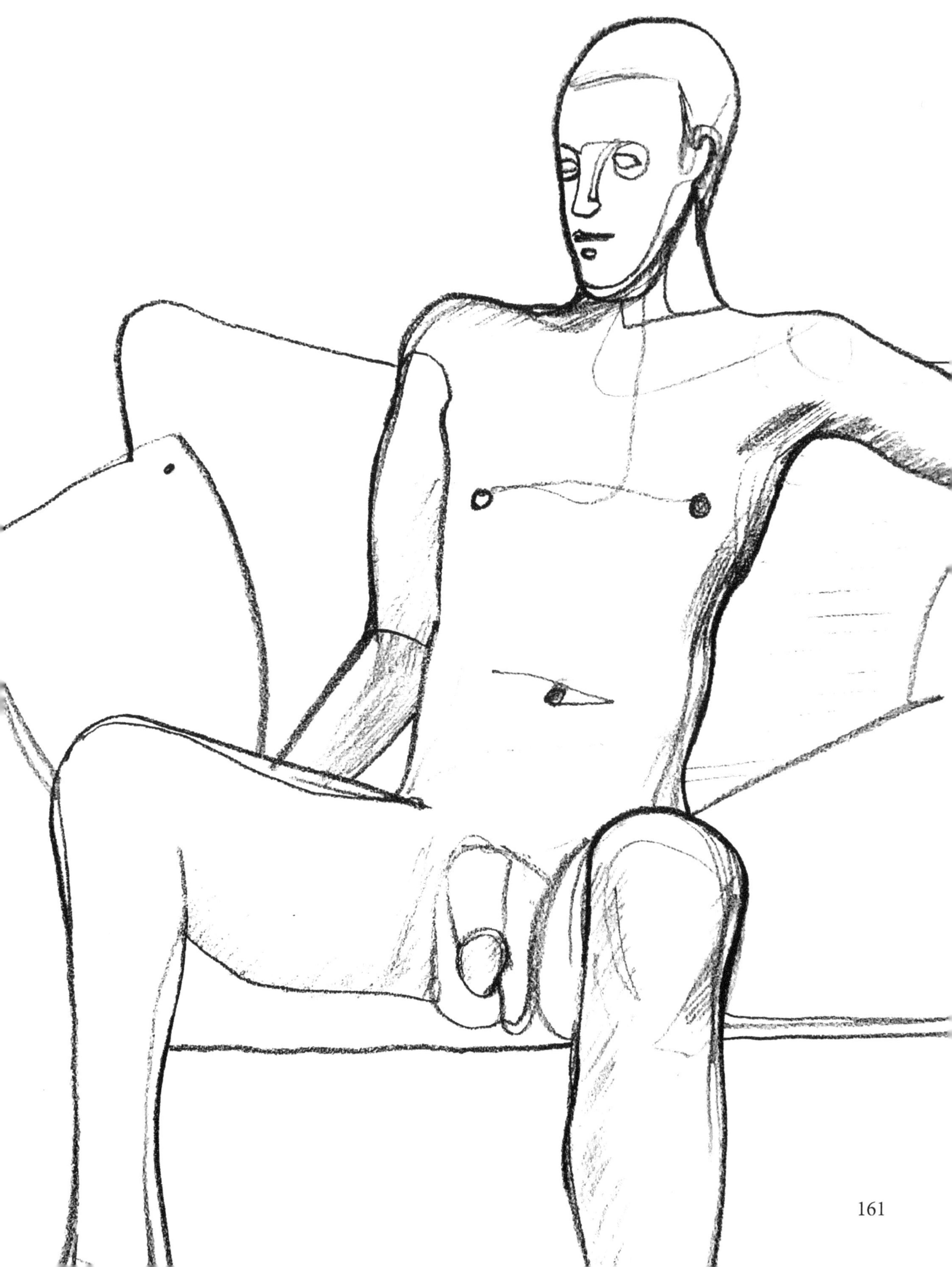

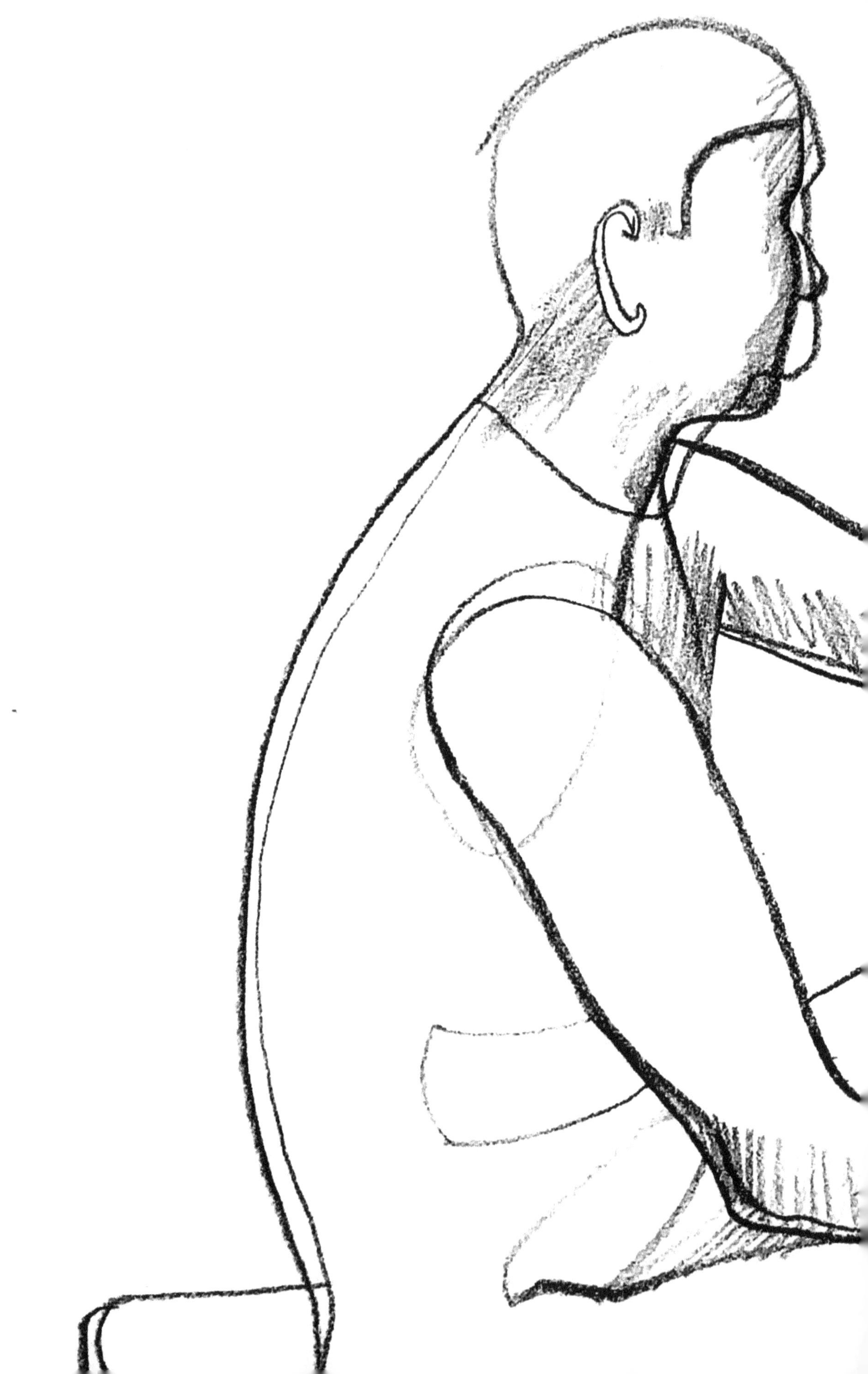

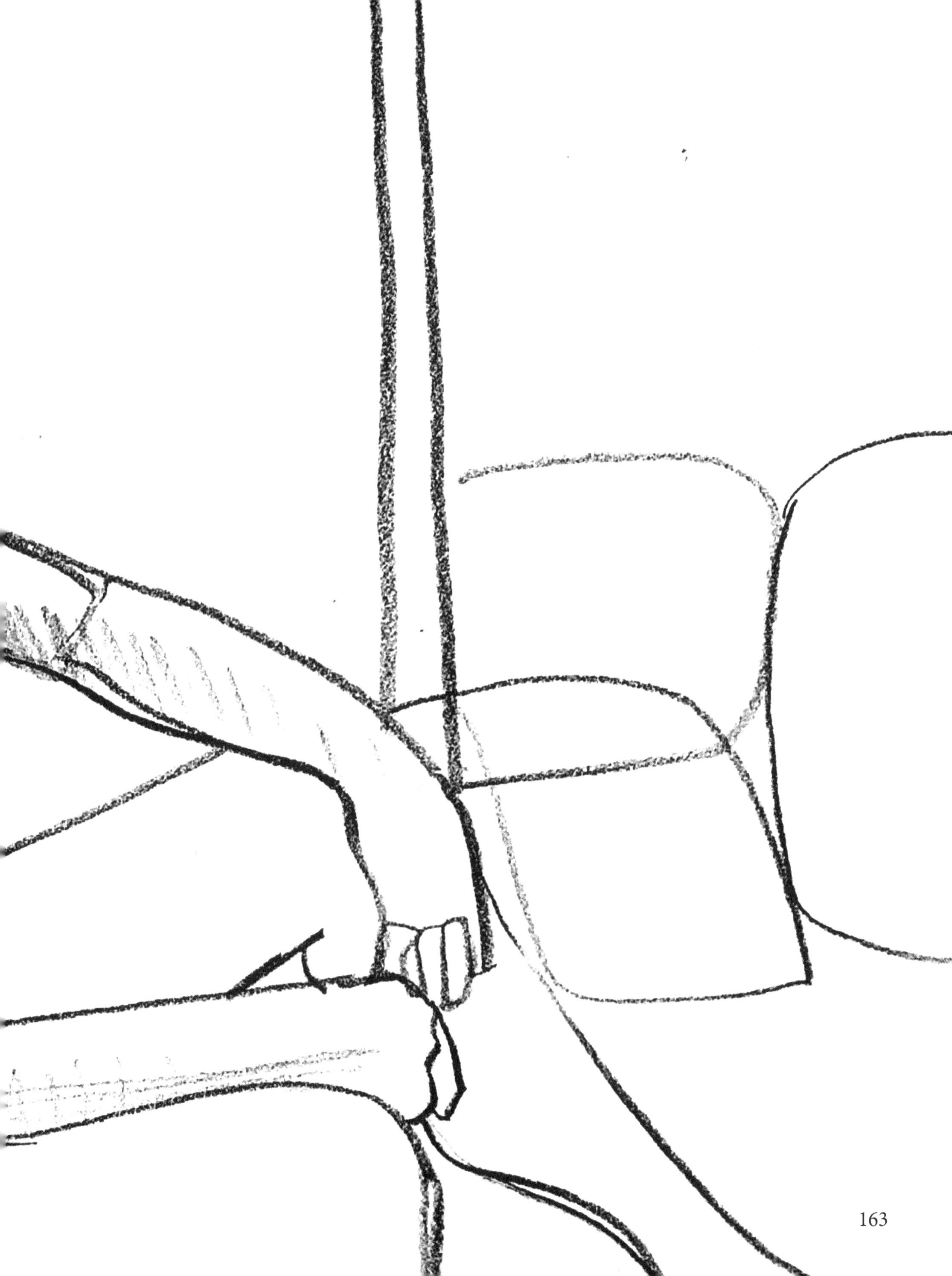

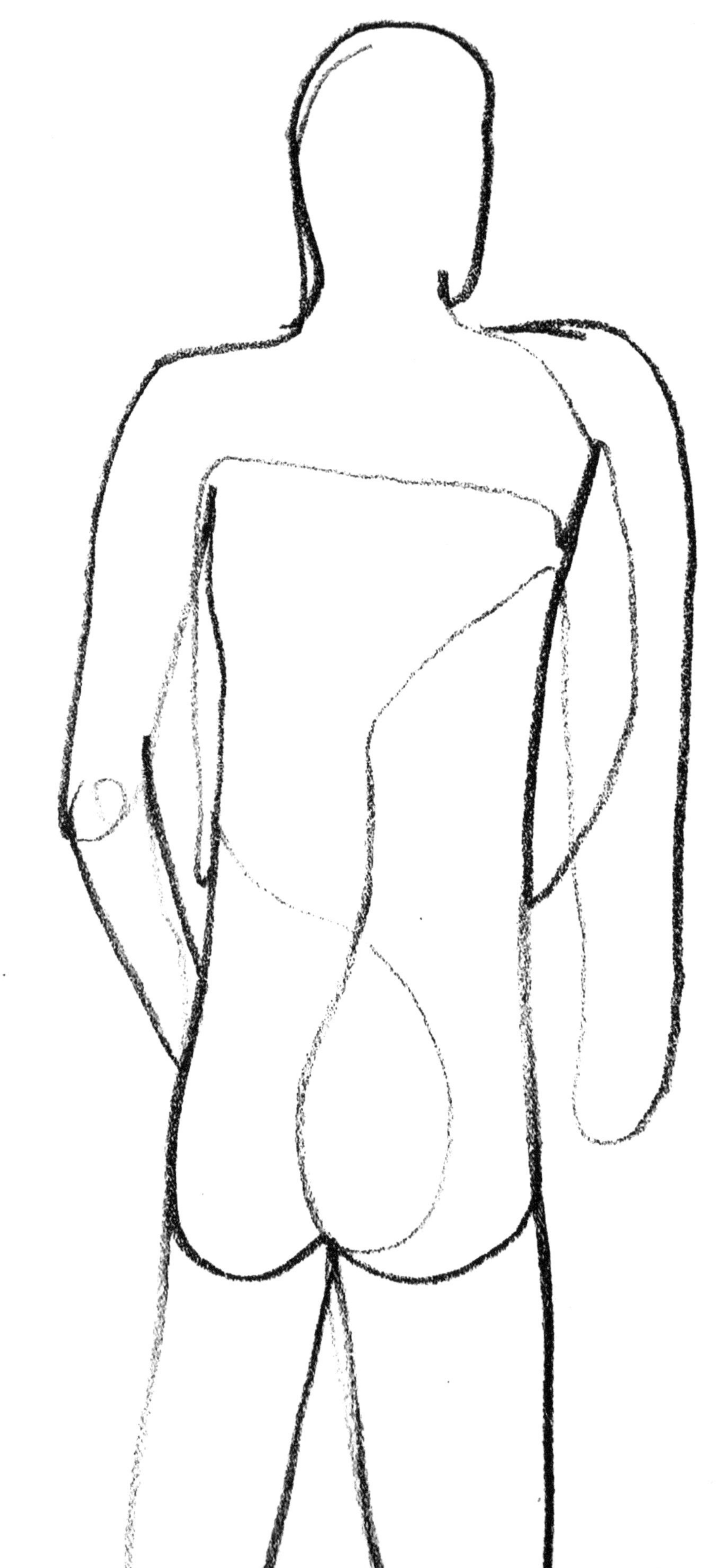

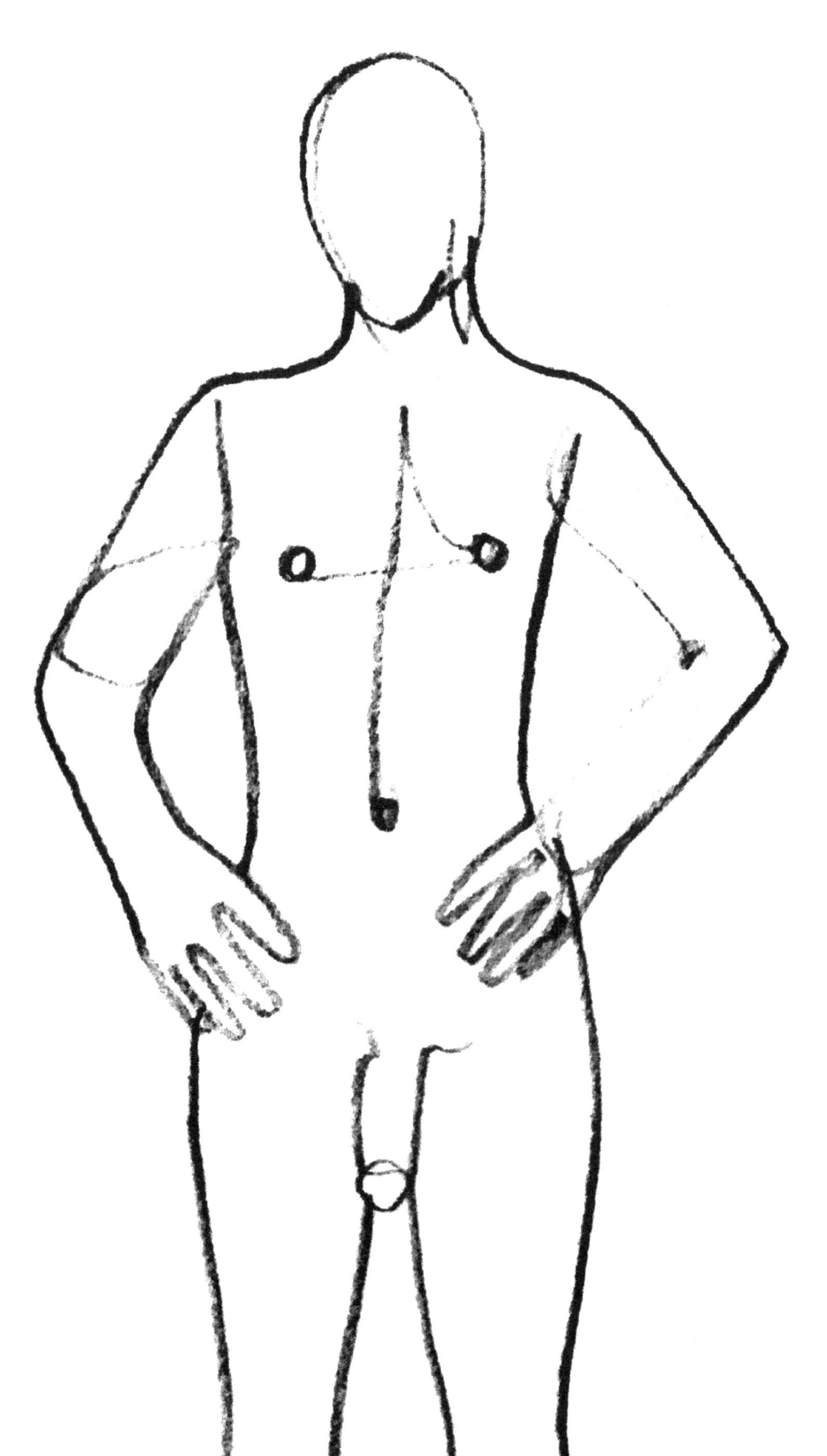

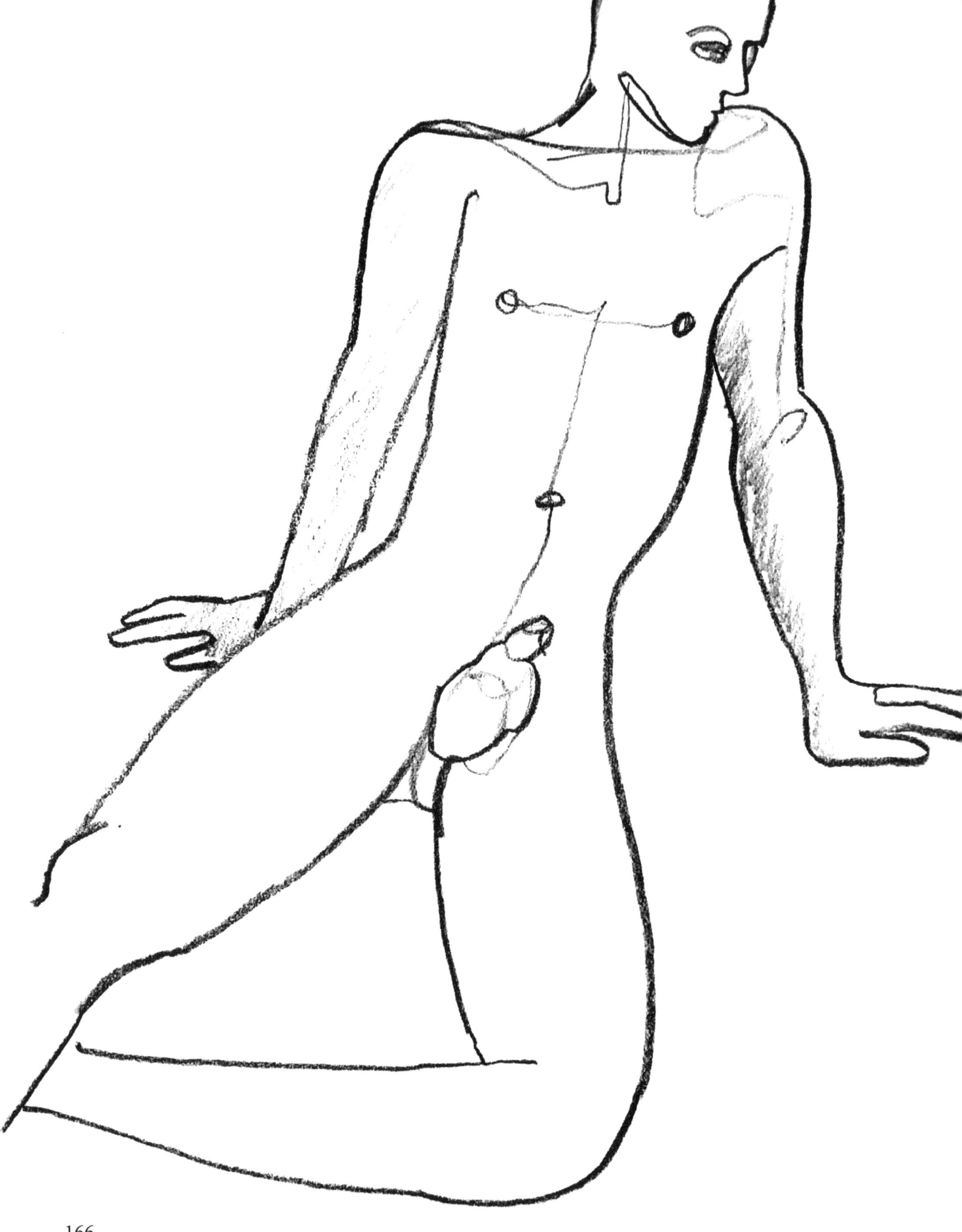

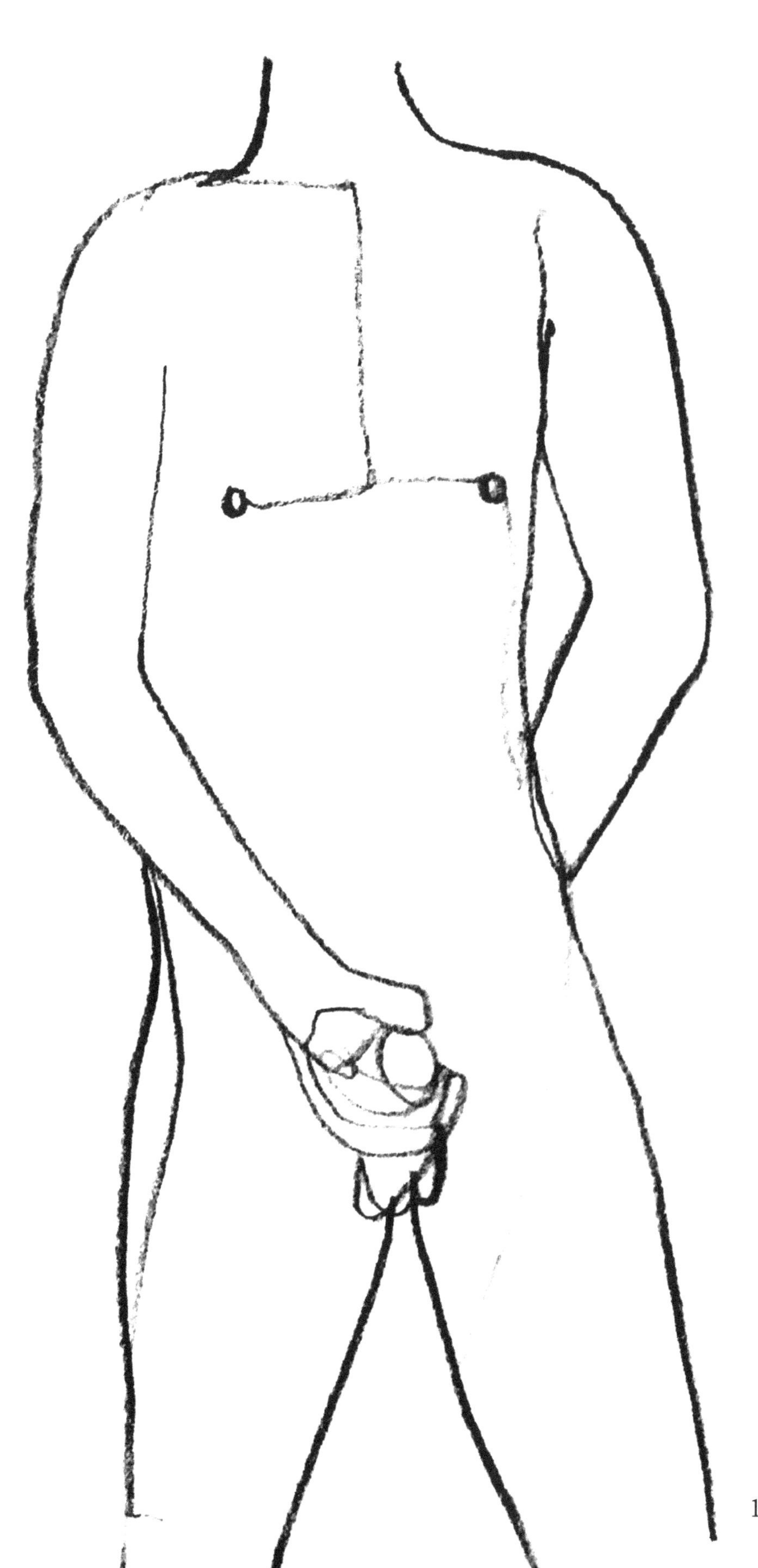

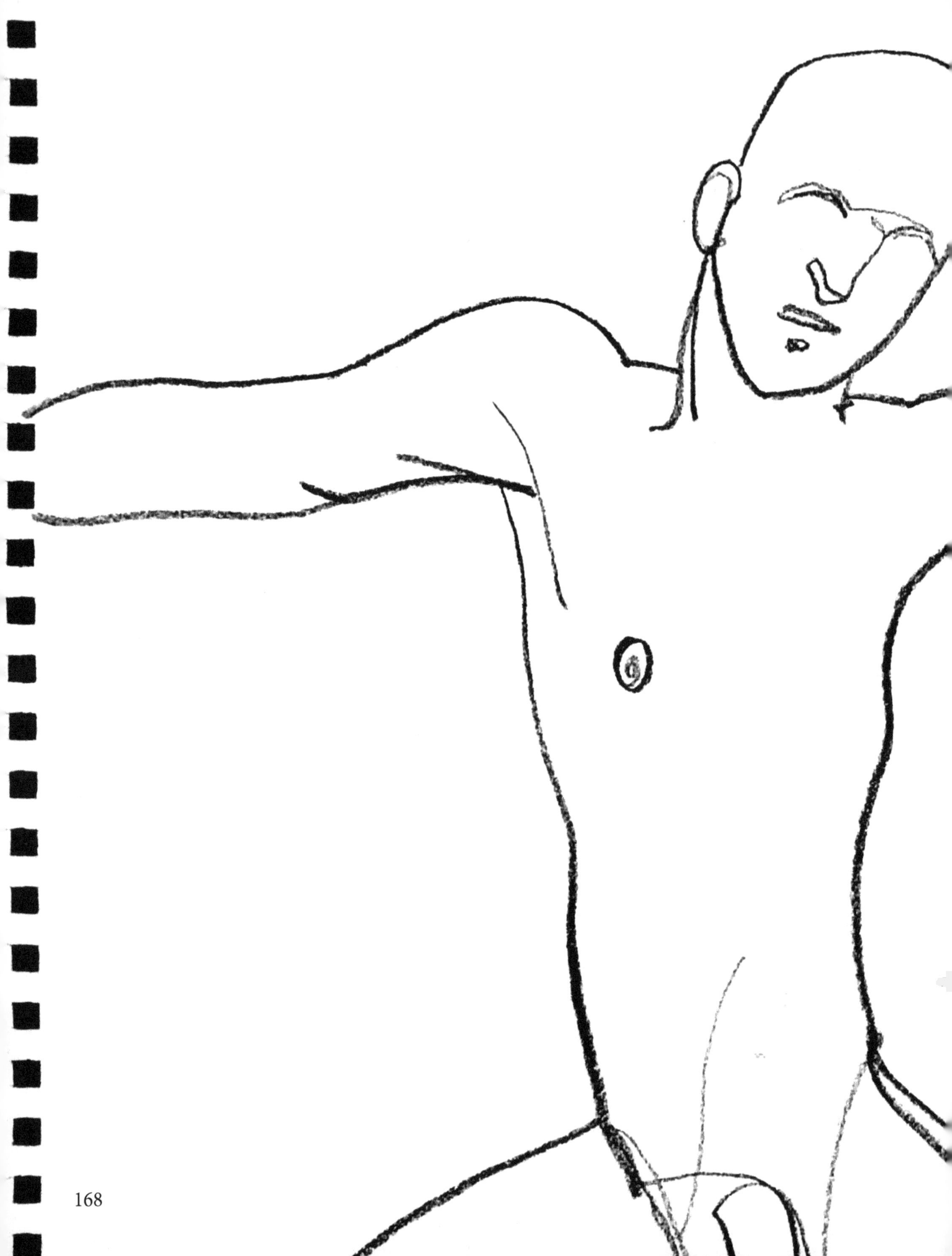

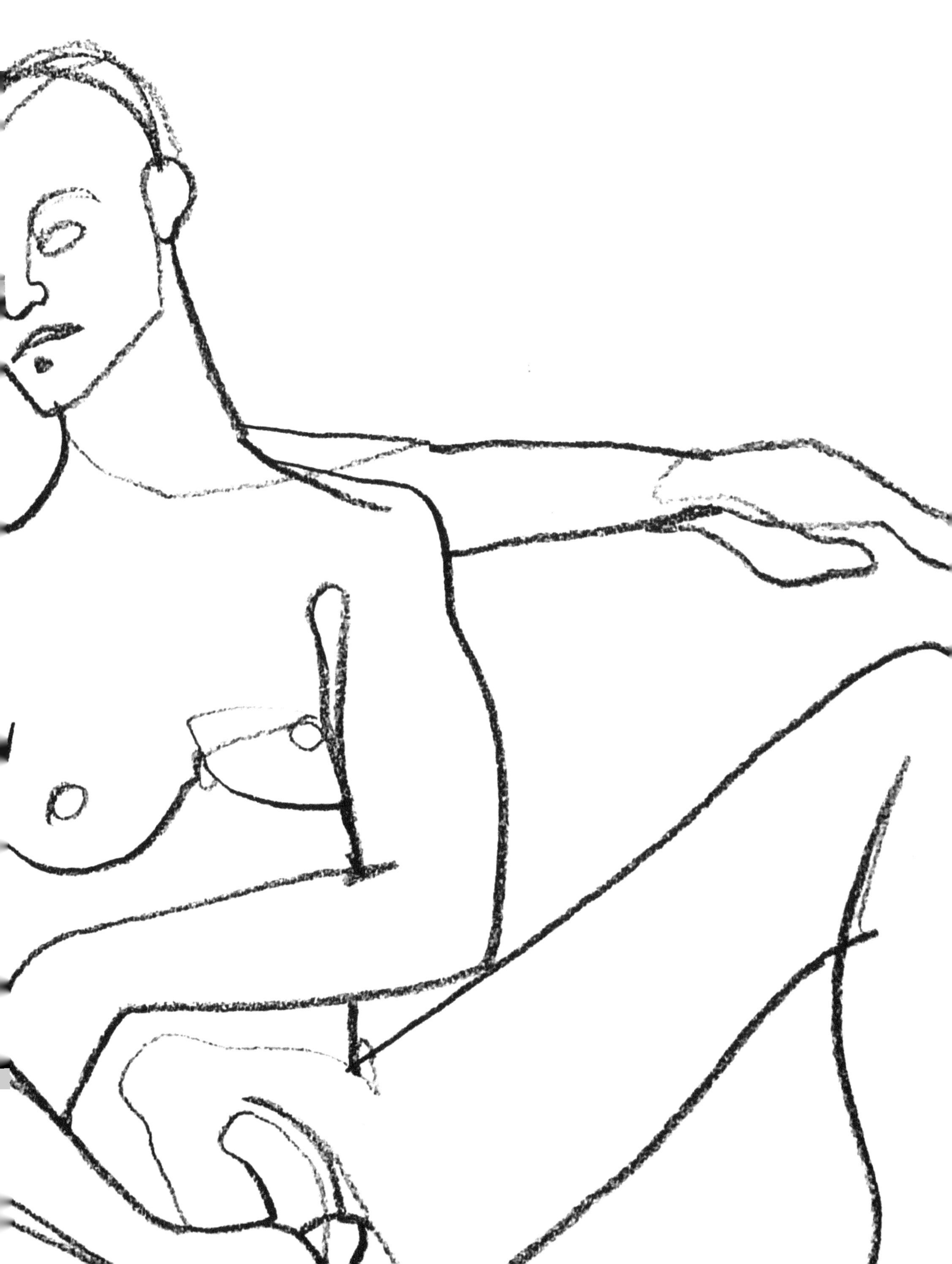

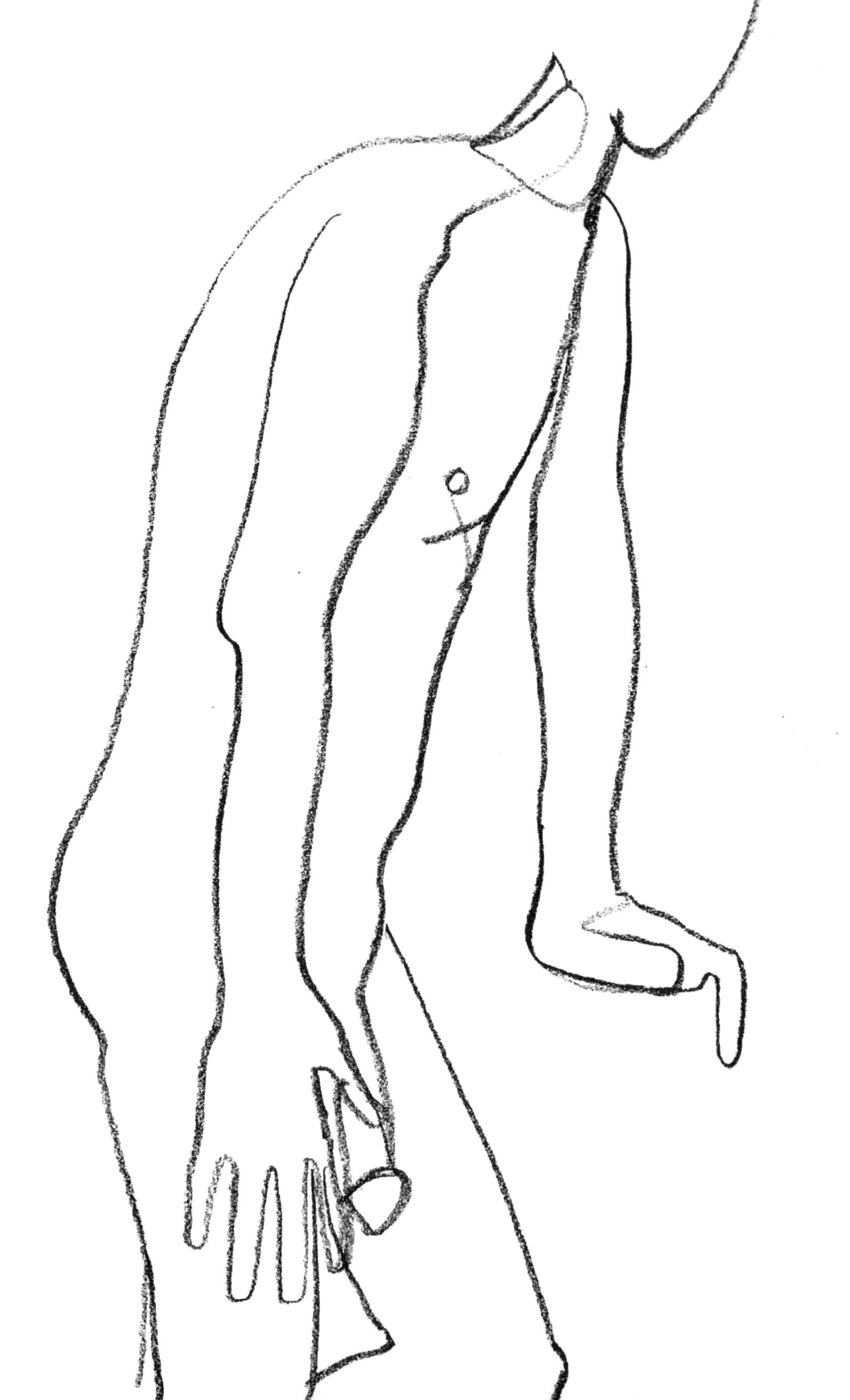

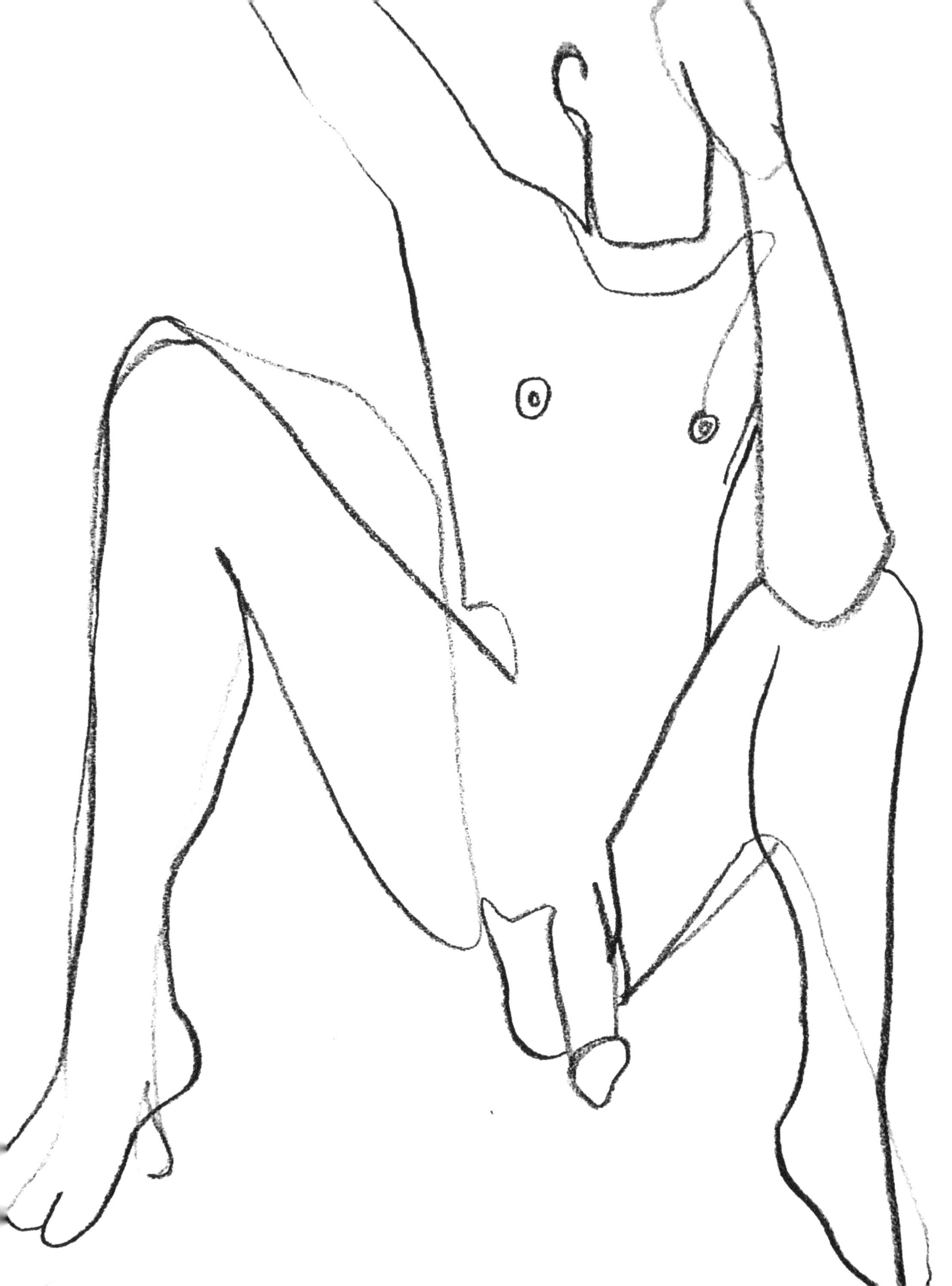

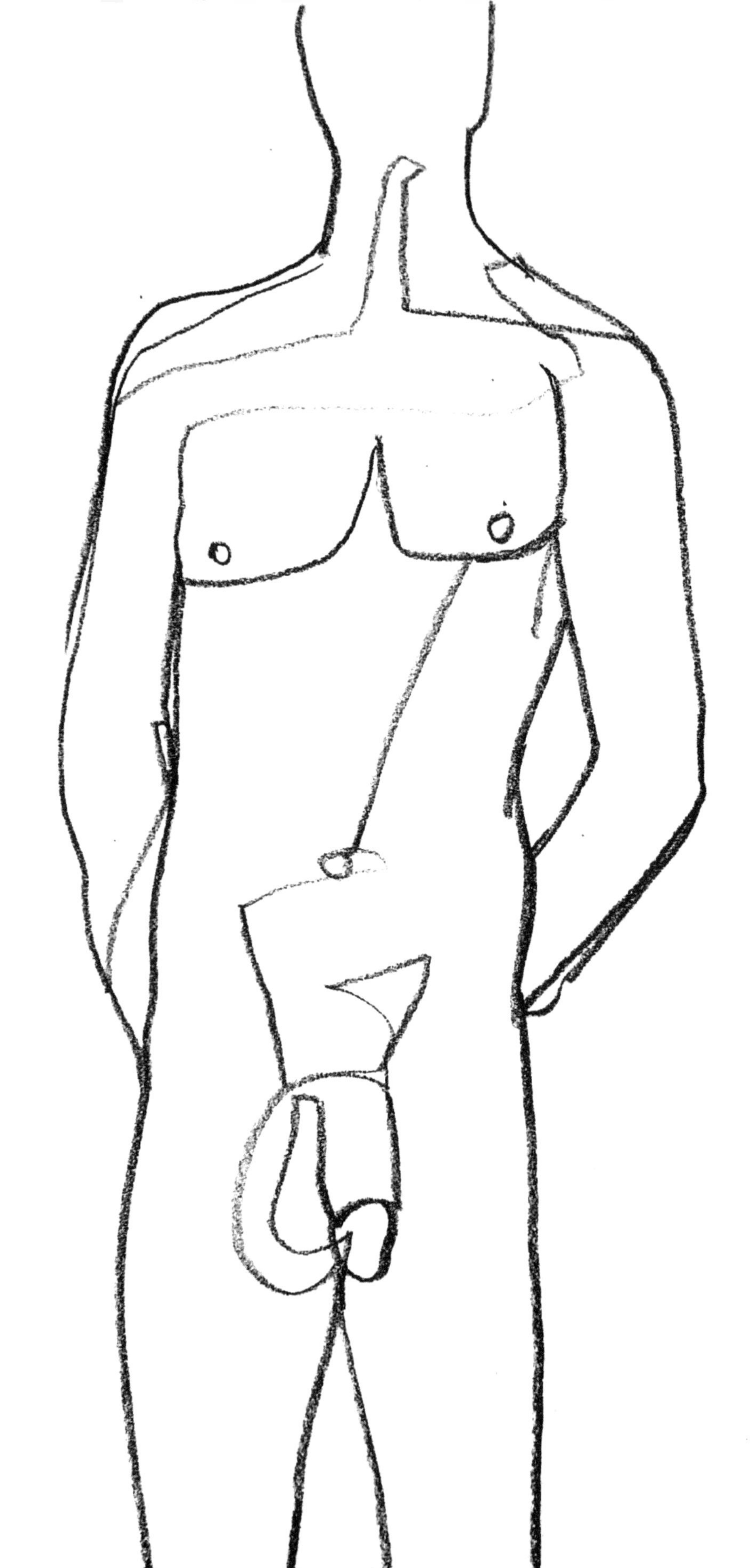

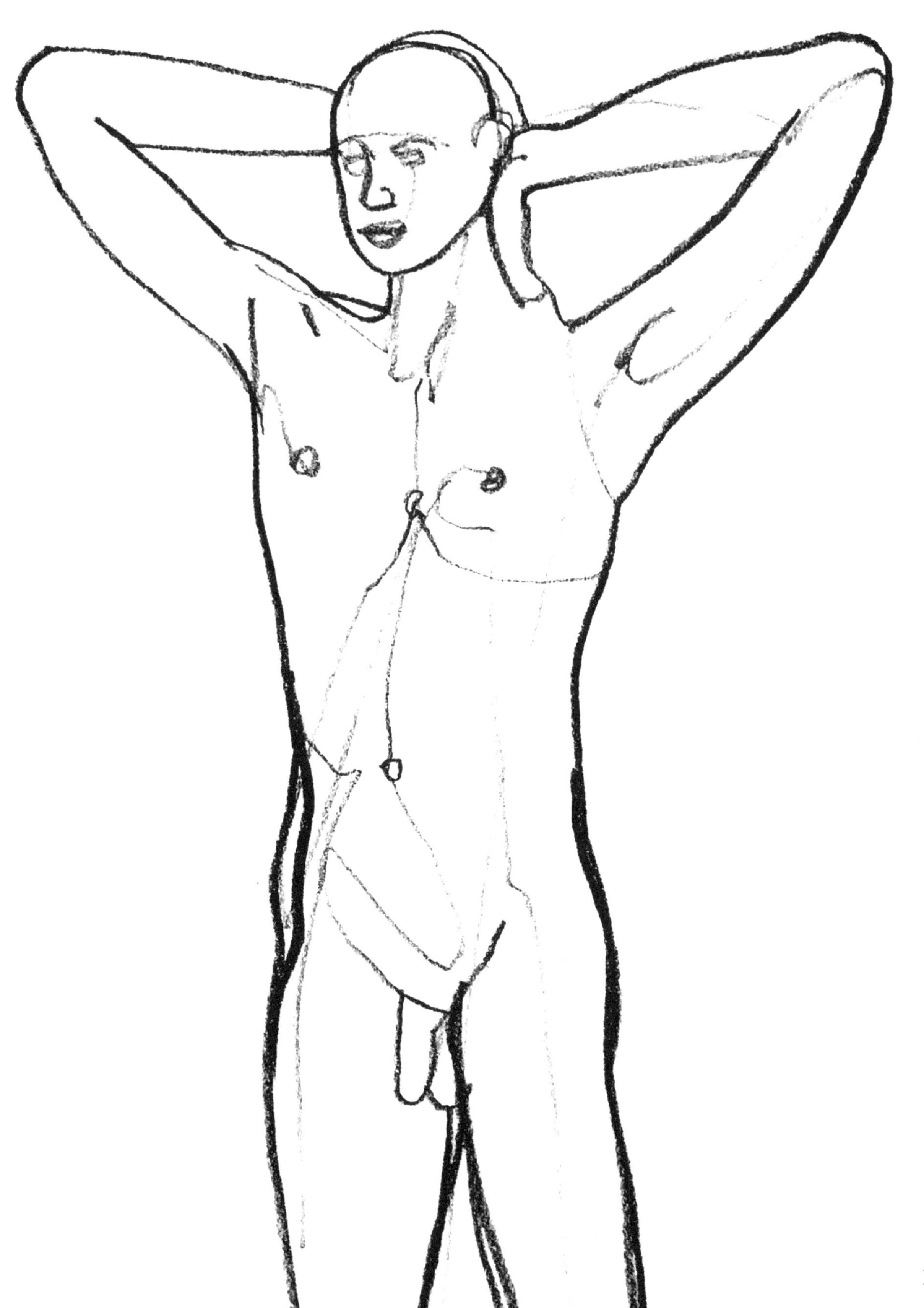

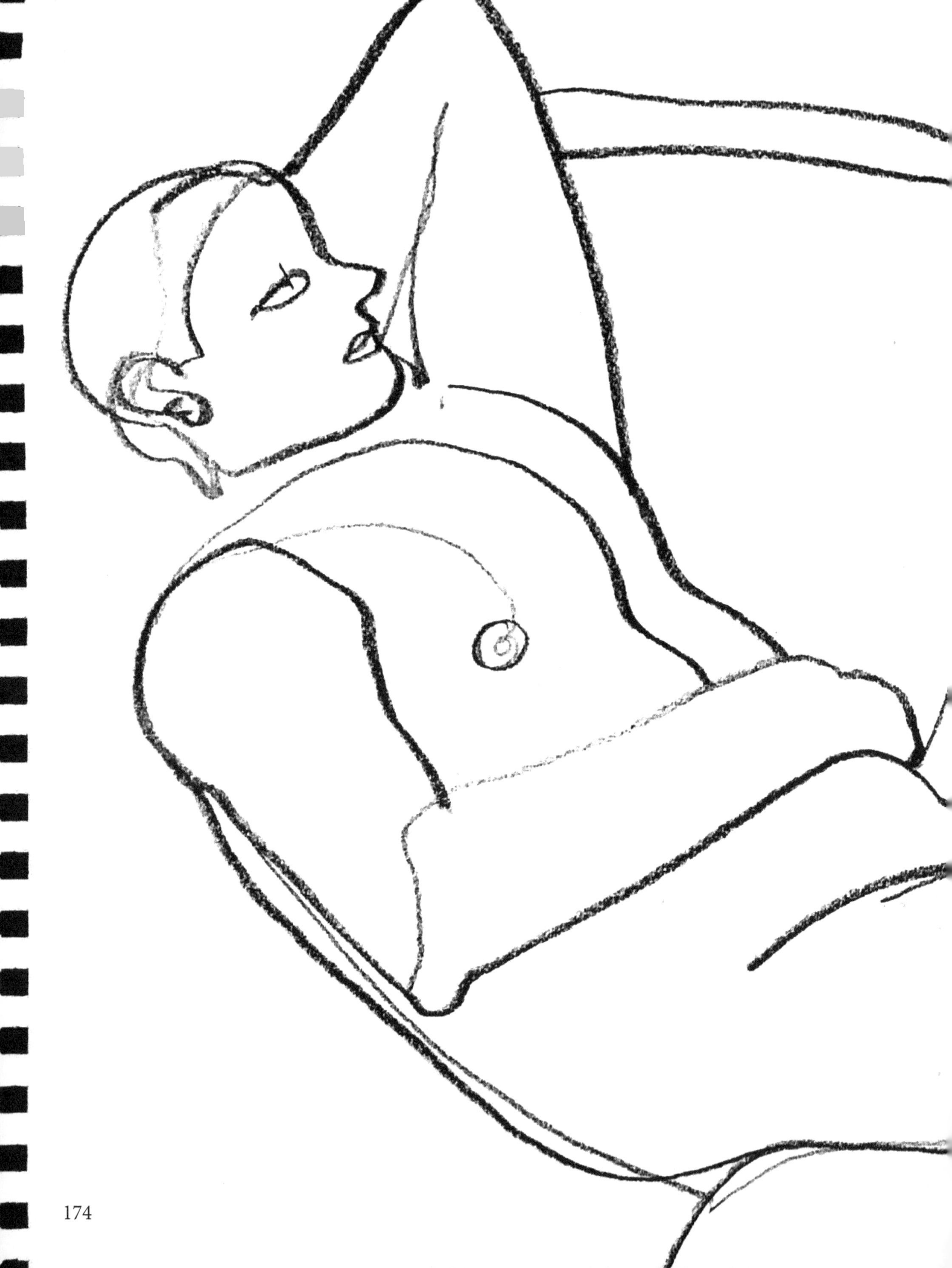

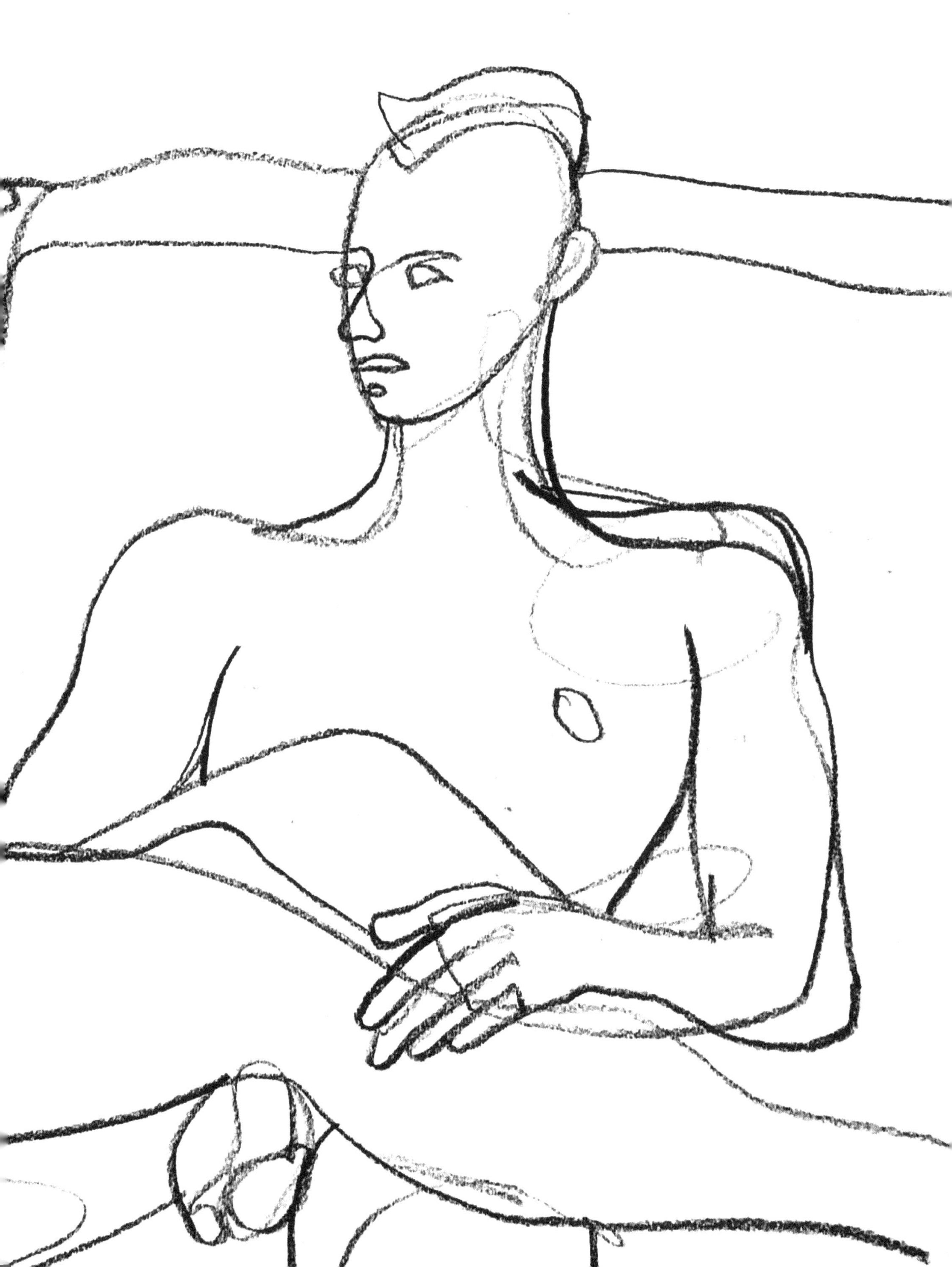

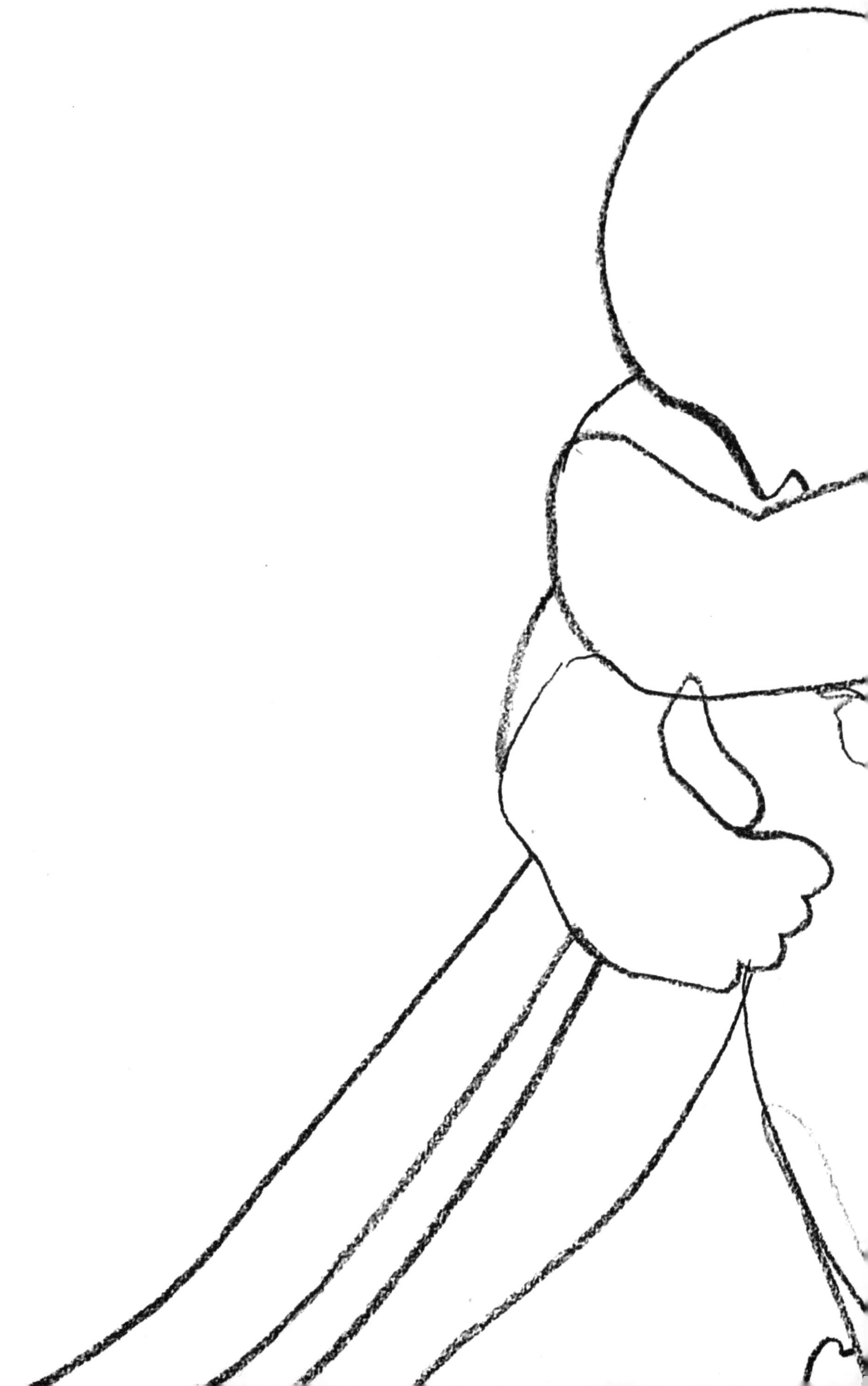

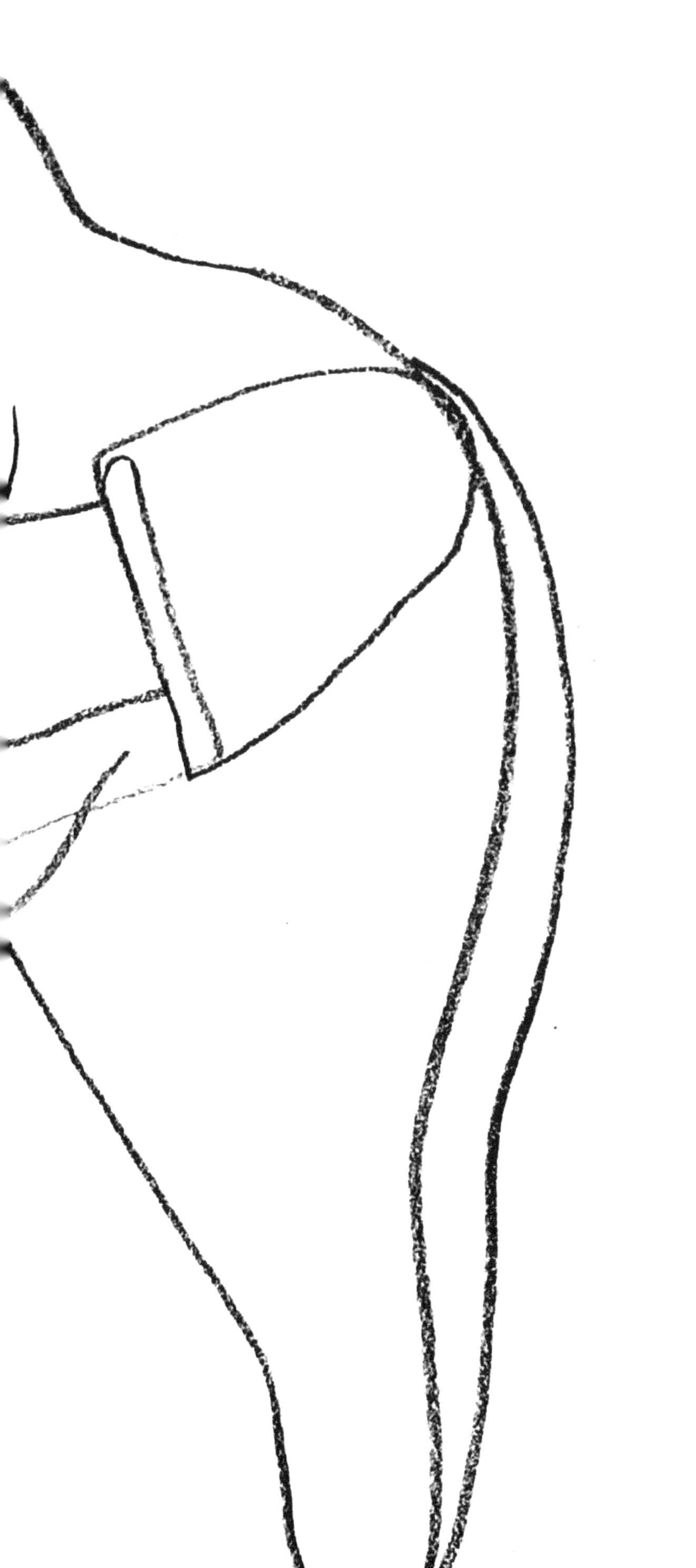

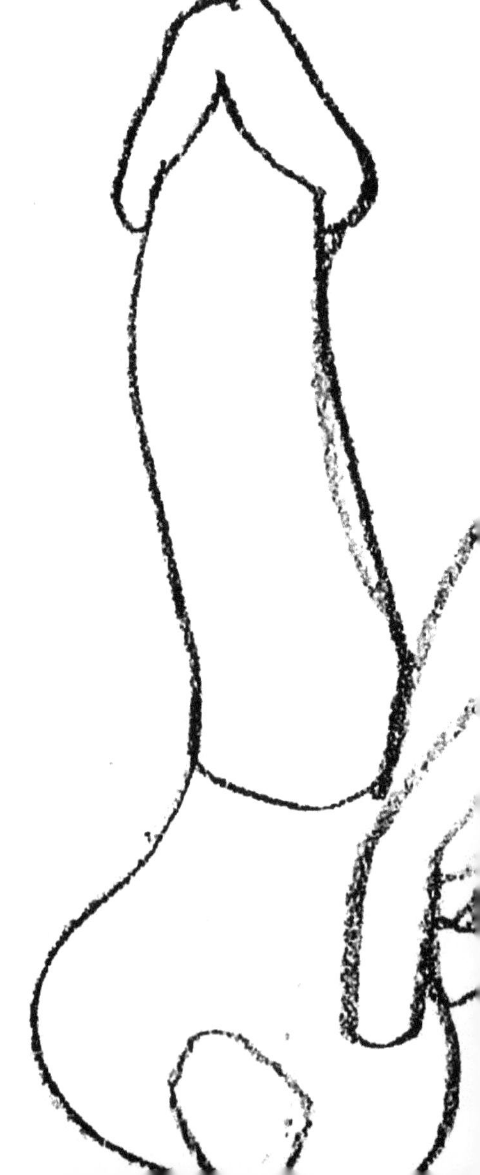

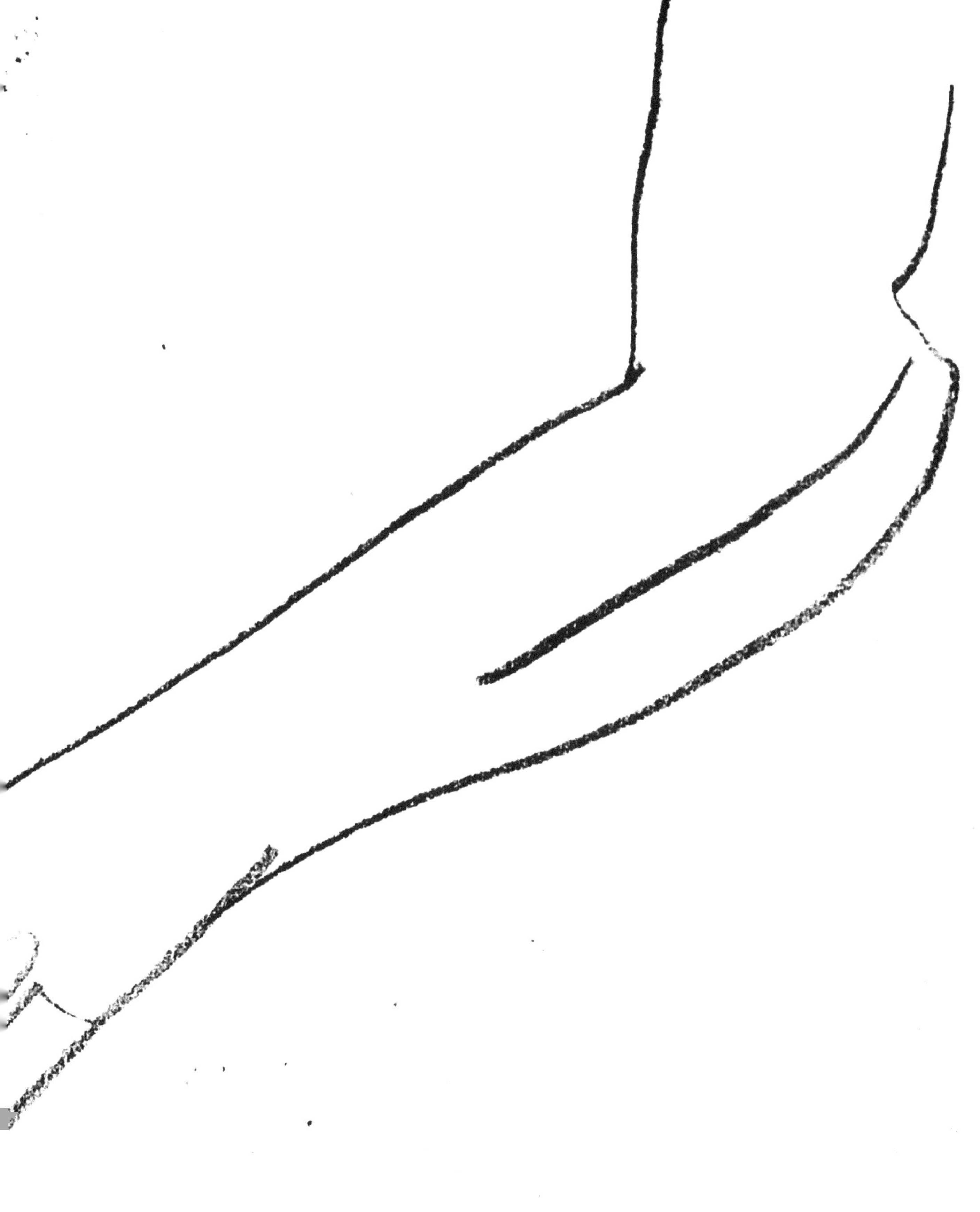

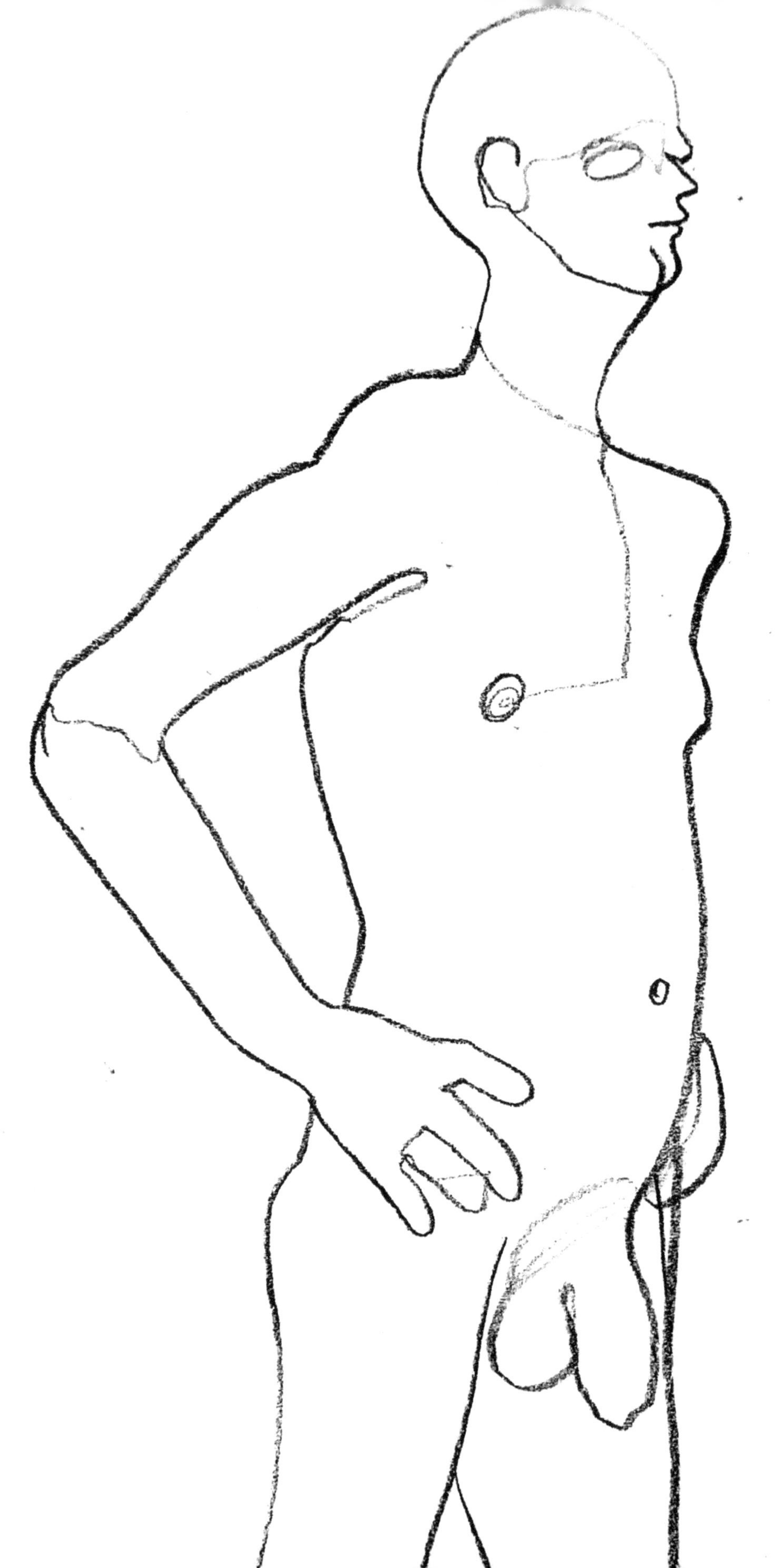

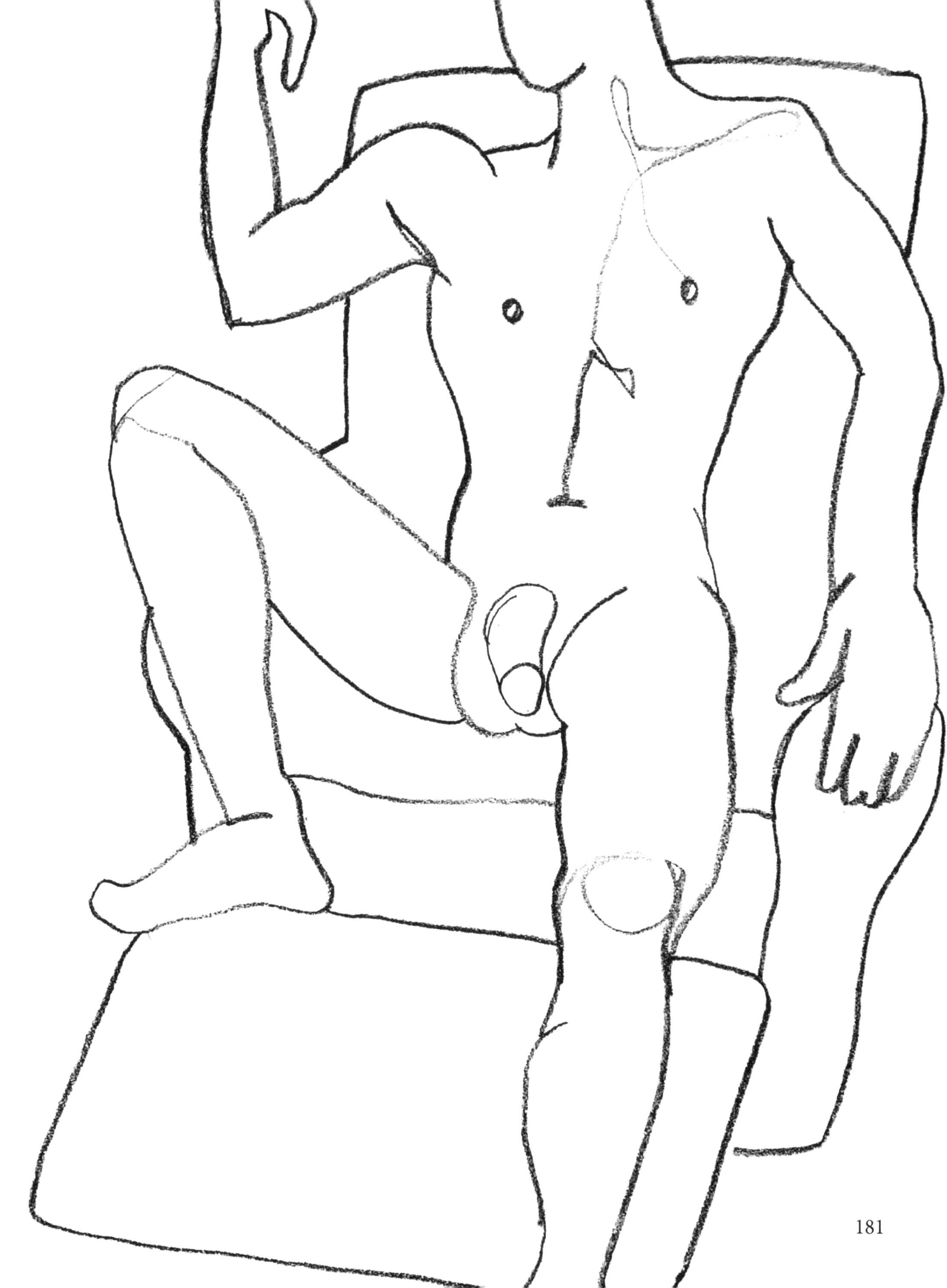

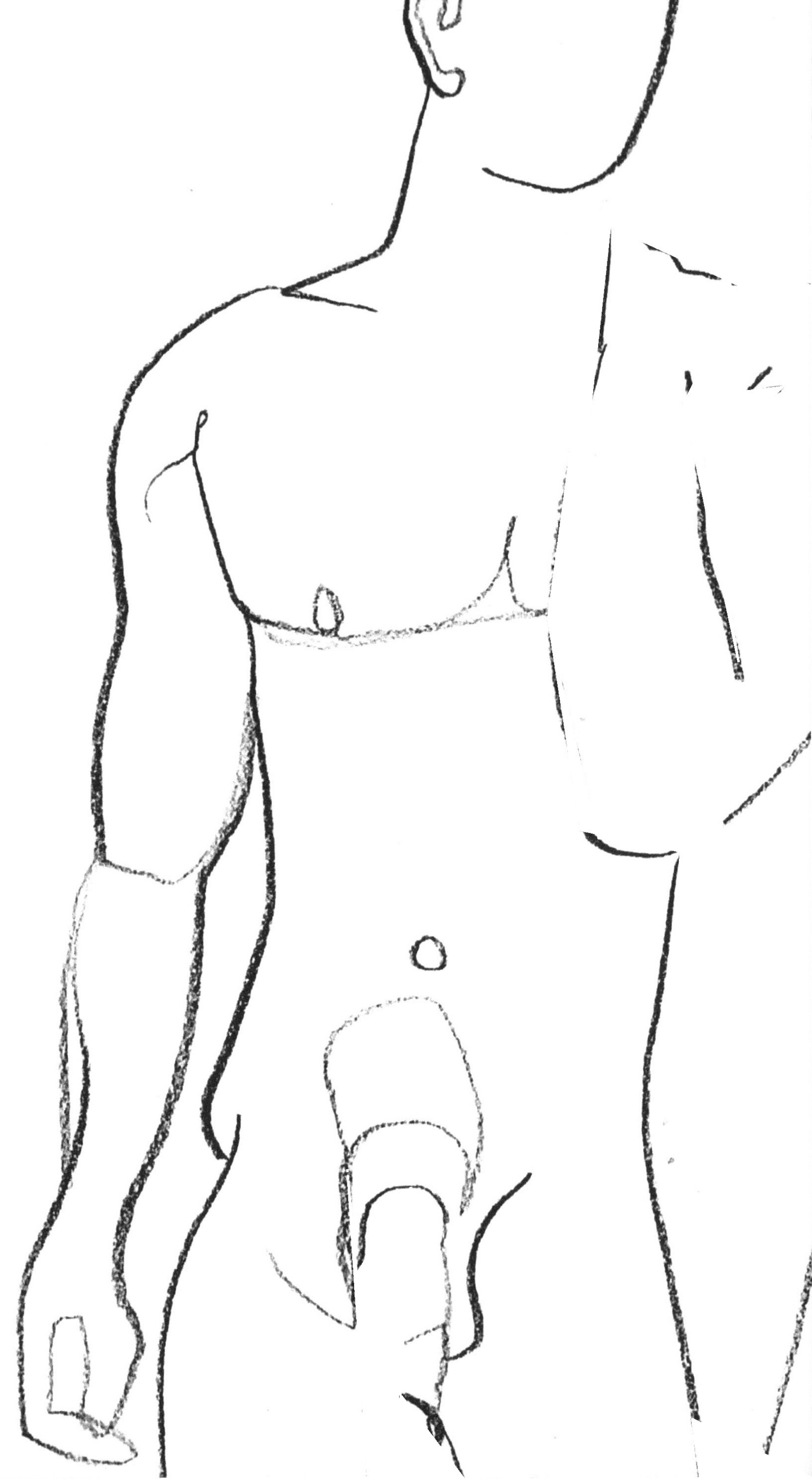

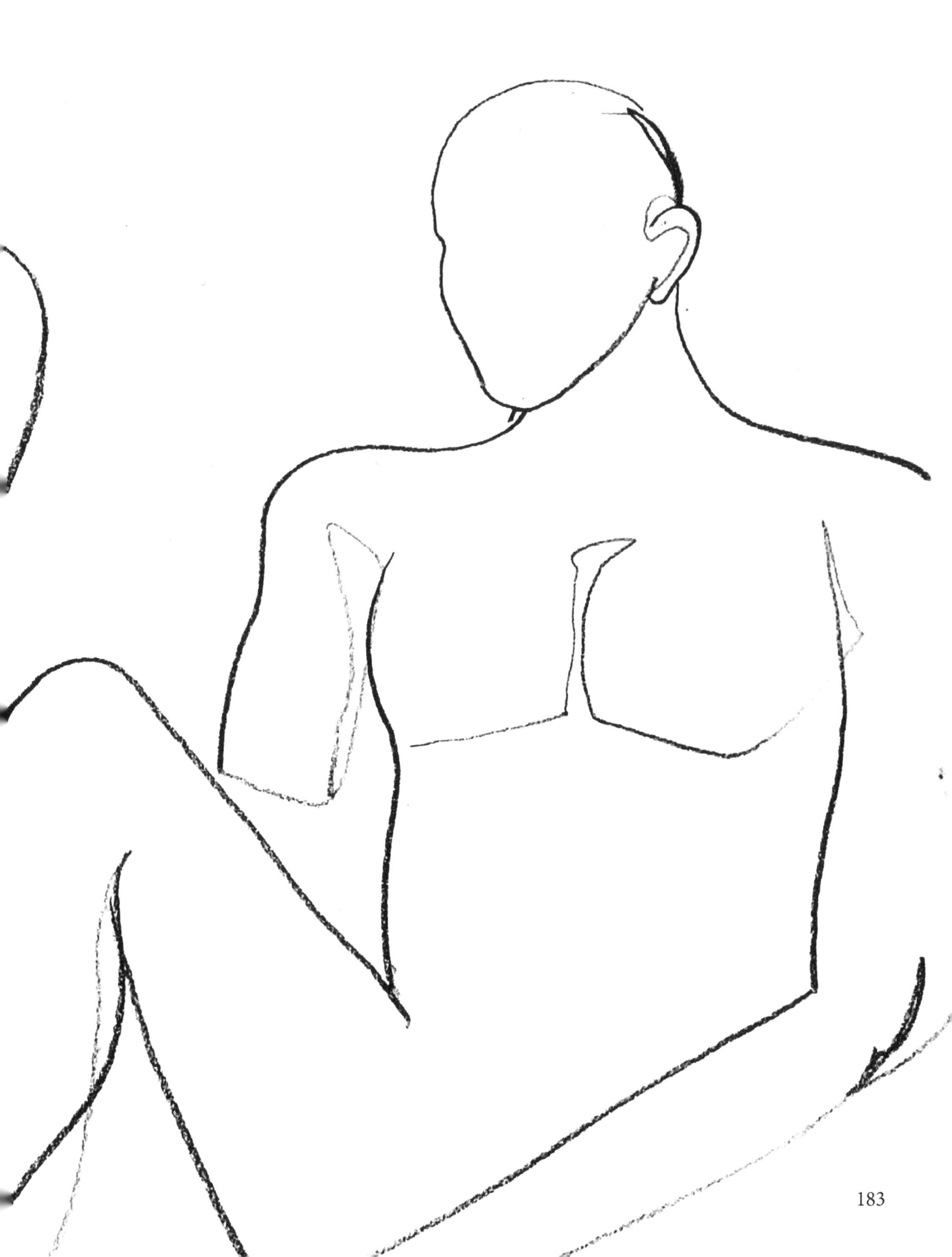

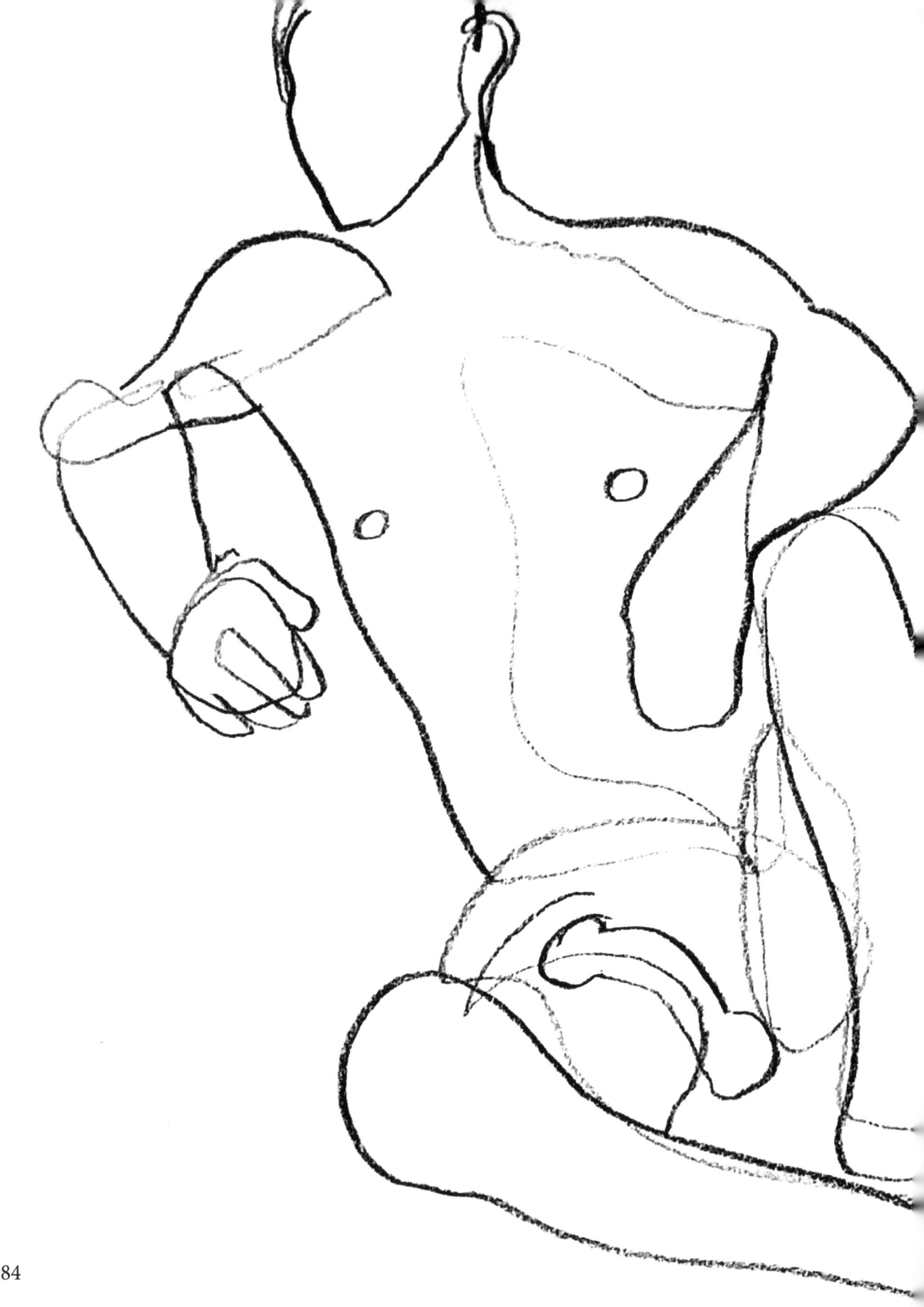

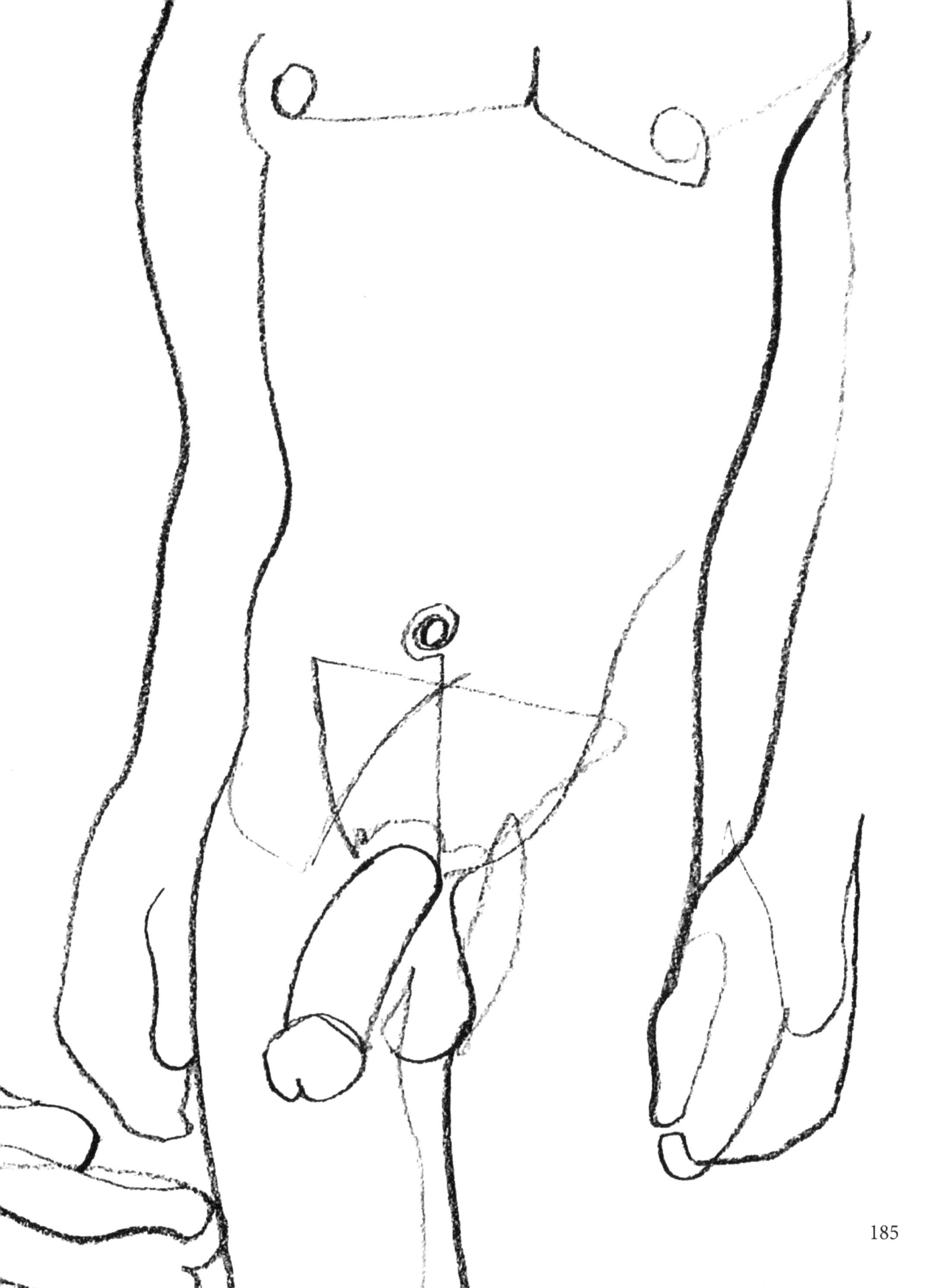

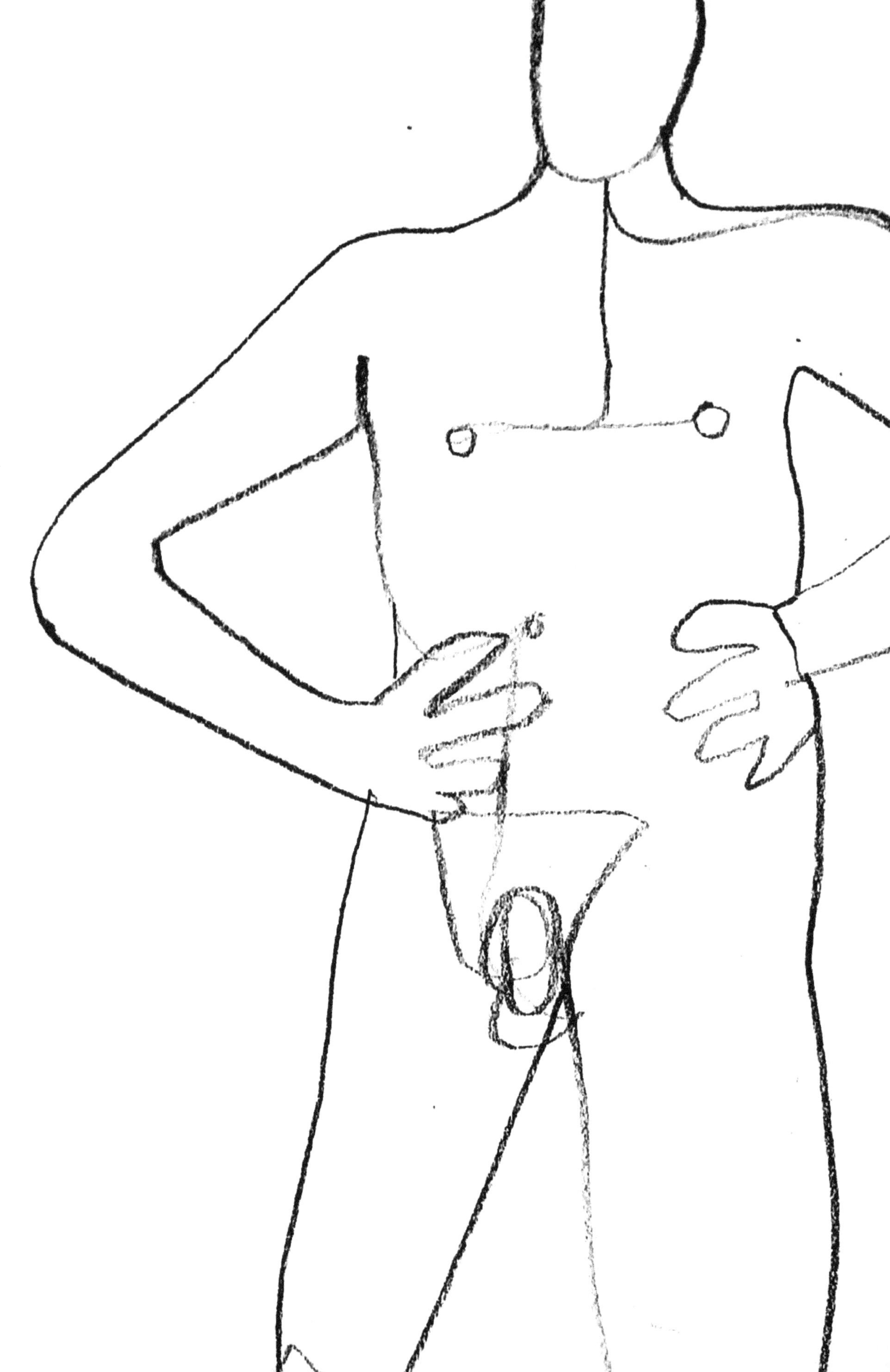

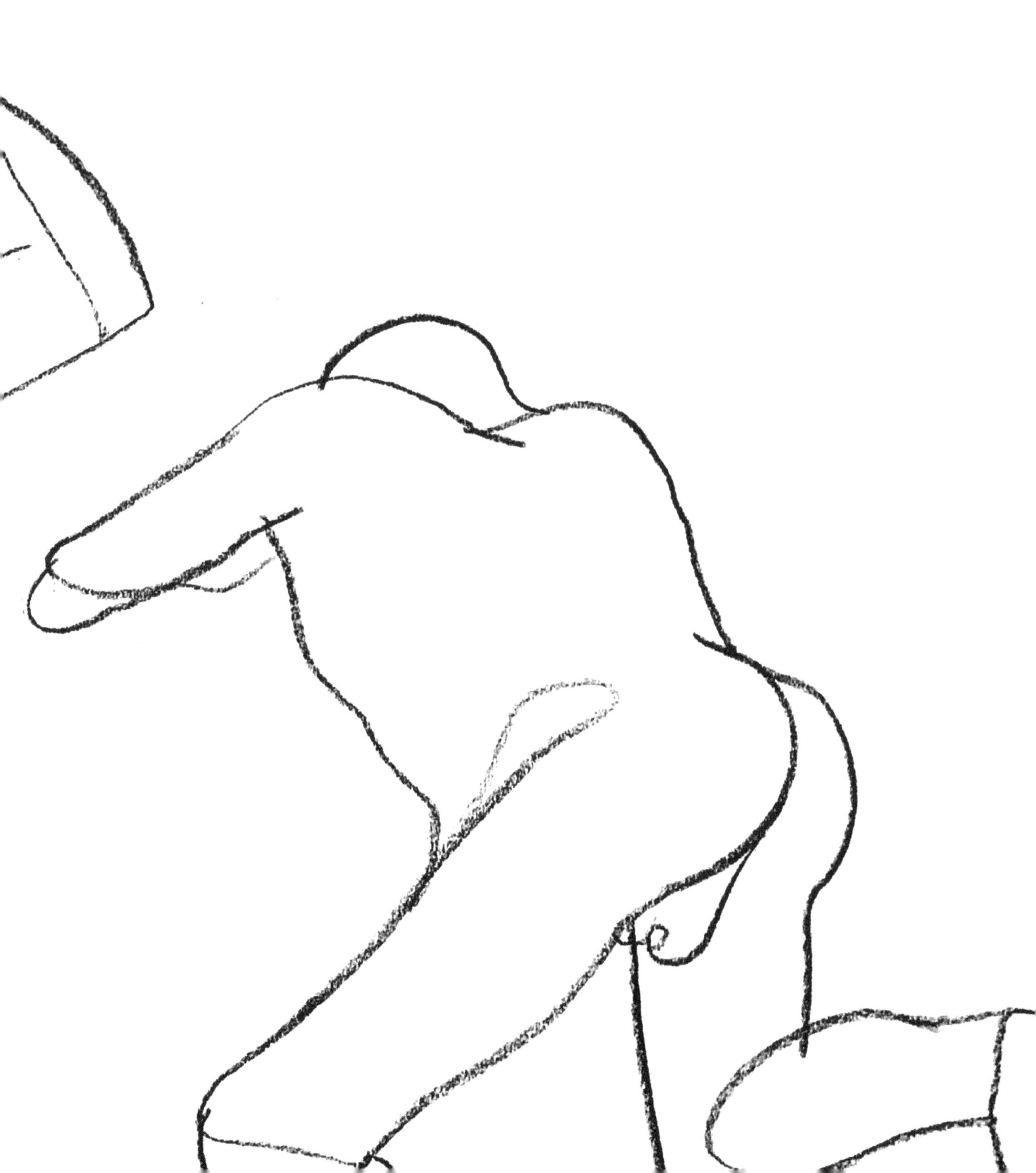

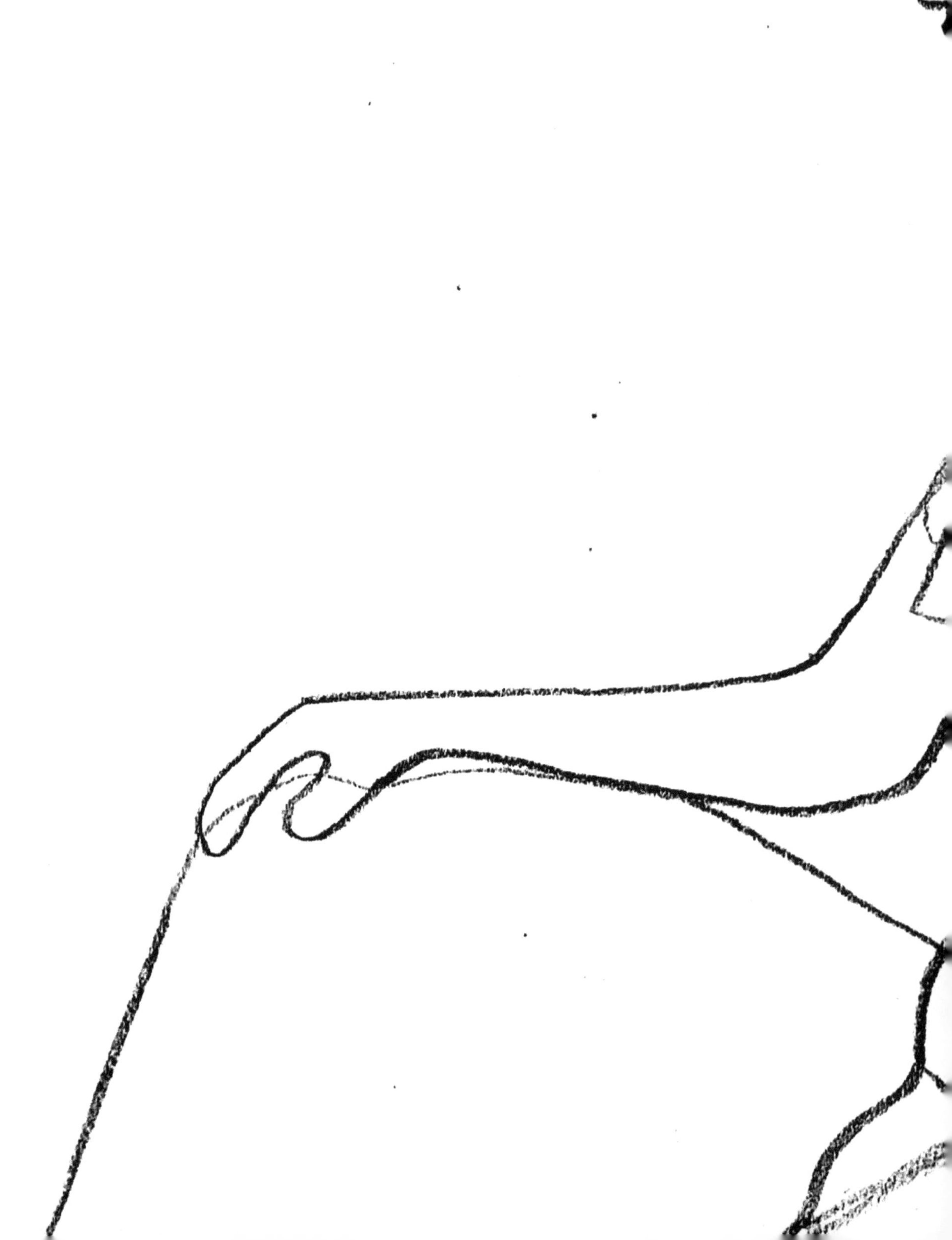

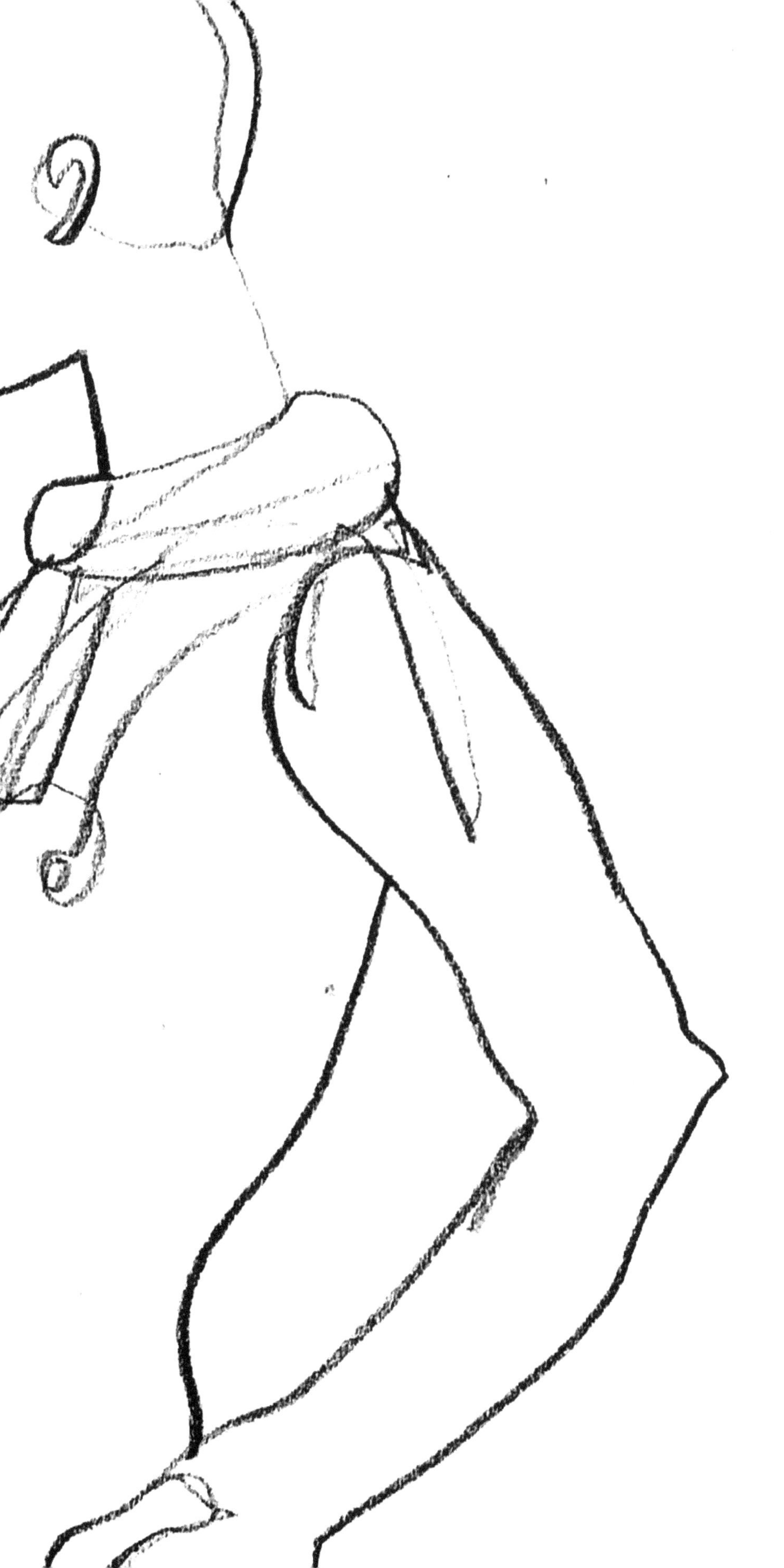

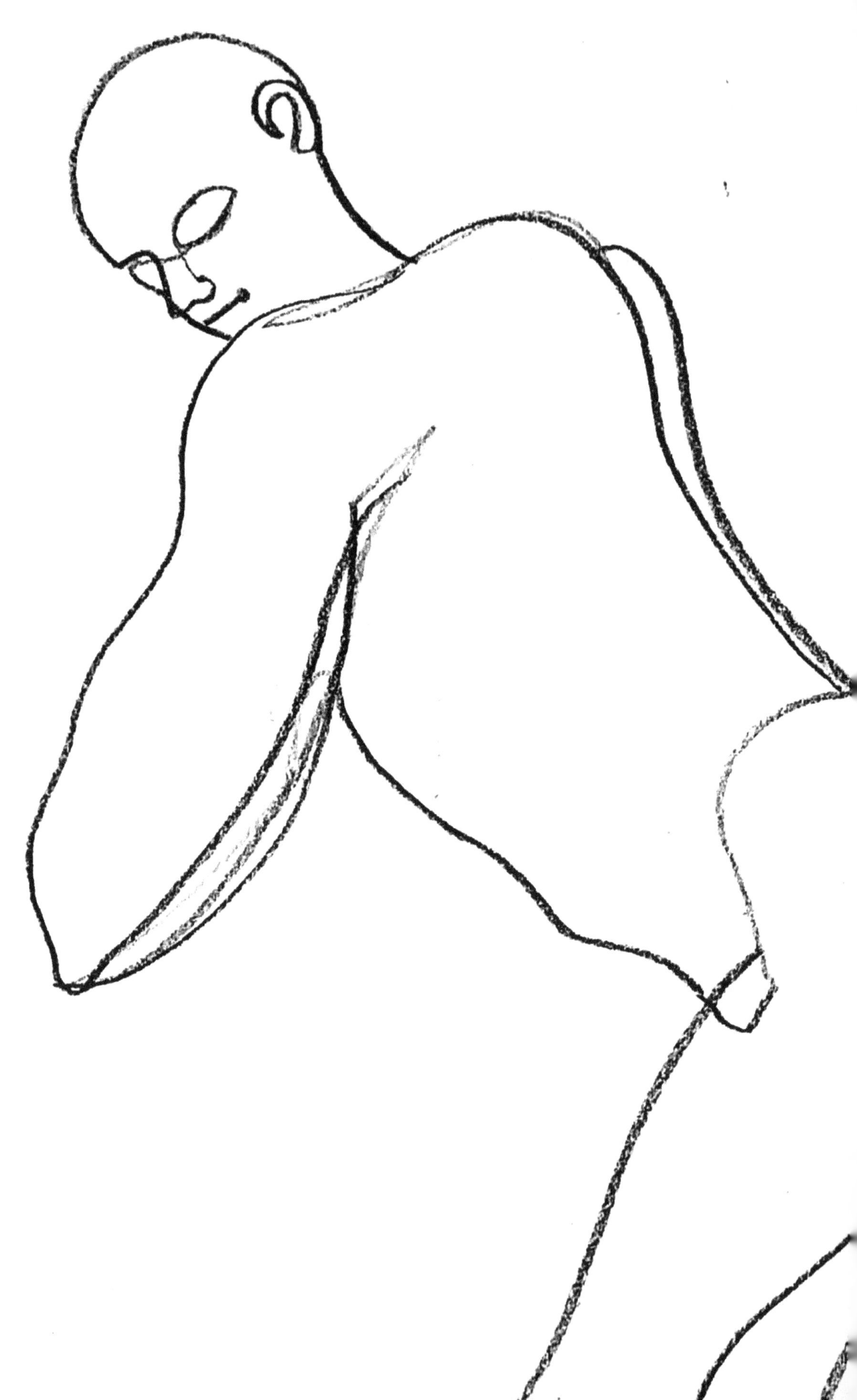

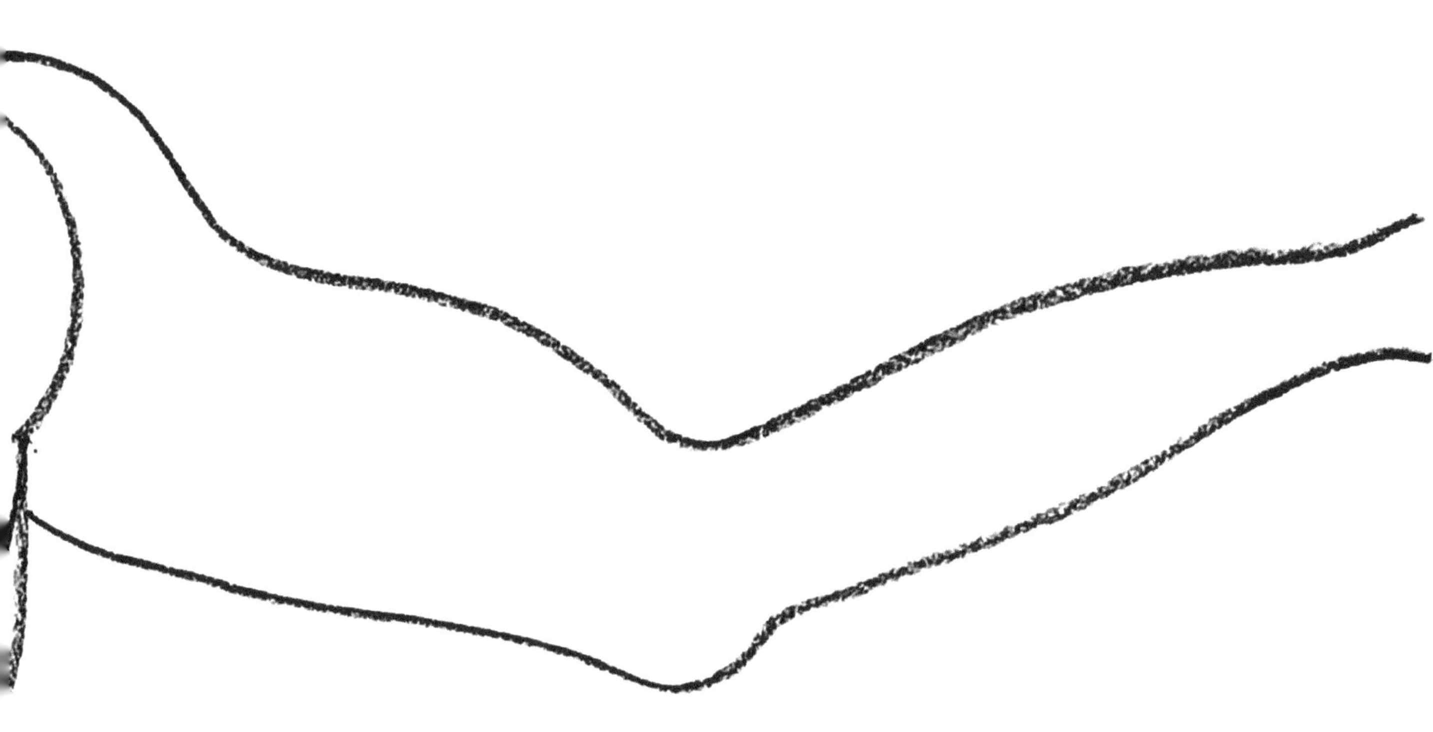

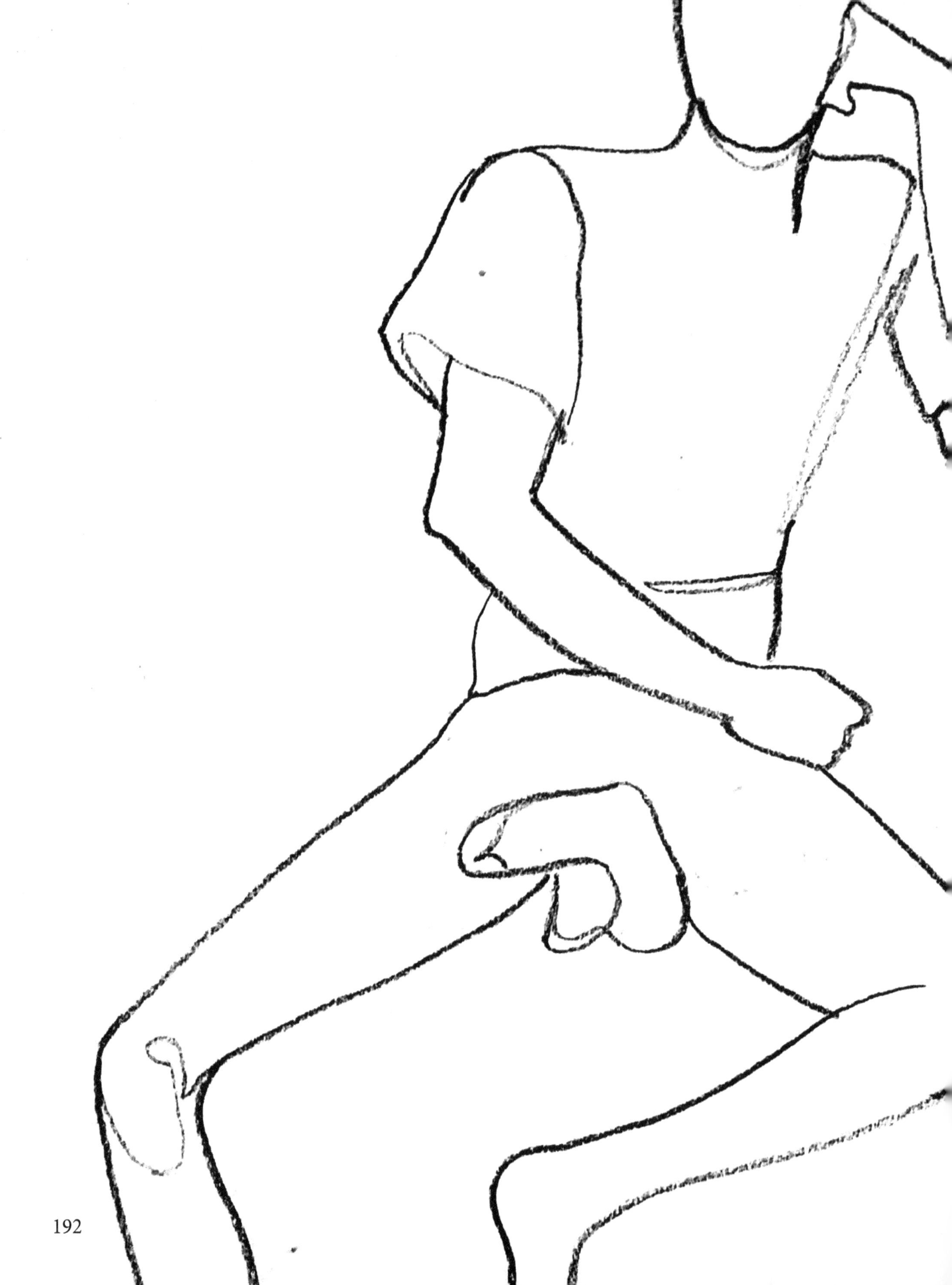

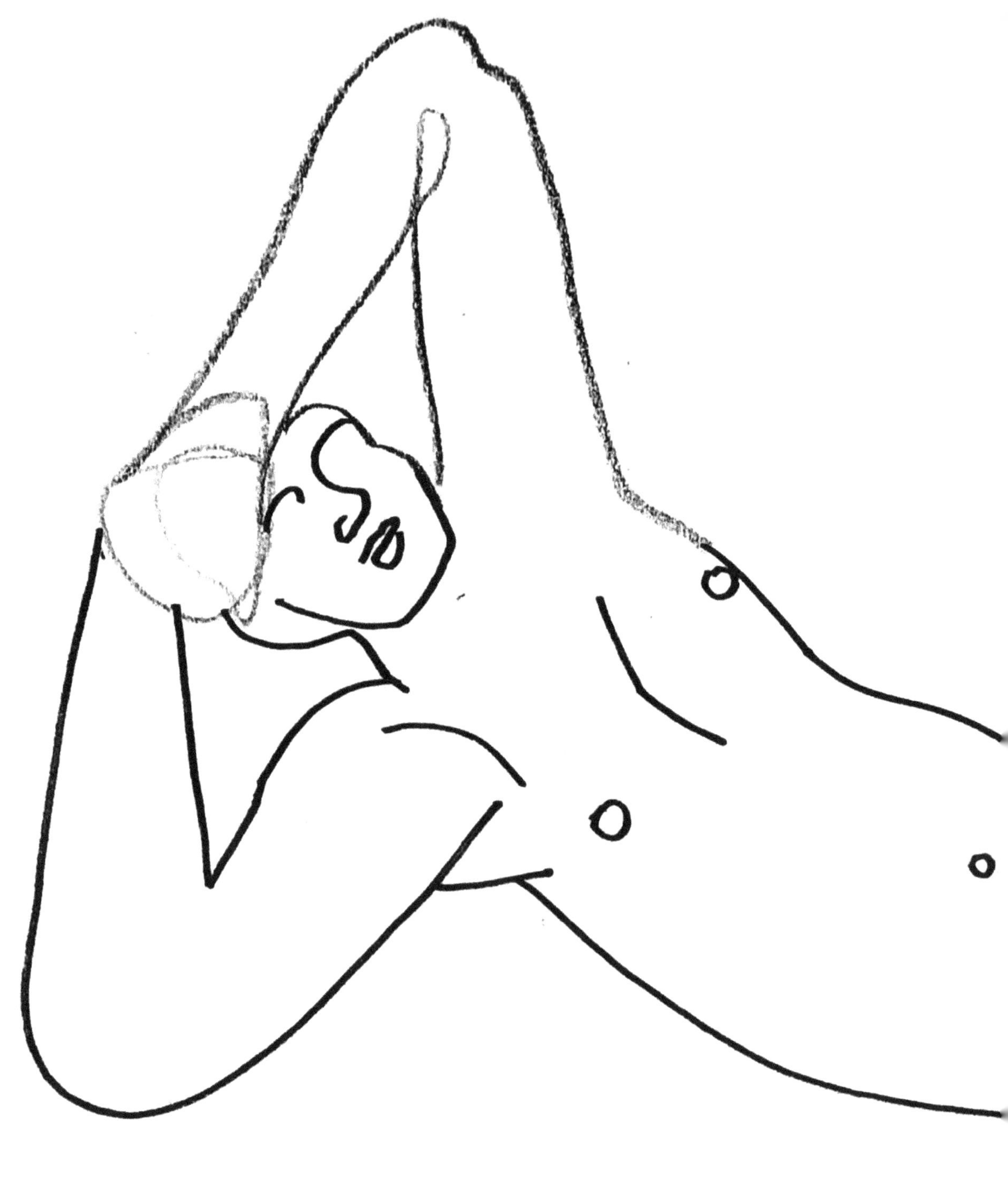

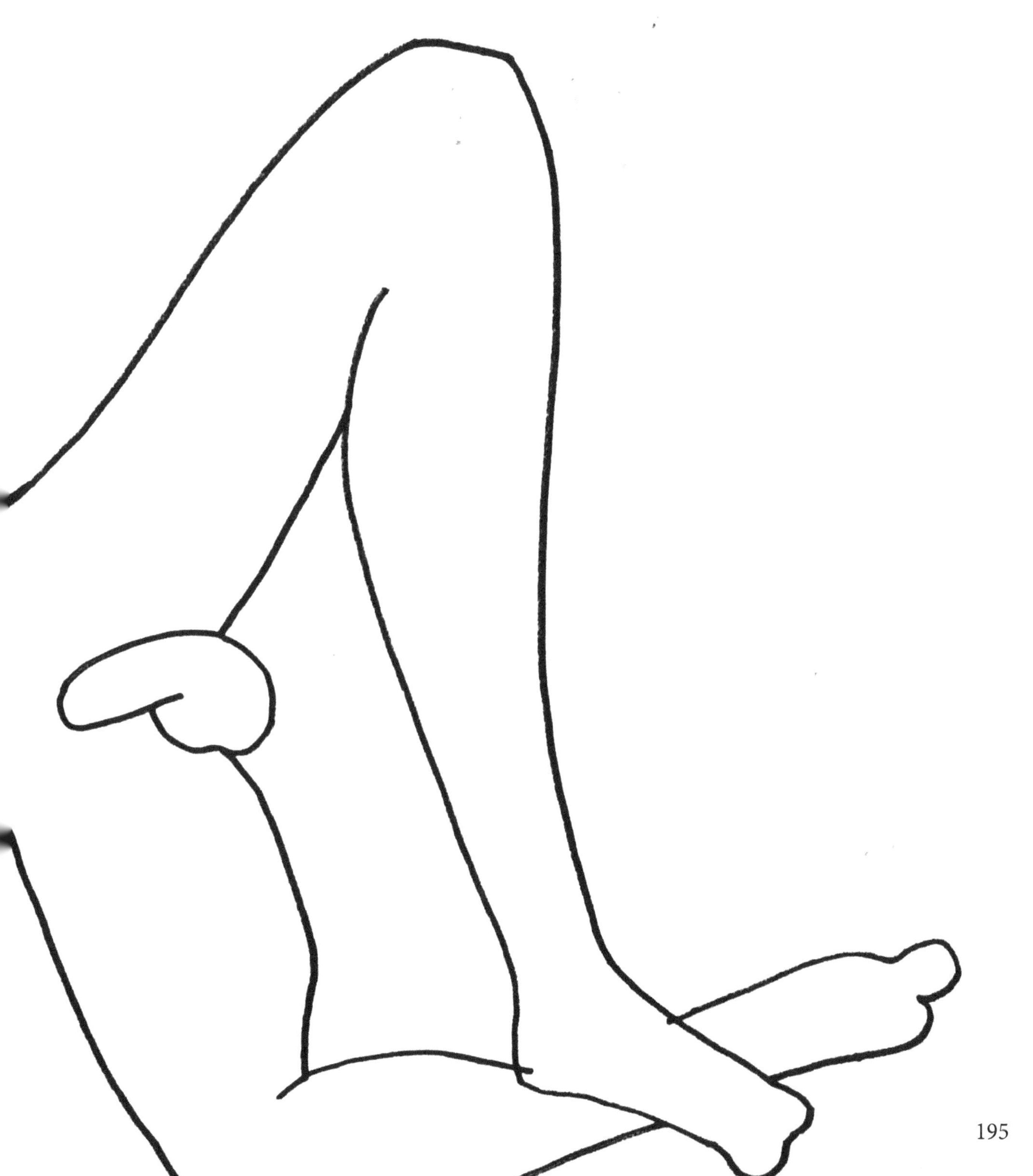

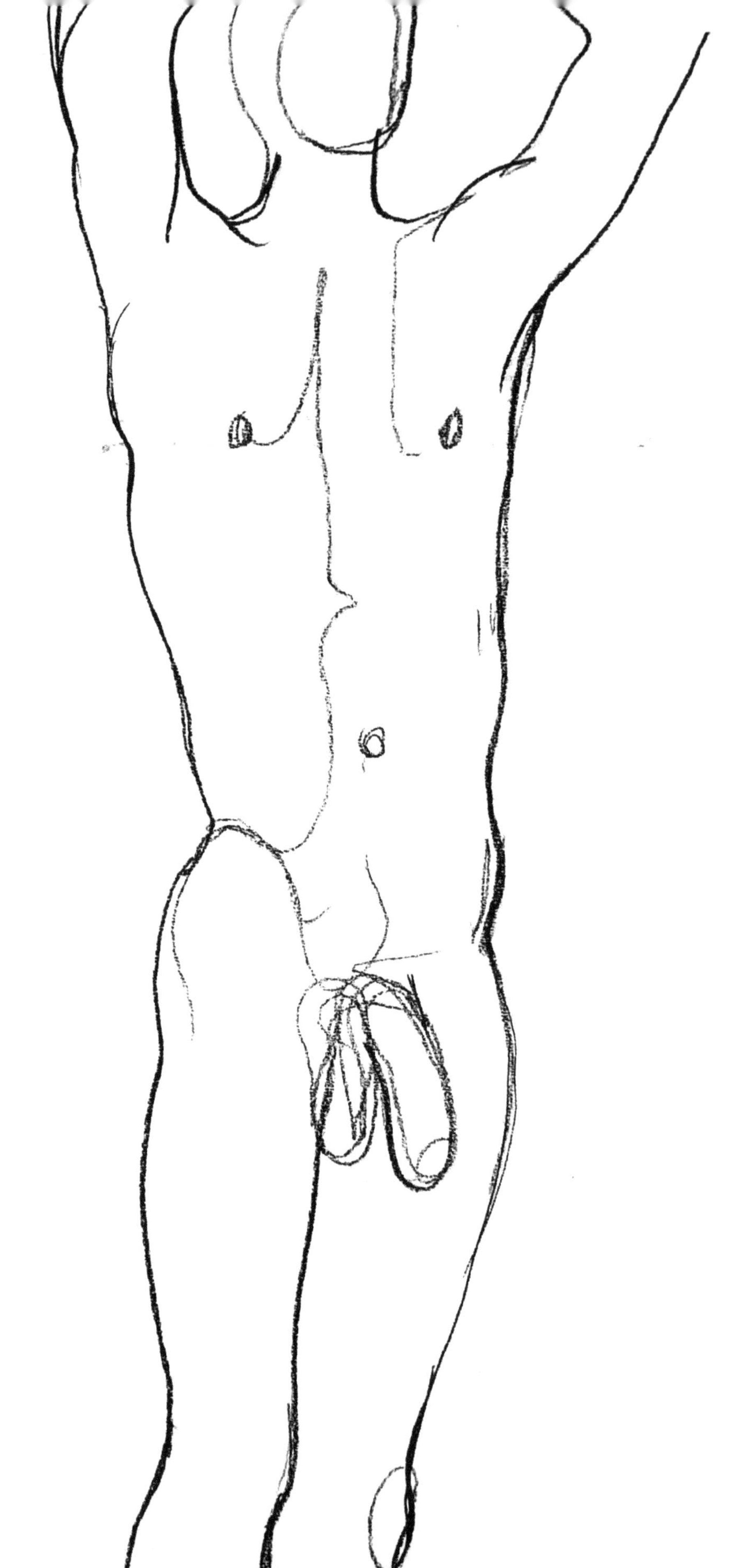

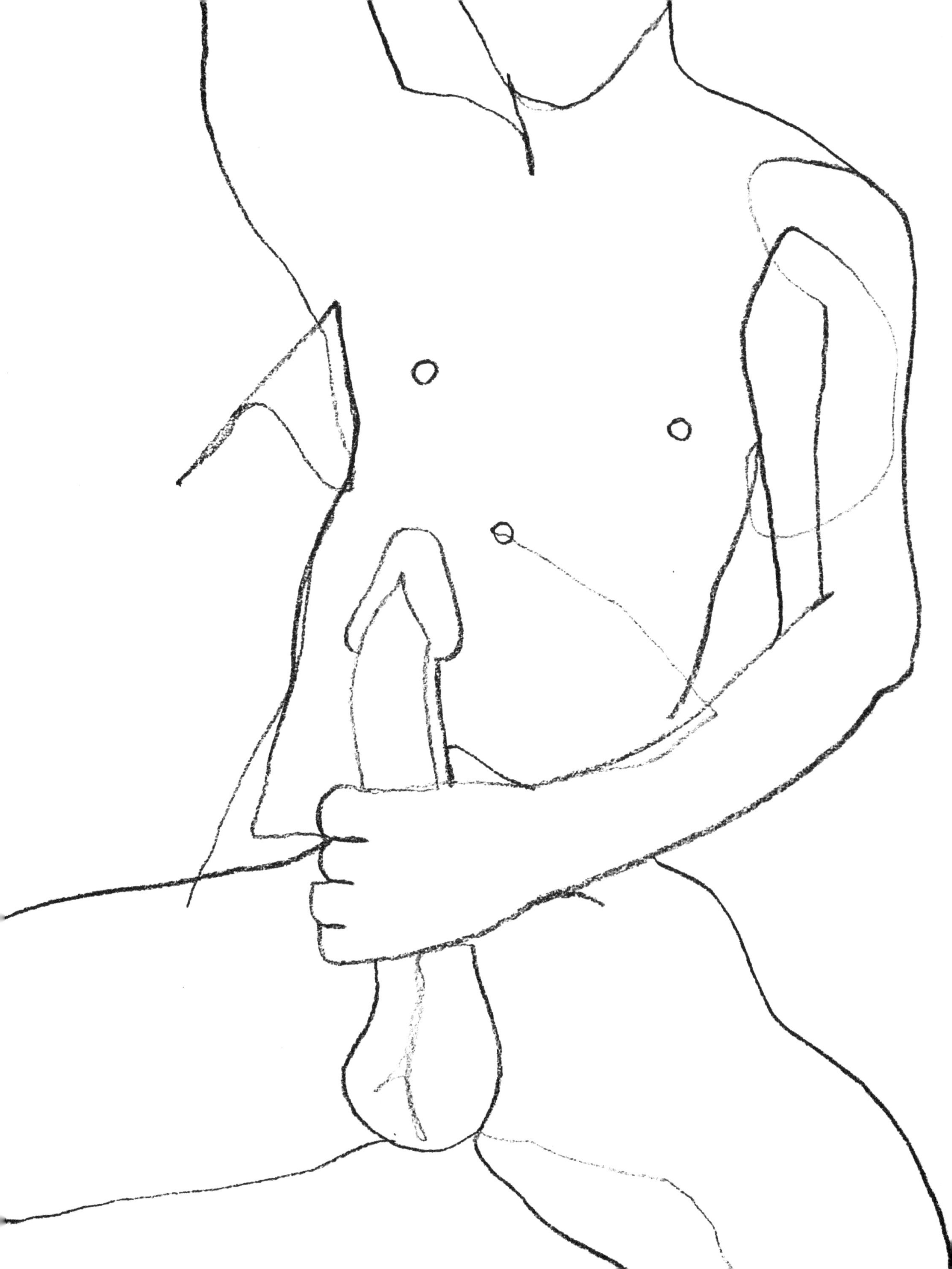

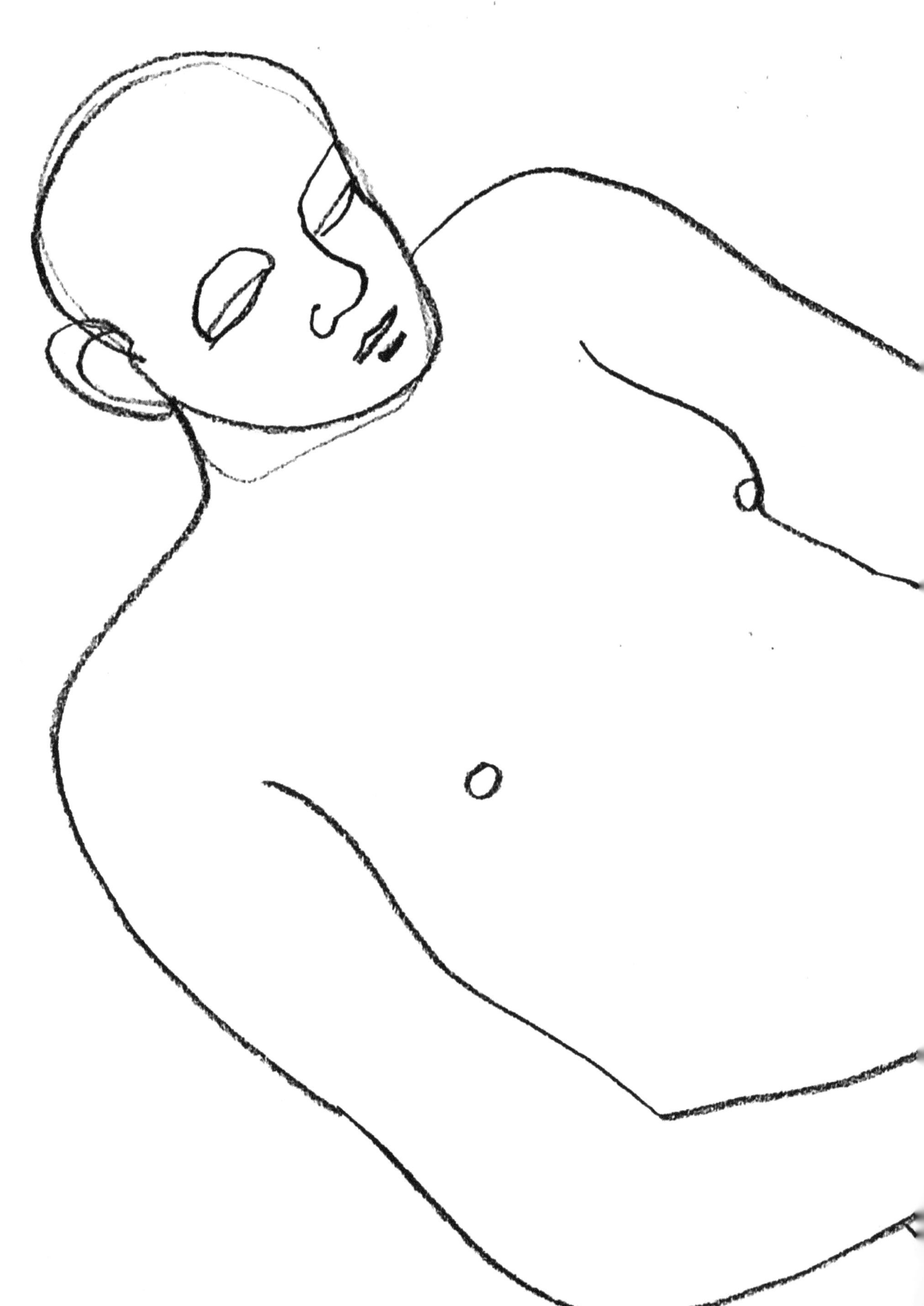

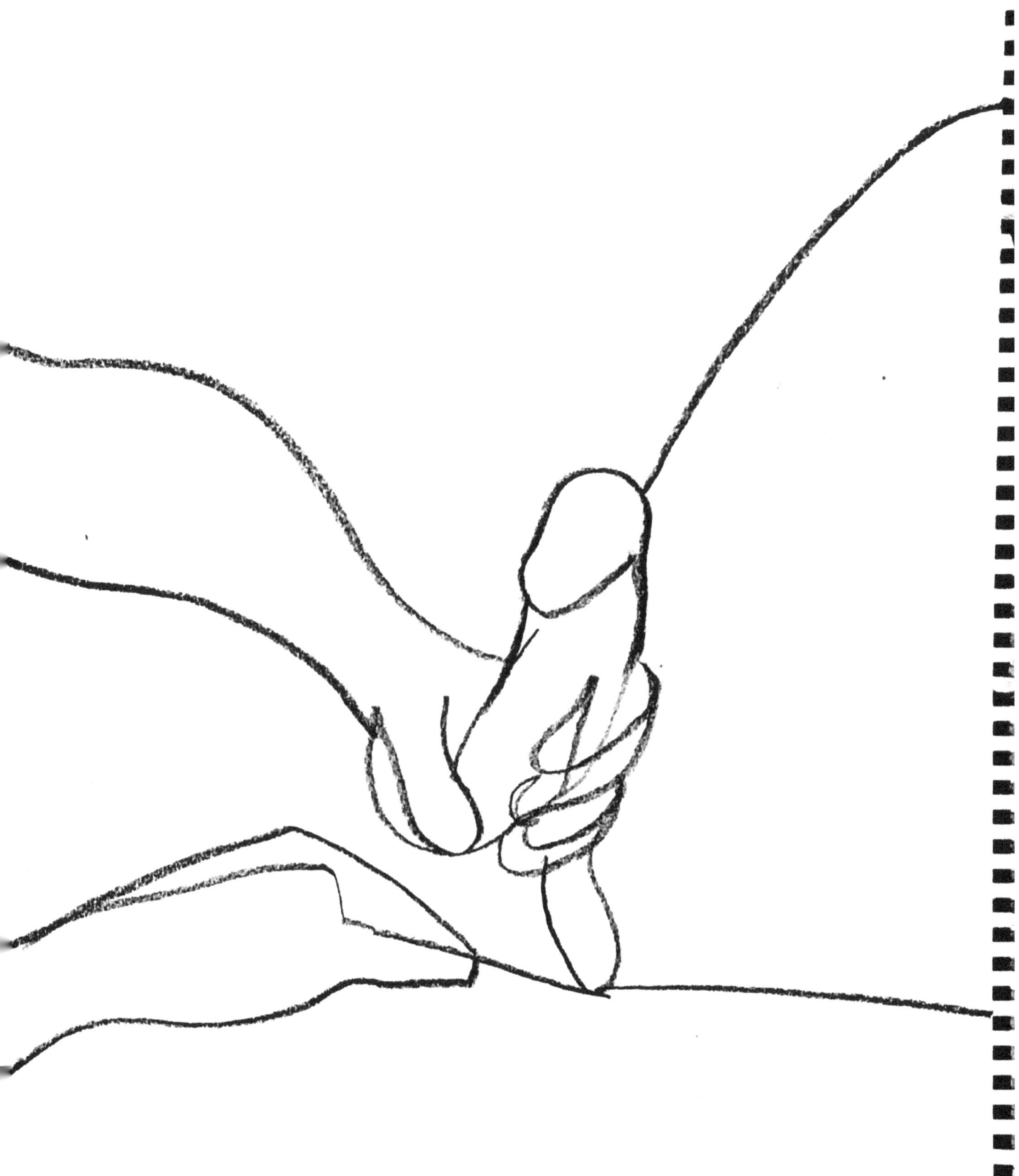

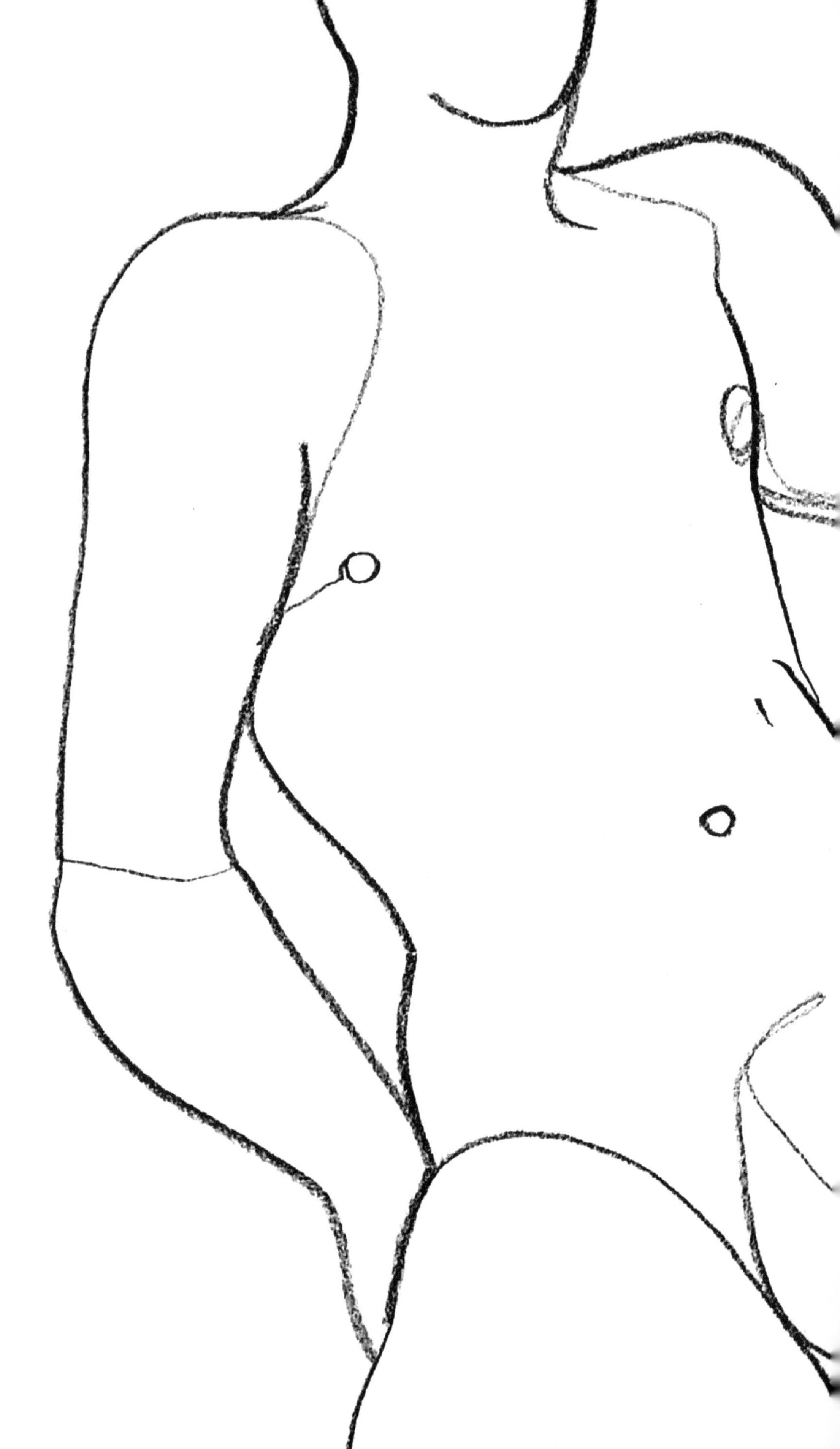

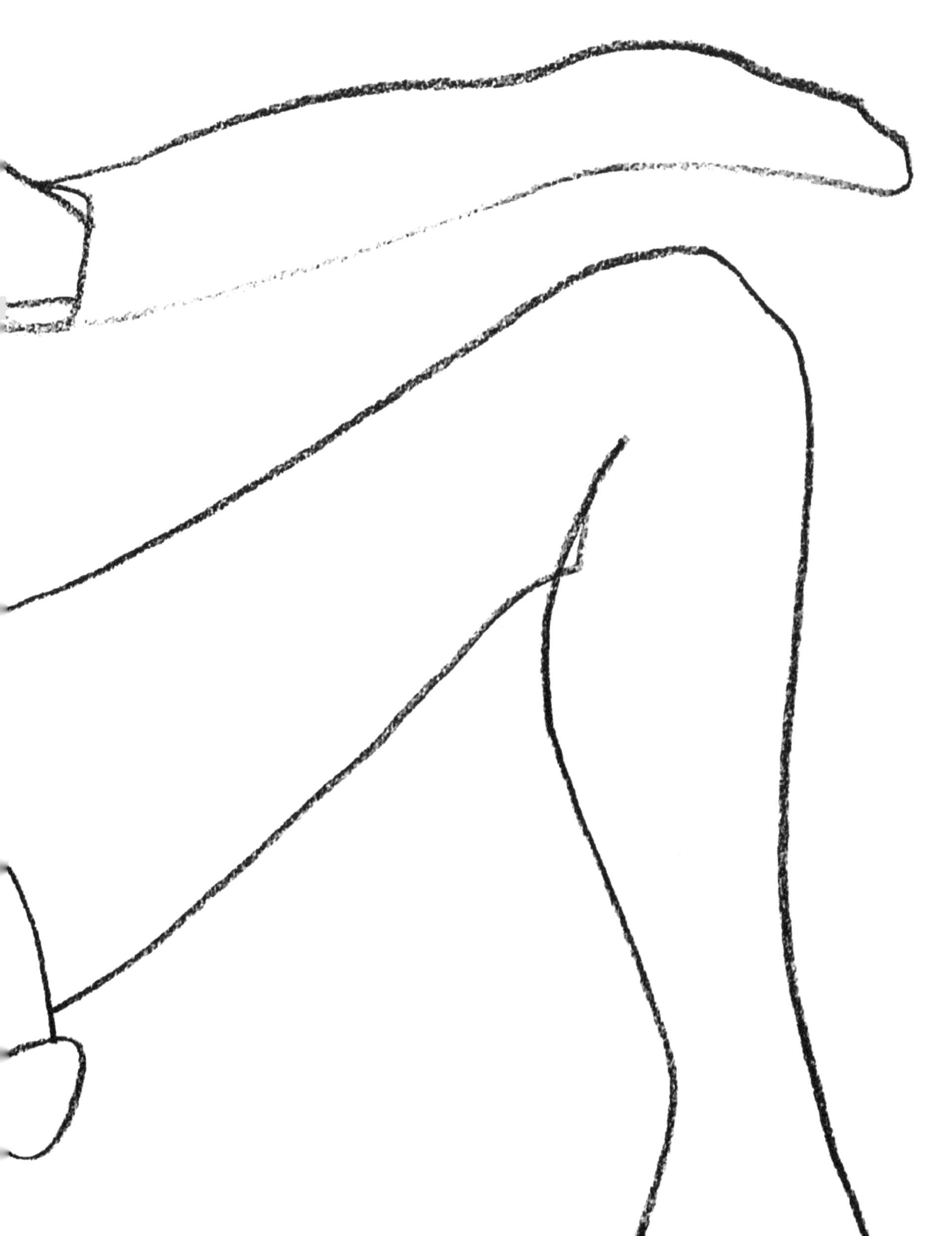

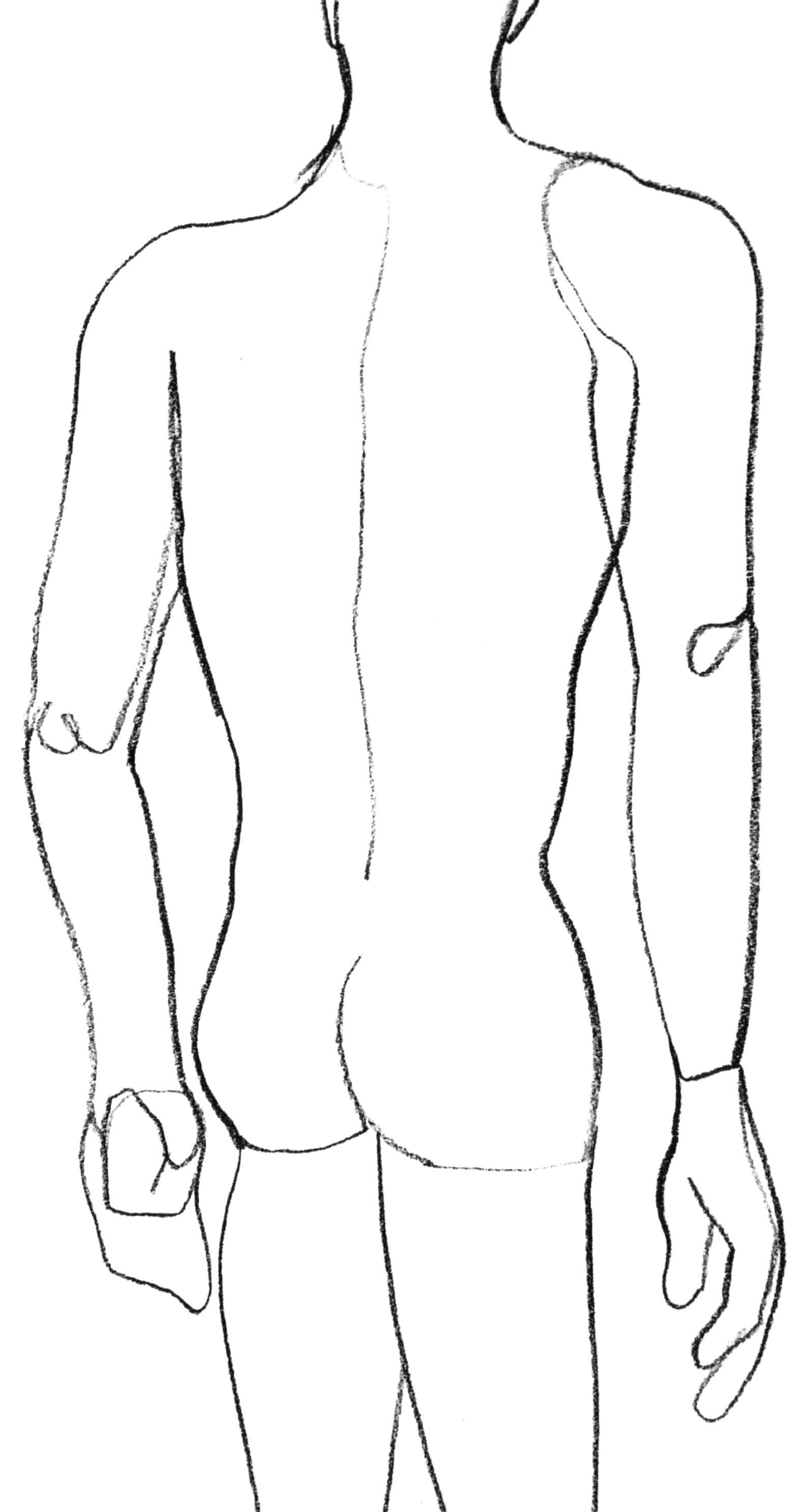

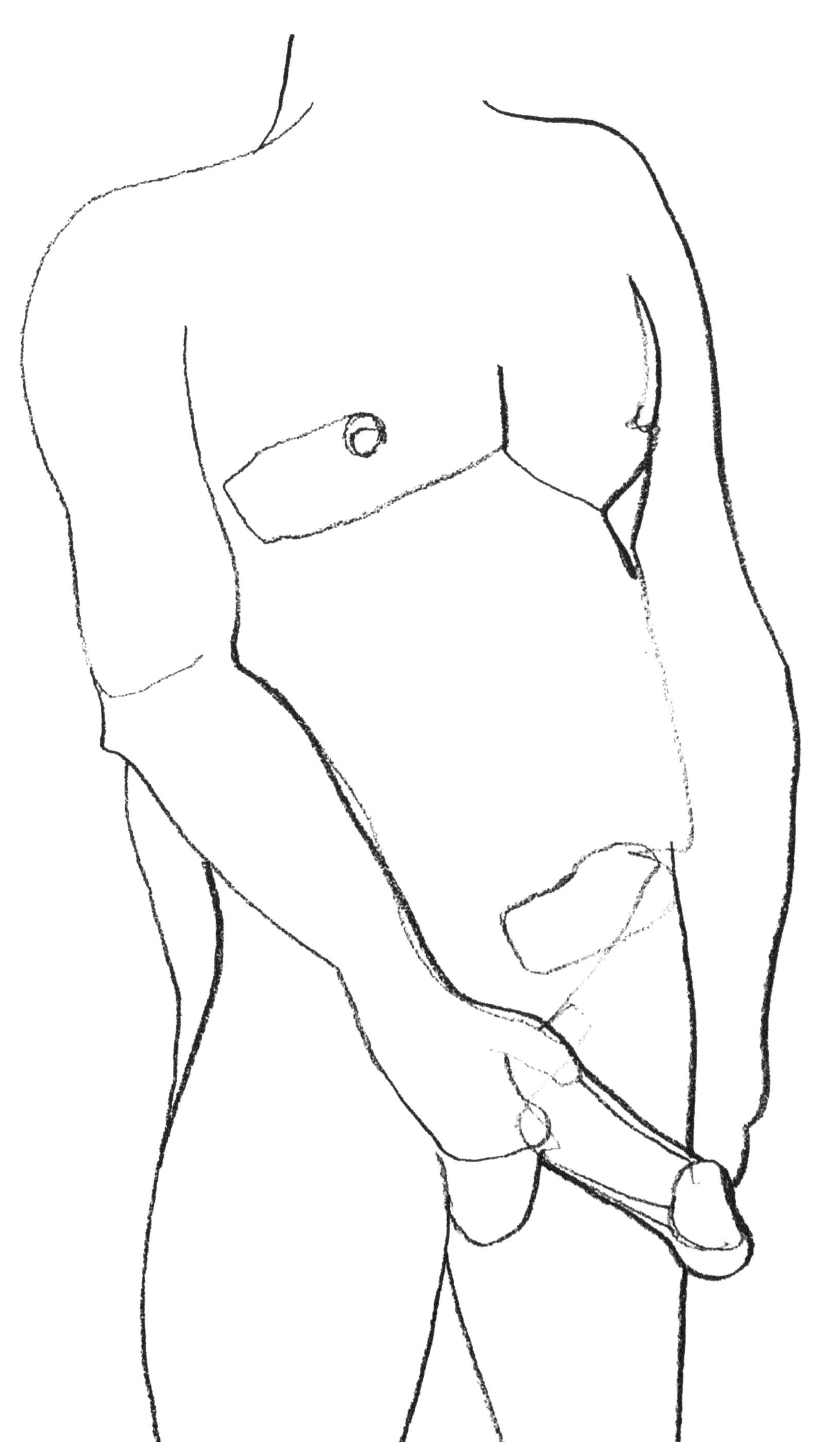

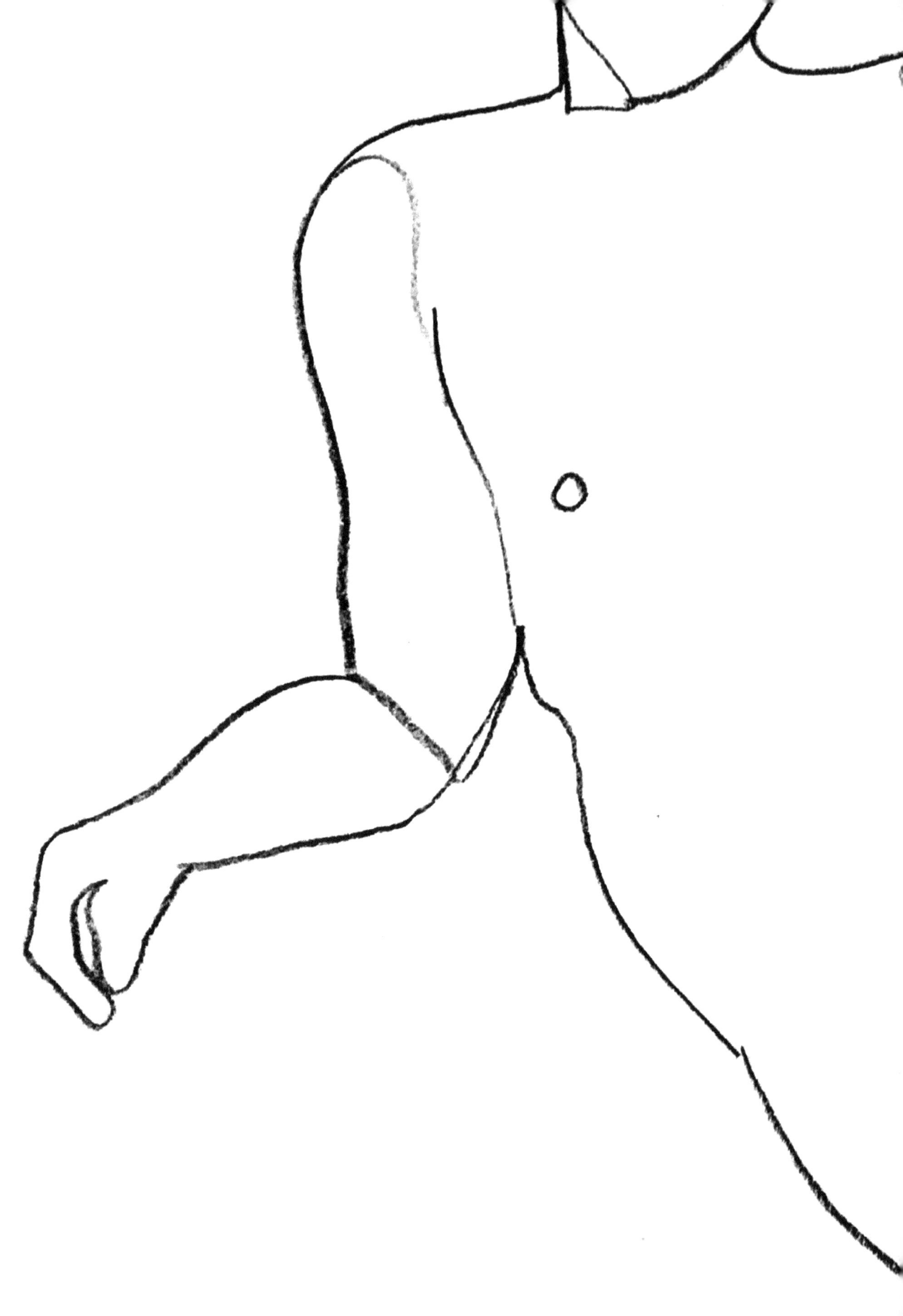

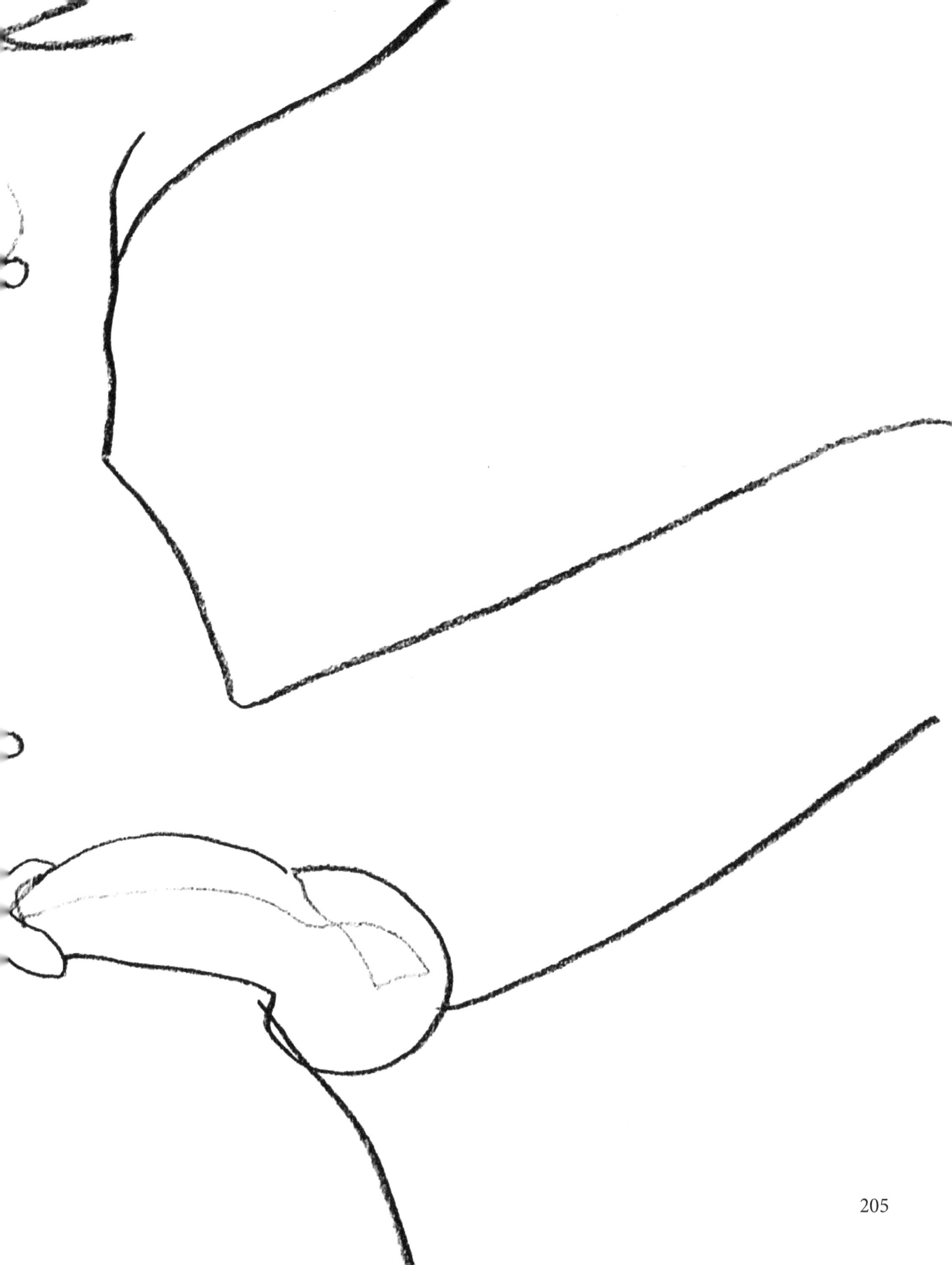

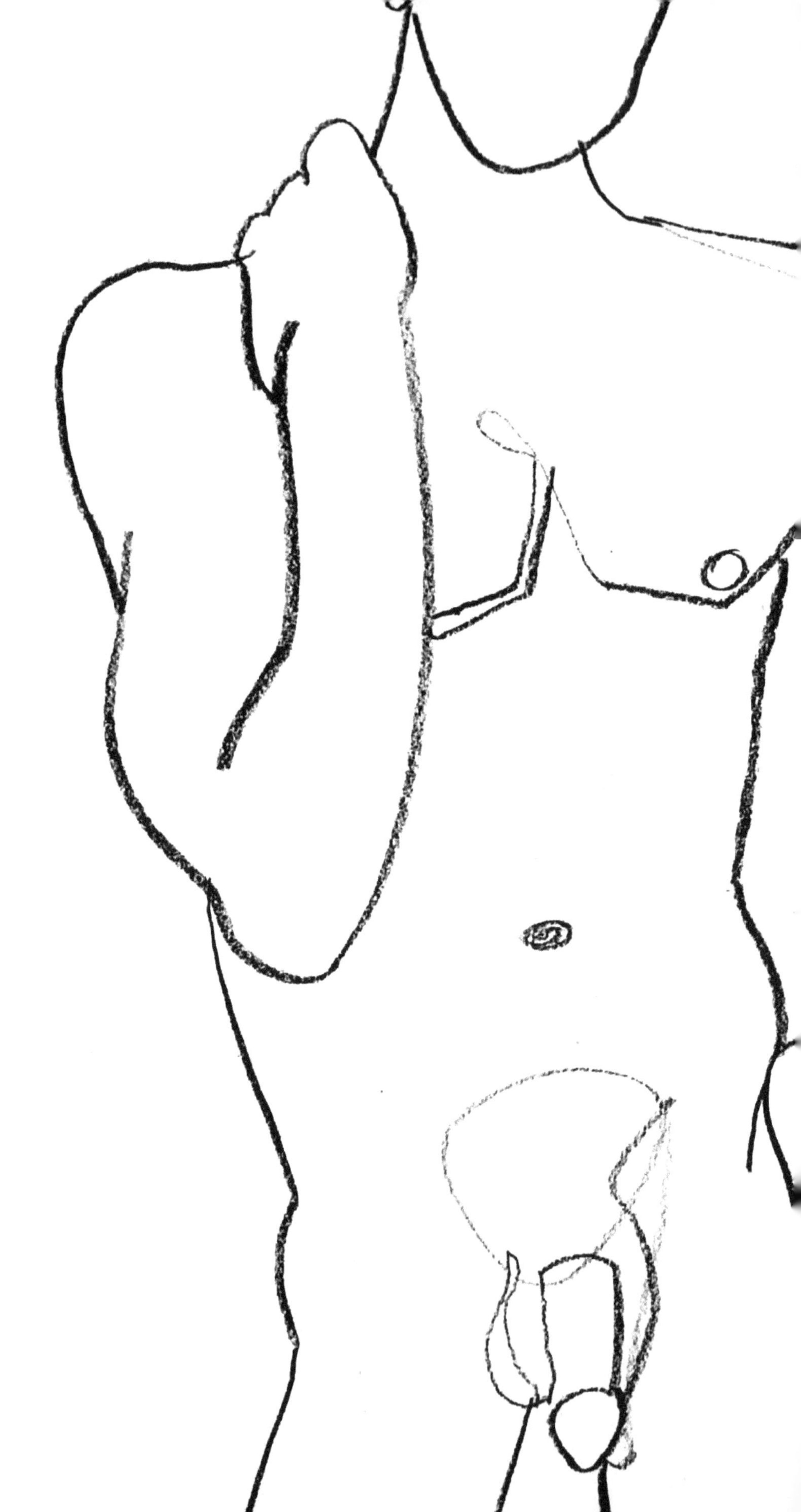

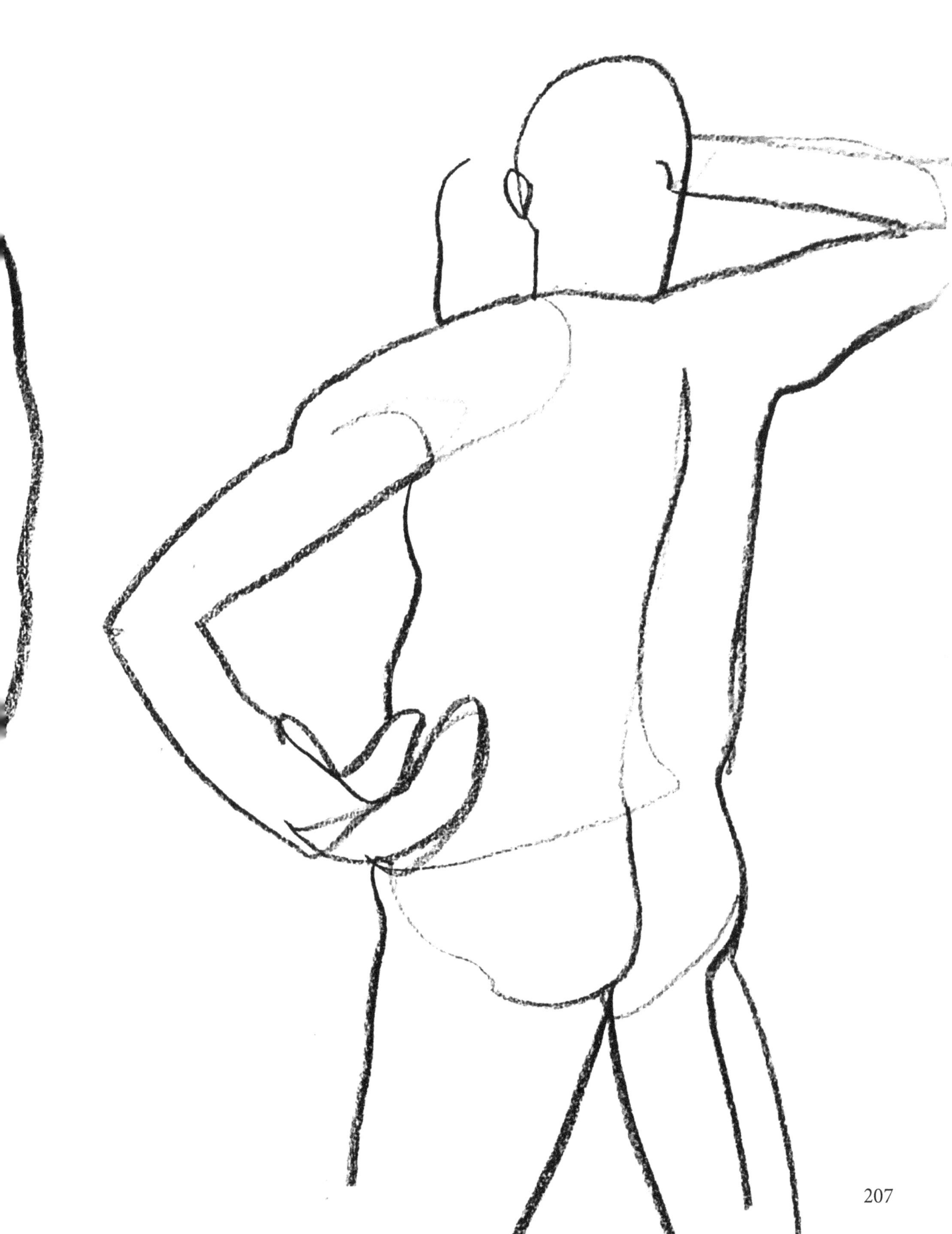

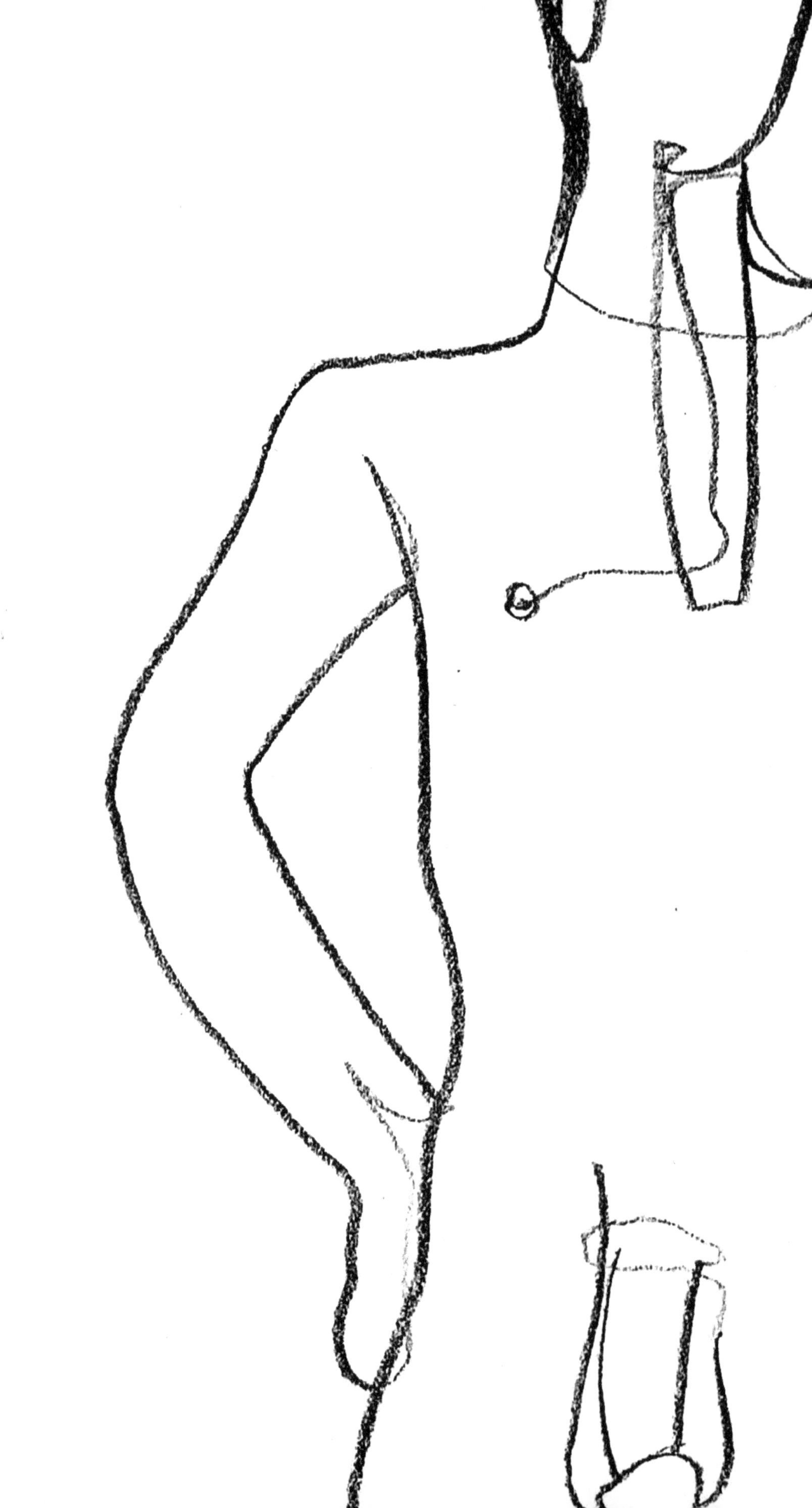

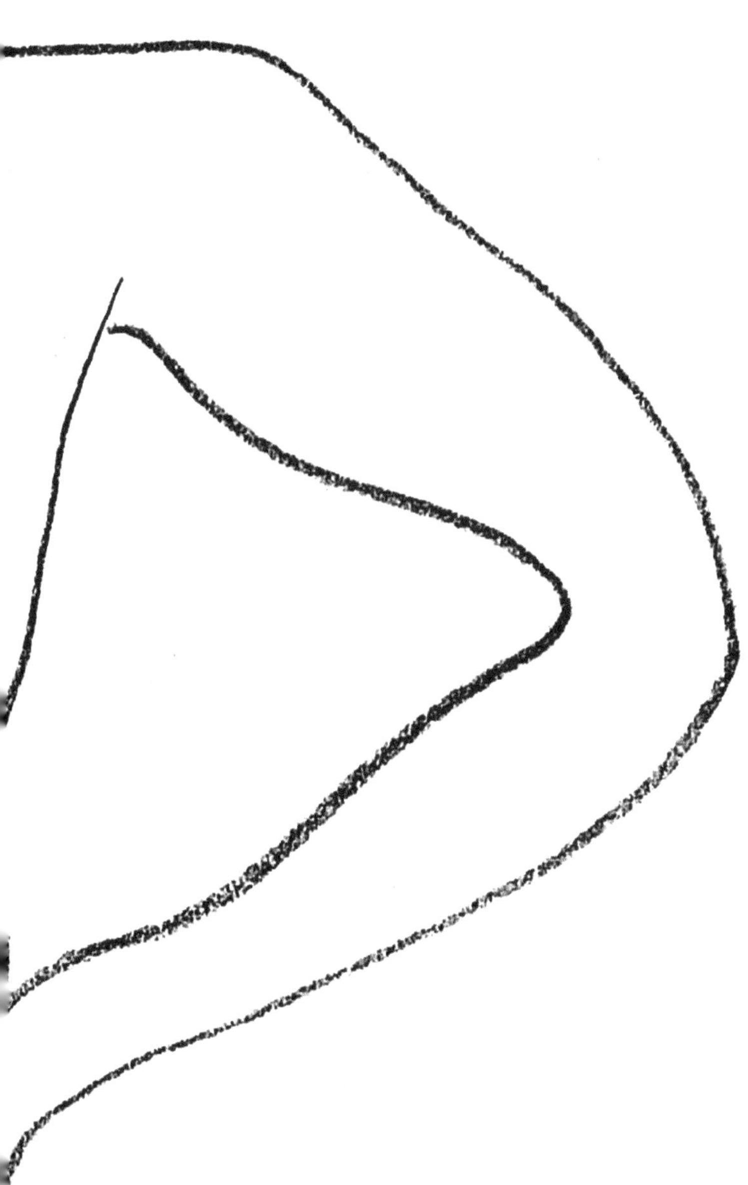

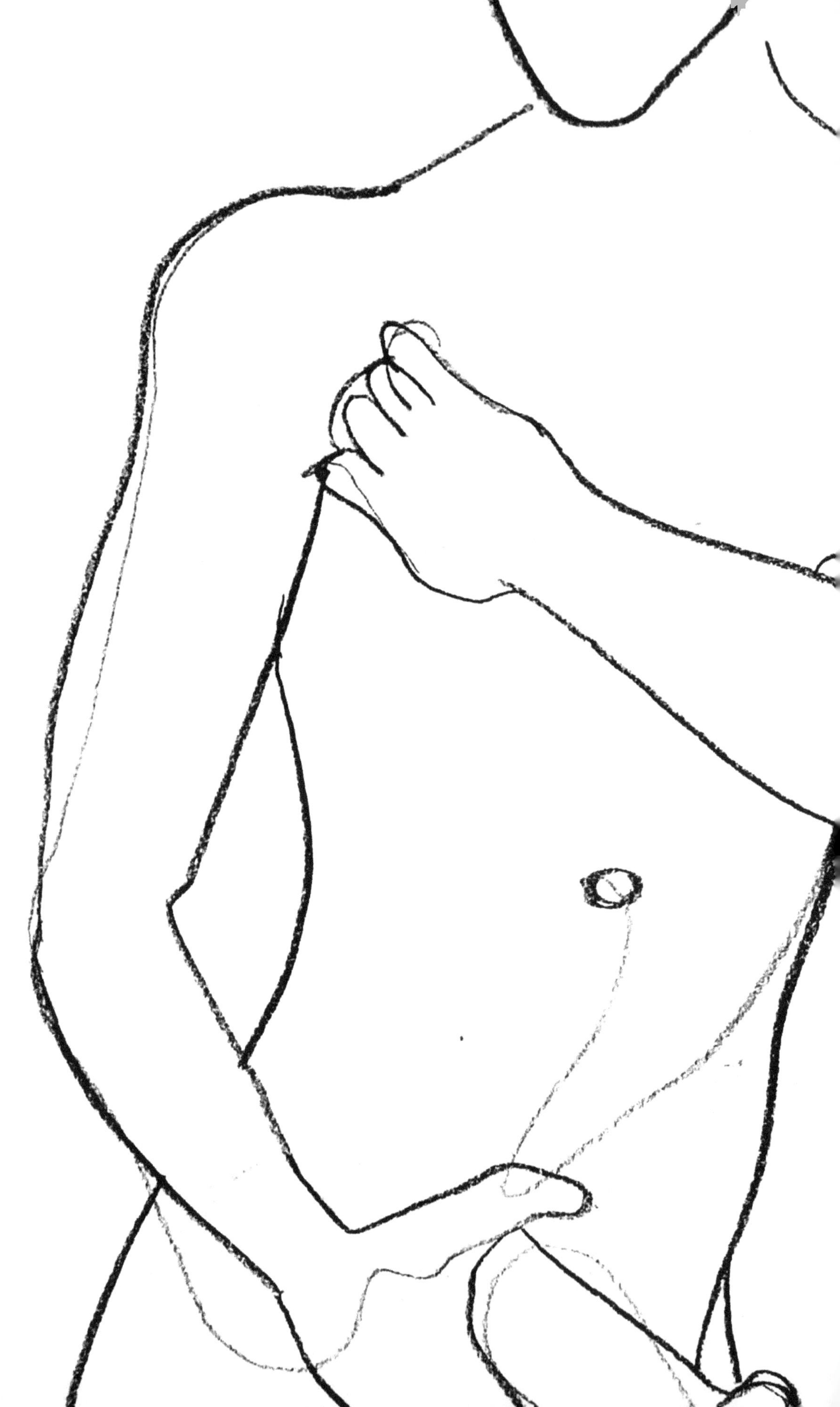

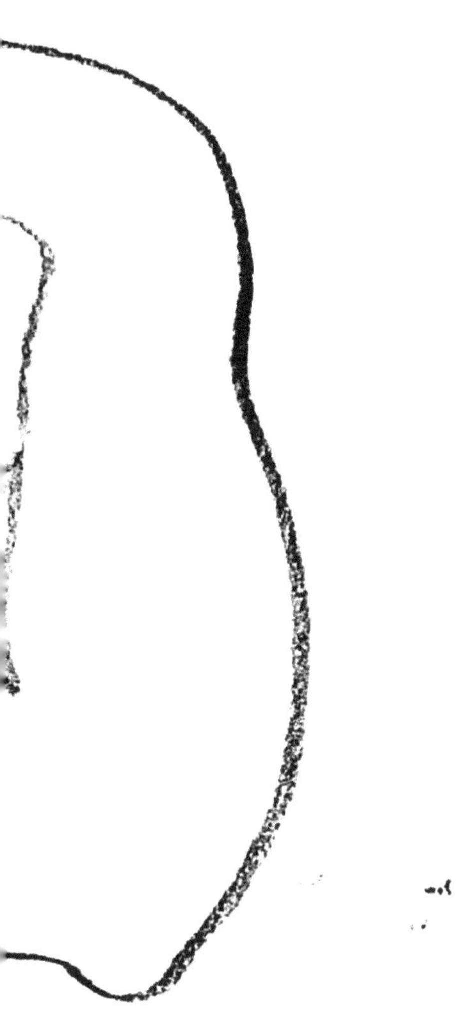

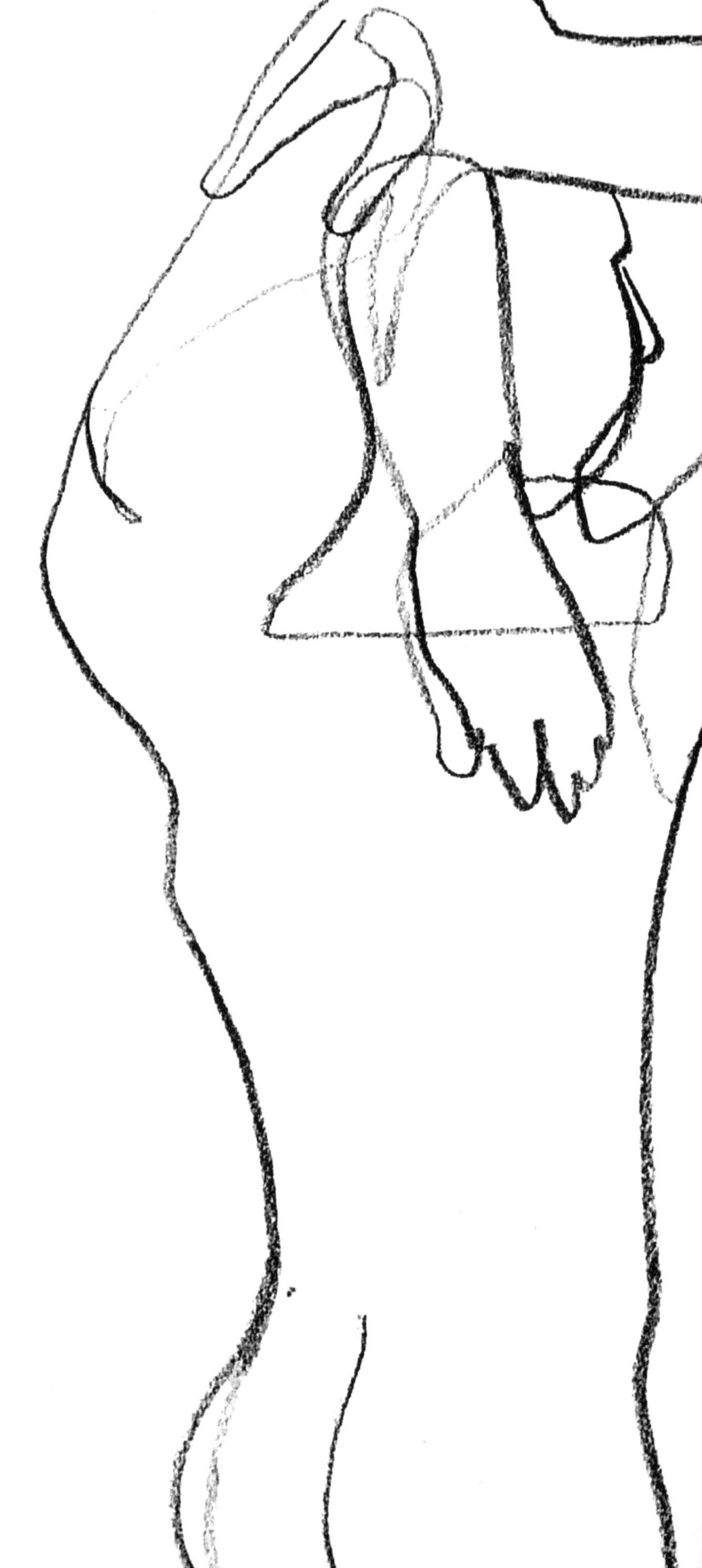

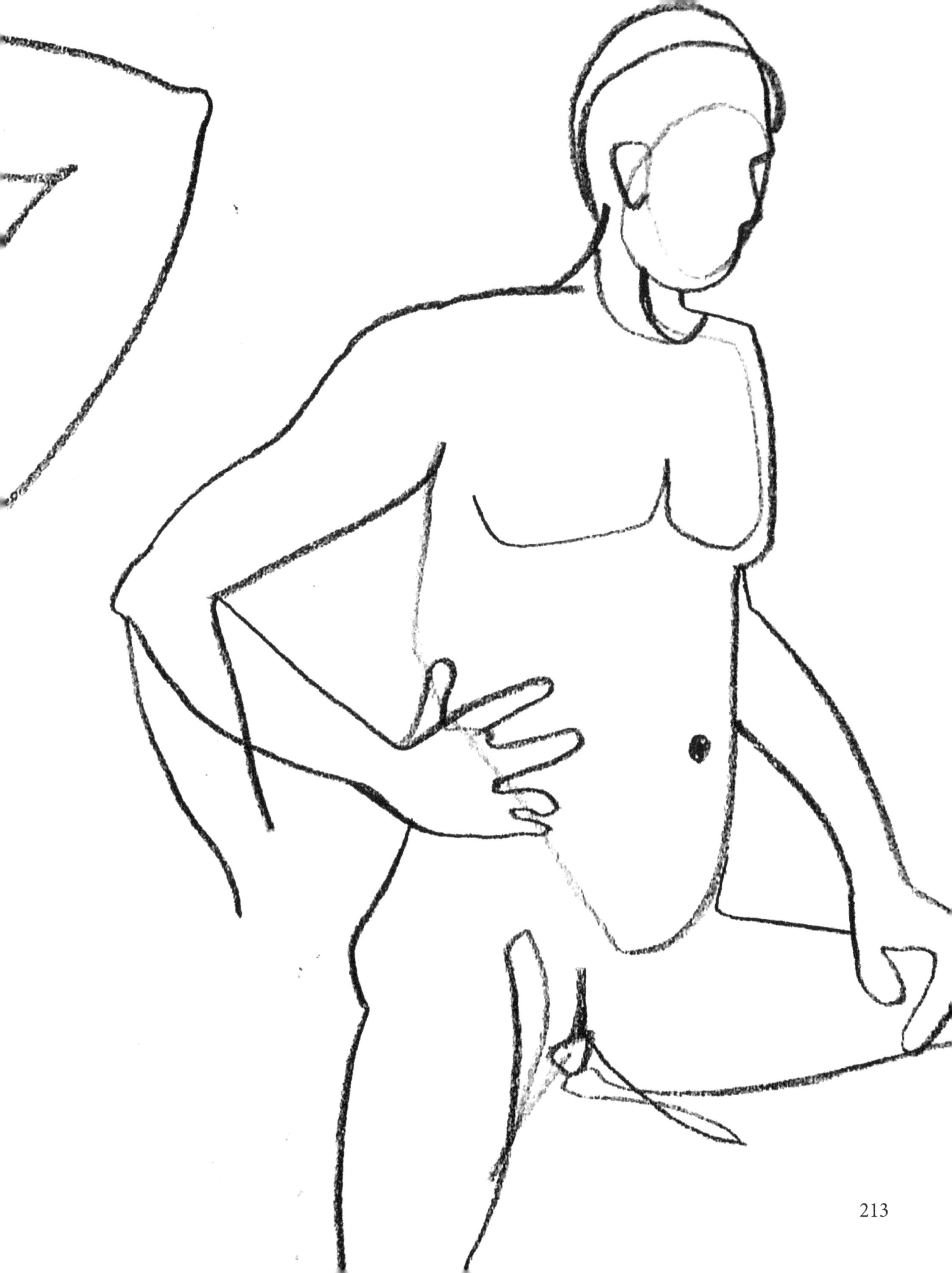

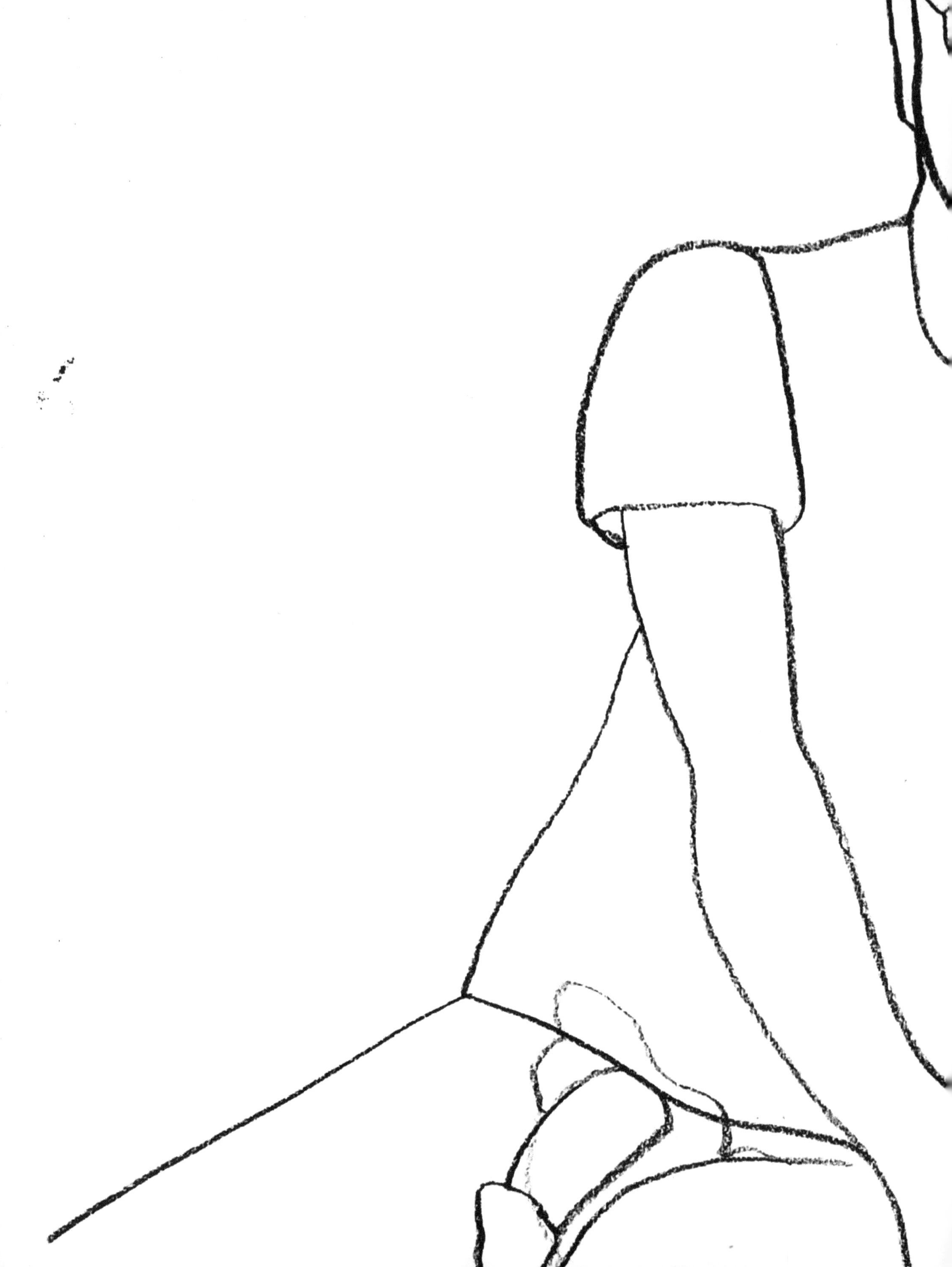

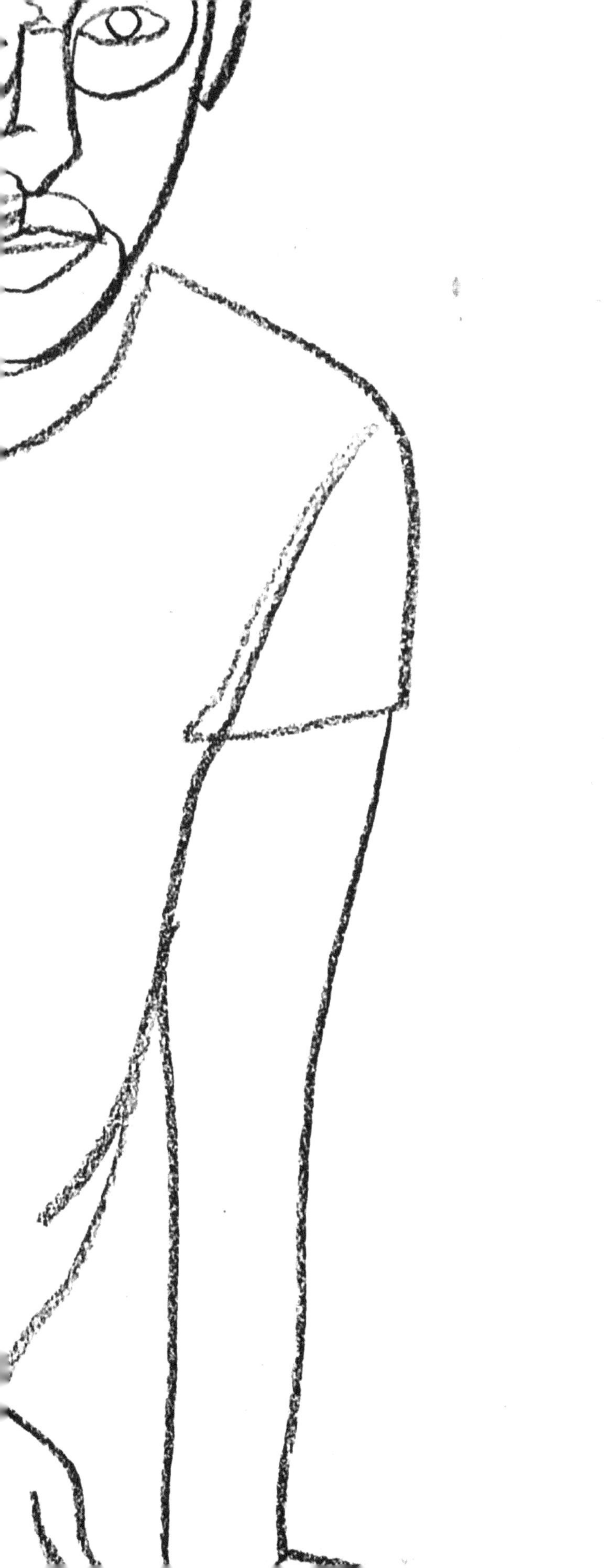

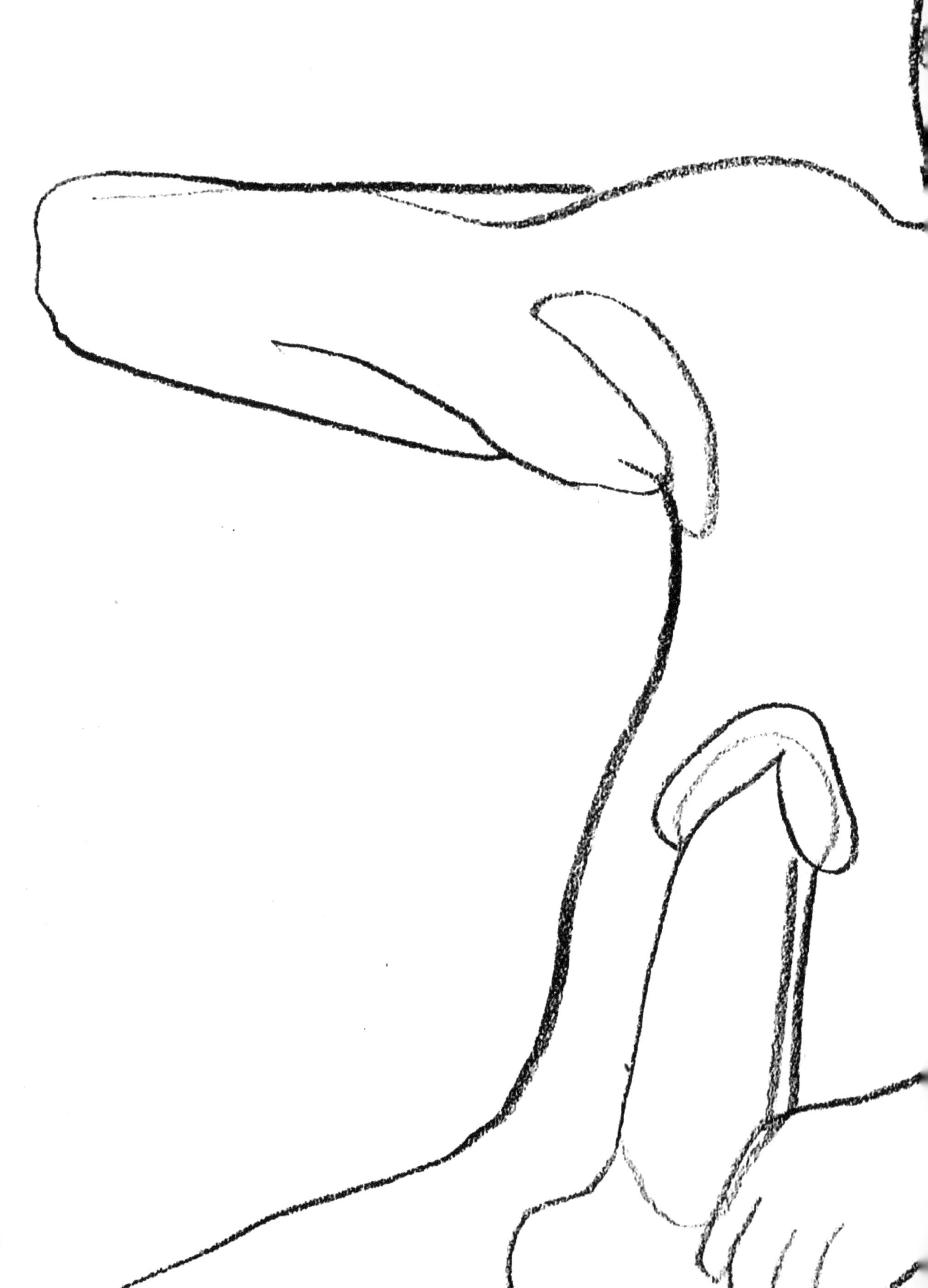

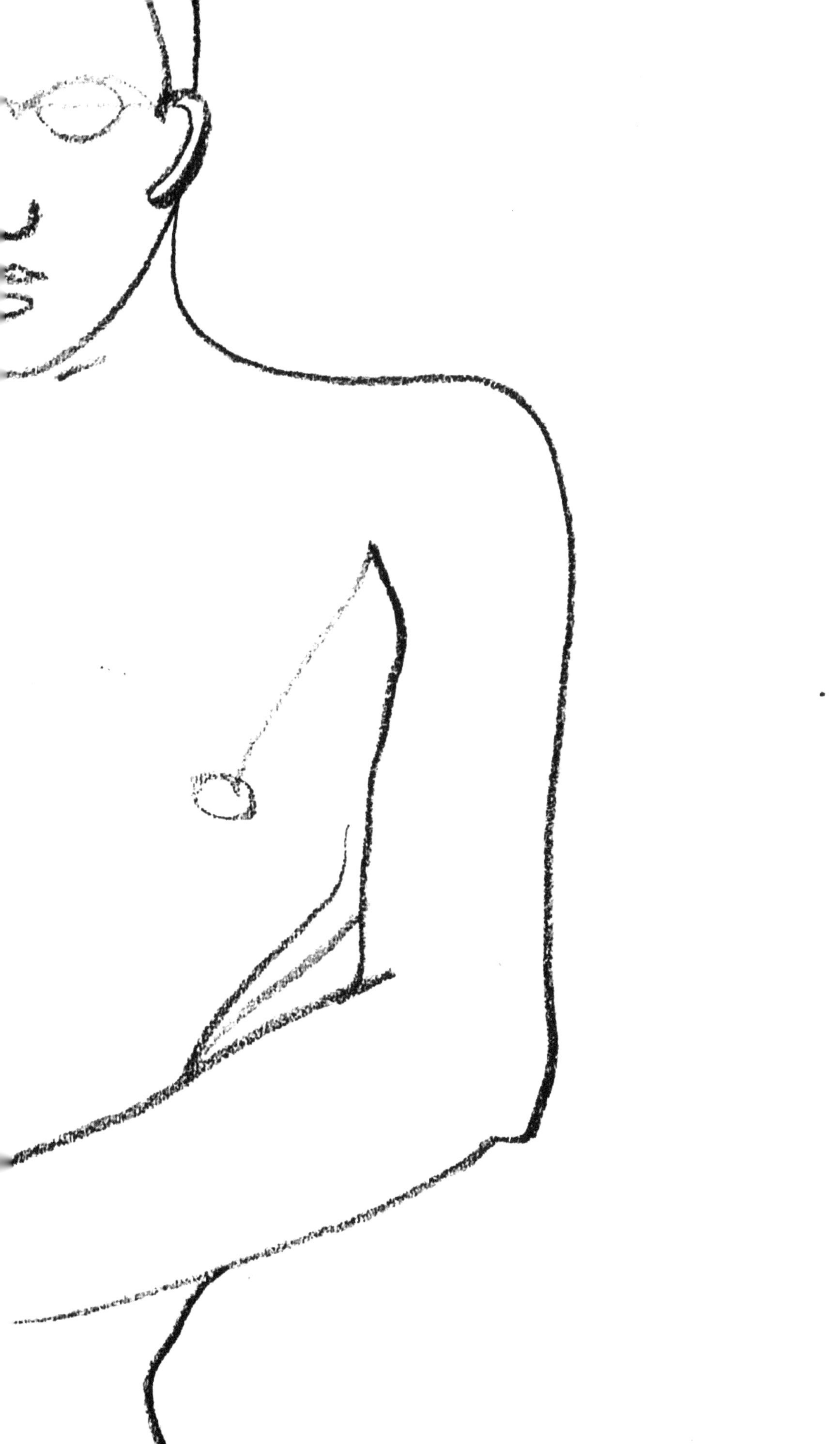

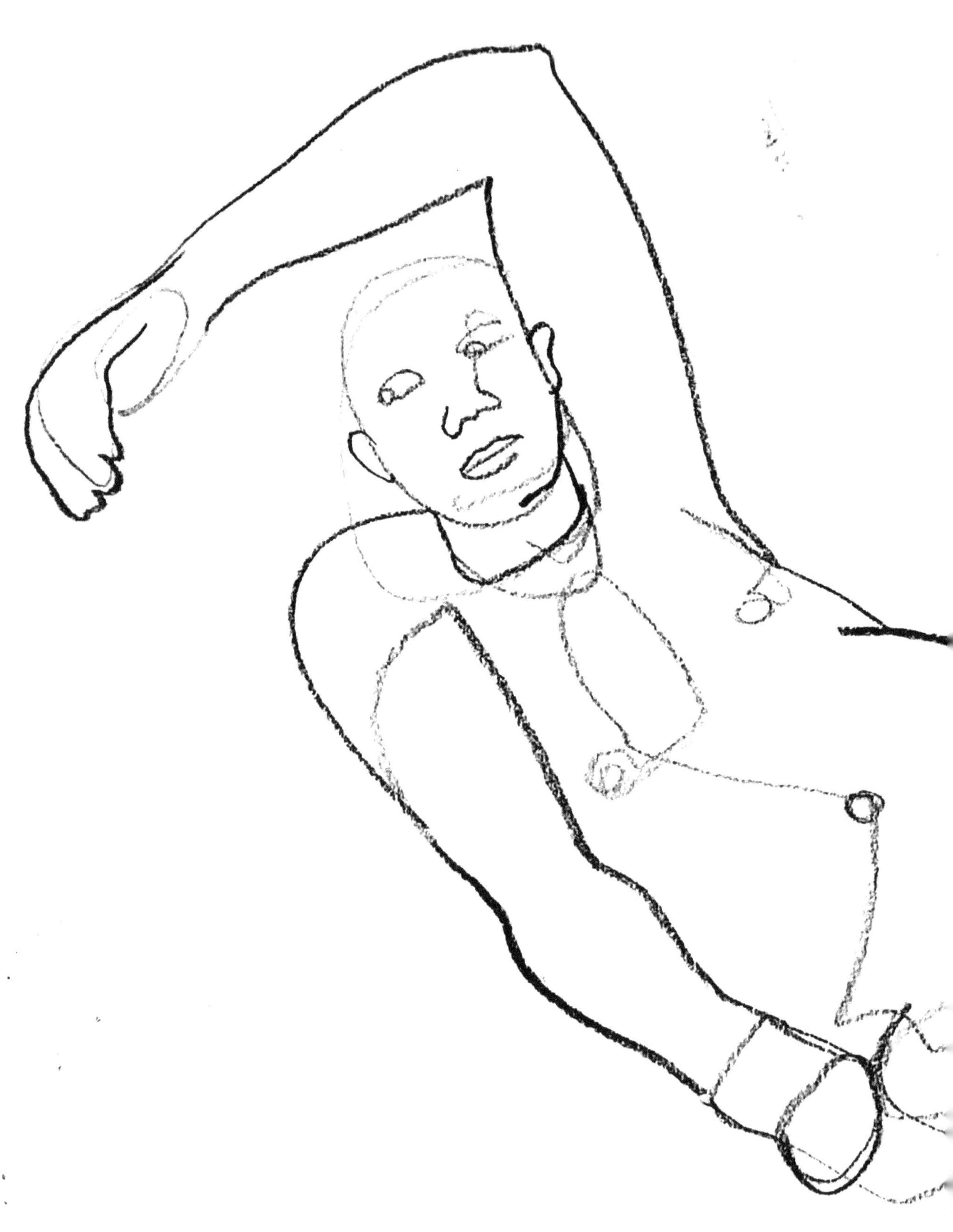

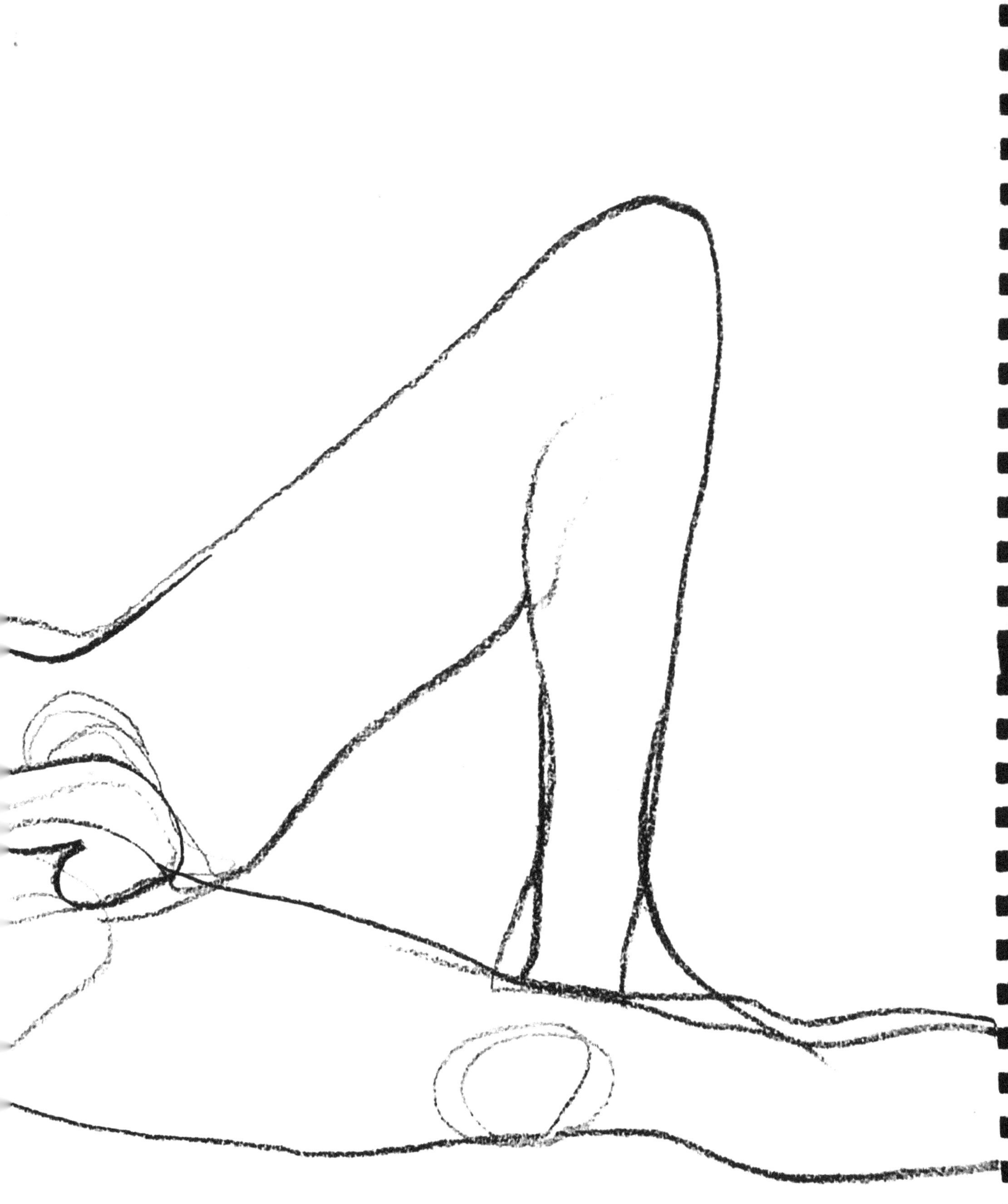

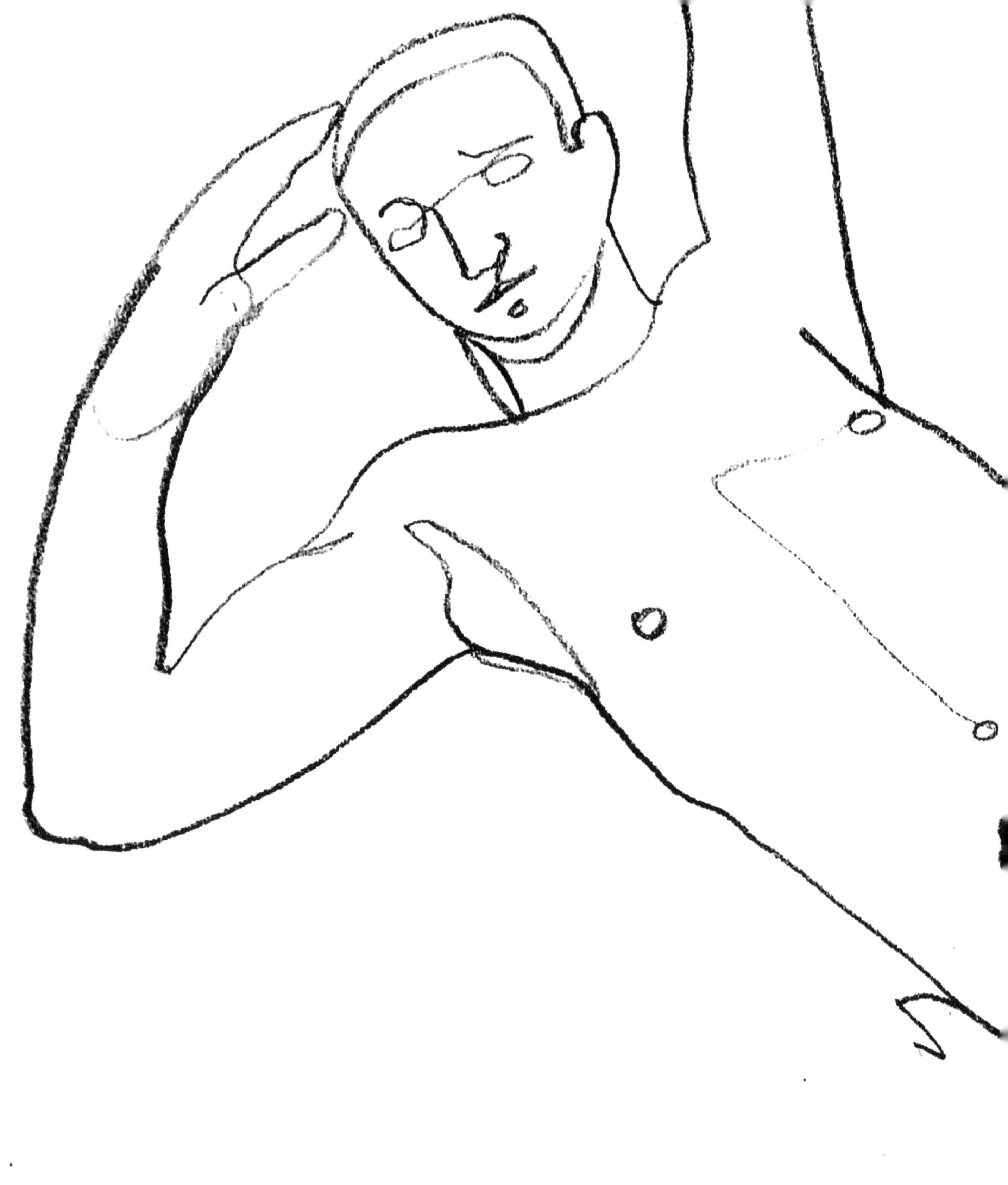

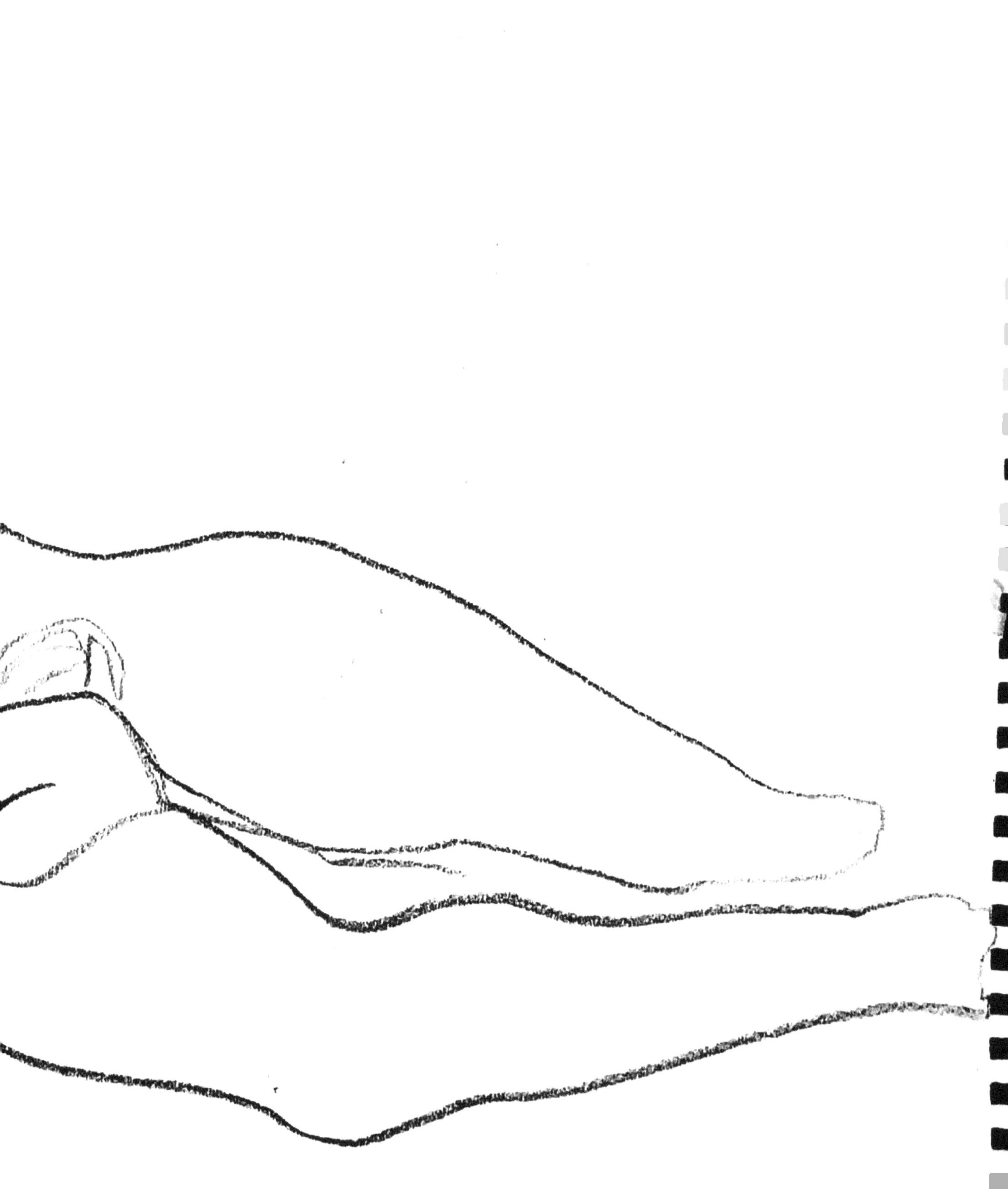

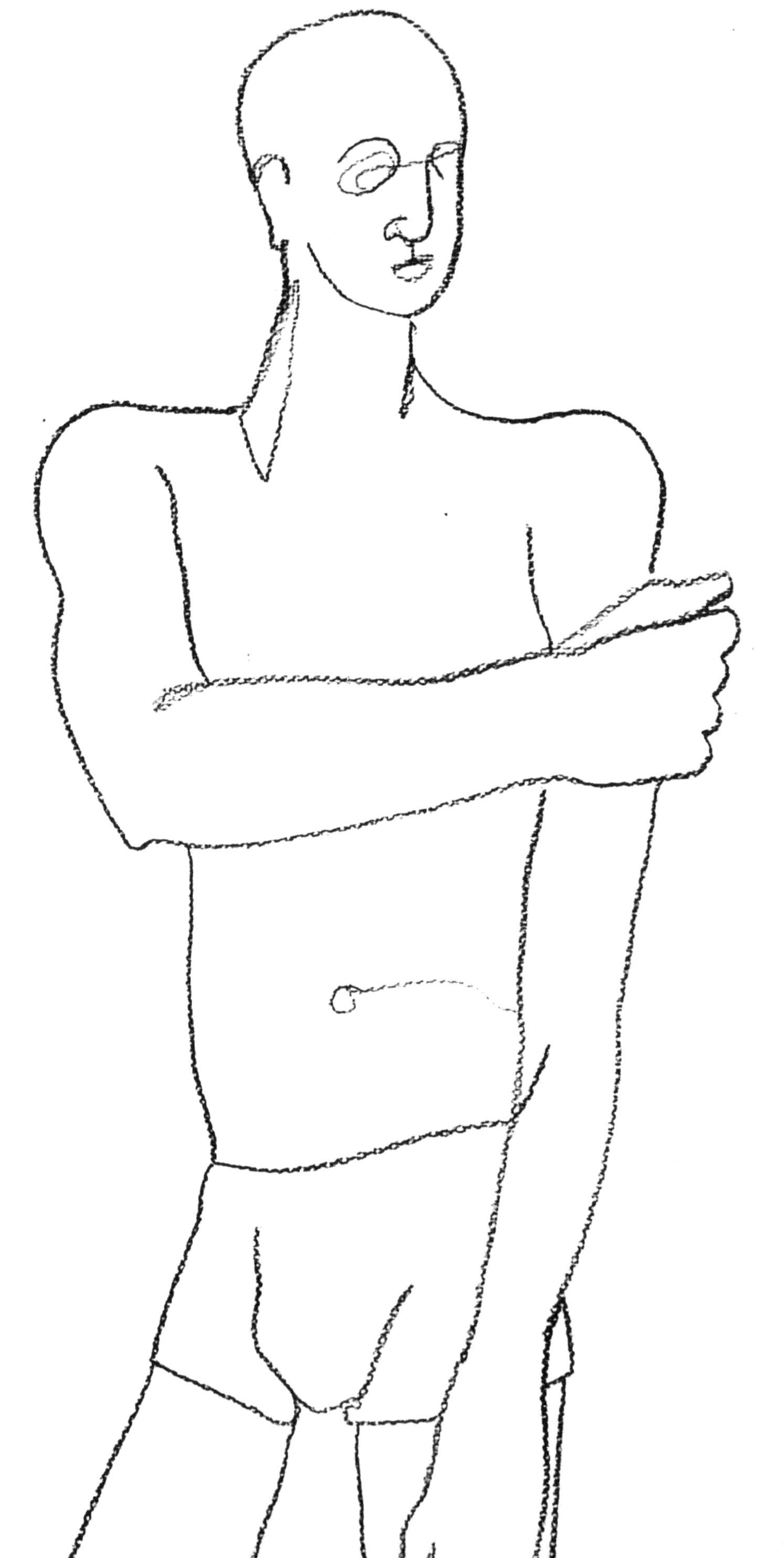

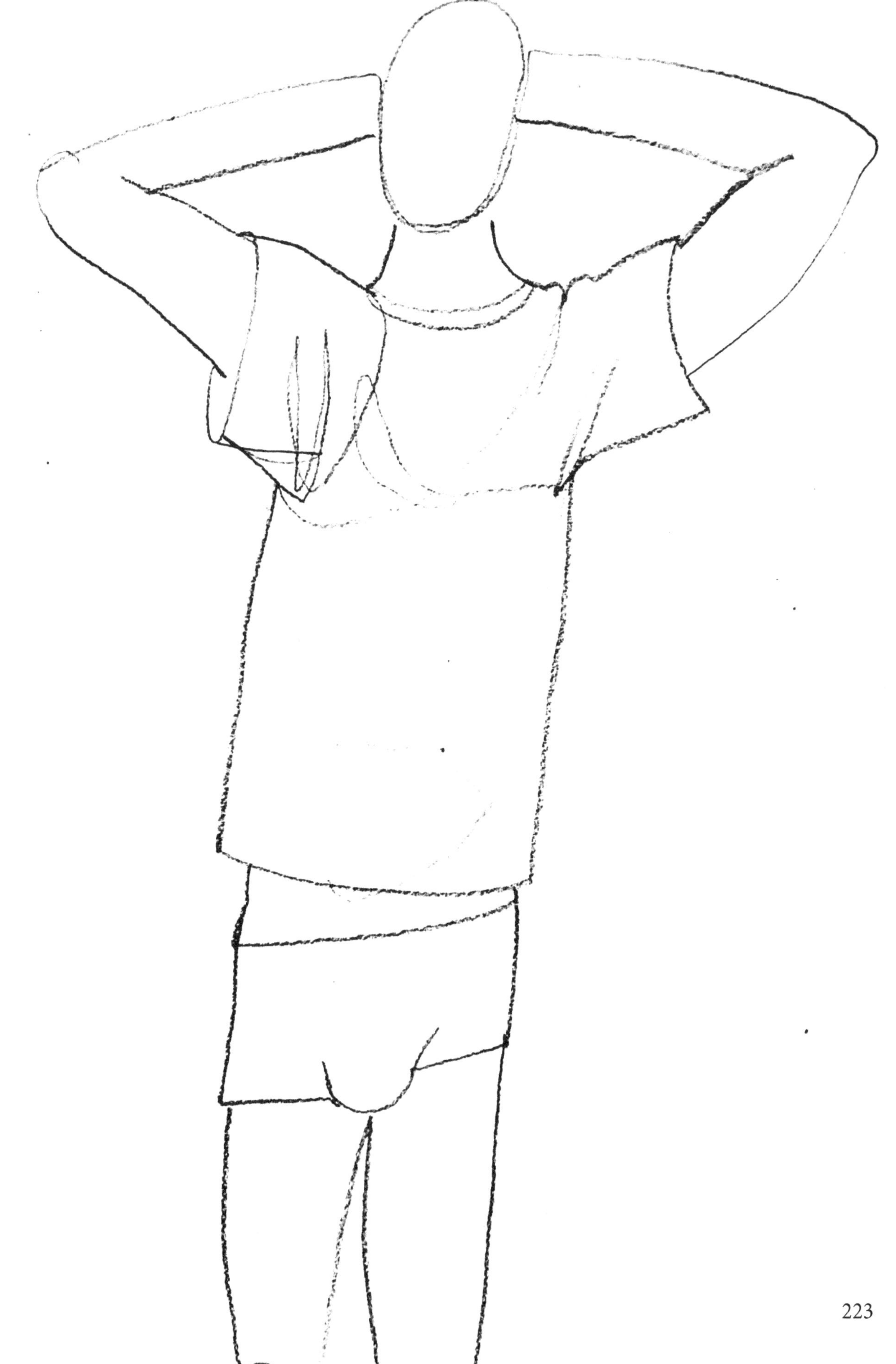

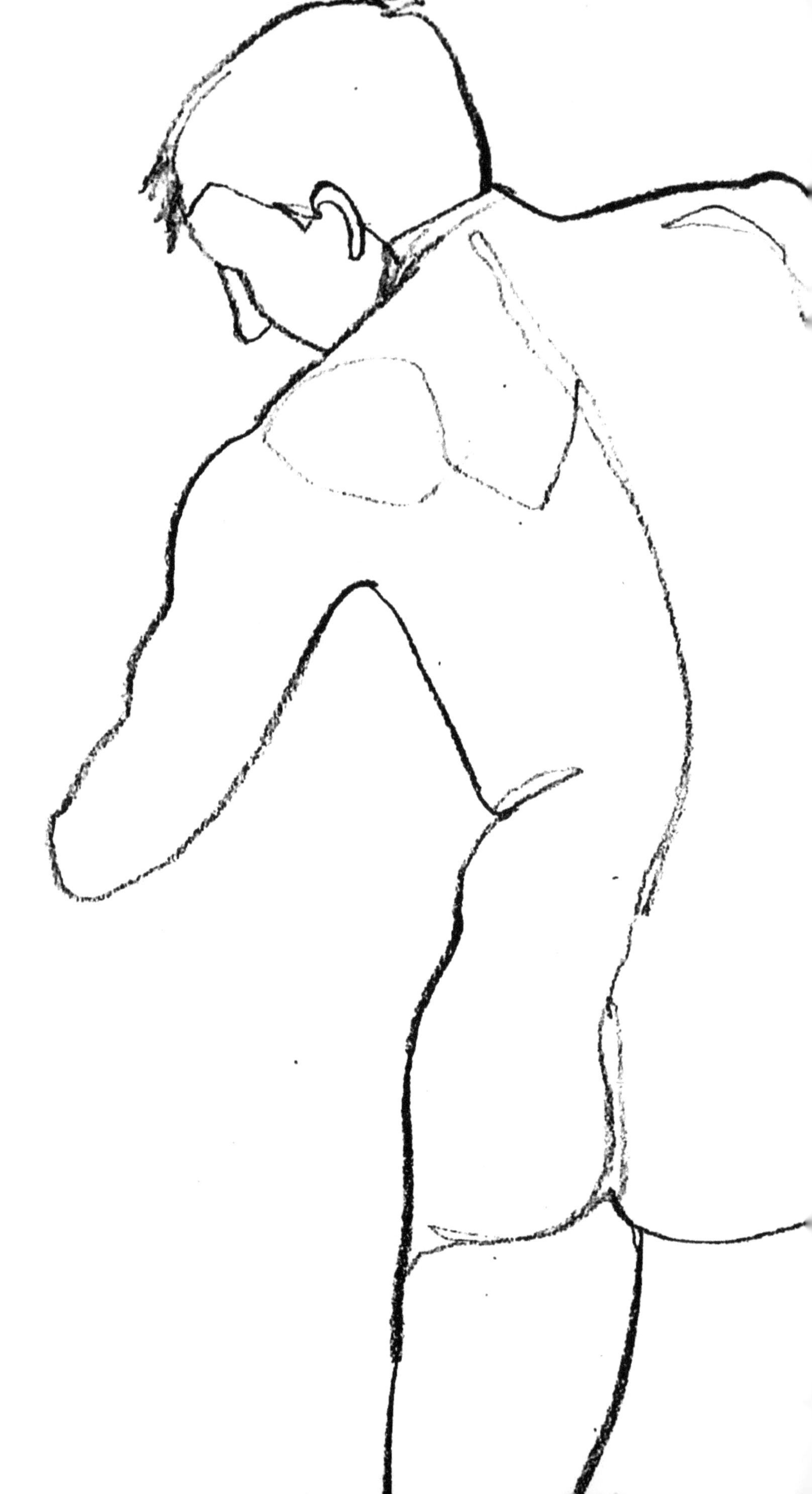

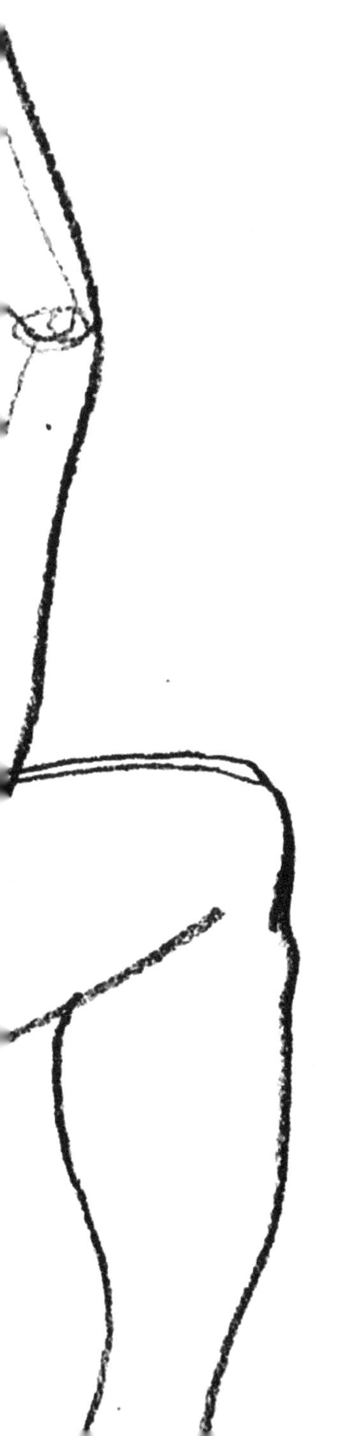

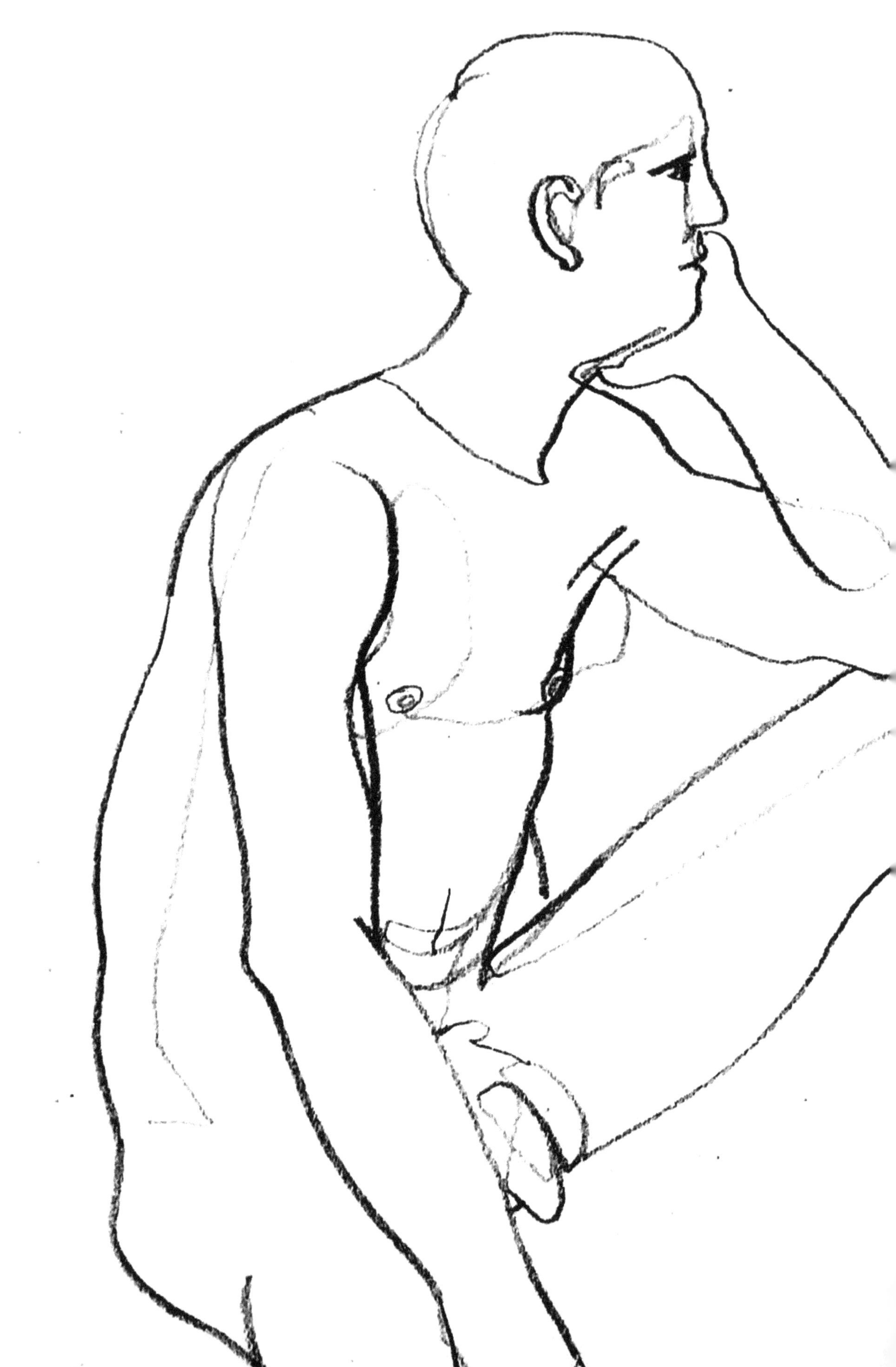

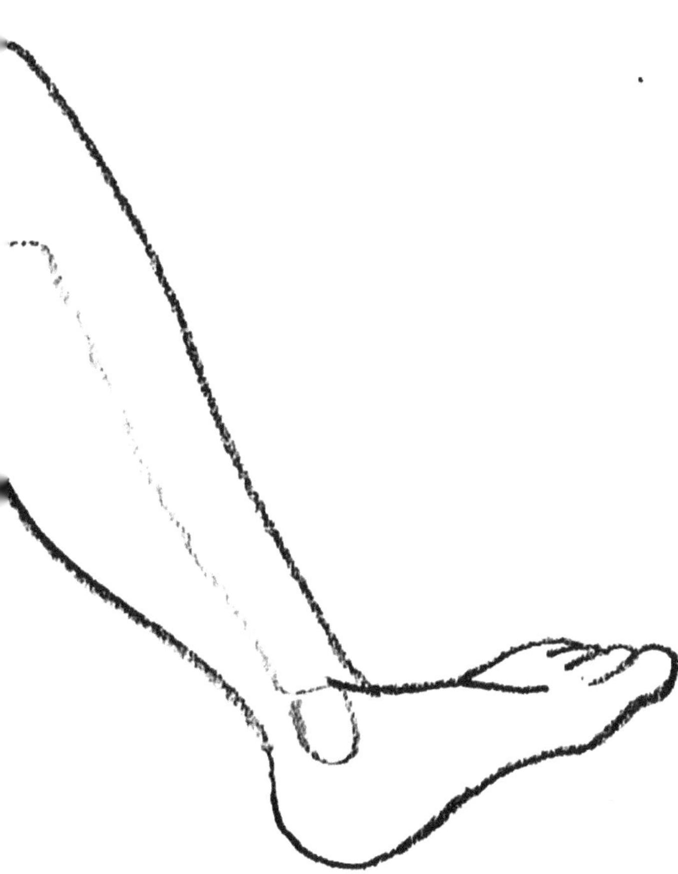

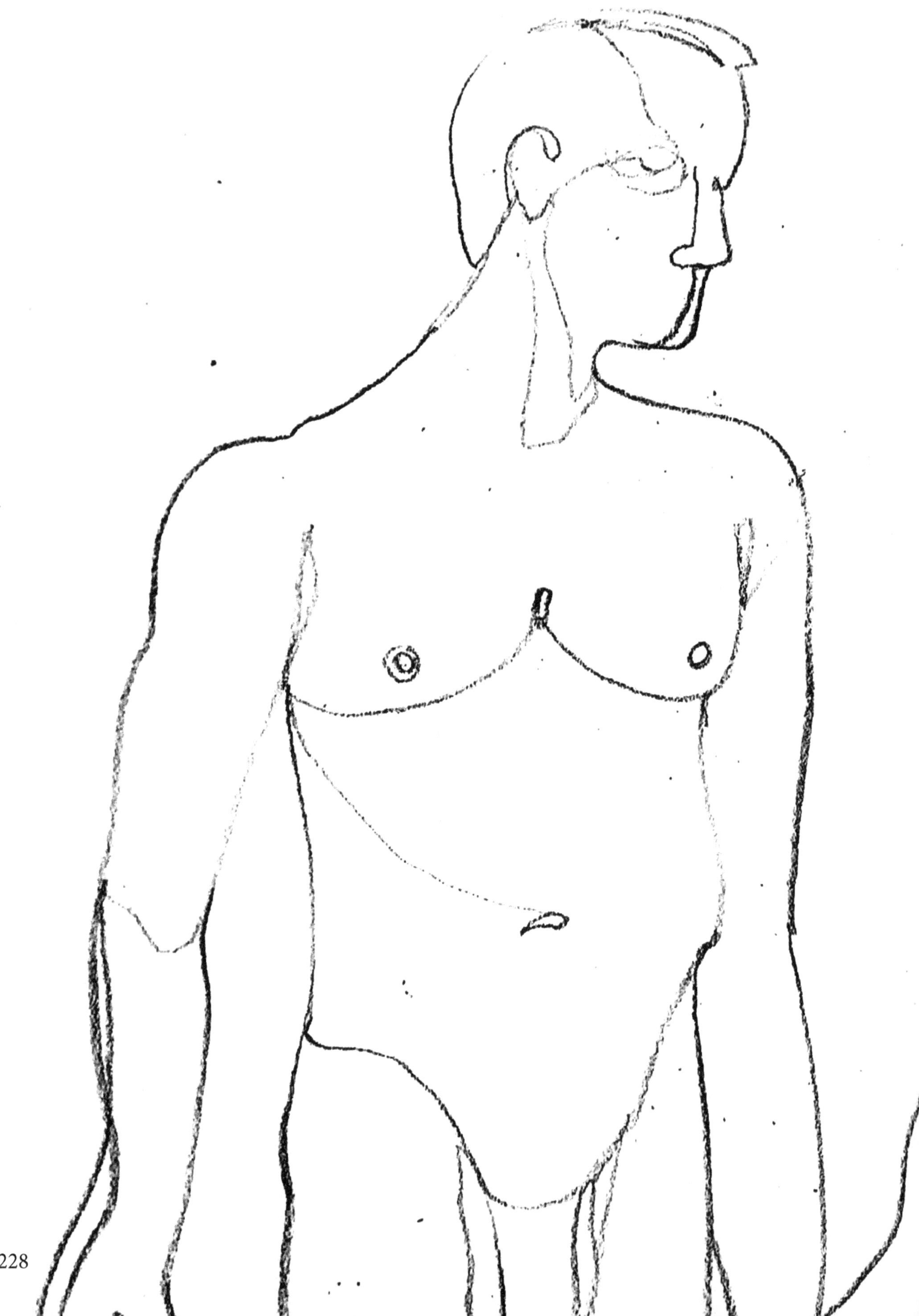

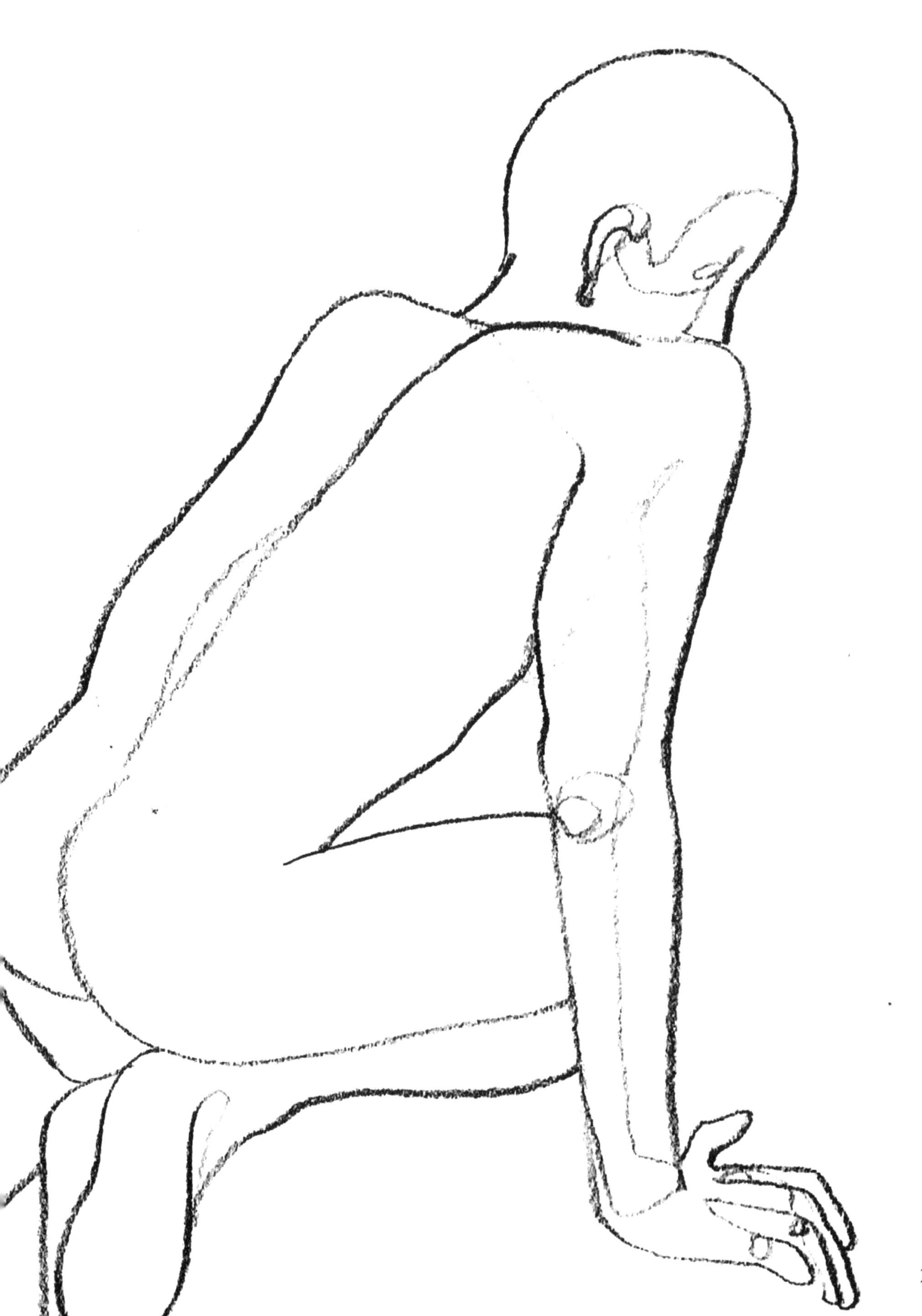

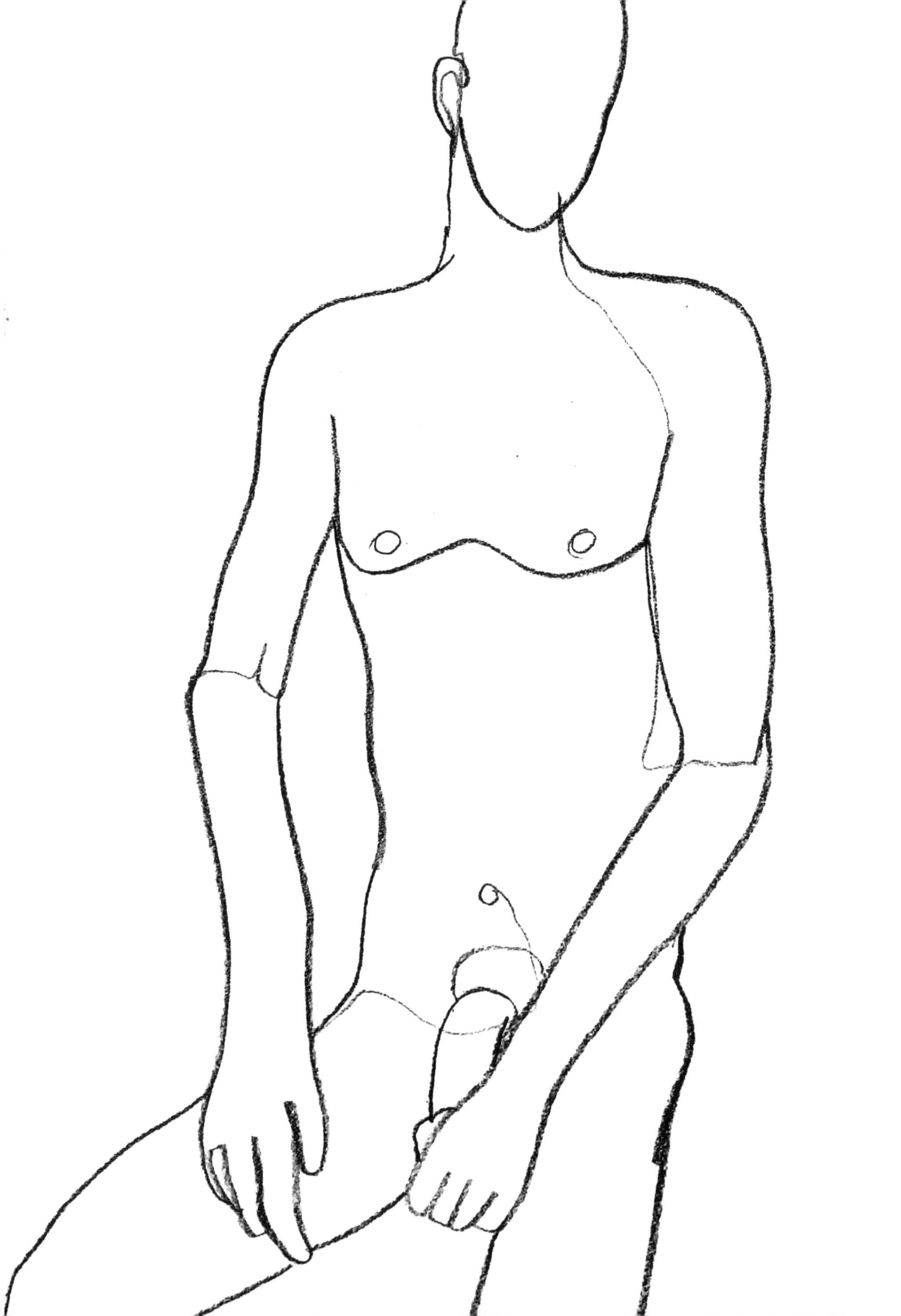

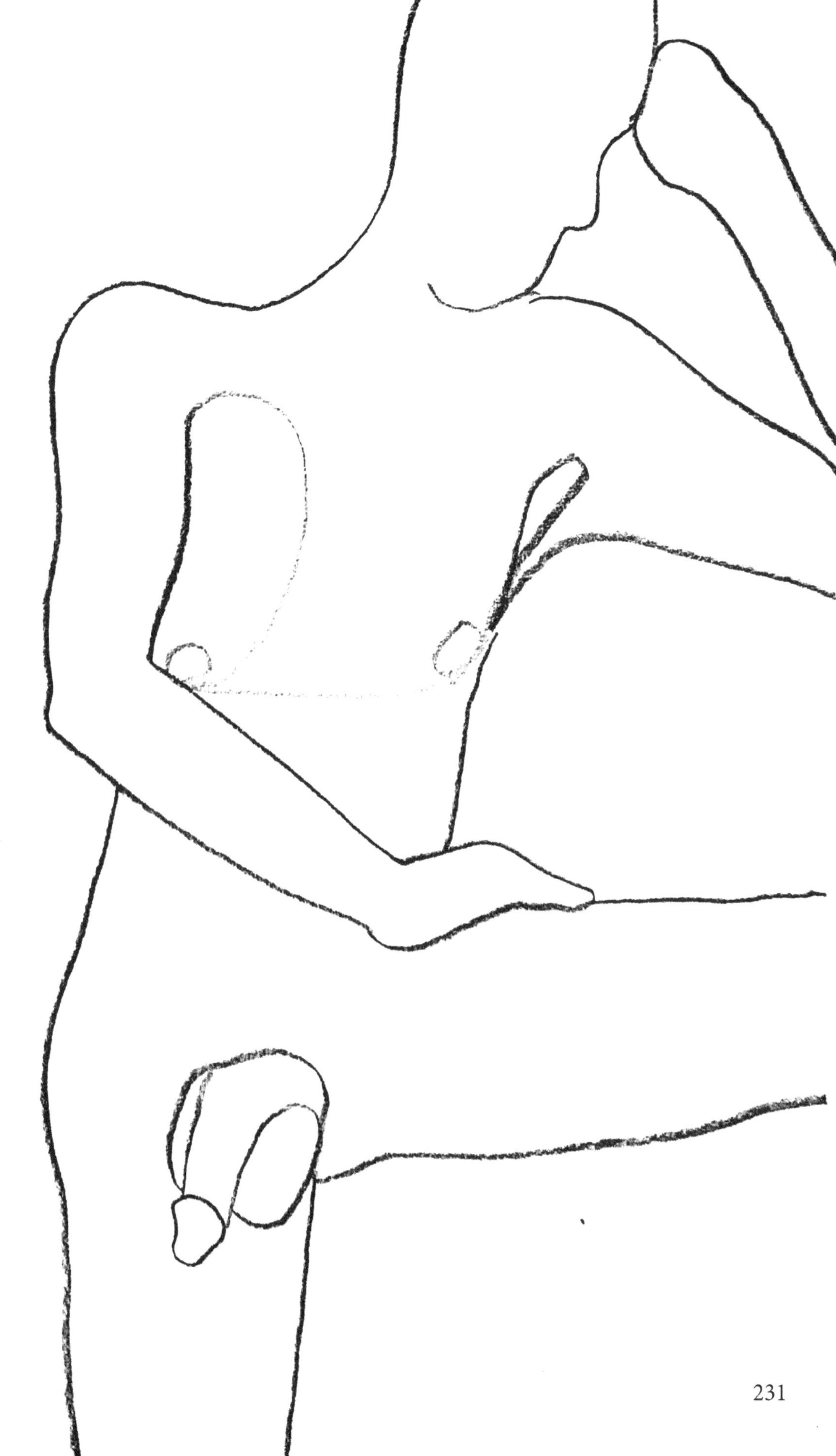

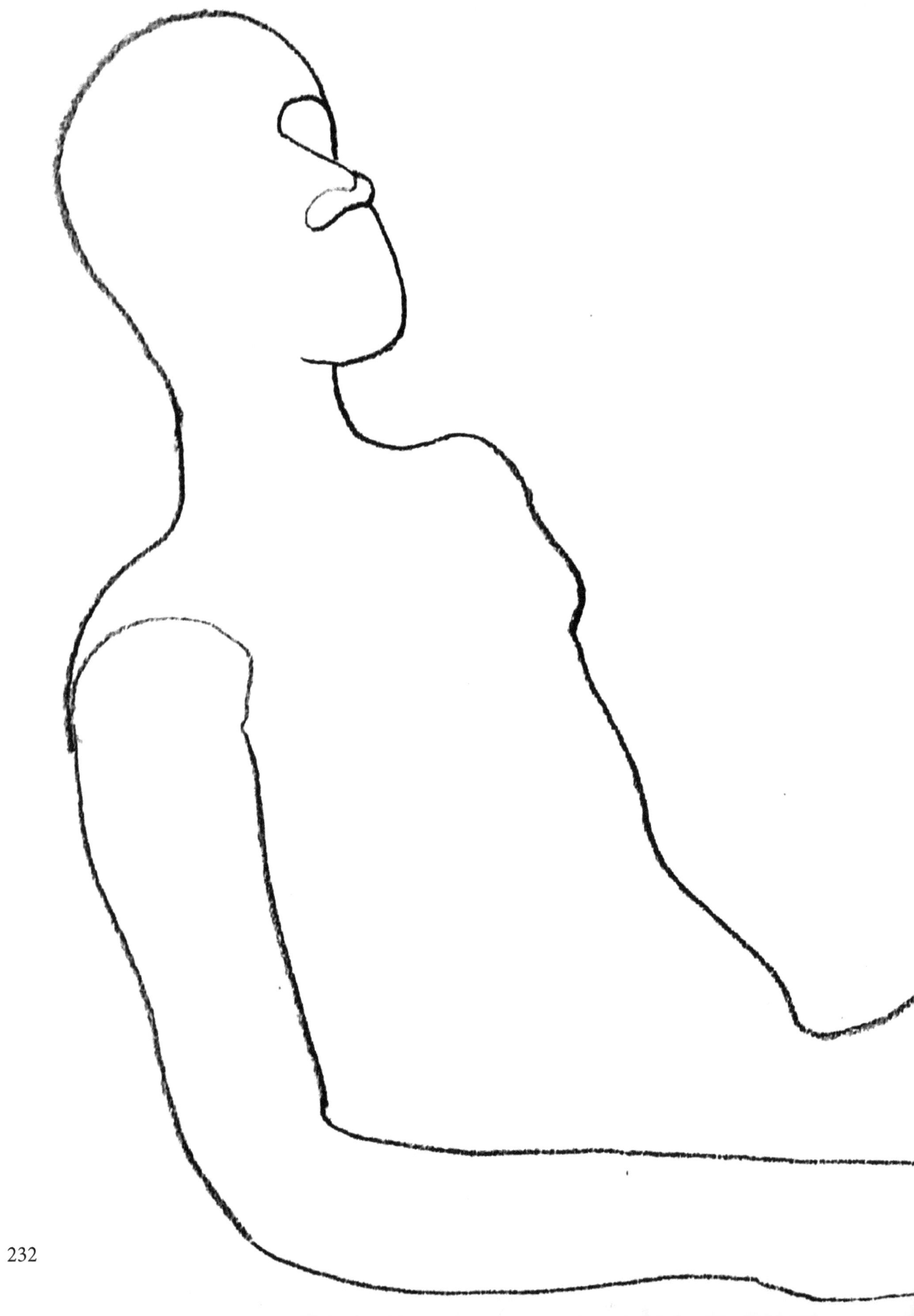

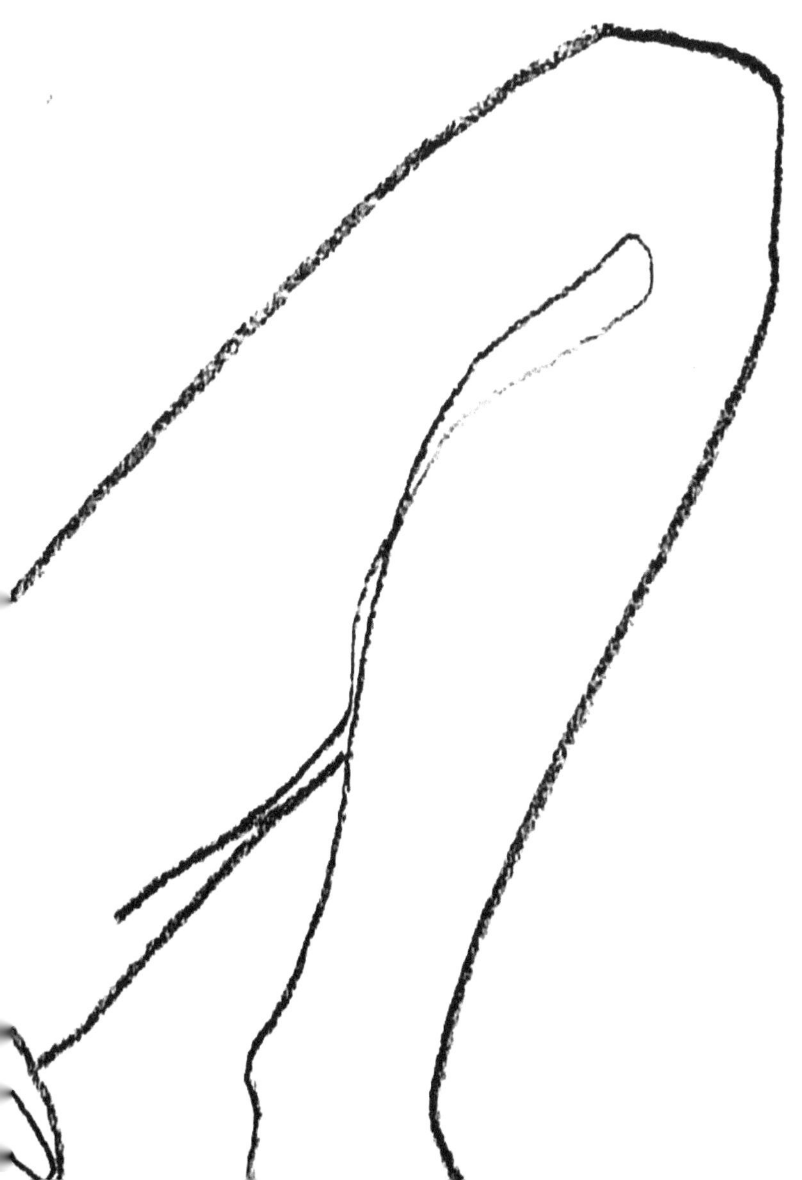

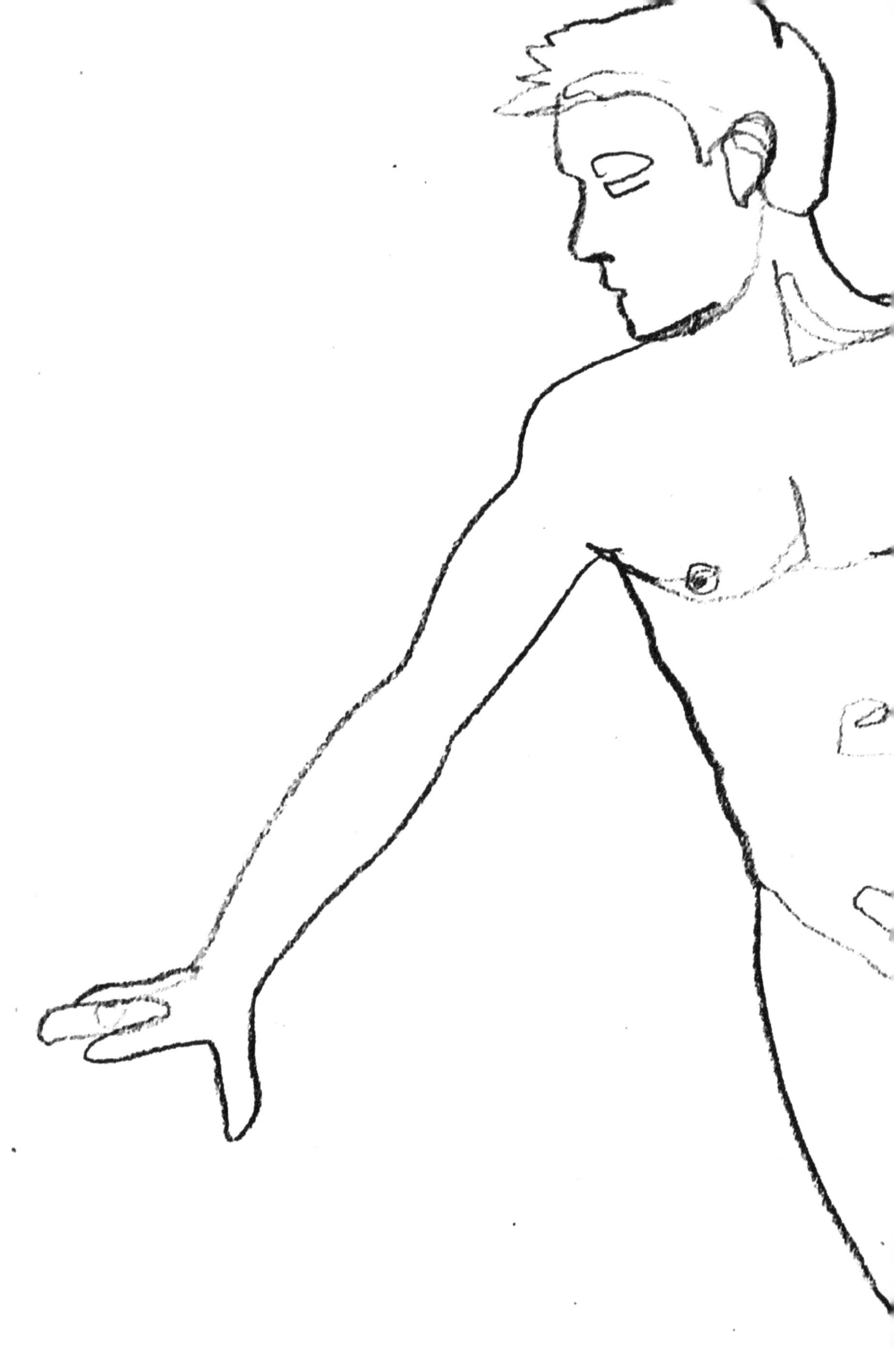

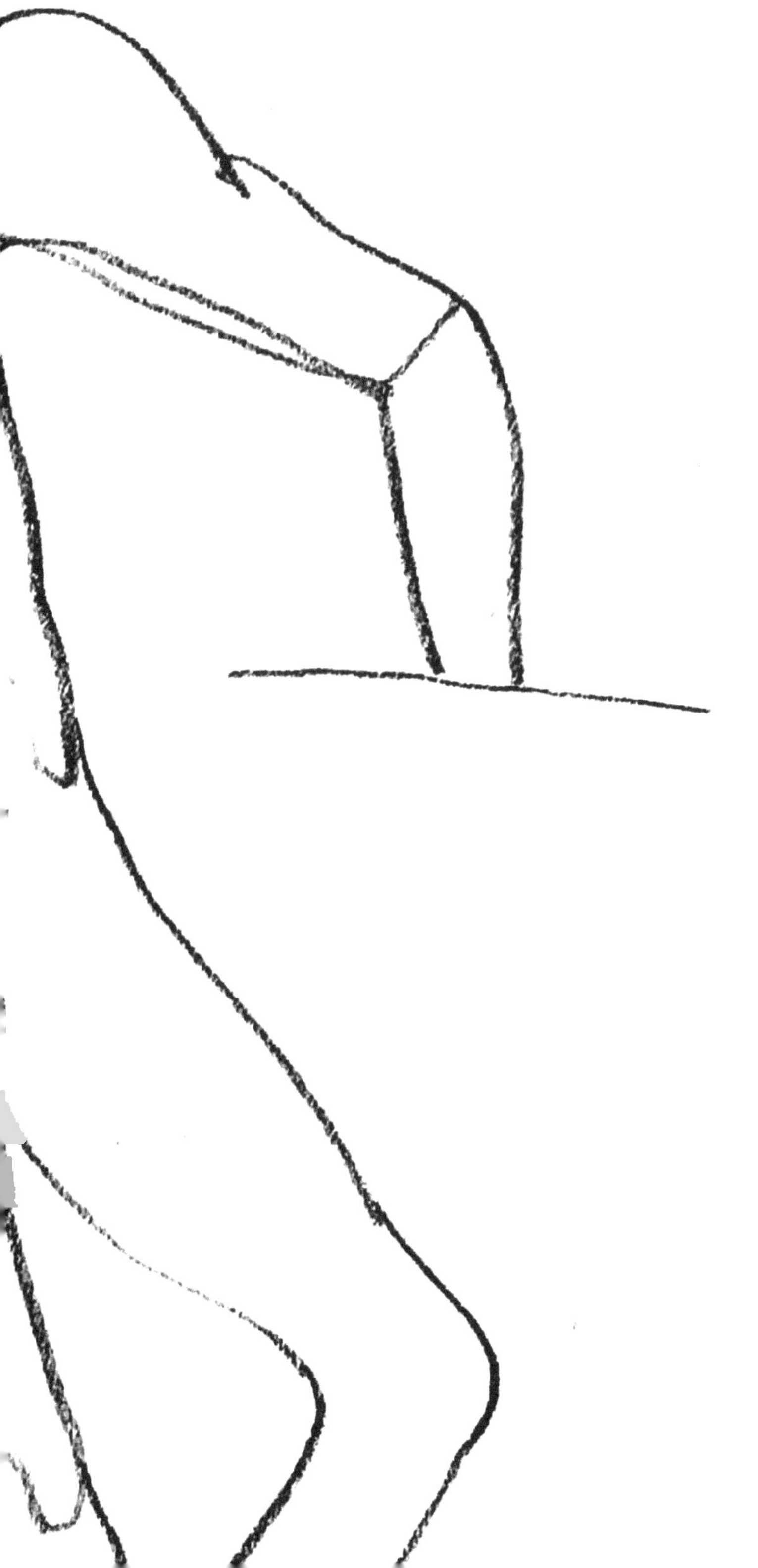

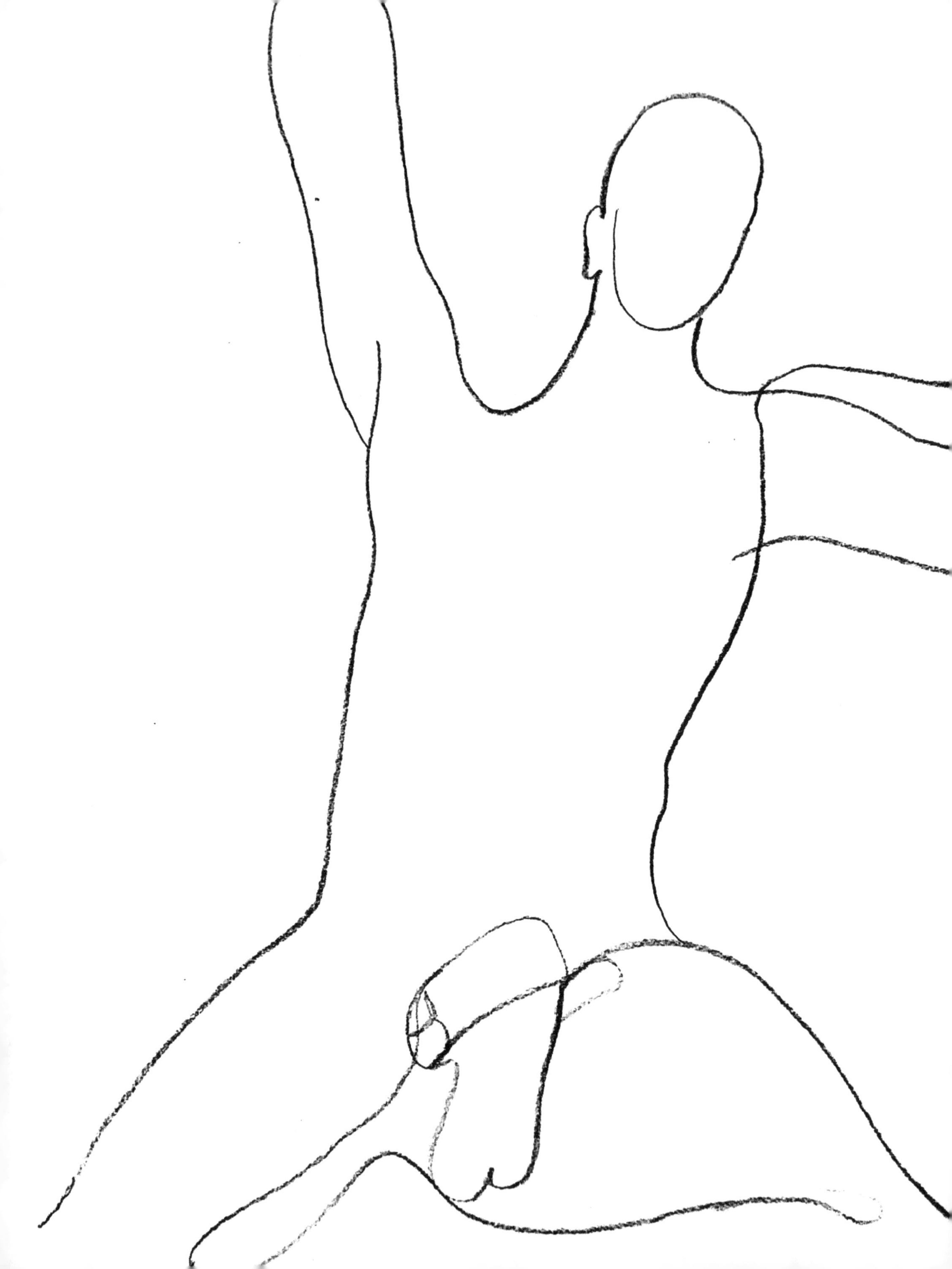

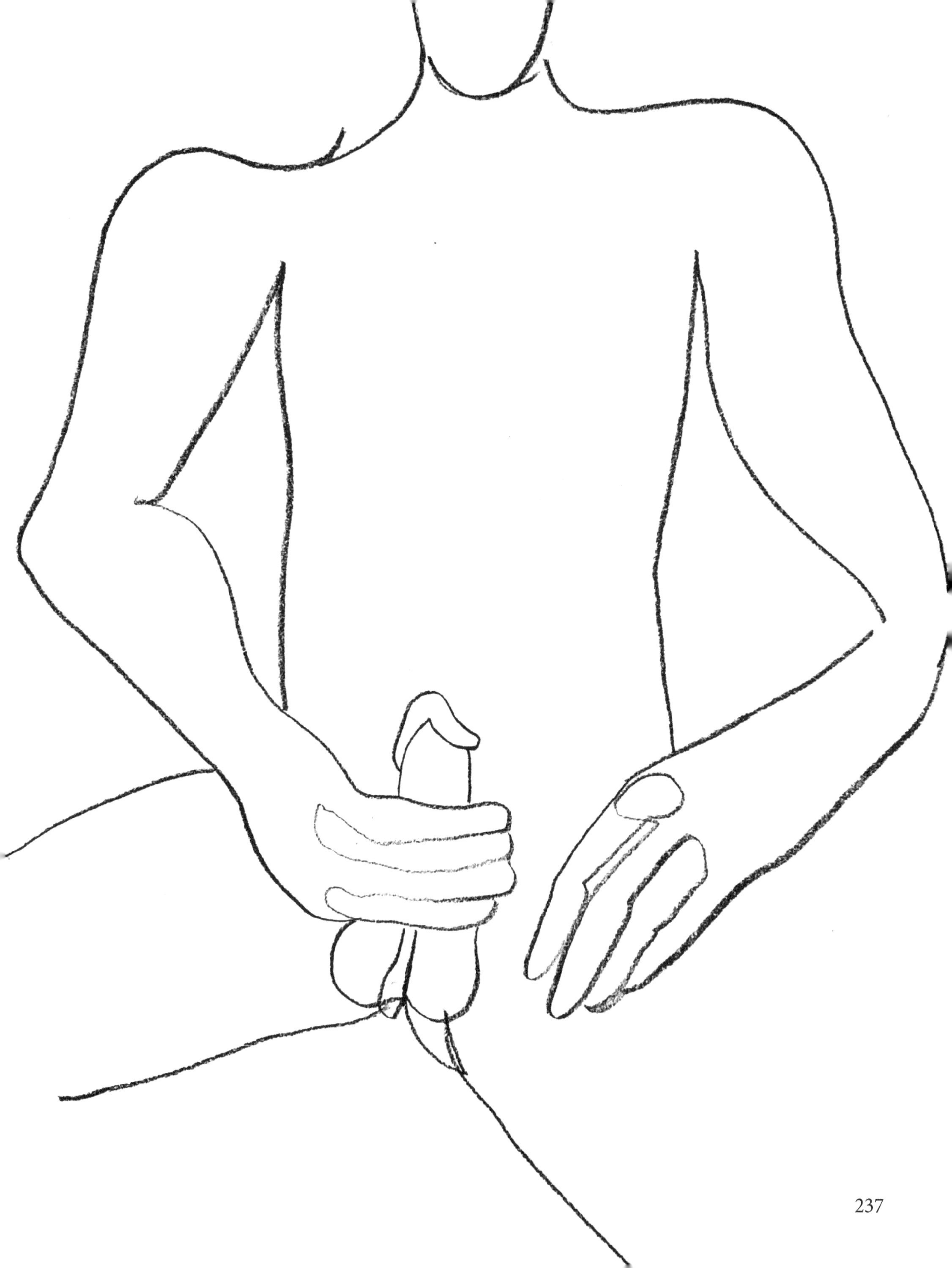

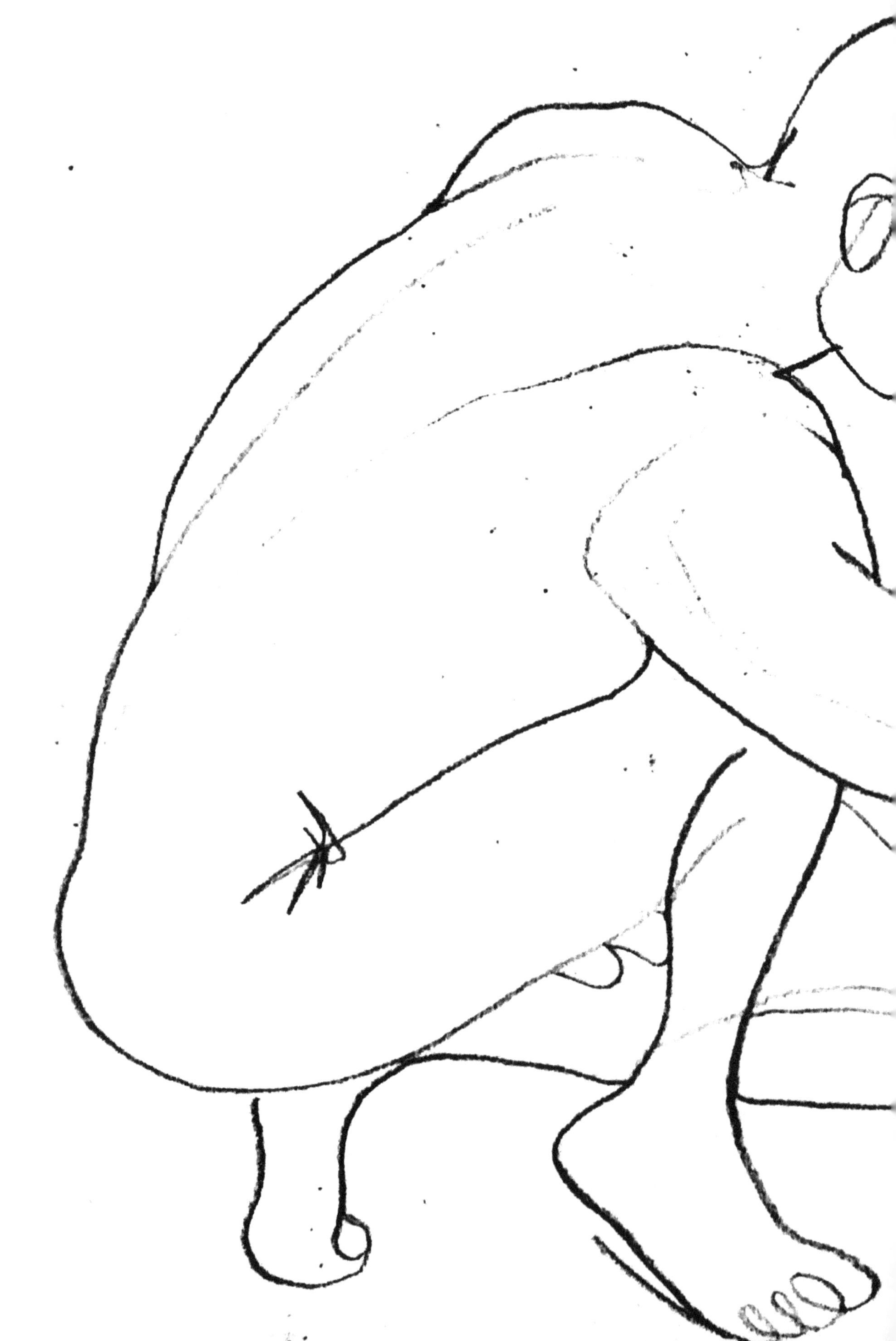

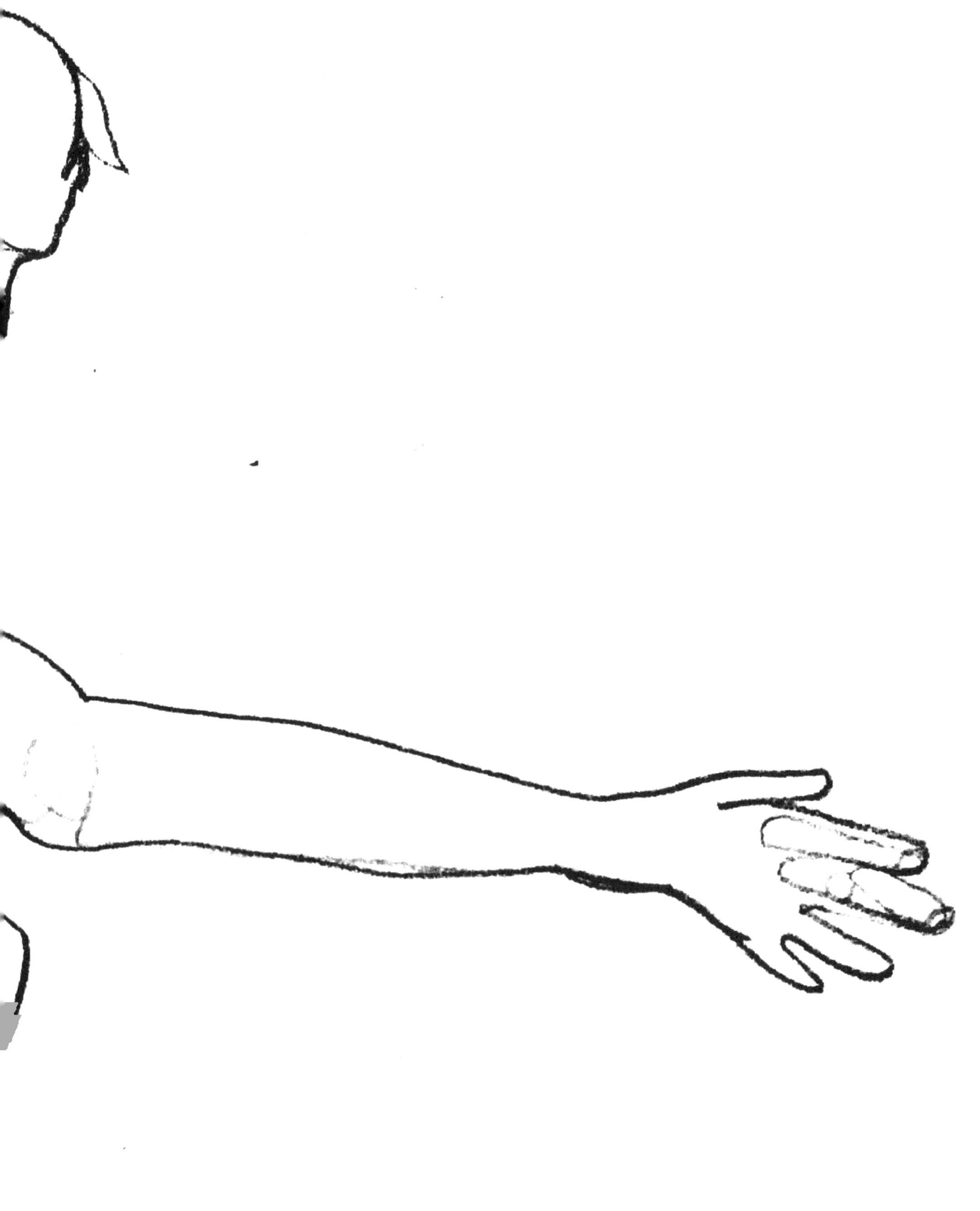

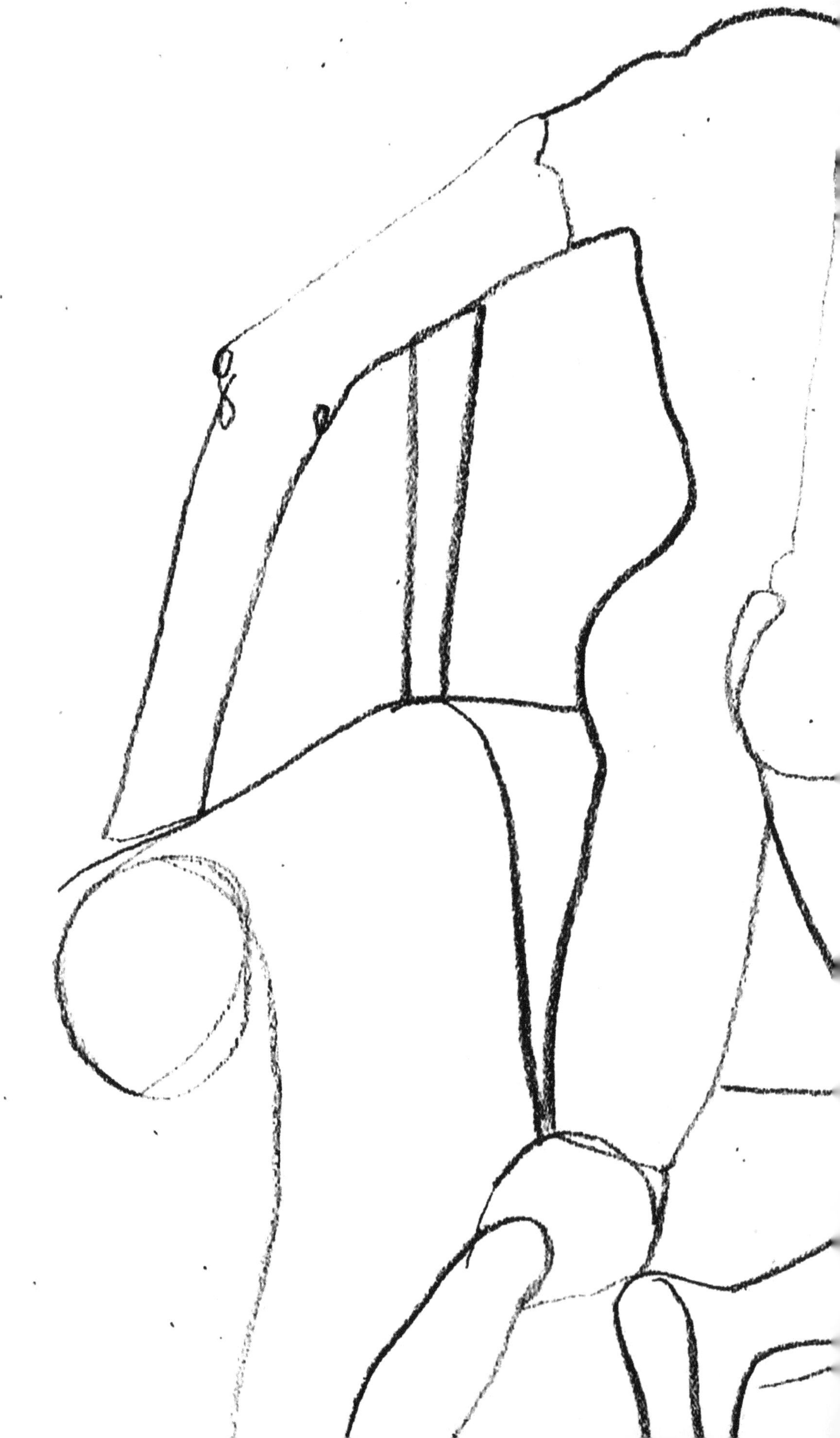

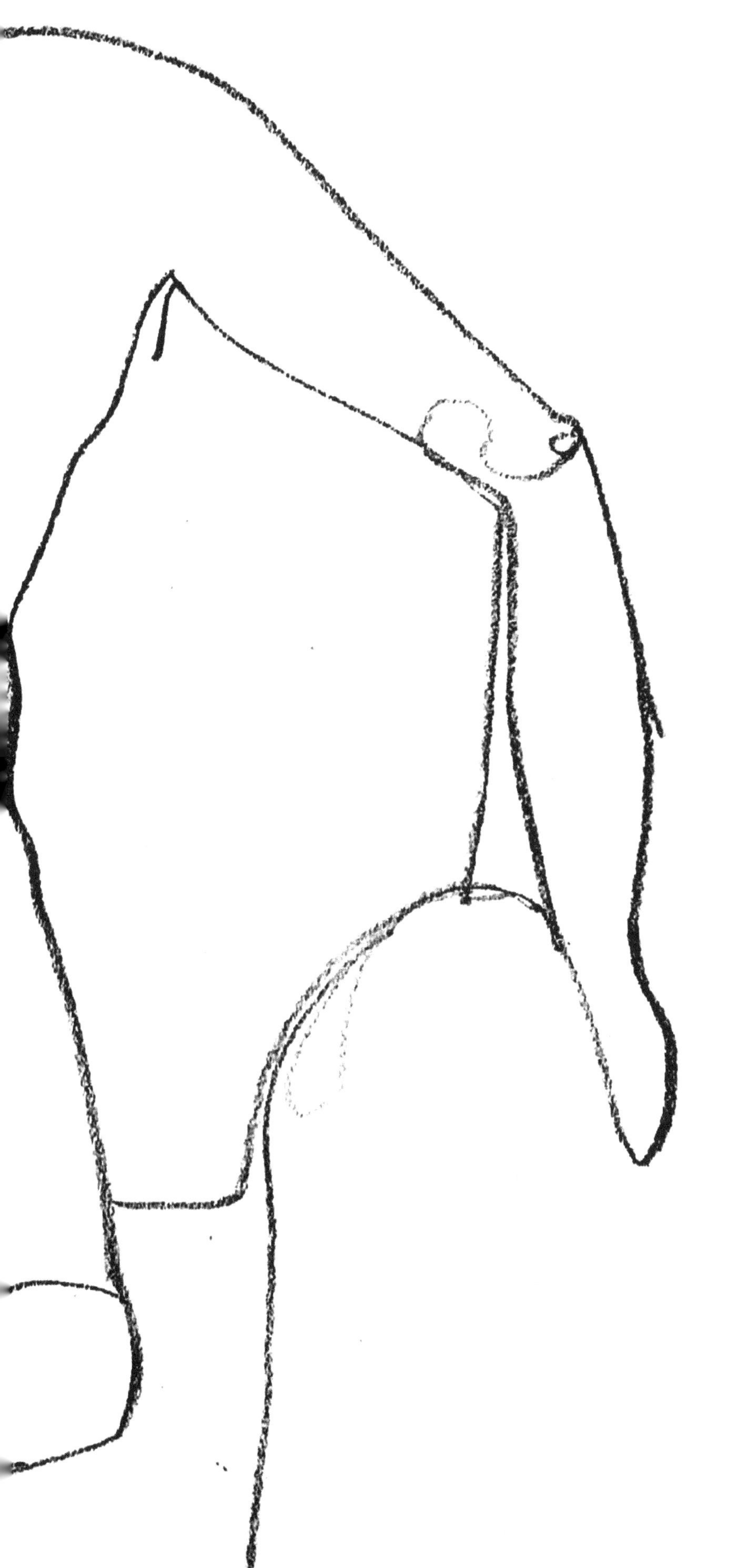

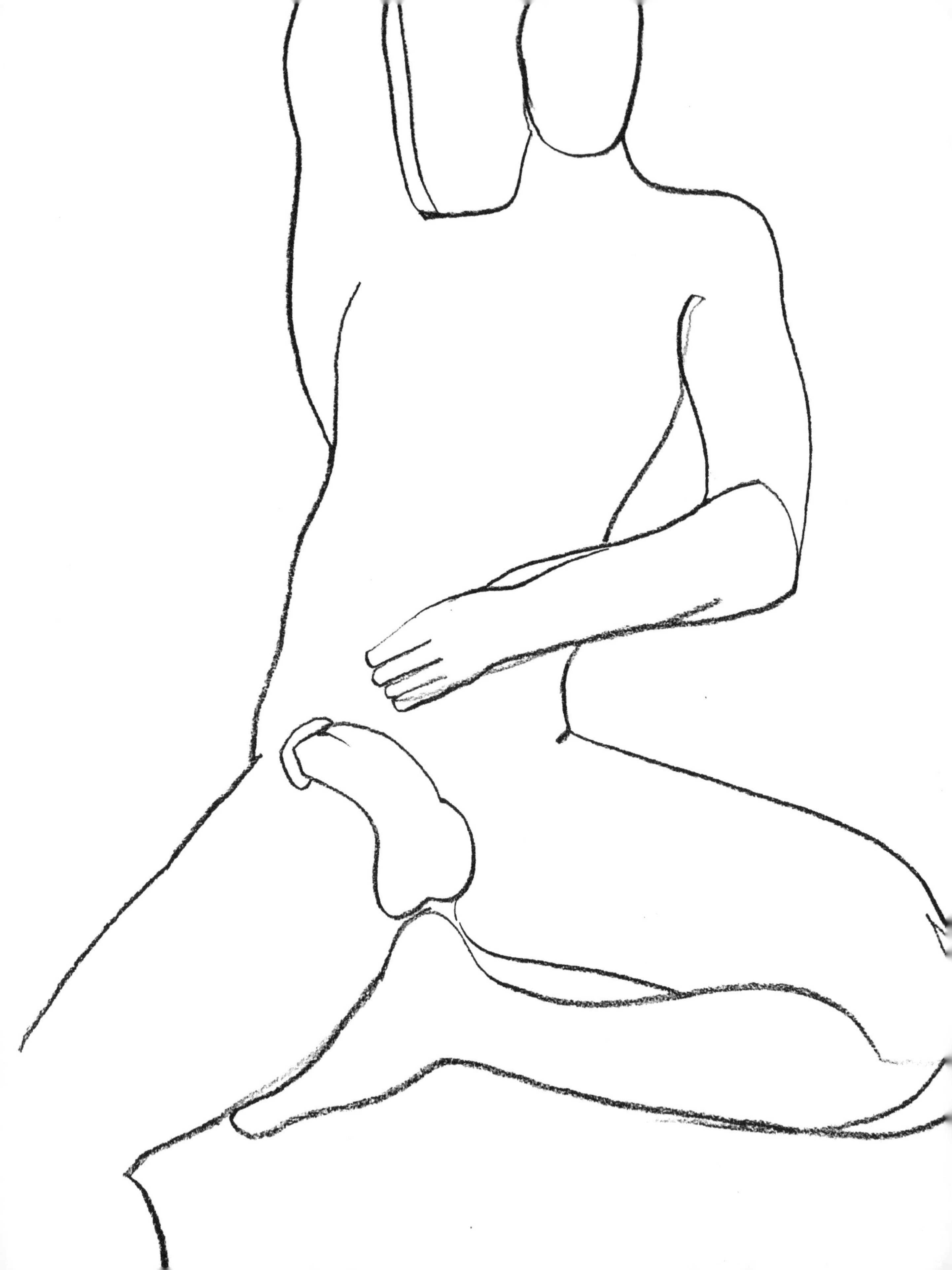

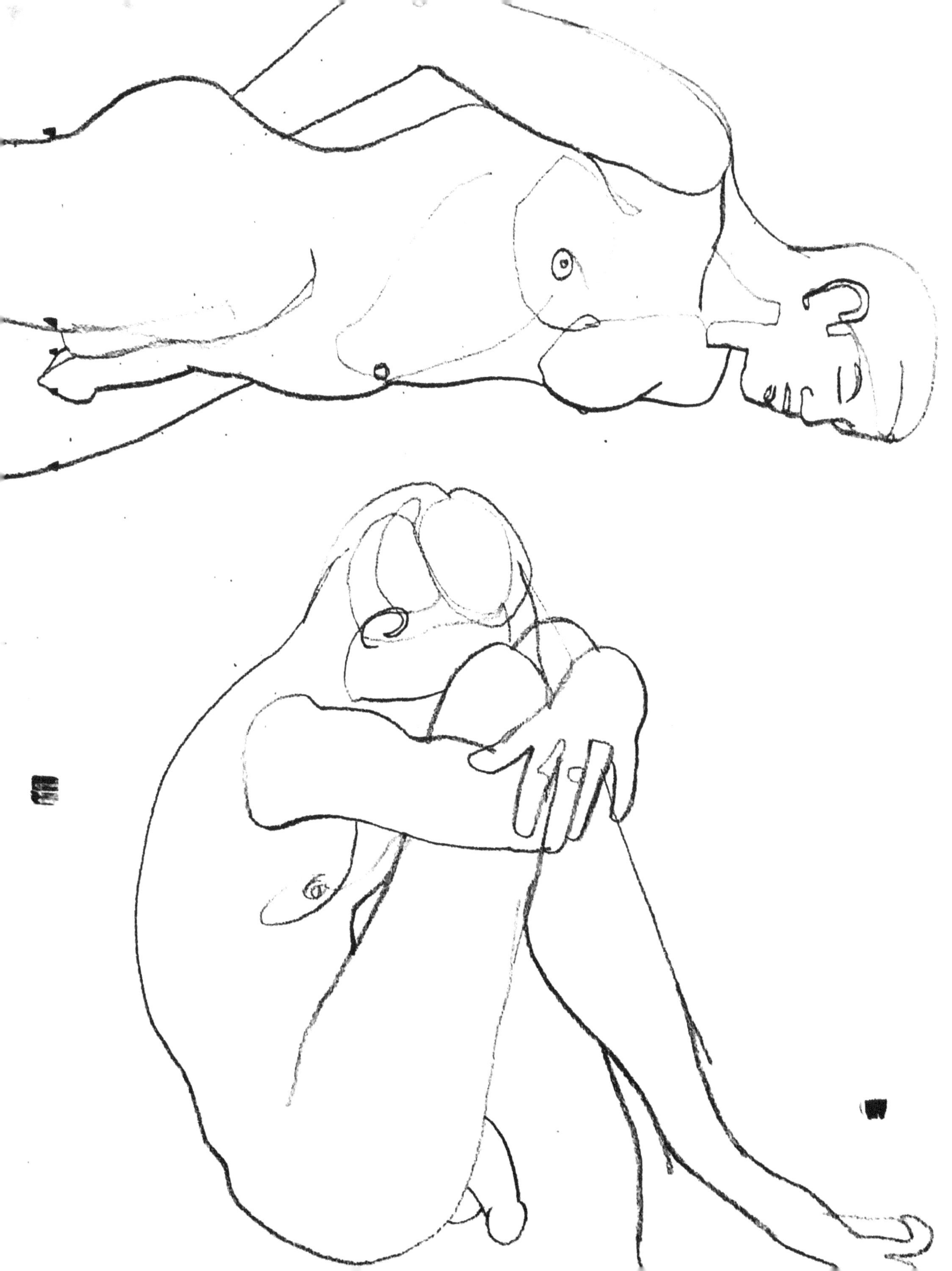

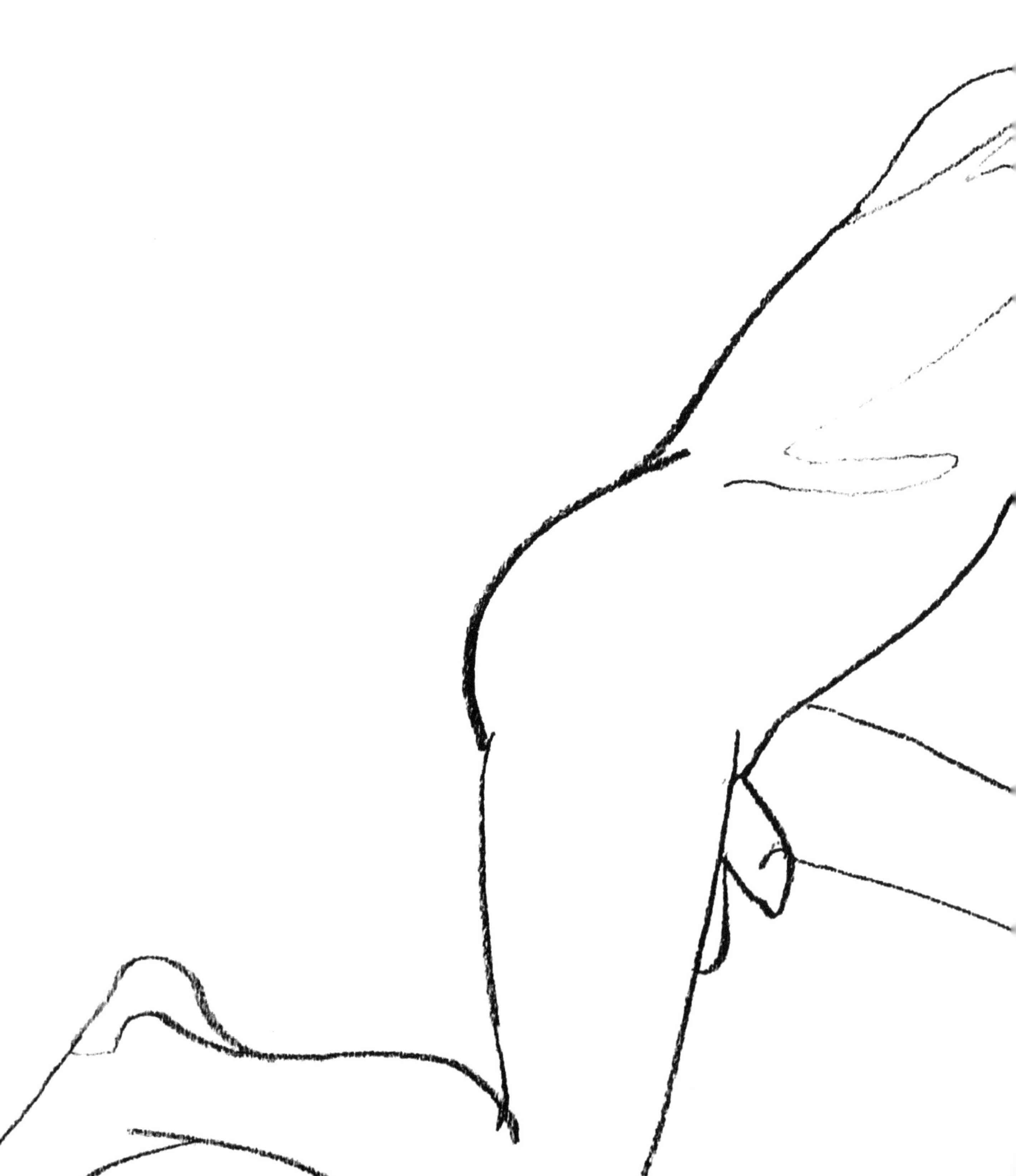

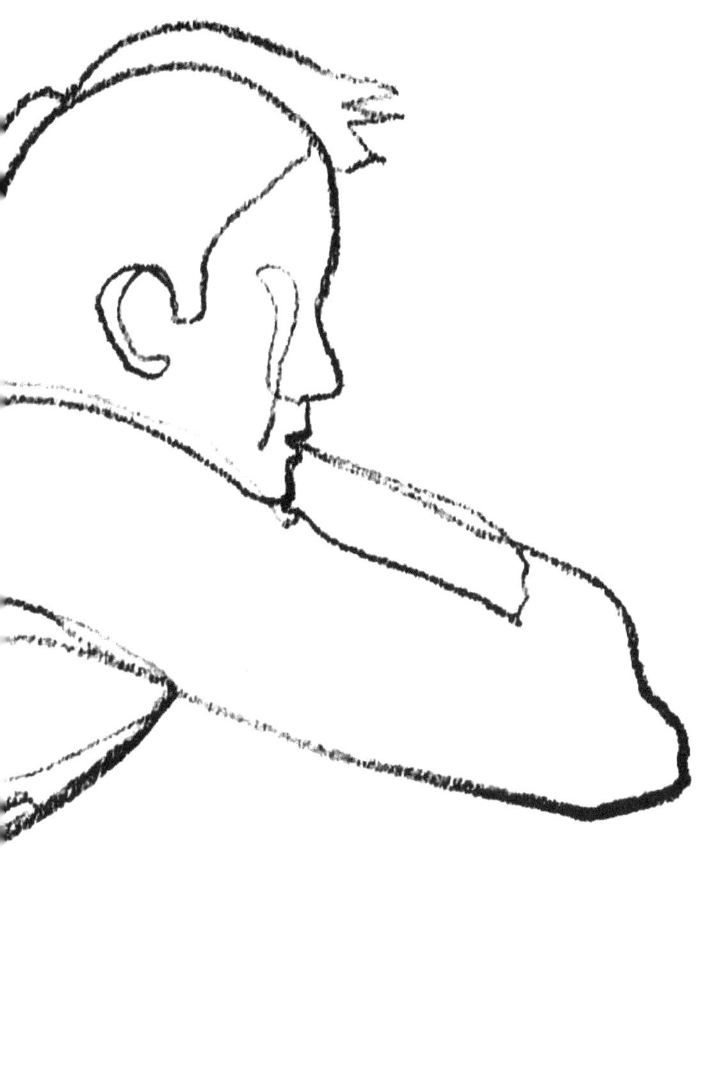

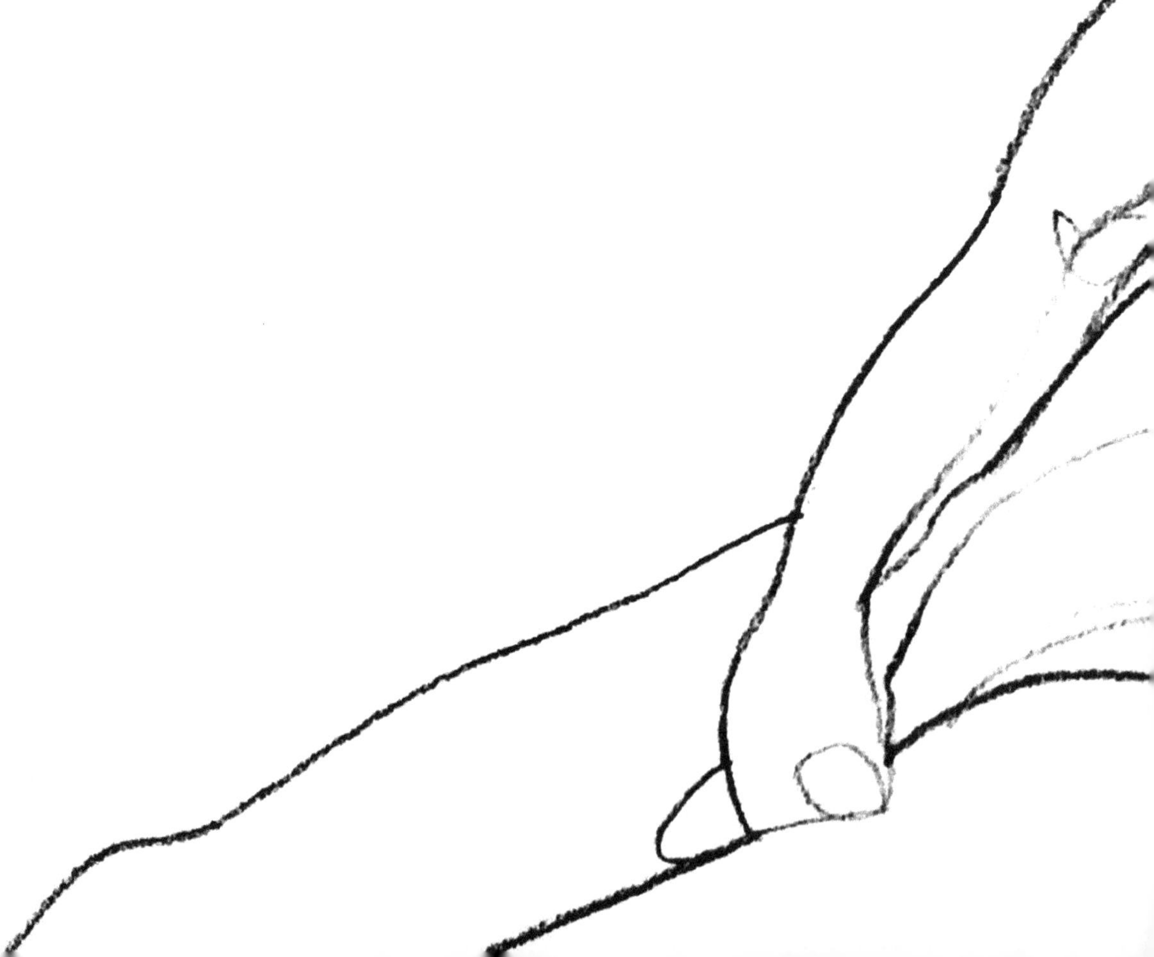

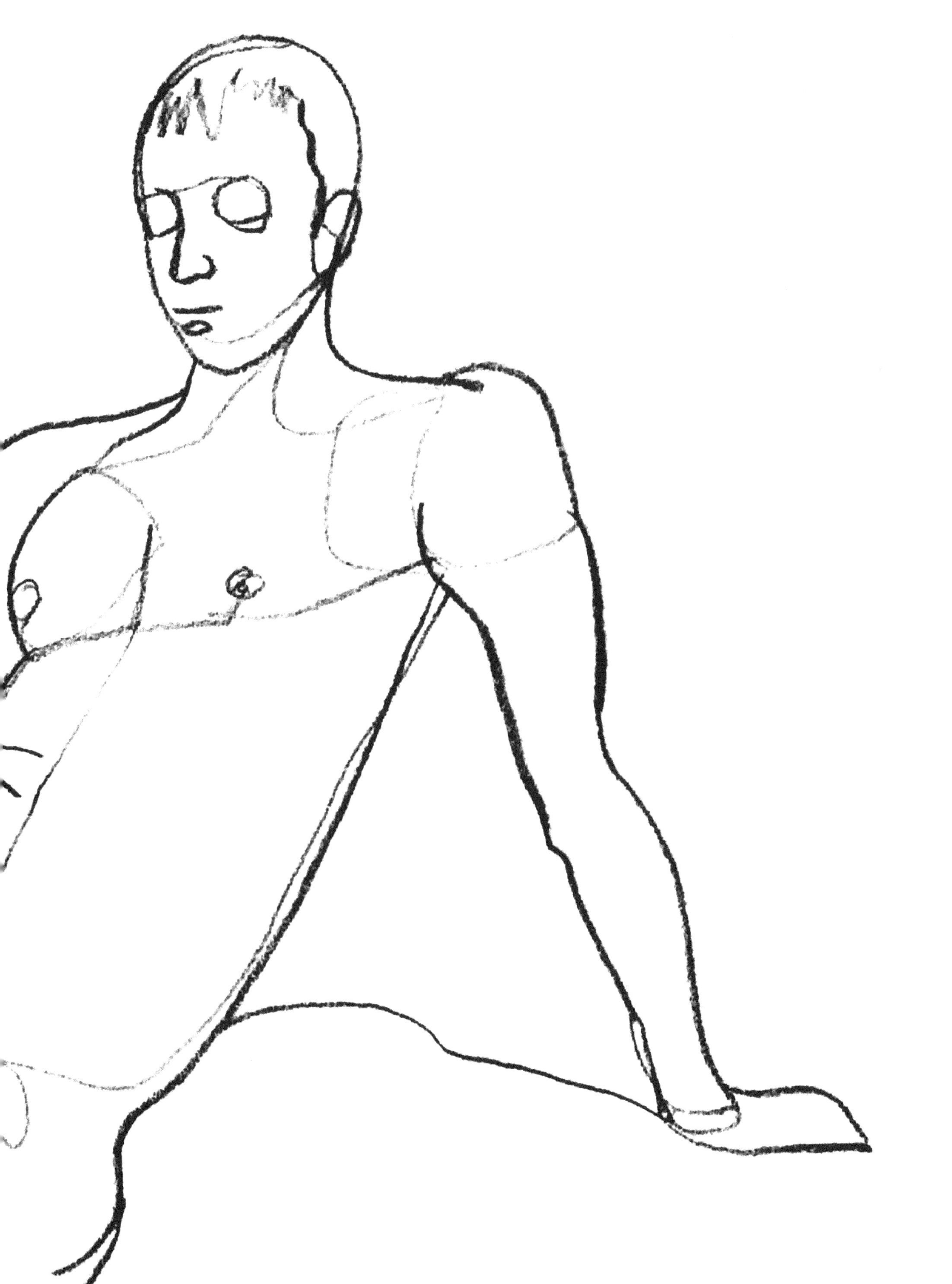

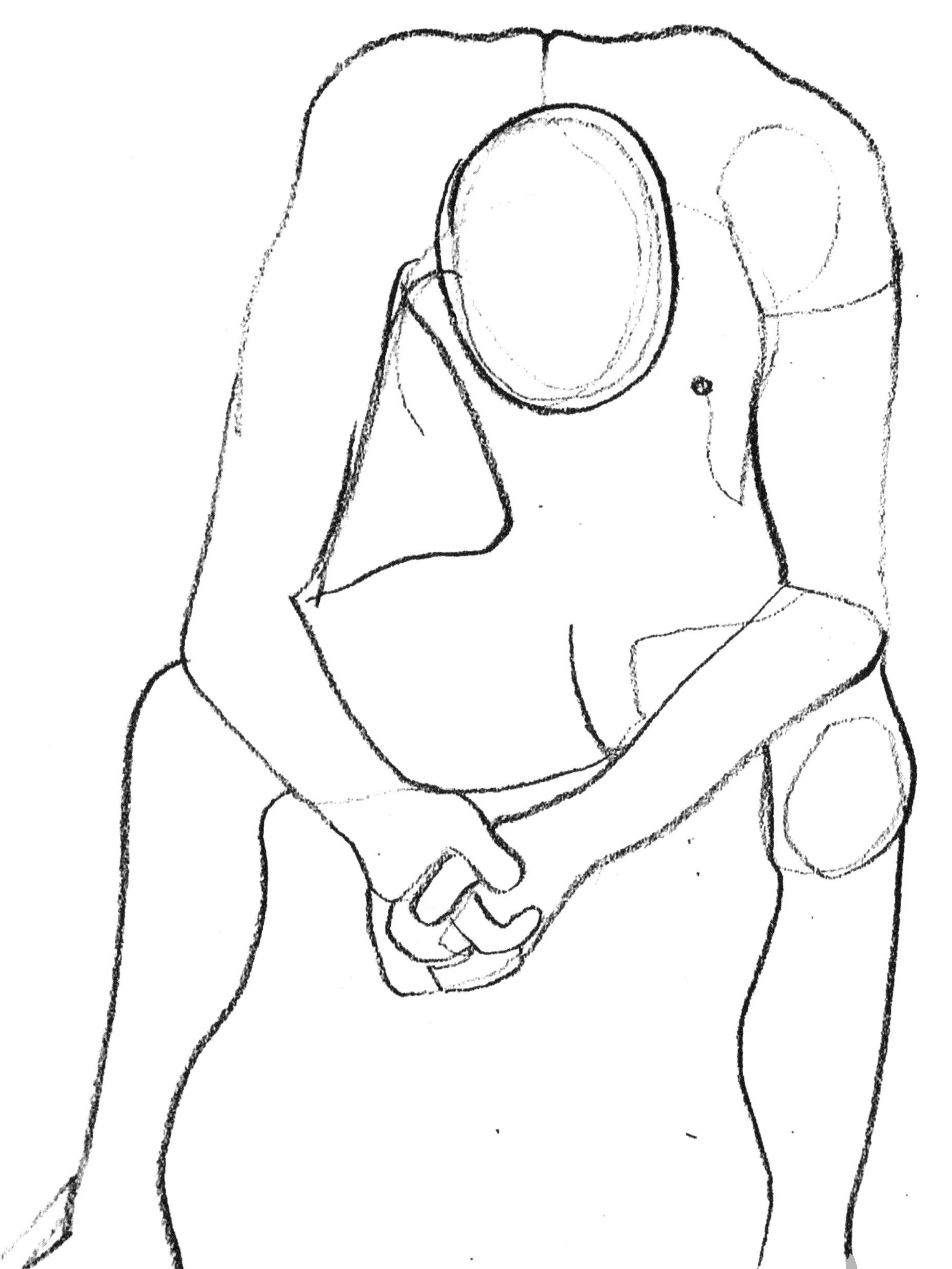

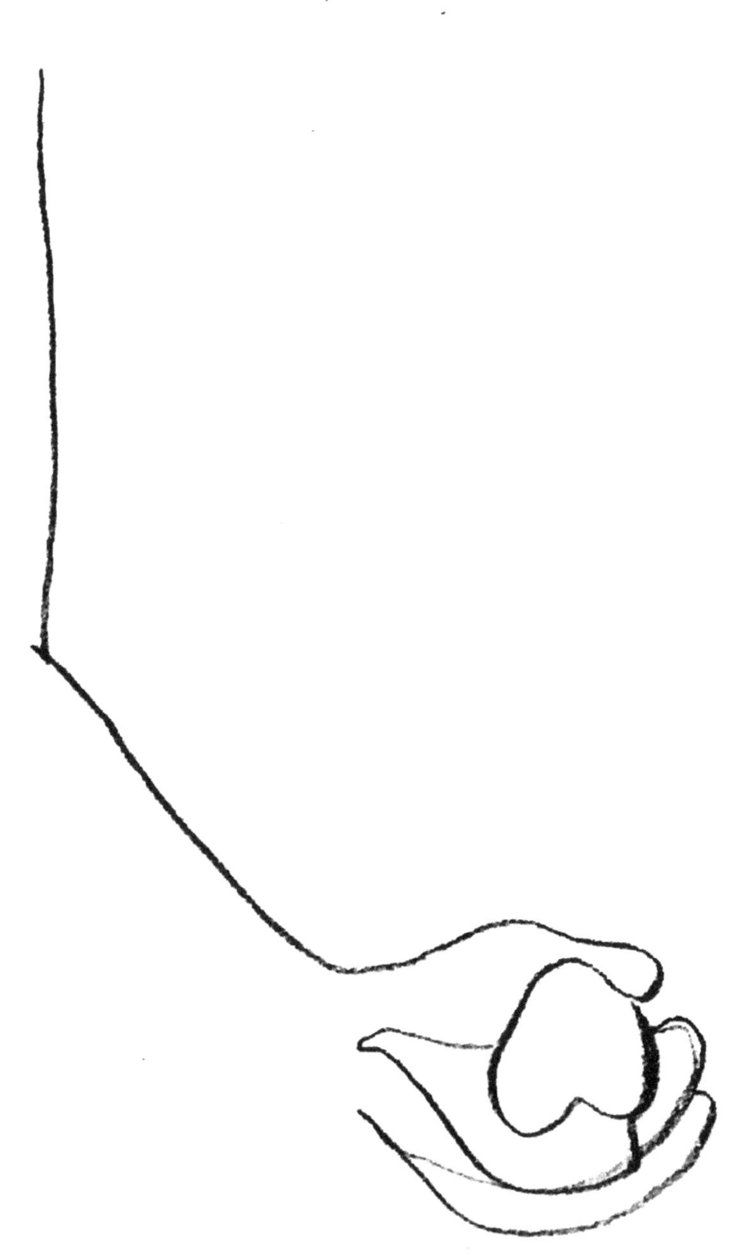

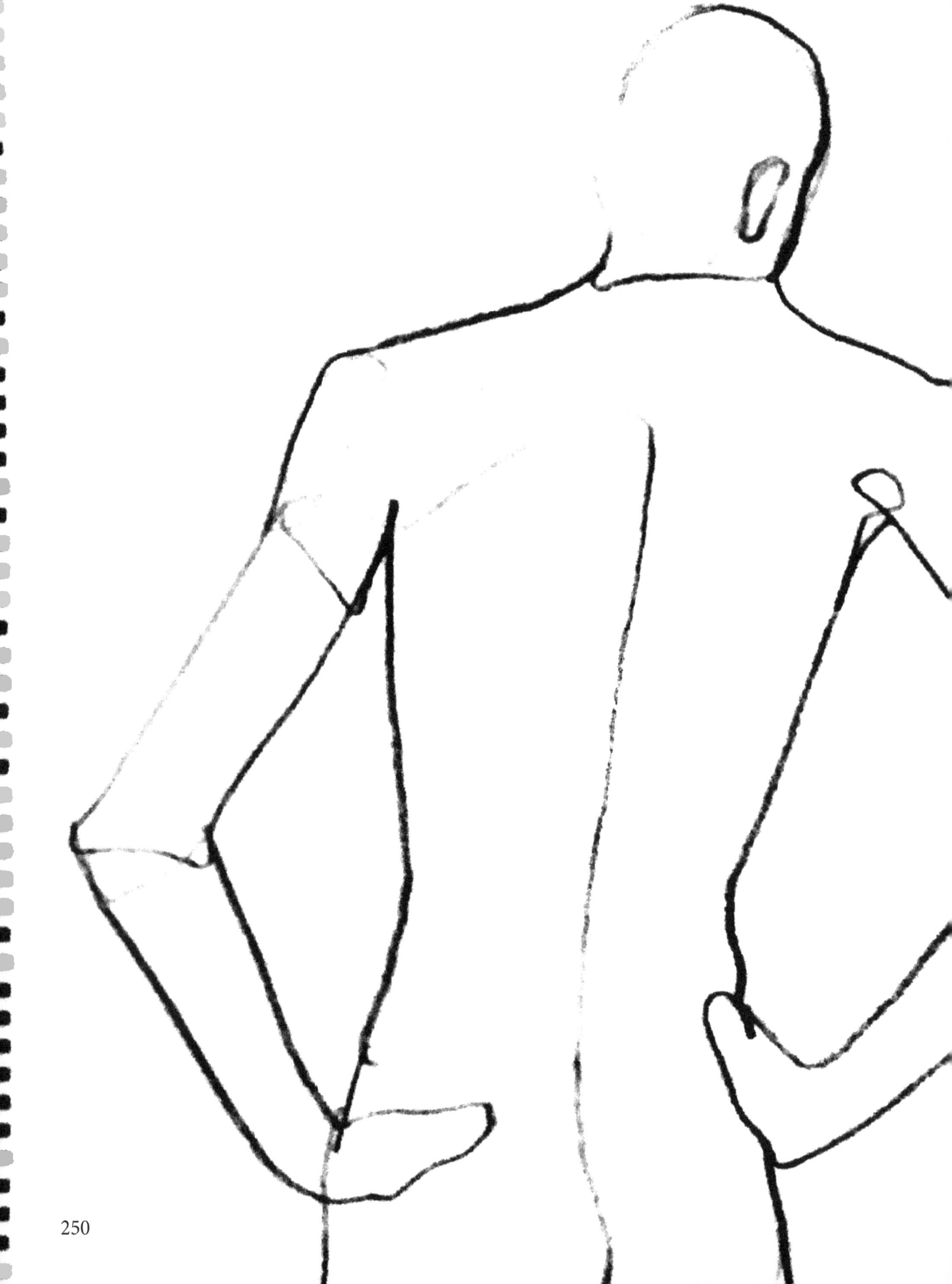

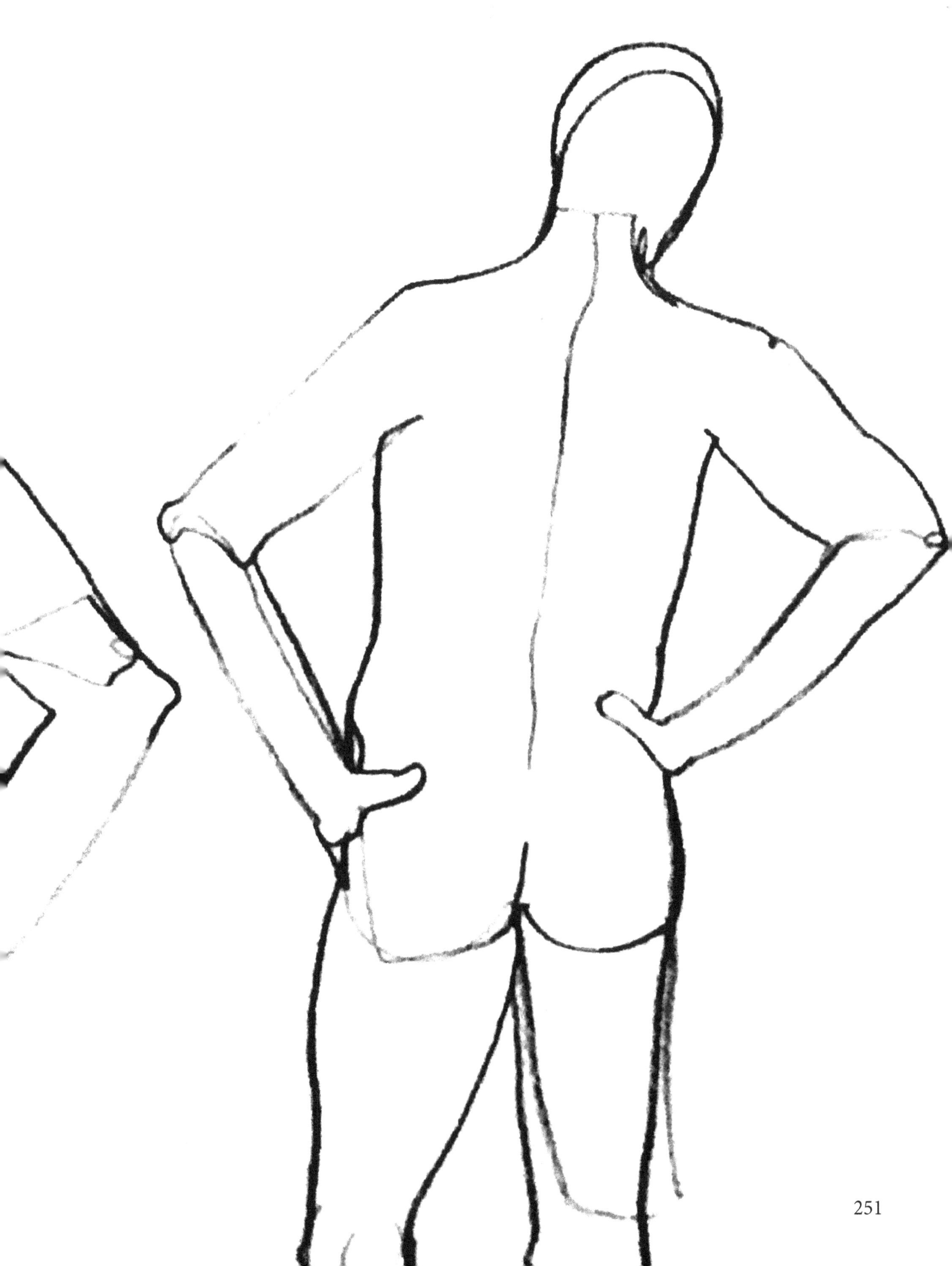

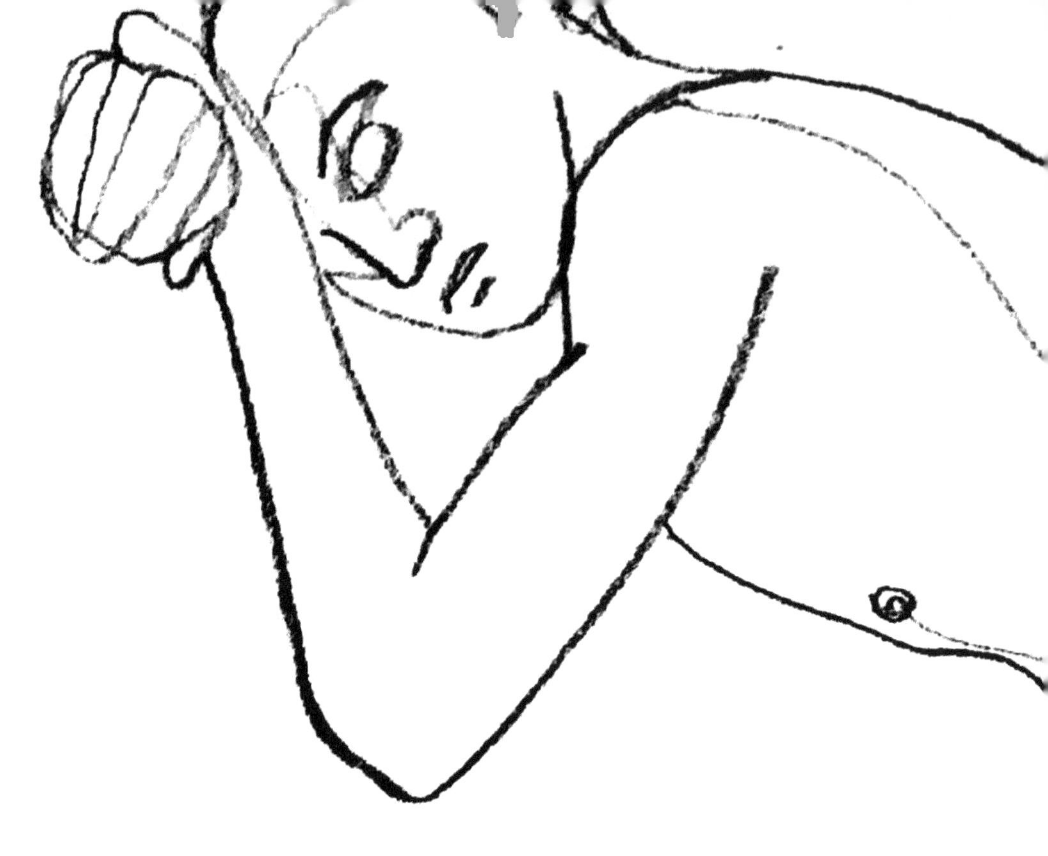

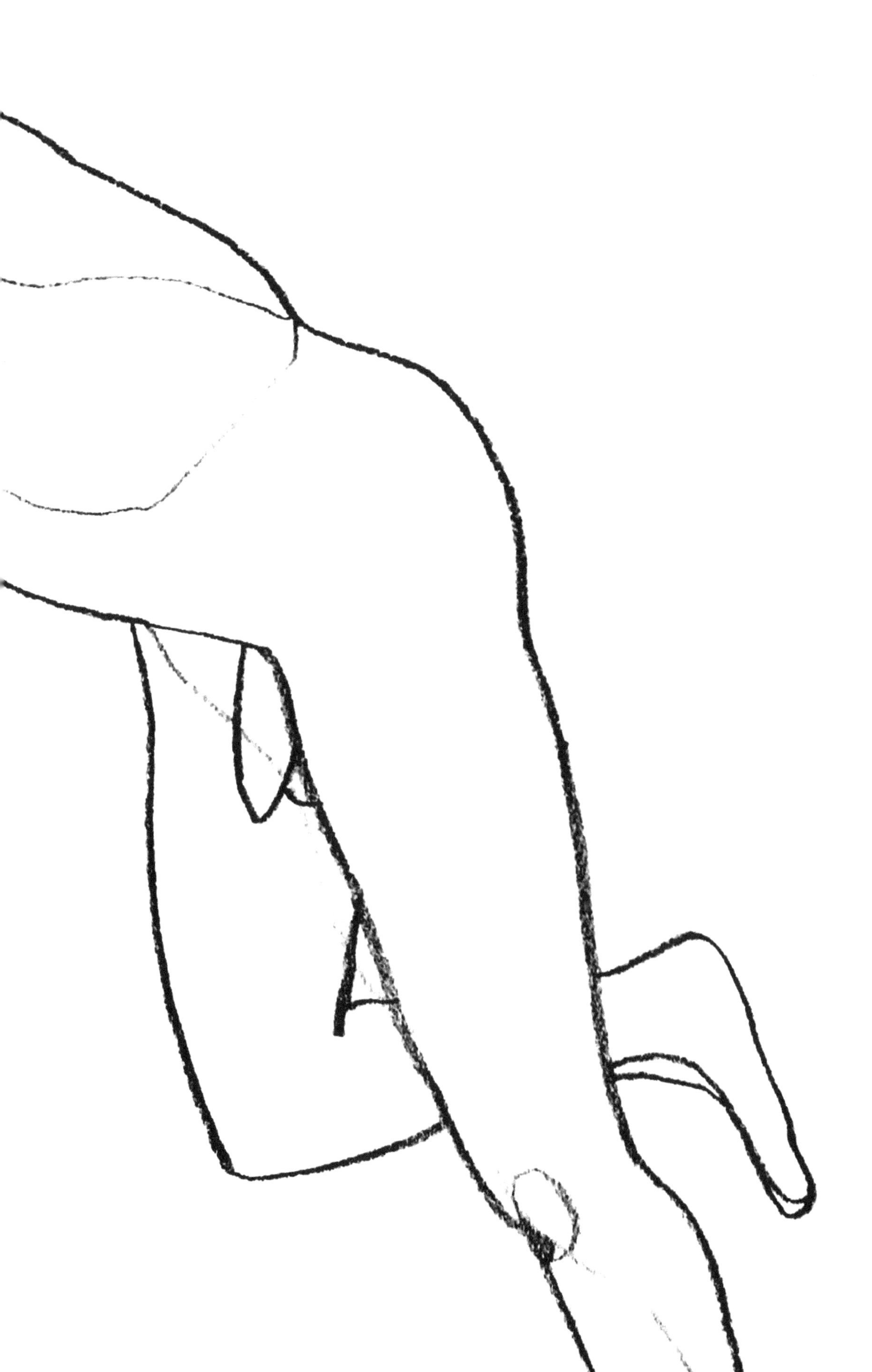

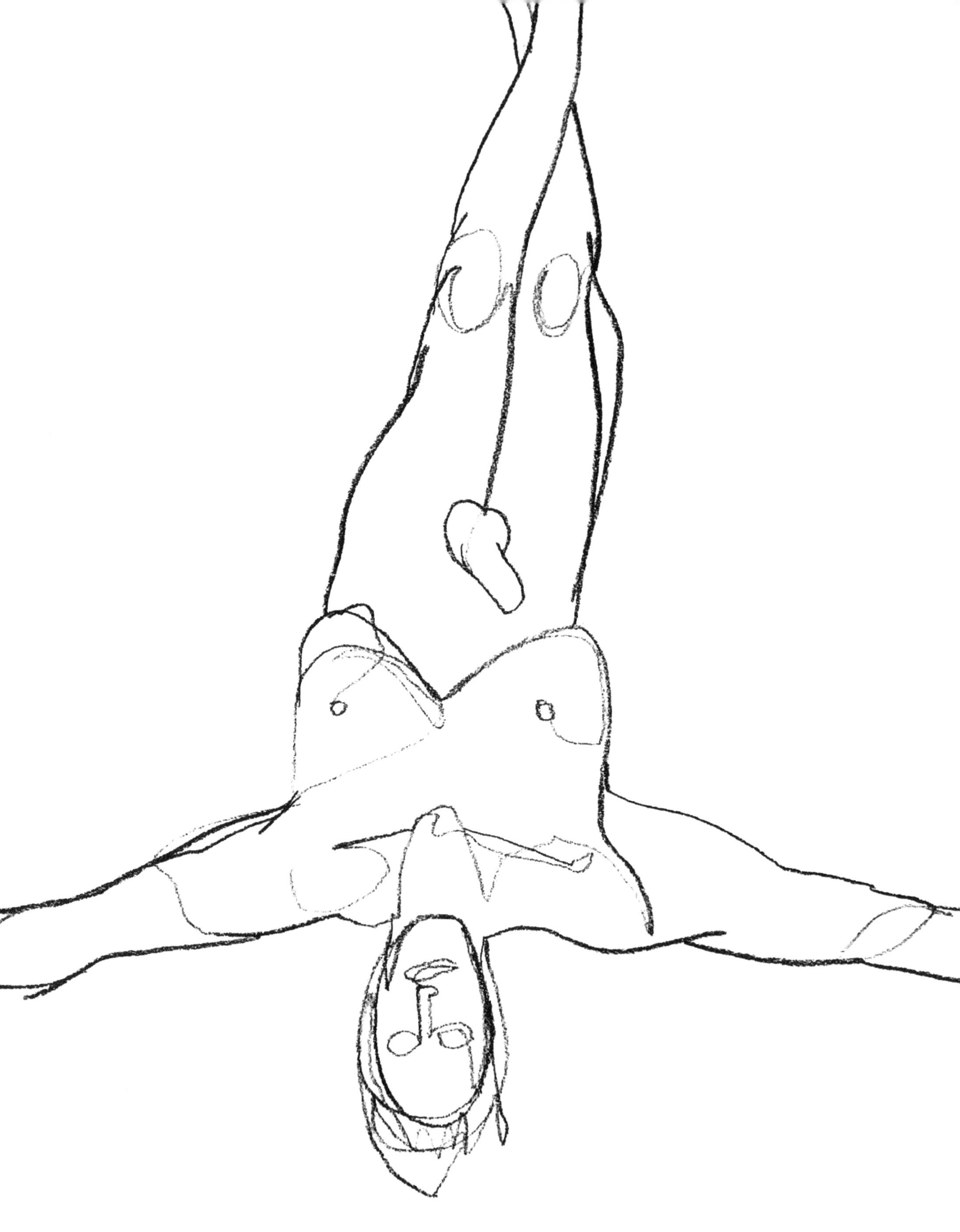

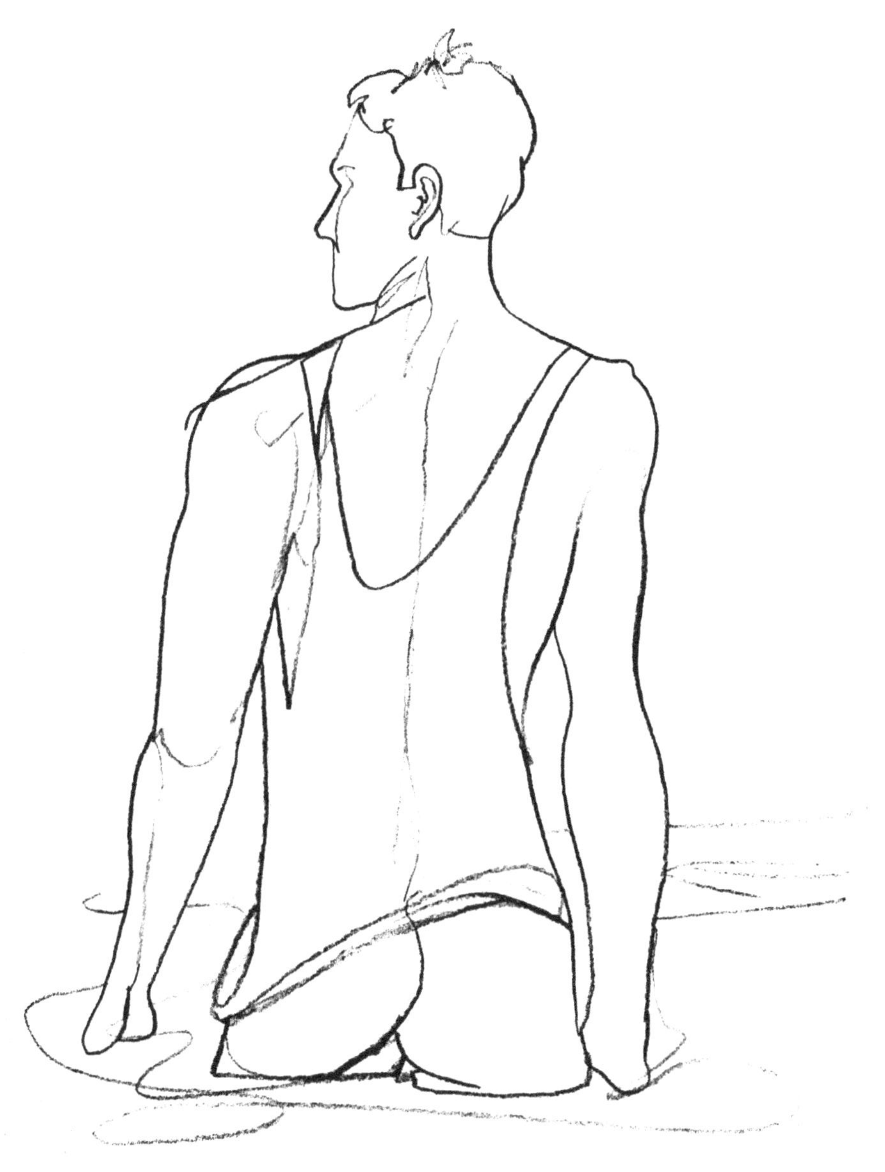

The Male Nude

Published by bd-studios.com in New York City, 2019
© 2019 Michael Tice

Art Direction and Design by luke kurtis

ISBN 978-0-9992078-9-5

also by Michael Tice

Retrospective

also published by bd-studios.com

Georgia Dusk by Dudgrick Bevins & luke kurtis
Route 4, Box 358 by Dudgrick Bevins
The Animal Book by Michael Harren
Tentative Armor by Michael Harren
exam(i)nation
the immeasurable fold: selected poems 2000–2015 by luke kurtis
Angkor Wat book and album by luke kurtis
Visions of the Beyond by Stefanie Masciandaro
Puertas Españolas by Josemaria Mejorada & May Gañán
Here Nor There by Sam Rosenthal
Jordan's Journey by Jordan M. Scoggins
Just One More by Jonathan David Smyth